Japan

EDWARD J. LINCOLN

Japan

Facing Economic Maturity

THE BROOKINGS INSTITUTION
Washington, D.C.

Copyright © 1988 by
THE BROOKINGS INSTITUTION
1775 Massachusetts Avenue, N.W., Washington, D.C. 20036

Library of Congress Cataloging-in-Publication Data
Lincoln, Edward J.
  Japan—facing economic maturity/Edward J. Lincoln.
    p.   cm.
  Includes bibliographical references.
  ISBN 0-8157-5260-1   ISBN 0-8157-5259-8 (pbk.)
  1. Japan—Economic conditions—1945–   2. Japan—Economic
policy—1945–   I. Title.
HC462.9.L56   1988
330.952'047—dc19   87-26103
                                                              CIP

987654321

THE BROOKINGS INSTITUTION is an independent organization devoted to nonpartisan research, education, and publication in economics, government, foreign policy, and the social sciences generally. Its principal purposes are to aid in the development of sound public policies and to promote public understanding of issues of national importance.

The Institution was founded on December 8, 1927, to merge the activities of the Institute for Government Research, founded in 1916, the Institute of Economics, founded in 1922, and the Robert Brookings Graduate School of Economics and Government, founded in 1924.

The Board of Trustees is responsible for the general administration of the Institution, while the immediate direction of the policies, program, and staff is vested in the President, assisted by an advisory committee of the officers and staff. The by-laws of the Institution state: "It is the function of the Trustees to make possible the conduct of scientific research, and publication, under the most favorable conditions, and to safeguard the independence of the research staff in the pursuit of their studies and in the publication of the results of such studies. It is not a part of their function to determine, control, or influence the conduct of particular investigations or the conclusions reached."

The President bears final responsibility for the decision to publish a manuscript as a Brookings book. In reaching his judgment on the competence, accuracy, and objectivity of each study, the President is advised by the director of the appropriate research program and weighs the views of a panel of expert outside readers who report to him in confidence on the quality of the work. Publication of a work signifies that it is deemed a competent treatment worthy of public consideration but does not imply endorsement of conclusions or recommendations.

The Institution maintains its position of neutrality on issues of public policy in order to safeguard the intellectual freedom of the staff. Hence interpretations or conclusions in Brookings publications should be understood to be solely those of the authors and should not be attributed to the Institution, to its trustees, officers, or other staff members, or to the organizations that support its research.

Foreword

JAPAN is one of the leading industrial nations of the world, the result of a remarkable century of determined economic development. But that very success has now created adjustment problems that are testing Japan's ability to adapt to its new economic circumstances.

In this study, Edward J. Lincoln finds that the roots of Japan's present trade surpluses lie in the slowdown in economic growth that occurred in the 1970s and the resulting excess of savings over investments that emerged in the Japanese economy. Masked by the two oil crises in the 1970s and by Tokyo's initial willingness to follow an expansionary fiscal policy, the domestic imbalances led directly to enormous current-account surpluses in the 1980s, contributing to tense relations with the United States and other nations. Since 1985 the appreciation of the yen against the dollar has ushered in a new and troubling period. Too little time has passed to judge how well Japan will cope, but the current wrenching change could prove to be the most difficult adjustment of all.

These macroeconomic developments have had important implications for Japan's financial markets, and have led to considerable domestic deregulation and the reduction of barriers to international financial transactions. Although the Ministry of Finance has acquiesced in these changes reluctantly, the process, once started, has gained a momentum that is still continuing. Lincoln concludes with a consideration of bilateral relations. The central importance of savings-investment imbalances leads him to stress the critical need for Japan to stimulate domestic demand and for the United States to control its budget deficits.

vii

Edward J. Lincoln is a research associate in the Brookings Foreign Policy Studies program. He was assisted in the course of this project by officials of the Ministry of Finance and the Bank of Japan, as well as by friends and acquaintances at Japanese and American banks and investment houses in Tokyo and in the Japanese academic community. He extends to them his thanks, though the list is too long to thank them individually. The author is also grateful for generous and valuable comments and suggestions from John C. Campbell, Hugh T. Patrick, William B. Quandt, Kazuo Sato, Charles L. Schultze, and Philip H. Trezise, and the participants at the Japan economic seminar in New York in March 1986 who discussed chapter 3. The author also thanks James R. Schneider for editing the manuscript, Patricia Nelson for verifying its facts and numbers, Susan Nichols for making the many changes and corrections to the text, Margaret Lynch for compiling the index, and Akihiro Kimoto for providing research assistance.

Brookings gratefully acknowledges the financial support for this project provided by the German Marshall Fund of the United States, the John D. and Catherine T. MacArthur Foundation, the Andrew W. Mellon Foundation, and the Rockefeller Brothers Fund, Inc.

The views expressed here are those of the author and should not be ascribed to any of the persons or organizations acknowledged above or to the officers, trustees, or other staff members of the Brookings Institution.

Bruce K. MacLaury
President

October 1987
Washington, D.C.

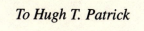

To Hugh T. Patrick

Contents

Tables

Figure

CHAPTER ONE

Overview

FROM THE OIL CRISIS OF 1973 through the first half of the 1980s, Japan experienced fundamental economic changes and faced significant problems in adjusting to them. The changes included drastic reductions in economic growth rates, severe imbalances between the domestic supply of savings and the domestic demand for investment, an enormous rise in the government fiscal deficit, the emergence of large current-account surpluses in the balance of payments, an increase in the number of serious international trade disputes, and extensive deregulation of capital markets.

When its record is compared with that of the United States and Europe, however, Japan has responded to its problems with relative success. Since 1973 its growth rate has been higher than that of other industrial countries while inflation and unemployment have been lower. Nevertheless, the economic changes have posed serious difficulties for Japanese policymakers, who have been constrained by Japan's cultural, social, and institutional settings and pushed by criticism and pressure from the rest of the world.

Many of the economic developments and policy responses have directly affected relations with the United States because they have led to a widening of the bilateral trade imbalance. In the search to solve these problems, Washington often fails to realize that policies appropriate in the United States are not necessarily appropriate in Japan, or may evolve in entirely different directions. Of course, better knowledge of the Japanese economic situation does not mean that the United States ought to accept Tokyo's bargaining positions on bilateral issues or refrain from pressing for policy changes. However, increased understanding ought to result in more appropriate goals for U.S. economic policy and the realization of those goals with fewer histrionics.

This study addresses the macroeconomic events that have taken place in Japan since 1973 and assesses their implications for bilateral economic relations. While a smattering of articles have dealt with these dislocations, information about and analysis of them have been scant. And although many topics at the microeconomic level could be addressed, this study focuses on financial markets, in which changes have been particularly rapid and significant.

Why pick 1973 as a starting point? The October war in the Middle East and the subsequent oil supply cuts and price increases provide an obvious answer; they were traumatic events that demarcated major periods in Japan's economic development. But 1973 also provides a convenient dividing line for other reasons. Japan had faced rapidly rising wholesale and consumer price inflation before the oil crisis. These were symptomatic of the other long-term changes that were coalescing to bring an end to the postwar era of very high economic growth. Some had been in motion since the late 1960s and by 1973 were strong enough to make a noticeable difference. But the much slower growth after 1973 triggered significant structural and institutional changes in the economy, a process that is still continuing. Japan today is very different from what it was in the early 1970s.

There is another reason for choosing 1973. A previous Brookings study of the Japanese economy analyzed postwar economic developments through the early 1970s.[1] While it remains an excellent analysis of the high-growth era, the institutional restructuring and the reorientation of policy in the ensuing years demand a new analysis.

A Different Japan

After expanding at an average annual real (inflation-adjusted) rate of 12.1 percent in the 1960s, Japan's growth from 1974 to 1985 dropped to 3.8 percent. The slowdown had actually begun earlier; between 1970 and 1973 growth averaged only 7.5 percent (table 1-1), suggesting that the

---

1. Hugh Patrick and Henry Rosovsky, eds., *Asia's New Giant: How the Japanese Economy Works* (Brookings, 1976). This multiauthored study covers many aspects of the Japanese economy.

Table 1-1. *Average Annual Real GNP Growth Rates, by Country, Selected Periods, 1960–85*[a]

Percent

Country	1960–69	1970–73	1974–85
Japan	12.1	7.5	3.8
United States	4.1	3.2	2.2
West Germany	5.7	4.2	1.8
France[b]	5.8	5.6	2.1
Great Britain[b]	3.1	3.7	1.3

Source: International Monetary Fund, *International Financial Statistics Yearbook, 1986* (Washington, D.C.: IMF, 1986), pp. 334–35, 346–47, 420–21, 684–85, 690–91.

a. Based on 1980 prices.

b. Data are for GDP.

causes lay in longer-run forces emerging in the early 1970s and not solely in the 1973 oil shock.

All industrial countries experienced sharply lower growth rates in the 1970s, so Japan's record is not exceptional in that sense. And Japan continued to do relatively well. During the 1960s it had grown three times as fast as the United States; from 1974 to 1985 the ratio dropped to a little more than one and a half times. Is it Japan's absolute or relative performance that is the most important fact deserving explanation? This book concentrates on the former.

Table 1-2 summarizes other economic shifts characterizing the years

Table 1-2. *Japan's Economic Performance, 1973, 1985*

Indicator	1973	1985
GNP		
Nominal (trillions of yen)	113	317
Real (trillions of 1980 yen)	186	291
Per capita (dollars)	3,760	10,997
Per capita rank among OECD members	14	8
Labor		
Unemployment rate (percent)	1.3	2.6
Job opening–job seeker ratio	1.96	0.68
Annual labor productivity growth in manufacturing in previous ten years (percent)[a]	11.5	6.5
Trade		
Exports (billions of dollars)	36.9	175.6
Merchandise trade balance (billions of dollars)[b]	−1.4	46.1
Current-account balance (billions of dollars)	−0.1	49.2

Sources: Management and Coordination Agency, *Japan Statistical Yearbook, 1986* (Tokyo: Statistics Bureau, 1986), p. 307; *1985*, p. 70; *1983*, p. 113; *1978*, p. 65; *1973–74*, p. 49; International Monetary Fund, *International Financial Statistics Yearbook, 1986*, p. 421; Economic Planning Agency, *Annual Report on National Accounts, 1987* (Tokyo: EPA, 1987), pp. 106–07, 118–19; Bank of Japan, *Balance of Payments Monthly* (October 1986), pp. 1, 7, 11; (January 1984), pp. 1, 7, 11; and "The OECD Member Countries," *OECD Observer*, no. 74 (March–April 1975), pp. 19–26; no. 145 (April–May 1987), pp. 17–24.

a. Value added per employee day.

b. Exports f.o.b.; imports c.i.f.

since the first oil shock. As a result of two and a half decades of extraordinarily high growth rates, Japan was the world's second largest market economy by 1973, and its per capita gross national product was fourteenth among the member countries of the Organization for Economic Cooperation and Development. Thereafter, its relative position advanced more slowly, reaching eighth among OECD members by 1985. The very large appreciation of the yen against the dollar in 1985 and 1986 finally pushed per capita income to the level of that in the United States.

Unemployment in 1973 was only 1.3 percent, and a widely used indicator in Japan showed almost two job openings for each job seeker registered at an official employment agency. However, by 1985 the unemployment rate had risen to 2.6 percent and the ratio of job openings to job seekers had fallen to 0.68. While the unemployment rate was still enviable by comparison with that in the United States (7.2 percent in 1985), what matters most is the direction of change—a doubling of the unemployment rate and a much weaker job market.[2]

Labor productivity in manufacturing from 1963 to 1973 rose at an astounding 11.5 percent annual rate. For the decade ending in 1985 the annual increase was only 6.5 percent. This performance was very respectable, but the slowdown is again striking.

Japan also experienced a major shift in its international balance of payments. In 1973, as the result of the increases in oil prices and an appreciating currency in the newly begun system of floating exchange rates, Japan ran a small current-account deficit of $136 million. In 1985 it produced a postwar high surplus of $49.2 billion, which was still rising rapidly. This surplus resulted from macroeconomic developments in Japan and elsewhere that will be major subjects of this study. It has been an important cause of the international trade problems in which the country has become embroiled.

National moods are also significant. The early 1970s were a time of exuberant enthusiasm about the future. After believing for many years that economic prosperity was fragile or unreal, people became convinced that

2. The official survey in Japan does not count laid-off workers, those waiting to report to a job, or those looking for work in the current month but not the reference week as unemployed. See Koji Taira, "Japan's Low Unemployment: Economic Miracle or Statistical Artifact," *Monthly Labor Review*, vol. 106 (July 1983), pp. 3–10. Adjusting the official Japanese data (possible with special surveys done in Japan between 1977 and 1980) yields an unemployment rate close to double the official one (3.8 percent instead of 2.2 percent in 1980). This adjustment does not include discouraged workers, many of whom were women.

it would continue indefinitely and would quickly push income to levels higher than those in the United States. Accompanying this belief was a long-standing desire to be accepted as an advanced, successful country, as good or better than others in terms of economic and social organization. These expectations and desires were temporarily dashed when the oil crisis and the first real recession of the postwar period struck in 1973–74. Although pessimism was relatively short-lived, it was followed by a more realistic, sober outlook conditioned by expectations of slower economic growth. Nothing demonstrates this new realism better than the behavior of labor unions. In 1974, spurred by their desire to continue the rapid real gains of the preceding years, they successfully negotiated enormous wage increases to compensate for high inflation. After 1974 they quickly readjusted to the new reality, lowering wage demands and dramatically reducing strike activity.

By the 1980s a different kind of confidence was returning to Japan. No one expected a return to high economic growth, but there was a rising sense of industrial prowess and accomplishment. The world might be a less vibrant place, but the Japanese now saw themselves at or near the top of the international economic hierarchy. Indeed as expressed by some, this confidence approached hubris with its strong element of contempt for the manufactured goods and general economic performance of other industrial nations.

Economic Changes Writ Large

The sharp reduction in Japan's rate of economic growth since the early 1970s has been fundamental. Most of the structural shifts considered in this study follow from or were seriously affected by this fact.

Of the factors that coalesced to moderate Japan's growth, the most important was the closing of the technology gap. Lagging behind other industrial countries in the 1950s and 1960s, Japan had been adept at importing and adapting foreign technology. The rapid gains in productivity this made possible meant that investment in the private sector was highly profitable. But when Japanese industry finally caught up in the 1970s, productivity gains became smaller and profitability declined, leading to reduced investment in new plant and equipment.

This slowdown caused a surplus of savings in the private sector. During the high-growth era, extremely high demand for private-sector investment had been matched by high levels of private-sector savings. The household sector's savings were transferred to the corporate sector, which invested much more than it could save. But when domestic investment demand dropped, the households continued to save as much as they always had. This excess of savings meant that the private sector was not absorbing through consumption, housing investment, and business investment as much as it was producing. Without government action the economy might have stagnated or gone into recession until savings and investment came back into balance.

Several solutions to the problem were possible. The government could use expansionary monetary policy—lower interest rates—to reduce the incentive to save and increase the incentive to invest. Alternatively, it could accomplish the same end by reducing tax incentives to save, increasing tax incentives for investment, or removing economic regulations that impeded investment. More directly, the government could run a fiscal deficit: bonds issued to cover the deficit would soak up the surplus savings. In effect, government would provide the demand missing in the private sector. Finally, the government could gamble that the rest of the world would provide the demand. Allowing a current-account surplus in the balance of payments would mean that the rest of the world was absorbing the goods and services produced but not consumed in the domestic economy. At the same time, the surplus savings would flow abroad as a net capital outflow.

Although Japan did experience a recession in 1974, caused mainly by the disruption of oil supplies and the subsequent price increases in the fall of 1973, it has since managed to avoid recession or stagnation, going through several phases in its response to surplus savings. From roughly 1975 to 1979 the principal adjustment came from fiscal policy. The government's deficit expanded rapidly, absorbing most of the surplus savings. Only small current-account surpluses developed. During the second phase, from 1980 through 1985, the fiscal deficit fell steadily while the current-account surplus rose sharply. Reducing government deficits was a deliberate policy based on deep concern over their long-run implications. This change of policy could have pushed the economy into recession, but the current-account surplus expanded to pick up the slack as rising U.S. federal deficits and current-account deficits provided an external outlet for Japan's exports of goods and services as well as its surplus capital.

By 1986 a third phase had begun. Between early 1985 and mid-1986 the yen appreciated more than 50 percent against the dollar, making Japan's exports more expensive for foreign buyers while imports became less expensive. Thus, allowing for some time lag, the current-account surplus would decline in the late 1980s, which posed a new dilemma. Since the private sector's desire to save still exceeded the demand for investment, and the government was reluctant to abandon its goal of reducing fiscal deficits, in the absence of deliberate policy changes, recession loomed as a means of adjustment (and economic growth in 1986 did slow considerably). In 1987 the government was still seeking concensus on a new set of policies involving monetary stimulus, abandonment of deficit-reduction goals, and implementation of tax changes to reduce private-sector saving and increase investment. It took some actions, including modest fiscal expansion, but it was not acting forcefully.

These developments are the focus of this book. Most of the emphasis is on the first two phases of adjustment. The third phase is still evolving, but possible outcomes are explored in the concluding chapter.

Much of the discussion in later chapters deals with fiscal policy because it played such an important role after 1973. Monetary policy was also an important means of adjusting to slower growth, but was unable by itself to create the necessary decrease in savings and increase in investment. First, the savings behavior of individuals was relatively insensitive to changes in interest rates, and investment, while it did increase, could not achieve the high levels of the 1950s and 1960s, even with lower interest rates. Second, Japan's increasing integration into world capital markets and the liberalization of regulations governing financial transactions allowed more capital to flow abroad where interest rates were higher, reducing the potentially positive impact of lower interest rates on domestic investment. The Japanese government was very sensitive to this problem, especially in the 1980s, and sometimes refrained from lowering interest rates to stimulate the economy out of fear that capital outflow would increase, lowering the value of the yen and increasing the trade and current-account surplus.

Economic Changes Writ Small

Slower economic growth brought about microeconomic as well as macroeconomic changes. Between 1973 and the mid-1980s industry, labor markets, and the institutional framework for regulating industry underwent considerable alteration. This book emphasizes government relations with the financial sector, where considerable deregulation took place.

Financial Deregulation

In the 1950s and 1960s Japan had a highly regulated financial system that served the economy well. Virtually all interest rates were controlled by the government, and financial institutions were restricted to narrow lines of business. Loans from financial institutions to corporations fueled the plant and equipment investment necessary for rapid economic growth. Regulation reduced risk and directed funds toward the industries considered most important for that growth.

The macroeconomic changes of the 1970s strained this tightly controlled system. More moderate growth meant that corporations were less dependent on loans from banks. Controlled interest rates made it difficult to float government bonds to finance rapidly expanding fiscal deficits. The emergence of current-account surpluses led to pressure to deregulate international transactions to allow the surpluses to be recycled abroad. Demographic change, especially an aging population, brought a rapid increase in the number and size of corporate pension funds. These changes pushed Japan toward a financial system characterized by a wider variety of financial instruments, greater use of market-determined interest rates, and less strict specialization within the industry. Although the Ministry of Finance eschewed sweeping actions in favor of gradual, marginal adjustments, by the mid-1980s financial institutions had been significantly altered, and the pace of change was accelerating.

Pressure from foreign institutions and governments was also a factor in causing the restructuring of financial-sector regulation but not the primary factor; the domestic economic shifts mentioned above were more important. Nevertheless, because some aspects of Japanese markets, especially the increasing capital outflow and rising value of pension funds, were attractive to foreign financial institutions, they wanted a piece of the action, and the pressure they applied, along with backing from foreign governments, played a catalytic role in promoting deregulation.

Besides altering the pattern of financial flows in the economy, deregulation held important implications for the conduct of monetary policy. In the years when most interest rates had been fixed, the Bank of Japan carried out monetary policy by telling the major banks how much their loans could expand each quarter. With the changes in the 1970s and 1980s the bank could affect economic activity by manipulating the central bank discount rate and intervening to influence certain market-determined rates, although the potential success of such actions has not yet been fully tested.

The Shifting Economic Structure

Just as in other industrial countries, the service sector in Japan has enlarged its share of economic activity, but the changes since the early 1970s have been moderate. During the 1950s and 1960s Japan experienced a rapid, sustained movement of resources out of agriculture, forestry, and fishing into mining, construction, manufacturing, and services. This movement diminished considerably in the 1970s since the labor and capital remaining in agriculture were less mobile and were protected by government assistance. The other significant change during the 1970s and 1980s was the increasing movement of employment and output from manufacturing to services, which not only reversed earlier trends but also ran counter to official expectations in the 1970s that although other countries might be moving toward postindustrial structures, Japan would remain the industrial heartland of the world. Those expectations were wrong, but at least the gains of the service sector were very slow and the changes thus not as traumatic as they could have been.

The more moderate economic growth and changes in the structure of the manufacturing sector created a number of depressed industries, a particularly unpleasant development for a country accustomed to seeing virtually every manufacturing industry expand. By 1978 the situation was serious enough that the Diet passed a special law providing some government assistance, mainly in the form of allowing collective action under government supervision to cut back industrial capacity.[3] The law was extended in 1983 to include the possibility of legalized cartels to maintain prices.

These declining industries primarily suffered from the rise in energy costs because Japan relied more heavily on oil than other industrial countries, and most of the oil came from the Organization of Petroleum Exporting Countries (OPEC). High energy costs especially affected such energy-intensive industries as aluminum smelting and electric furnace steel. Producers of petrochemicals, chemical fertilizers, and synthetic textiles also suffered, partly because of import restrictions on refined petroleum products that could have been substituted for expensive domestic products. Shipbuilding was affected because world demand for large tankers was drastically reduced as nations economized on oil and grew more slowly.

3. Edward J. Lincoln, "Depressed Industries in Japan," *Council Report,* no. 56 (November 27, 1978), pp. 1–8; and "New Depressed Industry Law to Take Effect in Japan," *JEI Report,* no. 19B (May 1983), pp. 1–8.

Rising relative wages also contributed to industrial decline. Labor-intensive industries such as textiles were unable to match the competition from low-wage countries. Other industries, including paper and plywood, in which import protection was weakening and domestic demand was stagnant, also faltered. Thus although Japan did not have regional concentrations of unemployment or failing companies as severe as those in parts of the United States, the industrial landscape was marred. The American image of an industrially secure and vibrant Japan has come primarily from imported products, which represent the internationally successful Japanese companies. Japan has had its share of losers.

Labor markets reflected changes as well. Rapid economic growth in the 1950s and 1960s absorbed the large pool of agricultural workers who were eager to move into manufacturing or service jobs. By the early 1970s the market experienced increased levels of labor turnover as firms began to hire workers from one another, which led to stronger wage demands by unions. With the combination of strong productivity growth and a tighter labor market, real wages rose at an average annual rate of 6.6 percent from 1961 to 1973. But from 1974 to 1985 they rose at only a 1.6 percent real rate.

A central feature of employment in large firms is an informal, unwritten job guarantee for most workers until the mandatory retirement age.[4] Faced with stagnant or declining labor demand in many industries after 1973, labor unions could either bargain for higher wages and accept cuts in employment or try to maintain the guarantee of lifetime jobs for existing employees and be more conciliatory on wage demands. Unions chose the latter. Companies maintained the job commitments to unionized workers; labor adjustment was handled largely by cutting overtime work, reducing the number of nonunionized workers and women within the company, and relying on attrition.

By the 1980s the rapid aging of the population, combined with continued slackness in the labor market, accelerated union attempts to raise the mandatory retirement age, traditionally fifty-five at large companies with unions. Companies did not want to extend the retirement age because the wage structure rewarded seniority, making older workers very expensive.

---

4. Not all workers even in large firms are covered by this system. All firms have "temporary" workers who do not belong to the union and have no job guarantee. In addition, women are generally expected to leave when they get married or have their first child.

However, pressure from workers and moral suasion by the Ministry of Labor have liberalized retirement policies, and far more employees now work beyond age sixty.

Pressure on the Institutional Framework

The late 1960s and early 1970s brought an upwelling of public mistrust of corporate activity, leading to an increase in the antitrust cases pursued by the Japan Fair Trade Commission, especially in 1973–74 in response to public outcries about corporate hoarding and price speculation on essential consumer products. A popular amendment strengthening the antitrust law was finally passed in 1977. While the law did not bring antitrust enforcement activity up to the level of that in the United States, the ability to strengthen the law represented at least a modest retreat from the earlier heavy dependence on the Ministry of International Trade and Industry to shape policies regulating competition. During the high-growth era, MITI pursued policies that moderated competition in some industries through legalized cartels and the promotion of mergers and generally overran opposition from the JFTC. The new mood in Japan became more evident in a landmark oil cartel case in which the court rejected informal direction from MITI as a defense for collusive price increases. The alteration of the antitrust law and the oil cartel decision did not fundamentally change government-business interactions but at least modified them. In the 1980s the government (and MITI in particular) exercised less authority over industry than it had earlier.

The end of the 1970s also saw an administrative reform movement that addressed the responsibilities of the government at a broader level, proposing to reduce the size of the government deficit and to make the bureaucracy more efficient. This pressure resulted in the successful separation of some government-owned corporations from direct government control and permitted increased private-sector competition with these companies.

The number of government-owned enterprises in Japan dropped from 111 in 1980 when the administrative reform movement began to 97 in 1986, the first sustained decline in the postwar period.[5]

---

5. Administrative Management Agency, *Tokushu Hōjin Sōran, 1986* (Overview of Special Legal Entities, 1986) (Tokyo: Government Publications Center, 1986).

The International Context

Most of this study analyzes domestic developments engendered by Japan's slower growth, but there have also been important international implications. Conversely, developments in international trade and finance have had significant effects on Japan's domestic adjustment.

The two oil shocks and the adjustment to the resulting slower economic growth and surplus savings in the private sector masked Japan's tendency to run large current-account surpluses. Because of the external constraints, the country would have faced economic recession had the government not allowed the fiscal deficit to rise. The government's ability to reduce its deficit depended on the willingness of the rest of the world to accept Japan's rapidly rising current-account surplus. Much of that international adjustment came from the United States, which chose to expand its own deficit (the result of the Reagan administration's tax cuts and increases in defense spending), thereby creating large current-account deficits. The two countries moved in opposite directions and needed each other. Fiscal austerity in Japan would have led to recession had not the United States emerged as a destination for surplus savings; expansionary fiscal policy in the United States would have brought higher interest rates had not Japan conveniently become a major capital exporter.

By 1986 this second phase of adjustment was drawing to a close, with the rapid rise of the yen against the dollar once again placing external limitations on Japan. Unlike the two oil shocks, which were one-time disruptions with short-term effects on the balance of payments, the shift in exchange rates in 1985–86 appeared more permanent. If the stronger yen were to continue, Japan would have to adjust savings and investment, raise the government deficit, or face recession. The alternatives generated extensive discussion in Japan. Changes in tax structure to encourage investment and discourage savings, some increase in the fiscal deficit, and deregulation of domestic industry to encourage investment were all on the agenda. However, many of the proposals are too modest to resolve the problem and some are unlikely ever to obtain approval. Some tax changes were made in 1987, and the government finally began to allow the deficit to rise, but these changes were rather minor. Stagnation—or at least economic growth well below potential—remains a strong possibility.

During 1985 and 1986 the United States, breaking its silence on international macroeconomic issues in the first half of the decade, began pressuring Japan to adopt policies to stimulate domestic demand. Unfortunately, the Japanese response has been that only the United States could reduce the U.S. current-account deficit; stimulating domestic demand in Japan would have little impact. Economic models support that argument, but it represents a short-sighted view of reasons for Japan to alter its policies.

Who will suffer most if Japan fails to stimulate domestic demand in the presence of surplus savings and external constraints? Japan. Without new policies the country's economy will stagnate, its GNP growing at well below the 4 percent rate it is capable of. That failure to achieve its potential represents a serious economic loss to the Japanese public.

As the debate on appropriate policies has developed, the domestic benefits of stimulating demand have been virtually ignored. Too much attention has been paid to foreign criticism and the narrow debate about the relative impact of U.S. and Japanese policy changes on the U.S. and Japanese current accounts. Japan's Ministry of Finance, with its continued desire to reduce fiscal deficits, has also impeded movements to stimulate the economy by increasing expenditures or reducing taxes, and has led the argument that Japanese changes would not help the United States very much. By 1987 it was clear that even the MOF would accept some changes in the interest of stimulating the economy, but the reluctance remains.

The causes of the decline in growth in the 1970s and how Japan has come to face the resulting problems are considered in detail in the following chapters. Whichever policy direction Japan chooses in the late 1980s will be shaped by the economic forces and institutional framework explored here.

CHAPTER TWO

The Slowdown in Growth

JAPAN burst upon the world in the 1960s and 1970s with a flood of high-quality, competitively priced manufactured products, the result of its post-war economic "miracle." This success has created an enduring image of the country as an unstoppable phenomenon of rapid growth. The reality, however, is that the Japanese economy has been growing at much more moderate rates for better than a decade. While Japan is still relatively successful, the era of extraordinarily high economic growth is gone and will not return.

The Era of High Growth

From 1950 to 1973 the annual real growth of Japan's gross national product *averaged* 10 percent, probably the highest sustained rate of increase that the world has ever seen. Although there were some fluctuations in this performance, at no point during these years did Japan suffer a recession. What the Japanese called recessions were years when the growth rate dropped to levels of 4 or 5 percent. Even some of these short-lived periods were not the result of a domestic business cycle but were deliberately caused by tight monetary policy when continuous rapid growth had pushed the country into balance-of-payments problems: short doses of slower growth were needed to curb the appetite for imports so that the government would not be forced to devalue the currency under the rules of the Bretton Woods system.

The industrialization and modernization that made rapid growth possi-

Table 2-1. *Sources of Growth in Japan, 1953–71*
Percent

Sources	Contribution to growth[a]
National income growth rate	8.77
Labor	1.85
Employment	1.14
Hours	0.21
Age-sex composition	0.14
Education	0.34
Unallocated	0.02
Capital	2.10
Inventories	0.73
Nonresidential structures and equipment	1.07
Dwellings	0.30
International assets	0
Land	0
Productivity change	4.82
Advances in knowledge and "not elsewhere classified"	1.97
Improved resource allocation	0.95
Economies of scale	1.94
Irregular factors	−0.04

Source: Hugh Patrick and Henry Rosovsky, eds., *Asia's New Giant: How the Japanese Economy Works* (Brookings, 1976), p. 94.

a. Percentage points of total national income growth originating in each factor. For example, increased labor inputs contributed 1.85 percentage points to the 8.77 percent national income growth.

ble stretch back to the nineteenth century. It is often conveniently identi-fied with the Meiji Restoration of 1868, an event that initiated the creation of the modern political nation-state. In fact, the roots of economic success can be traced back even farther to factors such as the high literacy rate prevailing by the time of the restoration. But these facts hardly diminish the luster of the extraordinary postwar economic performance.

Causes of High Growth

One way to explain growth is to look at trends in the main factors of production: labor, capital, and growth of productivity, a term that encom-passes a variety of elements, including technological change. In their work for *Asia's New Giant,* Edward Denison and William Chung found that five factors contributed more to growth in Japan than they did in ten other industrial countries: increased labor input, increased capital stock, ad-vances in knowledge, reallocation of resources away from agriculture, and economies of scale. Their findings are summarized in table 2-1. Of the

8.77 percent average annual rise in real national income in the 1950s and 1960s, labor contributed 1.85 percentage points, capital 2.10 points, and changes in productivity 4.82 points. Thus the rising productivity of labor and capital accounted for more than half of the economic growth. What Denison and Chung called advances in knowledge (which might also be labeled technological change or the introduction of improved technology) was the most important source of productivity change, contributing 1.97 percentage points. Just slightly less important were economies of scale, representing the ability of industry to attain more efficient size as the Japanese market grew. Improved resource allocation, mainly the movement of resources out of agriculture, contributed another 0.95 percentage point to growth.[1]

Some of these developments are self-explanatory. Labor's contribution increased partly because population was increasing. The very success of growth itself allowed a reallocation of labor away from low-productivity work in agriculture. Growth and rising incomes also allowed for economies of scale in production. The key question, then, is why did capital stock and gains from improved technology grow so fast?

Capital stock lies at the center of the explanation of growth provided by Kazushi Ohkawa and Henry Rosovsky, an analysis that nicely pulls together the relationships among the various factors involved.[2] Their analysis rests on three principal observations: Japan lagged far behind the industrial countries in technology in the 1950s and 1960s, it had a large pool of labor eager to move out of agriculture, and it had the social capability to absorb and adapt foreign technology. The critical element, one largely beyond the bounds of traditional economic analysis, is the ability to absorb new technology from abroad. Many nations lag behind the developed countries and have large pools of underemployed labor, but few have been able to import technology efficiently and move up the industrial ladder.

Japan is a market economy; capital stock lies mostly in the hands of the private sector, and economic decisions about production, prices, and investments are motivated by a desire to earn profits. Direct government involvement has mainly been limited to railroads, telecommunications,

1. Edward F. Denison and William K. Chung, "Economic Growth and Its Sources," in Hugh Patrick and Henry Rosovsky, eds., *Asia's New Giant: How the Japanese Economy Works* (Brookings, 1976), pp. 63–151.
2. Kazushi Ohkawa and Henry Rosovsky, *Japanese Economic Growth: Trend Acceleration in the Twentieth Century* (Oxford University Press and Stanford University Press, 1973), esp. pp. 39–43.

and cigarette manufacture (and recent efforts have been made to get out even of these, as will be explained in chapter 3). In this private-sector setting, the lag in technology, the ready availability of labor, and the ability to absorb new technology stimulated investment after World War II. Corporations expected high profits from investments in new plant and equipment, bringing in foreign technology in the process and hiring from the pool of available workers without putting undue upward pressure on wages. Those expectations were realized, encouraging further investment. As investment expanded, the continued availability of workers meant that productivity tended to rise as fast or faster than wages, which helped keep corporate profits high. High profits do not normally accompany continuous rapid investment in a mature economy. During investment spurts, profits decline, bringing an eventual slowdown in investment activity. Thus what happened in Japan was unusual; the technological lag, the ability to absorb technology, and the pool of available labor allowed it to avoid this cyclical pattern.[3]

An additional cause of growth was that investing in manufacturing was more profitable than investing in agriculture, so that resources flowed out of agriculture. Agriculture lacked profitability because little of the capital-intensive foreign technology was appropriate to the fragmented land holdings in Japan and because the large families of farmers gave them little incentive to replace workers with tractors.

The gains that Denison and Chung attributed to advances in knowledge follow from this model of strong investment demand because the technology was incorporated in new plant and equipment. Ohkawa and Rosovsky supported these findings with evidence of a close correlation between investment spurts and productivity growth. Gains from economies of scale

---

3. These relations can be expressed more formally. Let π = profit, K = capital stock, L = labor, W = wages, and O = output. Profits are the difference between output and the cost of labor: $\pi = O - W \times L$. The rate of return on capital can thus be expressed as $\pi/K = (O - W \times L)/K = O/K - W(L/K)$. An investment spurt eventually leads to a decline in profitability (π/K) because the additional amount of output from investment falls as the most productive investment opportunities are used up (declining marginal productivity of investment). This means that O/K falls. In addition, rapid investment may put pressure on labor markets, driving up wages (although this effect may be offset if the amount of capital per worker increases, that is, if L/K declines). Japan avoided a large drop in profitability in the 1950s and 1960s because the increases in productivity possible with imported technology meant that O/K was actually rising and because $W \times (L/K)$ did not rise faster than O/K. Wages rose rather rapidly, but L/K fell as corporations substituted capital for labor. For more detail and data see Ohkawa and Rosovsky, *Japanese Economic Growth*, esp. pp. 147–53.

also follow from this investment model, since an important feature of new plant and equipment was production on a larger scale. The effect was more important in Japan than in other countries because capital stock was growing so quickly.

Rapid growth based on this model applies to both prewar and postwar Japan, with a widened technological gap between it and more developed countries at the beginning of the postwar period (due to isolation during the war and the occupation) and a greater ability to absorb technology. Denison and Chung found that people did achieve higher levels of education after the war (which ought to increase the ability to use foreign technology) but that better education contributed less to growth in Japan than in other countries. However, they may have missed part of the importance of education in their data. Better postwar education contributed less because changes after the war were less dramatic than in other countries. However, during the war Japan had built up a pool of workers, many of whom had acquired technical education and experience from their military service. This created a disequilibrium in the early postwar period; many well-educated and trained people were seriously underutilized, and they were ready to move into positions in which their skills could contribute much more.

While investment-driven growth provides a tidy explanation of Japan's experience that is consistent with growth-accounting evidence, other factors were also involved. First, the private sector generated high and rising savings to feed the strong investment demand. This was important because the government chose not to borrow heavily from abroad to finance domestic investment, a choice different from that made by most developing countries today. Had domestic savings been lower, investment would have been limited unless government changed its stance and allowed dependence on foreign capital inflow.

Second, Japan has been politically stable since the war, with a popularly supported, noncoercive government. The Liberal Democratic party has been in power for virtually all these years, but its success has been based on free elections and not military power or suppression of opposition groups. The experience of South Korea, where economic growth temporarily dropped below zero during the uncertainty generated by the transfer of power after the assassination of Park Chung Hee in 1979, demonstrates the impact of political instability on growth.

Third, the Japanese government provided supportive economic policies. At the macroeconomic level the government followed tight fiscal policies and expansionary monetary policies. It maintained a balanced budget until the mid-1960s, thereby avoiding competition with the private sector for use of domestic savings (foreign borrowing was largely prohibited). Furthermore, public works spending was skewed toward industrially useful investment rather than social amenities. The money supply was allowed to grow rapidly enough to meet the needs of economic expansion. Because Japan had a capital-scarce economy after the war, interest rates were not low by international standards, but the government managed to keep them low enough so that they did not seriously impede new investment.[4]

At the microeconomic level the government also adopted supportive policies, but experts question the importance of some of them.[5] It imposed high import barriers, supposedly to protect infant industries (and perhaps out of simple economic nationalism), behind which industries could grow without much competition from abroad. These barriers helped provide additional incentives for investment. At the industry level a variety of other aids were supplied, but many were minor and some were used in ways totally unrelated to goals for economic growth and development (some aids, such as support of the domestic coal industry in the 1950s in the face of cheap imported oil, even ran counter to stated goals). How much government macroeconomic and microeconomic policies together contributed to growth is impossible to quantify, but overall they seem to have been supportive.

Fourth, Japan faced a favorable world environment. Trade liberalization under the auspices of the newly created General Agreement on Tariffs and Trade, rapid economic growth worldwide, and an end to colonialism that enabled former colonies to diversify their trade patterns all helped Japan expand exports in the 1950s and 1960s. Raw material prices fell in the 1950s and then remained stable in the 1960s, allowing the country to improve its terms of trade (the ratio of the price of exports to the price of imports).[6] The favorable price movements in the terms of trade enhanced

4. Rates on loans were controlled, but evidence suggests that financial institutions had a variety of means to circumvent those controls (such as requiring borrowers to hold some part of a loan as a savings deposit, discussed in chapter 4). See, for example, Akiyoshi Horiuchi, "Economic Growth and Financial Allocation in Postwar Japan," Discussion Papers in International Economics (Brookings, August 1984). pp. 16–20.

5. For a review of that debate, see Edward J. Lincoln, *Japan's Industrial Policies: What Are They, Do They Matter, and Are They Different from Those in the United States?* (Washington, D.C.: Japan Economic Institute of America, 1984).

6. Lawrence B. Krause and Sueo Sekiguchi, "Japan and the World Economy," in Patrick and Rosovsky, eds., *Asia's New Giant,* esp. p. 403.

national welfare and may have increased the growth rate by improving Japan's balance-of-payments position. (As mentioned earlier, balance-of-payments problems periodically forced monetary authorities to slow the economy, but favorable movements in terms of trade meant that these problems were less severe than they would have been otherwise.)

Fifth, the Japanese have long valued education, hard work, and loyalty. These emphases found expression in an educated and dedicated labor force with the ability and willingness to accept rapid technological change. In addition, the destruction of the war forged a strong social commitment to economic growth as a national goal. People were willing to forgo leisure and social amenities in order to promote rapid industrial development. Other social features that probably contributed to growth in intangible ways include the relative homogeneity of society and language, the absence of debilitating regional disparities, and sufficient social mobility to prevent class conflict.

Sixth, labor-management relations evolved in a relatively nonconfrontational way. Although the union movement was militant in some industries and strikes were frequent in the early postwar years, by the late 1950s and early 1960s most of the radical unions had been crushed and replaced by more moderate ones. This was a divisive period for labor, but the fact that the radical unions could not command sufficient loyalty among workers to stay in power confirms the broad nature of the social consensus on rapid growth and hard work. Japanese workers accepted a system of enterprise-based unions with very weak national organizations, moderate strike activity (in which strikes are of limited, preannounced duration), transfers between jobs or factories within a company as technological change eliminated old functions, and moderation in wage demands when corporate profits fell. In general, unions have been flexible on wages and work rules.

Finally, the postwar occupation by the United States brought a number of political and economic reforms that may have been very important to economic growth. These included extensive land reform (essentially eliminating tenancy), legalization of labor unions, and dissolution of the powerful business conglomerates (*zaibatsu*) that had increasingly dominated Japanese industry before and during the war. The dissolution may have brought greater competition and thereby more aggressive investment activity in the corporate sector. The establishment of an antitrust law helped prevent a reemergence of the zaibatsu and some of the more egregious forms of anticompetitive behavior (even though antitrust enforcement was lax by American standards).[7]

The effects of most of these factors cannot be measured, but they must not be ignored in explaining why Japan grew. They created an atmosphere in which private business could realistically hold expectations of high rates of return on investment in plant and equipment. Thus they are essential to explaining Japan's rapid growth and the difference between its prewar and postwar experiences.

As a result of these years of growth, by the early 1970s Japan was transformed from an impoverished, war-devastated nation into a prosperous, industrialized country. As put succinctly in *Asia's New Giant*, "Japan's surge over the past quarter-century, seemingly from nowhere, to join the vanguard of the world's economies has been an unprecedented, exciting, and at times disruptive event. By any economic criteria Japan is now an immense, rich nation."[8]

Expectations in the Early 1970s

By the early 1970s the Japanese and the rest of the world were beginning to realize that Japan's prosperity was not just a temporary or fragile phenomenon. But analysts began to err in the direction of unbounded optimism, engaging in projections for the future that assumed endless growth. In *The Emerging Japanese Superstate,* a best-seller in Japan, Herman Kahn confessed that "the overriding reason for my interest in Japan is its spectacular past and expected future economic growth—better than 10 percent a year in the last two decades, and likely to be maintained at around that rate for at least the next two or three decades."[9] Such enthusiasm was not surprising considering the self-confidence and optimism many Japanese displayed. Students, for example, were using the

7. After the war, firms that had been part of the zaibatsu reformed into loose groups called *keiretsu*. These groups look similar to the zaibatsu, but what ties there are (mainly through mutual stockholding and loans from the group bank) are weak enough that they have not suppressed competition in any measurable way. See Eleanor M. Hadley, *Antitrust in Japan* (Princeton University Press, 1970), esp. chaps. 11, 12.

8. Hugh Patrick and Henry Rosovsky, "Japan's Economic Performance: An Overview," in Patrick and Rosovsky, eds., *Asia's New Giant*, p. 3.

9. Herman Kahn, *The Emerging Japanese Superstate: Challenge and Response* (Prentice-Hall, 1970), p. 3.

phrase *Nippon ichiban* (Japan is number one) as an expression of where they saw their country headed.

The optimism spilled over into discussions of policy. In 1972, just before he became prime minister, Kakuei Tanaka published *Nihon Retto Kaizō Ron* (*Building a New Japan* was the English title) in which he proposed that high growth could be sustained and great improvements made by the government in roads, schools, hospitals, and other works for the welfare of the public. "The period of rapid growth," he wrote, "has given rise to such distortions as pollution, inflation, urban overcrowding, rural depopulation, and agricultural stagnation. To solve these problems and to provide a worthwhile life in a pleasant country, we must waste no time in improving social overhead capital and the social security standards."[10] A key feature of his proposals was to encourage redistribution of economic activity away from the Tokyo-Osaka industrial belt and toward more rural areas.

When Tanaka became prime minister in the summer of 1972, he quickly ordered the Economic Planning Agency (EPA) to draw up a long-term economic plan incorporating the basic philosophy of his book.[11] The Basic Economic and Social Plan for 1973–77, adopted in February 1973 just before the outbreak of problems that dramatically reduced growth rates, represented the last major policy statement of the high-growth era. Following the Tanaka script, the plan recognized the problems stemming from rapid growth and the concurrent need to redistribute resources. An awareness of the problems of pollution, old age care, inadequate social overhead capital, and others, it said, "once confined to a small portion of the population, has now emerged as broad national demands, partly be-

10. Kakuei Tanaka, *Building a New Japan: A Plan for Remodeling the Japanese Archipelago* (Tokyo: Simul Press, 1973), p. 68. One can easily be cynical about Tanaka's motivation in offering this plan. His own background was in the construction industry in rural Niigata Prefecture, and the primary bastion of support for the Liberal Democratic party was in rural areas, so that the plan could easily be dismissed as an exercise in building political support. Furthermore, Tanaka was known as a master of pork barrel politics, making him enormously popular with his constituents. However, the book was more than a self-serving political piece, and Tanaka deserves at least some credit for a genuine desire to make Japan a significantly better place to live and a supremely confident belief that this could be done painlessly.

11. Japan has seen a series of these macroeconomic plans, which are a combination of forecast and hope about where the economy is heading, since the 1950s. However, they often do little to influence policy, so that they are far from plans in any real sense. When a new prime minister enters office, it is customary for the EPA to formulate a new plan, and Tanaka was certainly no exception.

cause of the tardiness of policy response, and it is therefore necessary now that there be a policy switch that will make it possible to meet these demands."[12]

Projecting much the same confidence as Tanaka himself, the plan forecast about a 9 percent real GNP annual growth rate (in 1965 prices), down from the 11 percent rate that prevailed from 1961 to 1970. That was hardly a change at all. Helping to buoy the projected rate was the assumption that Tanaka's plan for redistributing economic activity more evenly around Japan would be implemented—that there would be improvements in regional transportation infrastructure, controls on further development in urban areas, inducements for industry to relocate away from urban areas, and financial assistance to regional cities to promote development.[13]

As a whole, the plan was a very liberal document, endorsing a wide range of social programs, including increased spending on housing, expanded public park lands, more resources for home care and community care of the elderly and seriously handicapped, increased spending on medical facilities, and the institution of a five-day workweek. The authors of the plan did acknowledge that to achieve these goals increased government deficits would be necessary. With a modest slowdown in private-sector investment, they predicted that government expenditures on social programs would cause a ¥6.0 trillion deficit by fiscal year 1977, or approximately $22 billion at average 1973 exchange rates. By way of comparison, the actual government deficit in fiscal 1977 was ¥9.6 trillion.[14]

The EPA plan also anticipated that continued expansion at home would hold the current-account surplus to a moderate $5.9 billion, with an equal outflow of long-term capital yielding a zero basic balance.[15] The actual current-account surplus for fiscal 1977 was $14 billion (1.5 percent of

12. Economic Planning Agency, *Basic Economic and Social Plan: Toward a Vigorous Welfare Society, 1973–1977* (Tokyo: EPA, 1973), p. 5

13. Ibid., pp. 20–21, 29–30.

14. Ibid., p. 108. The ¥6.0 trillion is in current prices (that is, not adjusted for expected inflation). Exchange rates based on yen-per-dollar period averages are from International Monetary Fund, *International Financial Statistics Yearbook, 1986* (Washington, D.C.: IMF); and Bank of Japan, *Economic Statistics Annual, 1980* (Tokyo: BOJ), p. 211.

15. Economic Planning Agency, *Basic Economic and Social Plan*, p. 124. The term "basic balance" includes the current account plus long-term capital (investments in assets with a maturity greater than one year). This balance has no particular theoretical meaning, but it was popular with Japanese officials, who felt long-term capital was less volatile and therefore better than short-term capital in some undefined sense. The balance-of-payments accounting framework is considered in greater detail in chapter 5.

GNP), and most of the offsetting capital outflow was in short-term assets, so that the basic balance showed a surplus of $11.6 billion.

This optimistic forecast purported to show how Japan could continue to grow at very high real rates despite a moderate shift from private-sector investment to government spending in order to improve the quality of life. Continued rapid growth would allow the government to make these new or expanded expenditures without going too far into debt because tax revenues would rise rapidly. Finally, growth would absorb resources at home, keeping the current-account surplus under control so that Japan would not get into political trouble with its trading partners. None of these projections came true.

The EPA was not alone in its optimism. The Japan Economic Research Center, often at the upper end of private-sector Japanese forecasts, published an even rosier forecast early in 1974, just as pessimism was settling in elsewhere. It predicted 9.2 percent average annual growth for the 1970–85 period, but then in a bow to the uncertainty of the future said that a wider range of 7 to 9 percent would be realistic. The forecast assumed continued high investment levels with some moderate shift from plant and equipment toward housing and government investment. Plant and equipment investment was to drop from 20 percent to 15 percent of GNP, while housing investment would be up from 6.6 percent to 10 percent. Government investment would be up from 8.2 percent to 10.5 percent, a more moderate rise than anticipated in the EPA plan. All this investment would be supported by continued high savings rates. The research center also predicted domestic demand would rise rapidly enough that the current-account surplus would increase to only $9.4 billion, or 0.3 percent of GNP at expected exchange rates (compared to an actual surplus in 1985 of $49 billion, close to 4 percent of GNP).[16]

The research center's projection was so optimistic that it implied a GNP almost as big as that forecast for the United States in 1985, with Japan's per capita income 74 percent higher than that of the United States. Thus the center joined the school that thought Japan could continue to grow at extremely high rates and divert resources to improving social welfare for a number of years to come.[17]

16. Japan Economic Research Center, *The Structure of a Three-Trillion Dollar Economy: The Japanese Economy in 1985* (Tokyo: JERC, 1974), pp. 3–5, 9, 24; Bank of Japan, *Balance of Payments Monthly*, (December 1985), p. 1; and Economic Planning Agency, *Annual Report on National Income Accounts, 1987* (Tokyo: EPA, 1987), p. 7.

17. Japan Economic Research Center, *The Structure of a Three-Trillion Dollar Econ-*

Not everyone leaped on the high-growth bandwagon. In *How Japan's Economy Grew So Fast,* Denison and Chung concluded that Japan's growth rate would be 6.9 percent annually between 1974 and 1982.[18] Brookings scholars Philip Trezise and Edward Fried came to a similar conclusion. Using the same growth-accounting techniques, they forecast 6 percent annual growth from 1975 to 1985 because of slower labor, capital, and productivity growth.[19] Although both estimates turned out to be too high, they did focus on the central feature of Japanese economic growth: much of it was based on special, temporary factors that by the early 1970s were reaching the limit of their contribution. What happened to these influences explains why growth dropped so much after 1973.

While the conclusion that growth would not continue at an annual rate of 10 percent into the indefinite future may seem obvious in hindsight, predicting the future from straight-line projections of the recent past was an easy and satisfying exercise in the early 1970s. Rapid growth had become a way of life in Japan, and a sharp decline was almost inconceivable. When the break did come, it turned out to be much sharper and more traumatic than anyone anticipated.

The 1973–74 Watershed

The disruption of oil supplies in late 1973 in combination with other domestic and foreign events marked the end of Japan's phenomenal economic growth. Abandoning the euphoric mood of the long-term economic plan approved early in 1973, EPA Director General Tsuneo Uchida announced before the Diet in January 1974 that "for both the international economy and the Japanese economy, one age is to pass, and a new age is to start."[20]

---

omy, p. 25. In all fairness, by 1975 in the aftermath of the first oil shock, the research center had lowered its sights to 7 percent growth. See *The Future of World Economy and Japan* (Tokyo: JERC, 1975), p. 3.

18. Edward F. Denison and William K. Chung, *How Japan's Economy Grew So Fast: The Sources of Postwar Expansion* (Brookings, 1976), p. 126.

19. Edward R. Fried and Philip H. Trezise, "Japan's Future Position in the World Economy," paper prepared for U.S. Department of State, 1974, p. 74.

20. *Nihon Keizai Shimbun* (Tokyo) Evening Edition, January 21, 1974. U.S. embassy translation.

What happened to make these years so traumatic? Basically, Japan suffered from simultaneous high inflation and recession. Much of the inflation was caused by the sharp increases in world prices for raw materials (including but not confined to oil). Government macroeconomic policies designed to stimulate domestic demand also contributed because the potential for growth of supply was diminishing.[21] As inflation mounted, the country faced a temporary cut in oil supplies from the Middle East. This combination of events not only created Japan's first recession of the postwar period but also raised extreme fears about long-term dependence on basic resources, a dependence that seemed likely to limit the country's ability to grow in the future. Had these events not transpired, a softer, more gradual shift to slower growth rates could have taken place. With them, the transition from one era to another was much faster and more frightening.

The 1973 Shocks

At the opening of 1973 the Japanese economy was growing rapidly, part of a business recovery from a growth recession in 1971 that had been caused by the revaluation of the yen.[22] And yet by early in the year inflation was running at higher levels than expected, fed by excess demand and rising import prices. Table 2-2 illustrates what happened to prices. During the 1960s Japan had had a pattern of very stable wholesale and import prices with moderate consumer price inflation. This pattern continued in the early 1970s. But after falling by 0.8 percent in 1971 and rising

21. When looking at economic growth, economists often make a distinction between potential and actual growth. The potential (or full-employment) growth rate is an estimate of how much the supply of goods and services would expand if all factors of production were fully utilized. Actual growth measures the demand for goods and services, and demand may be less than the potential supply, leaving some factors underused. This situation may result from external events or from the failure of government to follow economic policies to maintain full employment. Attempts to follow policies that push actual growth beyond potential levels, however, may result in inflation (as a means of restricting the level of demand to potential supply).

22. In August 1971 the fixed exchange rate of 360 yen to the dollar came to an end after the United States stopped convertibility of the dollar into gold. An agreement to fix exchange rates at a new set of parities was signed in December, establishing a ratio of 308 yen to the dollar, a 16.5 percent appreciation of the yen. While small compared to later exchange rate swings, this initial shift was a greater surprise to Japanese exporters. As a result, real GNP growth dropped to only 4.3 percent in 1971 (from 9.5 percent in 1970). Economic Planning Agency, *Annual Report on National Accounts, 1987*, p. 123.

Table 2-2. *Inflation Rates, Selected Years and Periods, 1959-75*
Percent change from same period in previous year

Year	Wholesale price index	Import price index	Consumer price index
1961–70 average[a]	1.3	0.6	5.9
1971	−0.8	0	6.1
1972	0.8	−4.3	4.5
1973	15.9	21.0	11.7
1974	31.3	66.3	24.5
1975	3.0	7.6	11.8
1973			
January	7.6	12.9	6.2
February	9.2	11.5	6.7
March	11.0	13.1	8.4
April	11.4	11.7	9.4
May	12.3	14.1	10.9
June	13.6	18.4	11.1
July	15.7	24.0	11.9
August	17.4	27.4	12.0
September	18.7	25.4	14.6
October	20.3	25.3	14.3
November	22.3	32.6	15.9
December	29.0	34.7	19.1
1974			
January	34.0	42.8	23.1
February	37.0	69.3	26.3
March	35.4	69.2	24.0
April	35.7	74.8	24.9
May	35.3	74.8	23.1
June	35.4	71.9	23.6
July	34.2	70.5	25.2
August	32.9	71.8	25.4
September	30.6	71.3	23.8
October	28.7	69.3	26.2
November	25.1	59.1	25.8
December	17.0	53.3	21.9
1975			
January	10.4	37.0	17.4

Sources: Bank of Japan, *Economic Statistics Monthly* (January 1973), pp. 139, 145, 147; (January 1974), pp. 145, 151, 153; (January 1975), pp. 145, 151, 153; (January 1976), p. 163; and Bank of Japan, *Economic Statistics Annual, 1970* (Tokyo: BOJ, 1970), p. 259; *1971*, pp. 249, 262.
a. Figures for 1961–70 average are in 1965 base year. All others are in 1970 base year.

only 0.8 percent in 1972, wholesale prices began to accelerate rapidly. In January they were running 7.6 percent above levels of a year earlier, and by March the rate had reached double digits. Import prices rose even more rapidly. After falling 4.3 percent in 1972, by January they were already 12.9 percent higher than a year earlier and by July were up 24 percent, reflecting world inflation trends that predated the oil shock. Consumer prices followed wholesale prices, with the rate of inflation rising continuously from 6.2 percent in January to 10.9 percent by May and 23.1 percent by January 1974.

Inflation at the levels evident by the spring of 1973 was an unpleasant experience for Japan. From 1961 to 1970 the wholesale price index had risen at an average annual rate of only 1.3 percent, while the consumer price index had increased at a 5.9 percent rate. This pattern of stable wholesale prices, reflecting great strides in manufacturing productivity, and moderately high inflation in consumer prices, because imported technology did not apply to many labor-intensive services, is typical of newly industrializing countries. While consumer inflation in the 1960s was higher than that experienced in the United States, it was accepted by the Japanese as a minor price to pay for rapid economic growth.[23] But the experience of 1973 began to remind people of the hyperinflation of the late 1940s.

Besides rising inflation, 1973 was marked by other new concerns. At the beginning of the 1970s the Japanese were fiercely committed to the idea of fixed exchange rates; the stability of the Bretton Woods system was one of the rocks upon which postwar prosperity was built. The revaluation at the end of August 1971 had been an enormously difficult decision to make, and when the Smithsonian agreement on exchange rates was signed in December 1971, there was hope that stability would return at the new parities. But in March 1973 the agreement collapsed and currencies were allowed to float. Some Japanese firmly believed that the uncertainties generated by floating rates would be so severe that international trade would collapse. Therefore, it was with great trepidation (and a great deal of direct intervention in the exchange market) that Japan began the era of floating rates.

At the end of June 1973 the Japanese faced another surprise: the United States announced a complete embargo on exports of soybeans. Soybeans

23. Average annual consumer price inflation in the United States from 1960 to 1970 was 2.3 percent, under half the rate in Japan. Bureau of the Census, *Statistical Abstract of the United States, 1987* (GPO, 1986), p. 463.

are an important element in Japanese cuisine (in both an esthetic and nutritional sense), but Japan had not protected domestic producers from import competition as it had producers of some other agricultural products, and as a result only 6 percent of the country's supply was produced domestically. The United States accounted for 88 percent of soybean imports in 1973 and 84 percent of total supply.[24] The embargo turned out to be very short-lived once the U.S. government realized the damage it implied for Japan, and no contracted shipments for the year were actually prevented. Nevertheless, that a valued ally could do such a thing added to Japanese feelings of vulnerability.

The soybean shock fed broader concerns about imports. An editorial on June 29 in the *Nihon Keizai Shimbun* noted:

> Because of a series of problems, including contaminated fish, the miserable drought in West Africa, frequent earthquakes, rising inflation, and the world shortage of grain since last year, people have become extremely anxious. We are now close to the point at which even a minor bit of bad news will be blown out of proportion and "anxiety will beget anxiety."[25]

Representative of these fears were Japanese press reports that Washington would restrict log and lumber exports to Japan or that it would limit wheat exports because of lobbying pressure from the All-American Bread Manufacturers Association, which wanted to keep U.S. domestic prices down.[26] Such rumors led to panic among consumers, who feared restrictions would multiply and shortages would spread to other commodities. In the fall of 1973 came the famous toilet paper shortage, when new shipments disappeared from store shelves as soon as they arrived. Self-fulfilling prophecy then led to panic buying and hoarding of soy sauce, cooking oil, and other necessities, creating shortages when no real supply problem existed.

All these fears came to naught. In April 1974, with a possible drop in U.S. prices and overproduction already in the offing, Secretary of Agriculture Earl Butz visited Tokyo to reassure the Japanese government about

24. Management and Coordination Agency, *Japan Statistical Yearbook, 1978* (Tokyo: Statistics Bureau, 1978), pp. 113–14; Ministry of Finance, *Summary Report: Trade of Japan, 1974* (Tokyo: Japan Tariff Assoc., 1975), p. 84; and MOF, *Japan Exports and Imports: Commodity by Country, 1973* (Tokyo: Japan Tariff Assoc., 1974), p. 58.

25. *Nihon Keizai Shimbun*, June 29, 1973. U.S. embassy translation.

26. *Nihon Keizai Shimbun*, February 13, 1974; and *Nihon Keizai Shimbun*, January 15, 1974. U.S. embassy translations.

exports of foodstuffs. He guaranteed Minister of Agriculture Tadao Kuraishi stable supplies from the United States and recommended stockpiling as a way to ease problems in times of short supply.[27] These guarantees were followed in 1975 by the Butz-Abe agreement, an unusual bilateral document of "understanding" that set minimum annual quantities of wheat, feed grains, and soybeans the United States would supply to Japan in 1976–78.[28]

The possibility of embargoes and other disruptions of imports generated some calls for achieving self-sufficiency in food production, but no actions were taken. In fiscal year 1965, government measures showed 61 percent of the calories the Japanese consumed were produced domestically; by 1975 the figure had declined to 43 percent and by 1983 to 32 percent.[29] Thus, far from acting on the fears generated in 1973, Japan has actually followed the economically rational policy of decreasing dependence on uncompetitive domestic food producers (and could move much farther in that direction). Even for soybeans this was the case, despite calls for diversifying sources of supply after the 1973 shock. By 1984 the United States accounted for 86 percent of Japan's total soybean supply.[30]

Of all the events of 1973, the most dramatic was the October war in the Middle East and the accompanying oil market disruptions. On October 16 the Organization of Arab Petroleum Exporting Countries announced an increase in the price of oil from $3 a barrel to $5. The next day it announced a 5 percent cutback in oil shipments. On October 19 it imposed a total embargo on the United States and a 10 percent cutback for other countries. On November 4 the cuts were increased to 25 percent and were to be increased to 30 percent in December. On November 6 the restrictions were eased somewhat for the European countries but not for Japan, apparently out of a belief that Japan was still too closely tied to American diplomatic positions. On November 22 Japan finally issued a strong pro-

27. *Yomiuri Shimbun* (Tokyo), April 21, 1974. U.S. embassy translation.

28. Emery N. Castle and Kenzo Hemmi, eds., *U.S.–Japanese Agricultural Trade Relations* (Johns Hopkins University Press for Resources for the Future, 1982), p. 80.

29. *Japan Economic Journal*, January 1, 1985. When measured in value terms, the share of imports is smaller. In 1984 the gross value of agricultural output was almost ¥12 trillion and foodstuff imports just under ¥4 trillion, making imports 32 percent of total supplies. But this was a large increase from the 20 percent reported in 1970. See Management and Coordination Agency, *Japan Statistical Yearbook, 1986*, pp. 172, 343.

30. Management and Coordination Agency, *Japan Statistical Yearbook, 1986*, p. 160; Ministry of Finance, *Summary Report: Trade of Japan, 1985*, p. 84; and Ministry of Finance, *Japan Exports and Imports: Commodity by Country, 1984*, p. 59.

Arab statement, and in December, Deputy Prime Minister Takeo Miki was dispatched to the Middle East. During his trip OAPEC eased the restrictions on Japan to a 15 percent cut, the same imposed on the European countries. On March 13, 1974, the restrictions were lifted entirely.[31]

Coming on top of rising general inflation, the soybean embargo, and the panic-driven shortages, the oil shock was a truly traumatic experience for the Japanese. Among other things, they worried that the international companies handling most of the actual supply of oil would not treat Japan equally with their home countries. As one major newspaper noted, "There is no doubt that the shortage of oil supply will concentrate, after all, in the consumer countries having no international oil capital."[32] Although such fears were groundless, they demonstrate the deep belief of the Japanese that they are not fully accepted in the international community and will be discriminated against when the economic chips are down, a fear no doubt reinforced by the soybean fiasco.

This disastrous combination of events created strong concerns that Japan would not be able to cope with the problems. An editorial in *Sankei Shimbun* speculated that "economic and social confusion will be beyond all imagination." *Tokyo Shimbun* expressed similar fears: "It will be presumed that such a scene, where social unrest will whirl around in the Japanese archipelago, will arise." The more cautious *Mainichi Shimbun* shied away from predicting social turmoil but noted that "people will be compelled to endure austerity, which has not been seen since immediately after the end of the war."[33] Such dire predictions may seem examples of journalistic excess, but they did represent the widespread public shock that more than two decades of unparalleled growth and prosperity could be so abruptly compromised.

By the beginning of November the Ministry of International Trade and Industry dared to suggest that in the worst-case scenario growth in the next fiscal year could be as low as zero. But most other government pronouncements in November and December said Japan would manage to pull through with a real GNP growth rate of 4 to 5 percent, which demonstrates

31. Valerie Yorke, "Oil, the Middle East and Japan's Search for Security," in Nobutoshi Akao, *Japan's Economic Security* (St. Martin's Press, 1983), pp. 52–53; and *Sankei Shimbun* (Tokyo), December 27, 1973, and *Yomiuri Shimbun,* Evening Edition, March 14, 1974. U.S. embassy translations.

32. *Sankei Shimbun,* October 19, 1973. U.S. embassy translation.

33. *Sankei Shimbun,* November 12, 1973; *Tokyo Shimbun,* November 14, 1973; and *Mainichi Shimbun* (Tokyo), November 16, 1973. U.S. embassy translations.

how ingrained the high-growth mentality had become among government officials: even in adversity it was difficult to conceive of anything worse than the growth recessions of the 1960s.

The 1974 Recession

Despite official optimism 1974 was the first year since World War II that Japan suffered a real recession, and one combined with very high inflation. At the beginning of the year the government refused to accept this possibility. The Economic Planning Agency forecast for fiscal 1974 called for 2.5 percent real growth, with a 10.4 percent rise in the GNP deflator, a 14.6 percent rise in wholesale prices, and a very modest current-account deficit of $450 million. Even these figures represented a downward revision made between the time the forecast was discussed at a cabinet meeting at the beginning of the year and its announcement to the Diet at the end of January. The somewhat more cautious organization of big businesses, Keidanren, predicted 1.4 percent growth.[34] In fact, real GNP growth was −0.4 percent in fiscal 1974, the GNP deflator was up 18.9 percent, wholesale prices were up 23.5 percent, and the current account was in deficit by $2.3 billion. On a calendar year basis, GNP growth was −1.4 percent, wholesale price inflation was 31.4 percent (following a 15.8 percent jump in 1973), and consumer prices were up 24.5 percent.[35] For a country used to 10 percent growth this was a devastating blow.

Two decades of rapid economic growth had eliminated the large pool of underemployed labor in Japan, and in the tightened labor market conditions of the early 1970s, unions were determined not to lose economic ground when inflation heated up. Union wages in Japan are set by one-year contracts, and all unions negotiate their contracts in the spring, during a period known as the *shuntō* (spring offensive). The outcome, as measured by a government survey after the negotiations were over, was an average increase in wages of 32.9 percent, following a 20.1 percent rise in 1973. This figure is somewhat higher than the one shown by published wage data for all workers (in establishments of thirty or more employees) because only part of the work force is unionized. But even the data for all

34. *Nihon Keizai Shimbun*, January 20, 1974; February 27, 1974.
35. Economic Planning Agency, *Annual Report on National Accounts, 1987*, pp. 49, 61, 123; and Bank of Japan, *Economic Statistics Annual, 1977*, pp. 227, 285, 299.

workers show a 27 percent increase in wages for 1974.[36] These high wage settlements became a mechanism for spreading the effects of inflation broadly through the economy.

Faced with simultaneous inflation and recession, public attitudes were gloomy. A survey at the beginning of January indicated 22 percent of those polled expected shortages of goods to last three years or more (including 9 percent who said shortages would last forever). Those who felt that they personally suffered from shortages were predictably more numerous among younger Japanese than among the older generations, who were used to living in more austere conditions.[37] Another poll found that 73 percent felt the Japanese economy was frail and worried about what would happen to it.[38]

While external factors—the oil shortage and price rise and the increases in the prices of other imported materials—can be blamed for much of the economic problem facing Japan, government policies may have made the situation worse. At the macroeconomic level the government made mistakes in both monetary policy and fiscal policy, supplying too much stimulus when inflation was rising. At the microeconomic level the government responded to inflation by controlling prices of some goods and services, thereby postponing needed price adjustments and distorting prices in the economy.

Both monetary and fiscal policies had been expansionary in 1971–72 to stimulate the economy following the shock of yen revaluation. Not only did such action help the economy, but it also took some of the upward pressure off the yen-dollar exchange rate by diverting goods from exports to domestic demand (at that time monetary authorities were still resisting appreciation of the yen, hoping to keep it at the new parity of 308 to the dollar set by the Smithsonian agreement of December 1971). According to EPA statistics, real GNP growth in 1971 (measured in 1980 prices) had been only 4.3 percent but had rebounded to 8.5 percent in 1972, partly because of these policies. Fiscal expansion was also related to implementation in 1973 of Prime Minister Tanaka's ideas for improving welfare in a high-growth environment.

Some prominent Japanese economists, especially the new breed of

36. Hajime Ohta, "As Economy Slows, Wage Increases Decline," *Council Report*, no. 27 (July 1980), table 2; and Management and Coordination Agency, *Japan Statistical Yearbook, 1980*, p. 399.

37. *Mainichi Shimbun*, January 1, 1974.

38. *Sankei Shimbun*, January 4, 1974.

Table 2-3. *Money Supply Growth, Quarterly, 1972–75*[a]
Percent increase from same quarter of previous year

Quarter	M1	M2
1972		
First	27.7	24.0
Second	19.9	22.8
Third	19.5	22.0
Fourth	24.7	24.7
1973		
First	27.4	25.1
Second	29.9	24.7
Third	27.0	22.9
Fourth	16.7	16.8
1974		
First	15.4	15.1
Second	15.7	13.4
Third	10.1	10.9
Fourth	11.5	11.5
1975		
First	9.8	11.3
Second	7.4	11.4
Third	9.8	13.2
Fourth	11.1	14.5

Sources: Bank of Japan, *Economic Statistics Monthly* (January 1973–75), p. 13; (January 1976), p. 15; and Bank of Japan, *Economic Statistics Annual, 1971*, p. 11.

a. Figures are based on money supply at end of the final month for each quarter.

monetarists, have chosen to place the blame for inflation on monetary policy. They have argued that the government allowed the money supply to grow too fast in 1971–72 and that to some extent policy was out of control, since extensive unsterilized direct intervention in exchange markets had the side effect of increasing domestic money supply. According to a number of senior economists, including Yoshio Suzuki of the Bank of Japan, Ryūtarō Komiya of Tokyo University, and Seiji Shimpo of the EPA, the Keynesian economists in control of macroeconomic policy seriously underestimated the inflationary potential of excessive monetary growth.[39]

To evaluate the contention, table 2-3 presents data on the increase in money supply from 1972 to 1975. By the second quarter of 1972, both M1 and M2 were 20 percent higher than a year earlier. The measures peaked at 30 percent for M1 and 25 percent for M2 in the second quarter of 1973, then increases moderated for the rest of 1973 and all of 1974. By 1975 M1

39. Seiji Shimpo, *Gendai Nihon Keizai no Kaimei: Sutagufurēshon no Kenkyū* (The Contemporary Japanese Economy: A Study of Stagflation) (Tokyo: Tōyō Keizai Shimpōsha, 1979), pp. 28–36.

was rising at less than 10 percent and M2 at about 11 percent. Such rates of increase were not unusual—money supply growth exceeded 20 percent for several years in the 1960s. What was unusual in 1973 was that the economy responded with more inflation and less growth than in the earlier years. Monetary stimulus came at a time when the economy was operating close to capacity; the supply of additional goods and services could not meet the increased demand created by the increased supply of money.

The problem of inflation could be attributed to a timing error; governments should not stimulate their economies when they are at cyclical peaks. However, such a situation had not arisen in the previous two decades, when monetary stimulus had worked because the supply capacity of the economy had responded very flexibly. The mistake, then, was the failure to recognize that the era of extremely high potential real growth was coming to an end, so that stimulating demand would generate more inflation and less growth of economic supply than before. The neat and simple division of the world into profligate Keynesians and sensible monetarists (made by economists such as Shimpo) is hardly the point; the Japanese economy was changing, and very few people recognized that fact regardless of their theoretical stripes. When policies have worked well for twenty years, it is difficult to be critical of continuing to use them.

Authorities finally realized that inflation was becoming a problem and tightened monetary policy, but the action was slow in having any impact. The large current-account surplus and the previous period of monetary ease had increased liquidity so much that the corporate sector did not feel the bite for some time. In tightening monetary policy, the Bank of Japan relied primarily on two instruments: the discount rate at which it lends funds to the commercial banks and "window guidance," direct and forceful "advice" to commercial banks on the rate their lending activity should increase. From 4.25 percent at the beginning of 1973, the discount rate was raised in a series of steps between April and December to 9.0 percent. This in itself was an unusual move, since during the 1950s and 1960s the discount rate remained very steady while window guidance acted as the main monetary policy instrument.[40] Under the influence of tighter mone-

40. Although the rise in the discount rate was sizable and unusual, real interest rates (nominal interest rates minus the rate of inflation) were below zero, as they were in other countries. Therefore the quantitive restraints on lending through window guidance remained a principal policy tool. The impact of negative interest rates on the savings behavior of individuals is considered in chapter 4. Although real interest rates were negative, the discount rate is taken here to be a reasonable proxy for the overall stance of monetary policy.

tary policy, though, the rate of increase in money supply did not sink below 20 percent until the fourth quarter of 1973 (see table 2-3).

Once monetary stringency was implemented, the Bank of Japan was very slow to reverse policy. The discount rate stayed at 9.0 percent until April 1975 and was not back to 1973 levels until 1977. While this may seem an unduly long time to maintain brakes on the economy, it was intended to disrupt inflationary expectations.

As for fiscal policy, the budget for fiscal 1973 was intended to be expansionary, aided by the beginning of the greater welfare and social infrastructure expenditures pushed by Prime Minister Tanaka. By the time the budget was passed by the Diet at the end of March, though, Ministry of Finance authorities realized that the economy was overheating and expenditures should be scaled back or postponed. Actual expenditures for the fiscal year were 4.4 percent below budget, with the cutbacks concentrated mostly in public works spending, which were 14 percent below the budgeted level.[41]

The Tanaka plan may have contributed to inflation in another way as well. A key element of Tanaka's concept for maintaining high growth was to spread industrial investment more evenly around the country. When he became prime minister after propounding these ideas, land speculation intensified. Land prices in urban areas had been rising at 13 to 20 percent each year since 1968, followed by increases of 24 percent in 1973 and 23 percent in 1974. This bubble was then followed by falling prices—they did not return to 1974 levels until 1978. It may be incorrect to place the entire blame for the rapid inflation of land prices on the Tanaka plan, since high inflation predated his proposals by several years, but land speculation certainly fed the overall inflationary mood of the nation.

At the microeconomic level the government stepped in soon after the beginning of the oil crisis to control certain prices. The Diet passed two laws giving the government power to impose price controls, and under this authority, the Ministry of International Trade and Industry placed controls on petroleum products. During the winter of 1973–74, liquefied petroleum gas and kerosene prices were controlled, since they were important for home cooking and heating. Prices on these products were allowed to rise by 62 percent in March 1974, but those of certain other basic commodities

41. Budget Bureau, *Zaisei Tōkei, 1986* (Fiscal Statistics, 1986) (Tokyo: MOF, 1986), p. 225.

and essential consumer goods were then brought under MITI administrative guidance.[42]

These measures came with expected theatrics. Corporation presidents were hauled before the Diet, where angry politicians accused them of price gouging, while the oil industry countered that the controls left them operating at a deficit as the OAPEC price increases on crude oil came into effect. Price controls finally came off in a series of steps between August and September 1974 as MITI decided supply conditions had eased enough that the danger of hyperinflation was over.

This effort to control prices was a serious (though short-lived) mistake by the government, since the policy created distortions in relative prices. It also provoked threats by some international oil companies to cut crude oil supplies to Japan if prices for refined products were not allowed to increase (a threat arising not out of the nationalism earlier assumed by the Japanese press but out of basic profit motives). Perhaps the most egregious episode of price control, though, involved the Japanese National Railways. A government-owned entity, the JNR was required to have its basic fares approved by the Diet. In 1972 the railroad submitted a request for fare increases to the Ministry of Transportation, which accepted it and passed it on to the Diet, where it was approved in 1973. But implementation of the increase was postponed because of the oil shock and the desire of the government to hold down any price over which it had control. Not until October 1974 was the increase allowed to go into effect. By then the 21 percent adjustment that had been approved was considerably below the more than 50 percent rise in wholesale and consumer prices that took place over the same period of time, leaving the railroad with an even worse deficit problem that subsequently proved to be nearly intractable.[43]

Summary

The events of 1973 and 1974 are important for understanding subsequent economic developments in Japan. These two years included a vari-

42. Organization for Economic Cooperation and Development, *OECD Economic Surveys: Japan, 1974* (Paris: OECD, 1975), pp. 35–36.

43. Edward J. Lincoln, "Regulation of Rates on the Japanese National Railways," in Kenneth D. Boyer and William G. Shepherd, eds., *Economic Regulation: Essays in Honor of James R. Nelson,* MSU Public Utility Papers Series (Michigan State University Press, 1981), p. 143; and Japanese National Railways, *Tetsudō Yōran, 1980* (Railways Handbook, 1980) (Tokyo: JNR, 1980), p. 65.

ety of symbolic and real events that heralded an era of lower economic growth.

First, the problems were far more extensive than just the oil crisis of October 1973: the economy was overheated and inflation was building early in 1973; prices for imports other than oil were also rising; government provided too much monetary stimulus; and consumers reacted hysterically to reports of shortages of some basic goods.

Second, the monetary and fiscal policy actions taken in 1971 and 1972 that helped feed the inflationary burst of 1973 and 1974 demonstrate the economy was already undergoing a long-term structural change. Unrecognized by most analysts, growth potential was declining. Thus the effort to sustain the high growth of demand generated high inflation. Rather than the smooth decline in growth foreseen by such analysts as Denison and Chung, the pattern was a bubble of inflation followed by recession.

Third, recognizing Japan's extreme anxiety over the future is important for understanding later policy actions. It seems puzzling that the Japanese would describe their large and successful economy as frail, but events like those of 1973–74 helped further ingrain that attitude. That a real recession could occur after more than twenty years of uninterrupted growth only convinced them they should not be overly swayed by current conditions in setting policy. In the private sector, decisions on business investments depend on expectations about the future, and the combination of the oil shock, problems with supplies of other imported raw materials, and recession punctured optimistic expectations. The end of the technology lag between Japan and other industrial nations was reducing the expected profits from plant and equipment investment anyway, but these events lowered expectations more quickly and dramatically. Government also became more cautious. Large current-account surpluses might seem to call for easing import restrictions, for example, but some officials still worried that the day could come when Japan could have trouble paying for imports.

Finally, the burst of inflation made a deep impression on government officials responsible for macroeconomic policy. Japan had experienced hyperinflation of 200 percent a year and higher just after the war, and the 1974 experience raised the specter of a repeat performance, which was enough to instill a considerable dose of fear and caution in government officials. This affected later Japanese policy, with greater weight given to controlling inflation and less to stimulating demand, as considered in chapters 3 and 6.

Table 2-4. *GNP Growth, 1973–85*

Year	Real GNP (trillions of 1980 yen)	GNP growth rate (percent)	Percentage points of GNP growth due to net exports[a]	Share of GNP growth due to net exports[b]
1973	185.9	7.9	−3.0	−27.5
1974	183.3	−1.4	1.2	. . .[c]
1975	188.2	2.7	1.9	71.1
1976	197.2	4.8	1.0	20.9
1977	207.7	5.3	0.9	16.9
1978	218.5	5.2	−0.9	−14.8
1979	230.1	5.3	−1.4	−20.9
1980	239.9	4.3	3.4	79.8
1981	248.7	3.7	1.5	40.9
1982	256.4	3.1	0.3	9.7
1983	264.7	3.2	1.5	46.3
1984	278.1	5.1	1.3	25.7
1985	291.2	4.7	1.0	21.2

Source: Economic Planning Agency, *Annual Report on National Accounts, 1987* (Tokyo: EPA, 1987), pp. 118–21.
a. Growth of exports and imports is weighted by their shares in GNP. Net exports is exports minus imports. The figures thus show the percentage points of growth due to expansion (or contraction) of net exports. For example, in 1984 net exports contributed 1.3 percentage points out of the total 5.1 percent real expansion of GNP in that year.
b. Percentage points of growth due to net exports divided by GNP growth rate. Thus the 1.3 percentage points due to net exports in 1984 was 25.7 percent of the 5.1 percent GNP growth rate.
c. Item is meaningless.

The Era of Slower Growth

From 1974 to 1985 Japan suffered no more recessions, but growth was far slower than before. Average annual growth for the entire period was 4.3 percent (table 2-4), which was less than half the rate that prevailed in the previous twenty years. Still, Japan managed to outdistance all other OECD member countries, though by a smaller margin.

Since 1974 the share of growth due to the expansion of net exports of goods and services has often been high (see table 2-4). Despite the small share of GNP accounted for by exports and imports, net export expansion contributed 38 percent of all growth in the economy between 1980 and 1985.[44] Even in 1984, which the Japanese government tried to tout as a year in which domestic-led growth was returning, net exports accounted for nearly 40 percent of growth. Only when the yen rose strongly against

44. In 1984, for example, net exports of goods and services expanded by 59.3 percent in real terms. The impact of that large increase, however, was muted by the small size of net exports—2.8 percent of GNP. Growth for the whole period is calculated by weighing export and import growths by their respective weights in GNP. These weights are an average of their shares of GNP in 1979 and 1985.

the dollar in 1985 did net exports begin to decline in importance (to 21.2 percent of total growth). By 1986 the effect of yen appreciation became so strong that net exports began contracting, constituting a drag on the economy.

In Japanese the new era is labeled *antei seichō*, or stable growth. This is a highly inappropriate term in two senses. First, there was nothing unstable about the high-growth era; it was unusually high and would necessarily come to an end eventually, but it was not based on unpredictable or fragile factors. Second, "stable" could be taken to mean more steady, but growth between 1974 and 1984 was not particularly steady. Even if the exceptional recession of 1974 is excluded, GNP growth rates varied from 2.7 percent in 1975 to 5.3 percent in 1977 and 1979. From 1976 to 1979 growth was very steady (ranging only from 4.8 percent to 5.3 percent), but thereafter it declined continuously to 3.1 percent in 1982. Even in the late 1970s when the overall growth rate was steady, the relative contributions of the economy's components varied greatly. Exports were important to growth from 1975 through 1977 but acted as a net drag in 1978 and 1979.

When growth returned to the economy after 1974 and Japan continued to perform well compared with other industrial countries, government officials regained confidence. They pointed proudly to their ability to guide the economy through the oil shock of 1979 without double-digit inflation or a recession. This confidence is clearly evident in the comments of Yoshio Suzuki of the Bank of Japan: "We owe this success [in the second oil shock] very much to the transformation of the monetary policy during the recent five-year period."[45] The principal change was that controlling inflation was given a much higher priority. Tokyo eased monetary policy very slowly after inflation came under control in 1975 in order to wring inflationary expectations out of the economy. However, given the steady slide in GNP growth rates from 1979 to 1983 and the international frictions resulting from external surpluses, it is not clear that the government was as successful in responding to the 1979 oil shock as it originally thought. Nevertheless its confidence continued, and controlling inflation remained an important factor in policy.

Confidence returned in the private sector as well. Despite slower growth, lower profits, and greater uncertainty about the future, corporations in the export sector became increasingly certain of their international

45. "Why Is the Performance of the Japanese Economy So Much Better?" *Journal of Japanese Studies*, vol. 7 (Summer 1981), p. 412.

competitiveness. Put less politely, many corporate executives became arrogant and contemptuous of foreign competitors. To a certain extent this attitude was reflected by the public, who, for instance, expressed doubt that the United States had anything to export that they would want to buy. Even some academic economists espoused the ascendancy of Japan: Tsuneo Iida of Nagoya University argued that Japan was not unique in terms of the model that explains its economic performance, but that as an economy fitting the neoclassical model, Japan simply performed better than other countries. He saw the country as providing a more competitive environment in the private sector and exhibiting better internal information flows so that the economy could operate more efficiently and more smoothly than the economies of the United States or European countries.[46]

The newly recovered self-confidence did not lead to rising expectations about future growth. By the early 1980s long-term forecasts tended to converge upon 4 percent real GNP growth, a very reasonable figure. Once slower growth was fully accepted, even the optimists' predictions were not far above 4 percent. Considering the obvious disappointment in light of the expectations that prevailed before 1973, Japan managed this transition relatively well. Labor unions, for example, accepted without a great deal of strife the slowing of growth and its implications for smaller wage increases. Growing at less than half the rate of the earlier period but faster on average than other industrial countries, Japan could easily see its cup as either half full or half empty; it chose to see the cup as half full.

Causes of the Slowdown

Why has Japan grown so much more slowly than it did before 1974? Why has its performance relative to other industrial nations also dropped? The disruption and confusion of 1973–74 was so strong in Japan that it is tempting to blame the oil crisis for everything. But the country did not return to its former high rates of expansion even after the effects of the oil shock should have dissipated. Since oil again rose in price in 1979, one could argue that Japan suffered through a prolonged adjustment to both episodes, so that by the mid-1980s a renewal of higher growth rates would occur, especially when oil prices began dropping. Higher oil prices are clearly one element in explaining what happened, but they are only one element and not the most important one.

---

46. Hajime Ohta, "New Views of Competition in the Japanese Economy," *Council Report*, no. 17 (May 2, 1980), pp. 1–5.

The key to understanding Japan's slower growth rate is that the process of catching up with other industrial nations ended, which meant that rapid leaps in productivity could no longer be generated by importing foreign technology. However, other elements were also involved. The growth-accounting framework provides a useful way to organize and look at these factors. This is the same framework used by Denison and Chung and Fried and Trezise in their estimates of future Japanese economic growth.

If certain simplifying assumptions are made about the nature of production in the economy (unitary returns to scale and disembodied technological change),[47] then the production relationship can be described as

$$(1) \qquad Y_t = C\, L_t^a K_t^b R_t; \quad a + b = 1,$$

where Y is economic output (GNP), C is a constant, L is labor input, K is capital input, R is a residual accounting for all sources of output not included in labor and capital, a is the share of labor in national income, b is the share of capital in national income, and t is the time period.

The change over time can then be expressed as

$$(2) \qquad \frac{Y_t}{Y_{t-1}} = \frac{C\, L_t^a K_t^b R_t}{C\, L_{t-1}^a K_{t-1}^b R_{t-1}} = \left(\frac{L_t}{L_{t-1}}\right)^a \left(\frac{K_t}{K_{t-1}}\right)^b \left(\frac{R_t}{R_{t-1}}\right).$$

Expressed in logarithms,

$$(3) \quad \ln Y_t - \ln Y_{t-1} = a\,(\ln L_t - \ln L_{t-1}) + b\,(\ln K_t - \ln K_{t-1}) + (\ln R_t - \ln R_{t-1}).$$

Letting $\Delta y = \ln Y_t - \ln Y_{t-1}$ and so forth yields

$$(4) \qquad \Delta y = a(\Delta l) + b\,(\Delta k) + \Delta r.$$

Essentially, equation 4 says that the growth in GNP (expressed in logarithms) must be equal to the growth in labor and capital, weighted by their

47. Unitary returns to scale means that if all factors of production are doubled, then output will be doubled. In mathematical terms, if $Y = f(L,K)$, then $aY = f(aL,aK)$, where Y is output, L is labor, and K is capital. Disembodied technical change means that technical change can be measured as a separate factor of production rather than being entwined with either labor or capital. In mathematical terms, if T is technical change, then $Y = f(L,K,T)$ and $T \neq f(L,K)$.

Table 2-5. *Growth of Private Fixed Nonresidential Capital Investment, Selected Periods, 1956–85*
Percent

Period	Average annual real growth
1956–1960[a]	22.2
1961–1965[a]	10.8
1966–1970	21.7
1971–1973	4.7
1974–1978	−1.0
1979–1985	7.6
1956–1973	16.0
1974–1985	3.9

Sources: Economic Planning Agency, *Annual Report on National Accounts, 1987,* pp. 118–21; *1970,* pp. 86–87; and Bank of Japan, *Economic Statistics Annual, 1971* p. 289.
a. 1956–65 average annual real growth is in 1965 prices. Other periods are based on 1980 prices.

shares in national income, plus a residual that captures increased productivity from technological change and other elements that do not show up as either labor or capital inputs.

As mentioned earlier, Denison and Chung found that in the high-growth era all these factors grew more rapidly than in other countries. In the slower-growth era all factors grew more slowly than before. Growth of capital stock was affected by the end of the catch-up process, rising energy costs, diversification of social goals (redirecting investment to such "nonproductive" uses as pollution control or constructing sidewalks), and slower growth abroad. Of these, closing the technology gap appears most important. The change in labor input is a relatively straightforward and simple factor to measure and forecast, but slower growth of labor contributed relatively little to slower GNP growth. Finally, productivity change was affected by the end of the catch-up process, of gains from reallocating labor from agriculture, and of dramatic increases in economies of scale.

SLOWER CAPITAL FORMATION. From 1956 to 1973 real fixed nonresidential capital investment grew at a 16 percent real annual rate, though with some unevenness (table 2-5). From 1974 to 1985, however, investment growth dropped to only 3.9 percent annually. The reduction was heavily affected by average annual real declines of −1.0 percent from 1974 to 1978. This drop can be attributed to the one-time shock of the 1973 oil crisis and a temporary deceleration effect as the economy slowed:

corporations had invested in expectations of continued high growth and now found they had more capacity than needed, so investment temporarily dropped while output caught up with installed capacity. After this temporary adjustment, investment grew at a 7.6 percent real annual rate, but even this was far below the growth before 1973. Chapter 3 will consider further the factors producing the slowdown in capital formation.

END OF TECHNOLOGICAL CATCH-UP. The end of the technological gap between Japan and other developed countries was critical for the slower growth of both capital formation and productivity in Japan. The impact of technological equality on capital formation was straightforward: because rapid increases in productivity based on imported technology were no longer possible, corporations could no longer expect the high levels of profit from new investment to which they had become accustomed. With lower expectations, investment decelerated. What had once been a powerful incentive for investment quickly evaporated in the mid-1970s.[48]

The end of the catch-up process also meant the cost of acquiring new, more productive technology was higher. While importing technology is by no means inexpensive, research and development expenditures are far lower than when technology is entirely developed at home. The change in Japan's position is clear from increases in research and development expenditures. By 1982 these expenditures (exclusive of social science research) were 2.20 percent of GNP, up from 1.70 percent in 1973 and 1.27 percent in 1965 (U.S. expenditures were 2.61 percent of GNP in 1982).[49] Thus Japan's R&D expenditures provide further indirect evidence that it was moving to the world technological frontier.

By the mid-1980s Japan had become the acknowledged world technological leader in a number of fields (including iron and steel, dynamic random-access memory chips, and automobiles). But no matter how suc-

48. Dale W. Jorgenson and Mieko Nishimizu found from their very detailed sectoral growth-accounting model that differences in technological level between Japan and the United States disappeared by the mid-1970s, with the remaining difference in output per worker in various industries in the two countries attributable to the differing levels of capital per worker. See "U.S. and Japanese Economic Growth, 1852–1973: An International Comparison," Discussion Paper 566 (Harvard Institute of Economic Research, August 1977).

49. Science and Technology Agency, *Kagaku Gijutsu Hakusho, 1984: 21 Seiki: no Arata na Gijutsu no Sōshutsu o Mezashite* (Science and Technology White Paper, 1984: Aiming for New Technological Development in the 21st Century) (Tokyo: MOF, 1984), pp. 336–37, 339.

Table 2-6. *Impact of Changes in Cost of Imported Energy, 1970–85*

Year	Import price index for energy (1980 = 100)[a]	Percent change from previous year	Percent change in GDP deflator from previous year	Terms of trade[b] (1980 = 100)
1970	12.4	0.8	7.7	224.5
1971	14.3	15.3	5.6	221.3
1972	13.8	−3.5	5.6	223.6
1973	14.9	8.0	12.9	203.3
1974	43.7	193.3	20.8	162.3
1975	52.3	19.7	7.7	145.1
1976	56.1	7.3	7.2	137.0
1977	53.9	−3.9	5.8	136.7
1978	43.7	−18.9	4.8	154.7
1979	57.8	32.3	3.0	133.3
1980	100.0	73.0	3.8	100.0
1981	109.7	9.7	3.2	99.6
1982	121.3	10.6	1.9	95.9
1983	107.0	−11.8	0.8	97.8
1984	101.8	−4.9	1.2	101.8
1985	102.1	0.3	1.5	102.9

Sources: Bank of Japan, *Economic Statistics Annual, 1985*, pp. 311–12; and Economic Planning Agency, *Annual Report on National Accounts, 1987*, pp. 166–69.
a. Includes imported petroleum, coal, and natural gas.
b. Ratio of the unit price of exports to the unit price of imports.

cessful it is at generating its own technology (or even continuing to adapt advances from other countries), the profit incentive from investment incorporating these new technologies remains smaller than when it lagged behind and was catching up. With a smaller profit incentive, corporate investment grew at a slower pace (data on corporate profit rates are provided in chapter 3). Reduced growth of investment as a result of closing the technology gap thus becomes important in explaining reduced productivity growth due to technological change and economies of scale because these are closely linked to capital formation.

HIGHER ENERGY COSTS. By 1985 the wholesale price index for imported oil, coal, and natural gas was more than eight times higher than in 1970 (table 2-6). The big increases came in the oil shock years, with a 193 percent gain in 1974 and a 73 percent gain in 1980, although as in other countries, the trend in energy costs was uneven, with declines in some of the years after the oil shocks. These increases far exceeded the overall inflation rate in the economy represented by the GDP deflator. The changes were more important for Japan than most other industrialized countries since it depended on imports for such a large portion of its total energy needs (83 percent in 1984).

Among energy sources, Japan is most dependent on petroleum. In 1973 it relied on oil for 76 percent of its total energy needs; even as late as 1985 oil accounted for 57 percent of total needs (compared with 42 percent for the United States in 1984). And because Japan produces almost no crude oil itself, its import dependency is virtually 100 percent. It is especially dependent on Middle Eastern crude oil—in the early 1970s for more than 80 percent of its petroleum needs; in 1985, 69 percent.[50]

How did the rising price of oil affect the economy? First, like other oil-importing countries, Japan suffered a loss of income to the OPEC members. As table 2-6 shows, its terms of trade worsened (meaning that the unit price of imports rose relative to the price of exports) in the immediate aftermath of the 1973 and 1979 oil shocks. With 1980 as 100, the terms of trade deteriorated from 203.3 in 1973 to 137.0 in 1976 and from 133.3 in 1979 to 95.9 in 1982.

In the longer run, again like other oil-importing countries, Japan also faced adjustment costs in coping with the relatively higher price of oil, but its problems were more serious than theirs. Its petroleum, petrochemical, aluminum refining, synthetic textile, and other industries were dependent on petroleum or petroleum-derived inputs that became relatively more expensive than in other industrialized countries. And in some industries Japan relied on petroleum-based energy, whereas other countries did not. As a result, its petroleum-dependent industries lost their competitiveness. Government policy may have exacerbated these problems. Import barriers erected in the 1950s and 1960s encouraged investment in some industries that, even before the oil shocks, had little chance of becoming competitive.

The aluminum industry provides the outstanding example of this adjustment problem. Smelting aluminum requires a great deal of electric energy, and aluminum smelters are usually located near sources of cheap hydroelectric power. In Japan the industry depended on oil-fired electric power plants. Because of import protection and new plants incorporating state-of-

50. Keizai Kōhō Center, *Japan 1986: An International Comparison* (Tokyo: KKC, 1986), pp. 64, 67; Jon Choy, "Japan's Energy Policy: 1986 Update," *JEI Report*, no. 3A (January 1987), p. 7; Bureau of the Census, *Statistical Abstract of the United States, 1987*, p. 544; and Organization for Economic Cooperation and Development, *Energy Balances of OECD Countries, 1973–75* (Paris: OECD, 1977), p. 48.

the-art technology, investment was attracted to aluminum refining during the 1960s. By 1979, though, under the combined impact of the two oil-price hikes, the industry could no longer compete against imports. Despite efforts to smooth and slow the process of decline (a euphemism for providing protection from the cold winds of international competition), companies went out of business or shut down capacity at a very rapid rate, so that by 1984 imports accounted for 71 percent of domestic consumption of aluminum in Japan (compared with 7 percent in 1965).[51]

Higher energy costs, then, caused a significant loss of income and a severe reduction of capital formation in some industries. Productive resources had to be removed from the declining industries, and higher oil prices meant lower expected rates of return, slowing new investment in others. However, the implications of higher oil prices were complex, and where capital (such as added equipment for saving energy) could be substituted for energy, the oil shock may have actually stimulated capital formation.

DIVERSIFICATION OF SOCIAL GOALS. The late 1960s and early 1970s brought a surge of public protest over pollution, and outspoken demands for increased investment in better roads, better housing, and other amenities. In response, government and industry reallocated some capital investment from plant and equipment, which had been heavily emphasized since the war. These actions clearly improved the quality of life but at the risk of slowing the steady growth of the economy, since investment in factories expands an economy's capacity to increase the supply of goods and services, while investment in pollution control or other amenities adds nothing measurable to future productivity. Sidewalks separating pedestrians from busy roads make life more comfortable and safer, but only the initial construction cost shows up in GNP statistics. In addition, changed public attitudes can cause an unfavorable environment for investment. In the United States, for instance, the costs imposed by lengthy public protests have largely halted investment in nuclear power plants.

In Japan the shift in public attitudes did cause reallocations, but the overall climate for investment was not noticeably worsened. The changes were also ambiguous in their implications. In a strict growth-accounting sense, reallocation in investment slowed the growth of output per unit of capital investment. However, the shift came at a time when investment in

---

51. Managment and Coordination Agency, *Japan Statistical Yearbook, 1986*, p. 228.

plant and equipment was decelerating anyway. Thus the increased investment in social infrastructure helped keep total investment in the economy higher than it would otherwise have been, stimulating economic growth.

During the 1950s the Japanese shared a rather broad consensus on the desirability of rapid economic growth. People were willing to work long hours and endure a lack of investment in social amenities on the assumption that this represented the best road to future prosperity.[52] In fact, the belief that this was the only feasible route to follow was so strong that many Japanese do not see even in retrospect that any personal sacrifice was involved; there was no realistic choice except to work very hard and do without if the country—and the individual—were to prosper.

The disintegration of this broad public consensus in the late 1960s was most visible and dramatic on issues relating to pollution. Rapid industrialization had been accompanied by severe degradation of the environment that ultimately resulted in a series of incidents of pollution-induced illnesses. In Minamata, mercury from an industrial process that was routinely dumped in a river poisoned hundreds of people and deformed their offspring. In Yokkaichi, smoke and fumes from a new complex of petrochemical plants created an upsurge in asthma and other serious respiratory conditions. In various parts of the country, *itai-itai* episodes of severe cadmium poisoning were caused by dumping wastes from lead and zinc smelting operations into rivers. In addition to enduring these acute incidents, some of which led to protracted and highly publicized court struggles, a broad segment of the public was suffering from generally increased air and water pollution. By the early 1970s, police directing traffic in Tokyo were given special roadside booths where they could take turns breathing pure oxygen. Newspapers and evening television news programs carried stories of groups of schoolchildren suddenly afflicted with fits of coughing or difficulty in breathing as stray clouds of chemicals drifted over playgrounds. Children being rushed en masse to hospitals for treatment did not create a good public image for industry, and people severely criticized government policies that allowed industrialization to bring about such severe conditions.

52. The existence of radical unions in the early postwar years, discussed earlier, implies that the consensus was not universal, but the failure of these unions in the 1950s indicates the direction of social attitudes. Given the poverty, poor housing, and generally harsh life after the war, it is easy to imagine that a different society could have generated a strong, radical union system with an agenda of reallocating resources to improve social welfare at the expense of investment in plant and equipment.

As public pressure mounted, the government reacted with new legislation and administrative action. In 1970 the Diet passed pollution control legislation. From 1970 to 1973 the central government's pollution control budget more than tripled, and if investments in related organizations for pollution control are added, expenditures almost quadrupled to ¥430 billion ($1.6 billion at 1973 exchange rates). Regional and local government spending in these same years rose more than 2.5 times to ¥954 billion (more than $3.5 billion). Although by fiscal 1984 the central government's environmental spending (again including transfers to other organizations) was up to ¥1.15 trillion (approximately $4 billion), the enormous increases had reached their limit. Government budget deficits had forced reductions of 2.5 percent in environmental expenditures between fiscal 1983 and fiscal 1984.[53]

Increased government spending for pollution control was matched by rapid increases in expenditures by private industry. In the iron and steel industry, spending for pollution control as a ratio to total sales rose from 0.9 percent in 1970 to 1.8 percent in 1974. The paper and pulp industry ratio went from 1.1 percent to 3.0 percent, while in chemicals it rose from 0.4 percent to 1.3 percent. Total private-sector investment in pollution abatement was roughly double expenditures by the central government and almost equal to those of local governments.[54]

These increased expenditures brought about a significant and visible improvement in environmental quality. Daily warnings about air quality (issued when photochemical concentrations exceed certain limits for one hour) were down from a peak of 328 in 1973 to a low of about 60 in 1981, followed by a sharp increase to 131 in 1983.[55] The number of people officially recognized as suffering from the effects of photochemical air pollution dropped from 46,081 in 1975 to a low of 446 in 1982, followed by a modest increase to 1,721 in 1983. (The unwillingness of some people to be officially recognized or designated as suffering from pollution prob-

53. Environmental Agency, *Kankyō Hakusho, 1976: Shiren to Sentaku no Kankyō Gyōsei* (Environmental White Paper, 1976: Environmental Administration's Ordeals and Options) (Tokyo: MOF, 1976), p. 515; and Environmental Agency, *Kankyō Hakusho, 1984: Seijukukasuru Shakai ni Okeru Kankyō Mondai e no Arata na Taiō* (Environmental White Paper, 1984: New Opposition to Environmental Issues in a Mature Society) (Tokyo: MOF, 1984), pp. 117, 479.

54. Environmental Agency, *Kankyō Hakusho, 1976*, pp. 402–03, 513–15. Comparison of private and government spending may involve some double-counting because the private-sector figures do not provide sources of funding (some of which was from government).

55. Environmental Agency, *Kankyō Hakusho, 1984*, pp. 6–7.

lems may have contributed to the decline.) Regardless of the accuracy of official statistics of this sort, though, even casual observation provides striking evidence of the changes: local news programs no longer show children being rushed to hospitals from school playgrounds, Mount Fuji is visible on more days of the year from downtown Tokyo than in the early 1970s, and the major cities look and feel cleaner.

While less dramatic than pollution issues, gaps in social amenities also received increased government attention in the 1970s—and improvements in social infrastructure and social welfare confirm that the politicians' speeches were backed up by substantial increases in public investment. The mileage of roads newly paved in 1980, for instance, exceeded that of roads paved in all of Japan through 1960. The distance of roads paralleled by sidewalks doubled between 1970 and 1975, and almost doubled again by 1981. Investment in paved roads and sidewalks represented a general improvement in quality and safety, contributing to a dramatic drop in traffic fatalities. From 13.3 traffic deaths per million vehicle-kilometers in 1970, fatalities dropped to 3.5 per million in 1980 (the comparable figure for the United States is 2.0 per million vehicle-kilometers).[56]

Traffic safety was far from the only improvement. In 1970 only 20 percent of the population of Japan lived in districts served by public sewage treatment systems, a figure that rose to 32.5 percent by 1984. The situation is better than it appears. As table 2-7 shows, 58 percent of Japanese dwellings had flush toilets in 1983, up from 9.3 percent in 1963, with much of the expansion taking place after the late 1960s. A significant share of the improvement during the 1970s came from private investment in septic tanks, since the percentage of dwellings equipped with flush toilets expanded so much faster than the percentage of population living in sewage treatment districts.[57] Nevertheless, one is left wondering whether it is the improvement over time or the continued high percentage of houses with primitive facilities that is the more striking. By 1983, 74.3 percent of U.S. dwelling units were connected to public sewer systems, and only 2.4 percent of occupied dwellings lacked some or all plumbing facilities.[58]

56. Edward J. Lincoln, "Infrastructural Deficiencies, Budget Policy, and Capital Flows," in Michèle Schmiegelow, ed., *Japan's Response to Crisis and Change in the World Economy* (Armonk, N.Y.: M.E. Sharpe, 1986), p. 171.

57. Even in suburban areas where sewage treatment plants have not been built and a septic tank or cesspool is not feasible, the Japanese are allowed to install special treatment tanks that hold and chemically process sewage and then periodically pump it into city storm sewers.

58. Bureau of the Census, *Statistical Abstract of the United States, 1987*, p. 710.

Table 2-7. *Dwellings with Flush Toilets and Percentage of Population Living in Districts with Sewage Treatment Systems, Selected Years, 1963–83*

Year	Total dwellings (millions)	Dwellings with flush toilets (millions)	Percent with toilets	Percent of population in districts with sewage treatment systems
1963	20.4	1.9	9.3	. . .
1968	24.2	4.1	16.9	. . .
1970	. . .	. . .	. . .	19.6
1973	28.7	9.0	31.4	. . .
1975	. . .	. . .	. . .	24.7
1978	32.2	14.8	46.0	. . .
1980	. . .	. . .	. . .	28.0
1982	. . .	. . .	. . .	30.0
1983	34.7	20.2	58.2	. . .
1984	. . .	. . .	. . .	32.5

Source: Management and Coordination Agency, *Japan Statistical Yearbook, 1986* (Tokyo: Statistics Bureau, 1986), pp. 24–25, 516–17, 619.

Quality of life improved in other ways. The total area of local parks doubled from 1970 to 1981. The percentage of households with telephone service between 1970 and 1980 tripled from 25 percent to 77 percent.[59] (Since Nippon Telegraph and Telephone was a government-owned corporation, this change was also closely related to government policy decisions, which had favored business phone installations in the 1950s).

Housing, too, showed some improvement. The European criticism that the Japanese lived in rabbit hutches became something of a cliché in the 1980s. The share of government funds in the Fiscal Investment and Loan Program (FILP) directed toward housing rose from 11 percent in 1965 to 25 percent by 1980, while the share of FILP funds for the Japan Development Bank and the Eximbank (both of which lend exclusively to the corporate sector) dropped from 19 percent to 8 percent. These figures nicely demonstrate the government's movement from promoting industrial growth to encouraging a broader improvement of living conditions. But the picture is ambiguous because although greater resources were channeled into housing in the 1970s, the average dwelling remained significantly smaller than in the United States in the 1980s.

The greater availability of public funds, rising income levels, and

59. Lincoln, "Infrastructural Deficiencies," pp. 159–61.

changing demographics (fewer people per household because of both fewer children and fewer three-generation households) gradually produced a rising amount of space per person in Japanese houses. From approximately 14.5 square meters per household member in 1958, the figure rose rather steadily to 25.6 square meters by 1983. There is no indication of any acceleration of change in the 1970s; in fact, the average annual growth in space per person was 2.6 percent from 1959 to 1968 and 2.1 percent in the 1970s. But if one focuses on the increase in dwelling size, the picture changes. The average size of newly constructed dwelling units increased 1.4 percent annually in the 1960s and 3.3 percent annually in the 1970s, despite slower growth of personal incomes in the latter period.[60] The contrast with the space-per-person data comes from a stabilization in the number of family members per dwelling. Still, the increase in living space left the Japanese with dwellings just over half the size of American ones. In 1982 the total amount of heated space (excluding basements and attics, amenities that do not exist in Japanese houses) per household member in the United States was 49.5 square meters, almost double the 25.6 square meter value for Japan in 1983.[61]

How should Japanese housing be evaluated? It increased markedly in size, and the living space of dwellings increased more rapidly in the 1970s than before. Any visitor can also readily see that the quality of housing underwent an astounding change from the 1960s to the 1980s. Houses are no longer flimsy, drafty, or poorly constructed. And although space remains tight compared with housing in the United States, even if income levels were equal to those of Americans, the Japanese would not choose to build houses of similar size because land is more expensive and less available, and people want to live in individual units close to major urban centers (and must therefore squeeze together).[62] But while the improvements have been significant and size parity with the United States is not to be expected, the stock of Japanese housing in the mid-1980s can be still further improved. One-quarter of the housing was constructed in 1960 or

60. Management and Coordination Agency, *Japan Statistical Yearbook, 1985*, pp. 268, 514–15, 518. The average size of new dwellings was 59.1 square meters in 1960, 68.1 square meters in 1970, and 93.9 square meters in 1980. Thereafter, size dropped modestly to 84.4 square meters by 1984. Because these data refer to new dwellings, the impact of increased size on the total stock of dwellings was more muted.

61. U.S. data are from Bureau of the Census, *Statistical Abstract of the United States, 1984*, pp. 47, 756.

62. Historically, the Japanese have lived in crowded villages surrounded by their farm fields, rather than in the middle of their individual properties.

earlier, and much of it is inadequate by 1980s' standards for size and quality.

For a country where the common wisdom is that government policy tends to be heavily business-oriented, the strong position taken on pollution and social spending may seem surprising. Many reasons account for the policy shift, but two stand out: the deficiencies and problems were very obvious and serious, and the adoption of pollution and social welfare as issues by opposition parties (especially at the local level) called for a response from the central government.

The late 1960s were a time of serious student protests on a variety of other issues—the Vietnam War, rising tuition, government authority in general, and other fashionable causes. While much of this is not particularly relevant to the growth of the economy, a strong antigovernment, antibusiness, proenvironmental thread ran through it all, as when radical students joined with the local farmers to protest construction of a new Tokyo international airport in the middle of rice fields, a protest begun in the 1960s and still continuing. However, the movement peaked in the late 1960s, when some universities were shut down for months at a time, and largely evaporated by the mid-1970s except for the actions of a very few, very small, but very radical nuisance groups. As in other countries, though, the breadth of the movement in the late 1960s was sufficient to cause concern within the government that policies were out of touch with public needs or desires.

More to the point for the Liberal Democratic party than the student protests was its slipping majority in the lower house of the Diet. Had the LDP chosen not to respond to public desires, it could easily have lost political control by the late 1970s to some form of coalition of opposition parties. Table 2-8 shows the distribution of Diet seats among the political parties. After comfortable majorities ranging from forty-five to sixty-two seats in the 1950s and 1960s, the election of 1972 whittled the LDP majority to twenty-five seats. In 1976 and 1979, the party did not win a majority of the Diet seats, but retained its majority position because formerly independent candidates joined its ranks after the elections. And although the election of 1980 brought a majority of twenty-eight seats, the election of 1983 put the LDP back into a minority that it again made up through the acquisition of independents and a coalition with a small splinter group called the New Liberal Club. Not until 1986, when it once more achieved a large majority, did the party feel that it had returned to a strong position.

Table 2-8. *Number of Seats in Lower House of the Diet, by Party, Election Years 1958–86*

Party	1958	1960	1963	1967	1969	1972	1976	1979	1980	1983	1986
Liberal Democratic	287	296	283	277	288	271	249	248	284	250	300
Socialist	166	145	144	140	90	118	123	107	107	112	85
Democratic Socialist	...	17	23	30	31	19	29	35	32	38	26
Komeito	...	...	...	25	47	29	55	57	33	58	56
Communist	1	3	5	5	14	38	17	39	29	26	26
Other	1	0	0	0	0	2	17	6	15	11	10
Independents	12	6	12	9	6	14	21	19	11	16	9
Total	467	467	467	486	486	491	511	511	511	511	512
Liberal Democratic majority	53	62	49	34	45	25	–7[a]	–8[a]	28	–6[a]	44

Sources: Takayoshi Miyagawa, ed., *Seiji Handobukku, 1985 Handobukku, 1985* (Political Handbook, 1985) (Tokyo: Seiji Kōhō Sentā), p. 210; *1980*, p. 200; Hans H. Baerwald, *Party Politics in Japan* (Winchester, Mass.: Allen and Unwin, 1986), pp. 42–43; and Michael W. Chinworth, "The Elections: Oh What a Feeling," *JEI Report*, no. 25B (July 11, 1986), p. 2.
a. Deficit in LDP seats was made up by independents joining the party after the election.

The political shift of the late 1960s and 1970s was also evident in the proliferation of opposition party victories in local elections. On some issues, it was these progressive local governments that took the lead in instituting new social programs, becoming another prod for central government action.[63] The Liberal Democratic party was astute enough that by "responding skillfully to the challenge posed by the progressive local governments, it succeeded in removing the uniqueness of the progressive camp's policies by improving environmental protection and welfare measures."[64]

The success of the opposition parties at the local level began to wane in the 1980s, and by 1985 ten of forty-seven prefectural governors were from the LDP and an additional twenty-three were independents supported by coalitions that included the LDP. Most of the remaining governors were independents with no party affiliations or coalitions. Only three were officially endorsed by progressive parties or by coalitions of progressive parties that excluded the LDP.[65]

These political trends suggest why the LDP shifted its policies away from a strictly progrowth, probusiness stance to one of greater support for social demands in the 1970s. And the resurgence of the party in the first half of the 1980s may explain (along with concerns about budget deficits) the leveling off or decline in such policies.

Both the Tanaka proposal for remaking Japan and the subsequent long-term economic plan put forth by the Economic Planning Agency demonstrated the recognition of these public concerns. EPA Director General Tsuneo Uchida portrayed the new thinking when he said in his opening Diet speech in January 1974 that under the slower growth imposed by the oil shock, government policy would have to change from support of "quantitative growth" to "qualitative growth" and from "production theory" to "distribution ethics."[66]

---

63. John C. Campbell, "The Old People Boom and Japanese Policy Making," *Journal of Japanese Studies,* vol. 5 (Summer 1979), pp. 321–57, for instance, details the impact of local progressive government initiatives (especially in Tokyo) in establishing free medical care for the elderly.

64. Seizaburō Satō, "The Shifting Political Spectrum," *Japan Echo,* vol. 11 (Summer 1984), p. 30. Translated from "Kakushin Yatō ni Nokosareta Saigo no Michi," *Chūō Kōron* (March 1984), pp. 62–72.

65. Takayoshi Miyagawa, ed., *Seiji Handobukku, 1985* (Political Handbook, 1985) (Tokyo: Seiji Kōhō Sentā, 1985), pp. 297–304.

66. *Nihon Keizai Shimbun,* Evening Edition, January 21, 1974. U.S. embassy translation.

In summary, the changes in investment patterns represented movement away from the single-minded pursuit of economic growth. To the extent that this involved a real reallocation of resources, it reduced the measured rate of economic growth. However, much of the change did not represent such a reallocation. Because private-sector investment in new plant and equipment was decelerating, increased investment in social infrastructure did not compete with it. The alternative was not an equal amount of investment directed more toward plant and equipment (and business-oriented infrastructure) but simply less investment. Social investment thus lessened the imbalances between savings and investment and kept economic growth from diminishing even further.

A SLUGGISH WORLD ECONOMIC ENVIRONMENT. From 1975 to 1985 the volume index for Japanese exports rose at a 6.9 percent annual rate, compared with 17.9 percent from 1961 to 1970 and 12.7 percent from 1971 to 1974. Chapters 3 and 5 will discuss the emergence of large trade surpluses in the 1970s and 1980s as a response to domestic savings and investment imbalances, and the fairly heavy dependence on net exports as a source of economic growth has already been mentioned. However, as these export data indicate, rising external surpluses occurred in an environment of slower real export expansion.

Much of the slowdown in export growth can be attributed to slower economic growth in the rest of the world, but there is another dimension as well. When Japan was economically a small force in the 1950s, its exports could expand rapidly without making much difference in world markets. But by the 1970s its exporting industries were important enough to represent a significant factor in world markets. This success created two reasons for export growth to drop. In economic terms the rapid gains of exports could be limited either because of market saturation or because the significant size of Japanese penetration provoked more successful counter-strategies by foreign competitors. In political terms Japan's success meant that attempts to expand rapidly exports of particular products would engender threats of protection from trade partners or real protectionist actions.

A CHANGING LABOR MARKET. In the 1970s and 1980s labor input in the Japanese economy grew somewhat more slowly than before because of slower population growth, a decrease in hours worked, and fewer gains from increased education. Partially offsetting these factors was a modest

Table 2-9. *Labor Force Participation and Unemployment Rate,*
Selected Years, 1950–85
Millions of people unless otherwise specified

Year	Population aged 15 and older	Labor force	Labor force participation rate (percent)	Unemployment rate (percent)
1950	55.2	36.2	65.6	1.2
1955	59.3	41.9	70.8	2.5
1960	65.2	45.1	69.2	1.7
1965	72.9	47.9	65.7	1.2
1970	78.9	51.5	65.4	1.2
1973	82.1	53.0	64.6	1.3
1975	84.4	53.2	63.0	1.9
1980	89.3	56.5	63.3	2.0
1985	94.7	59.6	63.0	2.6

Sources: Management and Coordination Agency, *Japan Statistical Yearbook, 1986,* pp. 70–71; *1973–74,* p. 49; *1960,* p. 42.

reversal of the earlier downward trend in labor force participation rates for women.

During the very early postwar period Japan experienced a baby boom similar to that in the United States. Children born between 1947 and 1951 outnumbered the next younger five-year group (1952–56) by 37 percent and the next older five-year group (1942–46) by 23 percent.[67] Since the early 1950s the birthrate has almost continuously declined. Therefore, even if the boom is considered to have lasted until as late as 1955, that generation was in the labor force by 1975.

The slowdown since the early 1950s is clearly visible in both population and labor force data. The number of people aged fifteen years and older grew at an average annual rate of 1.8 percent from 1956 to 1973 but at only a 1.2 percent rate from 1974 to 1985. Labor force participation rates, the percentage of people fifteen years and older with jobs or actively seeking employment, declined steadily from 70.8 percent in 1955 to 64.6 percent in 1973, primarily because the shift of workers out of agriculture led to falling participation rates for women. However, from 1974 to 1985 participation rates stabilized; the rate was 63.0 percent in 1985, down only slightly from the 1973 level.[68]

Table 2-9 shows the effects of population growth and participation rates on the labor force. From 1951 to 1960 the annual growth rate of the labor

67. Management and Coordination Agency, *Japan Statistical Yearbook, 1986,* p. 24.
68. Ibid., p. 70; and *Japan Statistical Yearbook, 1973–74,* p. 49.

force was a high 2.2 percent. From 1961 to 1973 the rate of increase slowed to 1.3 percent, and from 1974 to 1985 dropped a bit further to 1.2 percent. In addition, after unemployment had dropped from a peak of 2.5 percent in 1955 to a stable 1.2 to 1.4 percent in the 1960s, it rose again from 1.3 percent in 1973 to a new peak of 2.6 percent in 1985 (and was still rising).

The labor force continued to be characterized by increases in the number of years of education in the 1970s and 1980s, but this too was changing more slowly. From 1960 to 1970 the percentage of the population aged fifteen years and older that had graduated from high school increased from 22.2 percent to 30.1 percent; from 1970 to 1980 it increased to 38 percent. Thus the portion of adults with high school diplomas rose by 36 percent in the 1960s and 26 percent in the 1970s. People with diplomas from all forms of educational institutions beyond high school increased from 5.2 percent of the population fifteen years and older in 1960 to 8.4 percent in 1970 and 13.7 percent in 1980, roughly equal rates of growth in each decade.[69] In the 1980s the percentage of each age cohort completing high school appears to have stabilized at just over 50 percent, although the percentage continuing on to higher education was still rising. Therefore the data on the rising educational level of those fifteen years and older indicate primarily that the generations educated before the reforms initiated during the occupation were declining as a proportion of the total adult population.

These trends in education suggest that gains in the quality of the labor force continued during the 1970s, but contributed less to economic growth than they had before. Any precise estimate of the contribution of changes in education though, ought to be viewed with a certain amount of suspicion—years of education are only crudely related to workers' productivity.

Growth of labor input was also limited in the 1970s and 1980s by decreases in hours worked. The average monthly hours per worker in all industry declined from almost 203 in 1960 to 182 in 1973. For manufacturing only the decline was from 207 hours to 182, an almost identical change (table 2-10).[70] This slow drift downward became a sharp drop as

69. Management and Coordination Agency, *Japan Statistical Yearbook, 1986,* p. 44. Data on population by educational level are available only for census years (the first year of each decade).

70. Japanese data display some inconsistency between average monthly hours and average weekly hours. According to the data series for weekly hours, employees—excluding

Table 2-10. *Average Monthly Hours Worked, Selected Years, 1960–85*

Year	All industry	Manufacturing
1960	202.7	207.0
1965	192.9	191.8
1970	186.6	187.4
1973	182.0	182.0
1974	175.5	173.2
1975	172.0	167.8
1980	175.7	178.2
1985	175.8	179.7

Sources: Management and Coordination Agency, *Japan Statistical Yearbook, 1986*, p. 110; and Bank of Japan, *Economic Statistics Annual, 1977*, p. 281.

demand fell in the recession following the oil shock. For all industry, hours dropped to 172 by 1975, and to 168 for manufacturing. One contributor to the decline may have been the so-called lifetime employment system in Japan. With a portion of the work force covered by an implicit job guarantee until the mandatory retirement age, corporations tend to rely on overtime work to put flexibility into their labor costs. Large corporations are more constrained than their American counterparts in reducing employment when a recession hits, but they can cut overtime work heavily.

Once the recession-related drop was over, hours worked in manufacturing recovered to almost 180 a month by 1985, and more moderately to 176 for all industry. This difference is probably due to the limited opportunity for overtime in sectors other than manufacturing. As a result of these changes, shifts in hours worked were actually less important to labor input after 1973 than before. The average annual decline in hours worked in 1961–73 was 0.8 percent, while in 1974–85 it was only 0.3 percent (concentrated in the recession-related drop of 1974–75).

Somewhat offsetting the effect of the decline in hours worked on total labor input, more women entered the labor force in the 1970s and 1980s.

---

self-employed and family workers—averaged 47.5 hours a week in 1986. Adjusting that figure to a monthly basis yields almost 206 hours a month. The weekly figures show that even in the 1980s the Japanese worked considerably more hours than their American counterparts. Average weekly hours in U.S. manufacturing fluctuated close to 40 in the first half of the 1980s; for Japan the figure remained close to 47 hours—almost a full day more a week. Bureau of the Census, *Statistical Abstract of the United States, 1987*, p. 394; and Management and Coordination Agency, *Monthly Statistics of Japan* (March 1987), p. 19.

Table 2-11. *Female Labor Force Participation, by Age Group,*
Selected Years, 1960–85
Percent

Year	Total	Age group						
		15–19	*20–24*	*25–29*[a]	*30–39*[b]	*40–54*[c]	*55–64*	*65 and older*
1960	54.5	49.0	70.8	54.5	57.8	59.0	46.4	25.6
1965	50.6	35.8	70.2	49.0	55.4	60.2	44.8	21.6
1970	49.9	33.6	70.6	45.5	52.9	61.8	44.4	17.9
1973	48.3	27.9	67.1	44.5	51.4	61.3	44.5	16.9
1975	45.7	21.7	66.2	43.2	56.9	59.8	43.7	15.3
1980	47.6	18.5	70.0	48.7	60.9	62.0	45.3	15.5
1984	48.9	18.5	72.4	52.1	63.7	64.1	45.0	15.9
1985	48.7	16.6	71.9	52.2	63.7	64.6	45.3	15.5

Sources: Management and Coordination Agency, *Japan Statistical Yearbook, 1986*, p. 71; *1978*, p. 49; *1973–74*, p. 49.
a. Includes ages 25–34 after 1973.
b. Includes ages 35–44 after 1973.
c. Includes ages 45–54, only, after 1973.

For all women 15 years and older participation rates dropped until 1975, then increased modestly to almost 49 percent by 1985 (table 2-11). Considered by age group, the data indicate some weakening of the traditional expectation that women should leave their jobs when they get married (or at the latest when they have their first child). This tradition did not apply to work on family farms or in small family enterprises, so that well over 40 percent of women beyond their mid-20s had always remained in the labor force. Following the first oil shock, though, more women chose to stay on the job or to return to work outside the home more quickly after having children. For the group aged 25 to 34 participation rates rose from 43.2 percent in 1975 to 52.2 percent in 1985, and for those aged 35 to 44 (who have presumably finished having children) rates rose from 56.9 percent to 63.7 percent.

Although Japan benefited from having more women choosing either to stay in or to return to the labor force, in a growth-accounting framework, this had both a positive and a negative effect. Had women not chosen to work, the labor force would have grown even more slowly than it did. However, because women are paid less than men, a higher share of women in the work force implies less growth in the measured value of output attributable to labor. Males made up 62.7 percent of the labor force in 1975 but 60.3 percent by 1985.[71]

71. Management and Coordination Agency, *Japan Statistical Yearbook, 1986*, p. 70.

Taken together these factors imply that labor's contribution to the Japanese economy grew somewhat less rapidly after 1973 than before. As labor force growth decelerated, creating a tight labor market, the continued rapid economic expansion of the late 1960s and early 1970s enabled unions to negotiate the very large wage increases of 1973 and 1974 mentioned earlier. This wage pressure was even more significant than implied by the wage settlements, since the strong seniority element in Japanese wage structures combined with the aging of the labor force implied rising wages even without annual overall increases.[72] After the recession of 1974, though, the situation changed. Slower economic growth and the longer-term effort of corporations to replace labor with capital moved Japan away from the tight labor market conditions. Growth in employment, in fact, was so slow that the unemployment levels rose (see table 2-9.)

Reductions in the growth of labor supply in Japan should not be considered a major cause of slower overall economic growth, however. First, slower labor expansion need not be a problem if capital or technological change can be substituted. Second, the slowdown in labor supply was relatively mild, accounting for less than 1 percentage point of the reduction of economic growth in the growth-accounting framework. Finally, the expansion of unemployment implies that the demographic changes slowing the expansion of the labor force were not a constraining factor in Japan's growth performance. Constraints lay instead in the slower growth of the capital stock and smaller increases in productivity.

SLOWER PRODUCTIVITY GROWTH. Endowed with the intellectual and social capacity to efficiently absorb and adapt foreign technology, Japan was able to achieve great leaps in productivity as the private sector continually discovered new investment opportunities using imported technologies in the 1950s and 1960s. But by the 1970s this situation was coming to its logical end. Productivity increases due to implementation of new

72. When economic growth was high, corporations hired large numbers of young employees, which helped keep the age and seniority structure of the work force biased toward the young, inexpensive end of the scale. In the adjustment to slower economic growth in the years just after 1973, though, firms hired fewer workers with an implicit lifetime employment commitment. This in effect increased average pay per worker as existing employees moved up the seniority ladder. Among large firms, the average seniority of male employees rose from 11.7 years in 1970 to 15.4 years by 1984. Management and Coordination Agency, *Japan Statistical Yearbook, 1986*, p. 97.

technologies slowed because the changes in technology became more incremental.

Productivity change in the growth-accounting framework includes all sources of change, not just increases due to new technologies. Of these other sources, Denison and Chung found economies of scale to be important during the 1950s and 1960s. Virtually every Japanese industry was starting from a small production base, so that economies of scale were achieved easily as output grew and larger production facilities were constructed. This effect was compounded in new industries, including most consumer durables, because domestic demand for their products proved highly income-elastic. Further economies were available as industries reached productivity levels high enough to be competitive in world markets. But by the mid-1970s these gains were largely realized, and economies of scale could be no longer be expected to contribute more to growth than they did in other industrialized economies. In addition, the slower pace of investment in new plant and equipment reduced the speed with which new, larger, more efficient production facilities replaced older facilities. Therefore, even if economies of scale could be realized, they were being realized more slowly.

Finally, there were fewer gains to be realized from the transfer of labor from low-productivity agriculture to other, more productive employment. The movement of labor out of agriculture was an important source of productivity growth between 1955 and 1973 because the shift took place so quickly. As table 2-12 shows, the proportion of employment in agriculture, forestry, and fishing dropped from 51.6 percent in 1950 to only 13.4 percent in 1973. This represented an absolute drop of 11.4 million people engaged in the primary sector. However, from 1973 to 1985 only 1.9 million people moved out, bringing the sector's proportion of total employment down to 8.8 percent. While the movement of workers did not come to a complete halt, it slowed from an average of 496,000 a year in the earlier period to 162,000 a year in the more recent period. Part of this absolute drop may not represent a movement of workers to other sectors as much as it does retiring workers not offset by new entrants: the population engaged in agriculture is older on average than the total labor force and is aging more rapidly. Future migration may be further limited because few farmers are engaged full time in agriculture. At what point Japanese statistics move a worker from one sector to another is unclear, but only 14 percent of farm households in 1985 were considered to be engaged full time in farming, and nonagricultural income accounted for more than half

Table 2-12. *Employment, by Sector, Selected Years, 1950–85*
Percent of total unless otherwise specified

Year	Total employment (millions)	Primary[a]	Secondary[b]	Tertiary[c]
1950	35.7	51.6	21.7	28.6
1955	40.9	37.6	24.4	38.1
1960	44.4	30.2	28.0	41.8
1965	47.3	23.5	31.9	44.6
1970	50.9	17.4	35.2	47.3
1973	52.3	13.4	36.6	49.8
1975	52.2	12.7	35.2	51.9
1980	55.4	10.4	34.8	54.5
1985	58.1	8.8	34.3	56.5

Sources: Management and Coordination Agency, *Japan Statistical Yearbook, 1986*, pp. 72–73; *1973–74*, pp. 50–51; *1960*, pp. 44–45.
a. Includes agriculture, forestry, and fishing.
b. Includes construction, mining, and manufacturing.
c. Includes services and government.

of all farm household income.[73] Thus the migration of workers from agriculture, forestry, and fisheries probably brought slower productivity gains because so much farm household activity was already off the farm by the mid-1980s.

Prospects

Most of the changes responsible for slower growth were longer-term shifts that implied high economic growth would not return. This can be seen in each of the factors of production.

LABOR. The labor force in Japan will continue to grow slowly. Official estimates of the population fifteen years of age and older in the year 2000 imply an annual growth of 0.84 percent after 1980, compared with 1.83 percent from 1956 to 1973.[74] How this will translate into labor force growth will depend on participation rates, of which the most uncertain aspect will be the participation of women. Will the modest upturn of the early 1980s continue as more women choose either to remain in the labor force or to return to it after marriage and children? This is impossible to predict, but the biggest part of the shift could be over. Certainly any straight-line extrapolation from the very recent past is suspect.

73. Ibid., pp. 149, 171.
74. Ibid., p. 25; and *Japan Statistical Yearbook, 1973–74*, p. 49.

Demographics will also affect participation. An increasing proportion of the population will be aged sixty-five and older, at which point labor force participation drops quickly. In 1985, for example, only 37.0 percent of males and 15.5 percent of women sixty-five and older were still in the labor force.[75] Unless senior citizens increasingly decide to keep working or return to work, overall participation rates will fall, so that the labor force will grow more slowly than the 0.84 percent projected annual growth in population.

There is certainly no reason to expect increased output from any substantial increase in hours worked: by the late 1970s overtime work stabilized at between thirteen and fourteen hours a month.[76] The more likely possibility would be a small and slow decrease in hours worked as industrial structure continues to shift away from manufacturing to services. Some downward influence could also occur as observance of a two-day weekend continues to spread among corporations, but this trend will also be very slow. Although the two-day weekend has been part of official Japanese government pronouncements since the early 1970s, even by the mid-1980s very few corporations actually gave their employees Saturday off every week.

CAPITAL. There is no reason to expect capital stock to grow quickly either. A recent study by the Japan Economic Research Center predicted a 6.34 percent annual real increase in capital inputs for 1980–90, slightly slower than the actual increase for 1975–80.[77] This estimate appears reasonable, with capital investment continuing a moderate expansion after the one-time downward adjustment immediately after the 1973 oil shock. Now that Japan is no longer catching up in technology, there is no reason why investment should return to its earlier high levels. Without the large

75. These participation rates are much lower than for workers younger than 65. Approximately 97 percent of males are in the labor force between ages 25 and 54, with a drop to 83 percent for ages 55–64; see Management and Coordination Agency, *Japan Statistical Yearbook, 1986*, p. 71. Data for women, showing lower participation rates (but still much higher than for women aged 65 and older) are presented in table 2-11. However, labor force participation rates for both men and women aged 65 and older are much higher than is the case in the United States. For men the rate in the United States in 1985 was only 15.8 percent and for women 7.3 percent; Bureau of the Census, *Statistical Abstract of the United States, 1987*, p. 376.

76. Bank of Japan, *Economic Statistics Annual, 1985*, p. 305.

77. Hisao Kanamori and others, *Japanese Economy in 1990 in a Global Context: Revitalization of World Economy and Japan's Choice* (Tokyo: Japan Economic Research Center, 1983), p. 34.

jumps in productivity available from imported technology, expected profits on new investment will remain lower than during the high-growth era.

Some optimists believe rates of investment will increase because of the wave of new technologies beginning to become important by the mid-1980s—personal computers, factory automation, new materials, biotechnology. Advances in high-technology industries will certainly have important repercussions for all societies, but their impact on investment rates is unlikely to be very great because while investment in these industries may continue at levels significantly higher than in other industries, they are a small part of total industrial capital stock. Other industries will, of course, also be affected, since some of these new products are intermediate inputs or capital goods (such as industrial robots), but this impact, too, is unlikely to be strong enough to make much difference in total investment.

Growth in export markets could also make a difference in capital investment. If the United States were to continue to grow and pull in Japanese exports as it did in 1983–85, profits and investment in exporting industries would rise. However, this growth was an unusual cyclical development (based on a low value of the yen against the dollar as well as an upturn in U.S. economic growth) that did not last. The rapid appreciation of the yen in 1985 and 1986 cut export-sector profits and resulted in sharp cutbacks in investment spending.

Finally, Japan is unlikely to reassemble that consensus on industrial growth that was a significant cause of the rapid gains of the 1950s and 1960s. For government, a return to tax and expenditure policies that heavily favored business would be difficult even if other conditions suggest such a redirection would raise investment levels. For labor, concern with the quality of life implies that a return to longer hours of work is unlikely. Recent attitudes could also result in a decline in dedication to the corporation, bringing slower productivity increases, though no major trend in that direction appears at all likely.

PRODUCTIVITY. Although Japan's productivity might improve because of new industries such as biotechnology, for the reasons discussed above any such gain will probably be moderate. A technological revolution may also have less impact than some anticipate because of the declining importance of manufacturing in the economy.

GROWTH ESTIMATES. Forecasts in Japan converged on an average 4 percent annual GNP growth in the mid-1980s, which is not unreasonable. Denison and Chung suggested in 1976 that growth would slowly decelerate from 5.7 percent in the 1980s to 4.6 percent in the 1990s to 3.2 percent by the year 2000. That scenario was overly optimistic because the oil shocks and recession of the 1970s kept actual growth below the potential. However, the basic point was valid: the factors producing very high growth were temporary, and growth rates will fall.

As of 1984 a Japanese government estimate for 1981–2000 placed annual real GNP growth at 4.0 to 4.4 percent, depending on assumptions about inputs.[78] A survey of public opinion done for the study came up with a weighted average of 4.36 percent, but in the text the authors stepped back from endorsing any precise figure. It is worth noting that this forecast was based on a rather optimistic 4.4 percent average annual increase in real final consumption spending, a level considerably higher than in the decade from 1974 to 1983. The long-term economic plan for fiscal years 1983 to 1990 also anticipated 4 percent growth and also avoided being very precise.[79]

Private-sector estimates converged at this 4 percent level as well. A forecast made in 1984 by the Nomura Research Institute predicted 3.9 percent growth for 1983–94 (identical to the 1973–83 average), but it was based on higher labor force growth than in the previous decade (a 1.2 percent annual increase instead of 1.0 percent) because of more working women—an assumption that could easily be challenged. Optimism on labor force growth was, however, combined with pessimism about employment, with a predicted increase in unemployment to 5.3 percent by 1994.[80]

The Japan Economic Research Center produces forecasts that are the product of different teams of researchers working with separate models, so that its forecasts are not entirely consistent. A five-year forecast for 1984–88 prepared in May 1984 estimated 4.2 percent annual growth in real GNP, but a year earlier a report predicted that growth from 1980 to 1990 would be 5.0 percent, while a report on Japan in the year 2000 called for 4.47 percent growth from 1980 to 1991 and 4.14 percent from 1991 to

78. Economic Planning Agency, *Japan in the Year 2000: Preparing Japan for an Age of Internationalization, the Aging Society and Maturity* (Tokyo: Japan Times, 1983), pp. 60–64.

79. Economic Planning Agency, *Outlook and Guidelines for the Economy and Society in the 1980s* (EPA, 1983), p. 17.

80. Nomura Research Institute, "A Long-Term Outlook for the Japanese Economy (Fiscal 1984 to 1993)," unpublished document (August 1984), pp. 2, 4.

2000.[81] This last forecast attributed the slowdown between the two decades primarily to a drop in hours worked; it anticipated approximately constant growth in capital stock and a modest rise in productivity growth. But the report went on to note that actual as opposed to potential growth would be about 4 percent because of slow expansion in the government sector (both current and investment expenditures by government) that would not be offset by higher growth in the private sector.

These government and private-sector estimates had several important features. First, they were not very far apart. Almost all were about 4 percent, with the Japan Economic Research Center somewhat more optimistic. Second, most of them anticipated U.S. growth to be about 2.5 percent and Europe's somewhat lower, so that Japan would continue to outperform other industrial nations. Third, all the estimates depended critically on assumptions about productivity change. The 5 percent annual growth anticipated in the 1980s by the Japan Economic Research Center assumed labor and capital would contribute only 1.74 percentage points; the remaining 3.26 points would come from growth in productivity. Lower estimates of growth produced by other organizations assumed roughly the same contribution from labor and capital but were more cautious about productivity growth.

A final point about all forecasts is that actual growth could be below the potential, depending on the handling of macroeconomic policy. All the figures cited are for potential growth (based on expansion of supply capacity), and at least the one Japan Economic Research Center forecast anticipated that actual growth (based on demand) would be slower because of government's failure to pursue full-employment policies.

Summary

Japan experienced unprecedented rapid economic expansion for two and a half decades, raising it from an impoverished, war-devastated nation to an advanced industrial giant. That extraordinary period was gradually coming to an end in the early 1970s, and the traumatic events of 1973 and 1974 hastened the transition. From 1974 through the first half of the

81. Nobuyoshi Namiki and others, *Five-Year Economic Forecast, 1984–1988* (Tokyo: Japan Economic Research Center, 1984), pp. 26–27; Kanamori, *Japanese Economy in 1990*, p. 36; and Japan Economic Research Center, *2000-Nen no Shōhi Shakai: Shin Gijutsu Kakumei no Inpakuto* (Consumer Society in the Year 2000: The Impact of the New Technological Revolution) (Tokyo: JERC, 1984), p. 5.

1980s, annual growth was less than one-half the earlier level, averaging just over 4 percent. Although Japan's economic performance continued to be better than that of other industrial nations, it was by a smaller margin. None of this was entirely unexpected; some economists had been predicting in the early 1970s that Japan's miracle would have to come to an end. But the actual performance has been below the expectations of even the pessimists.

Why did these changes take place? The starting point for any explanation must be the end of the process of technological catch-up. By the 1970s the technological gap was largely closed, reducing the productivity gains that could be realized by importing foreign technology, thus decreasing the expected profits from investment in new plant and equipment and causing investment to decelerate. Lower rates of investment also slowed the productivity gains realized from economies of scale. This primary cause of slower economic growth was supplemented to a lesser extent by other factors: slower expansion of labor inputs because of slower population growth, a decline in labor force participation, and a decline in hours worked; rising energy costs that brought both a one-time loss of income and longer-run costs from shifting resources out of labor-intensive industries; less favorable world market conditions for exports; and a shift in priorities away from economic growth per se to a broader set of social goals. This final element may have inhibited productivity change by reallocating investment to programs with less connection to increased output (such as pollution control or building hospitals) but helped to keep investment levels higher than they would have been otherwise.

Because these represented long-term structural changes for the Japanese economy, rapid growth of the sort that characterized the earlier postwar period is unlikely to return. If growth does not rise to earlier levels, then the changes in macroeconomic structure of the economy that form the topic of the next chapter will remain for some time.

These statements may seem incongruous. How can the reality of slower growth be resolved with the impression of Japan as a vigorous, hard-working exporter of superior manufactured goods? If Japan is such a successful manufacturer, why are not investment rates and economic growth higher? The answer is that exports represent only a small share of total economic activity—especially since they are concentrated in relatively few product categories. Continued international success of these products does not represent the state of quality, innovation, competitiveness, profits, or investment levels in other sectors of the economy. Japan is doing relatively well, but it is no longer a high-growth country.

CHAPTER THREE

Macroeconomic Balances and Policy Responses

JAPAN'S declining rates of economic growth in the 1970s and 1980s were, by themselves, unremarkable. Extremely high rates of growth could not last forever, and all industrial nations experienced slower growth after 1973. But slower growth in Japan brought about fundamental shifts in basic macroeconomic balances within the economy that created new problems and required different policy responses.

When growth moderated, so did the need for investment. Because the economy continued to generate high levels of savings, an imbalance developed that had not existed before. The excess of savings over investment in the private sector had to be absorbed elsewhere in the economy to avoid stagnation and recession. This chapter explores the reasons for these developments and the options for adjustment.[1]

The Accounting Framework

The easiest way to visualize what happened to Japan in the 1970s and 1980s is through the macroeconomic accounting identity, which describes the interrelationships of key elements of the economy. This framework for

---

1. In 1984 the Economic Planning Agency of the Japanese government discussed macroeconomic developments in its annual economic white paper: see *Keizai Hakusho, 1984: Arata na Kokusaika ni Taiō suru Nihon Keizai* (Economic White Paper, 1984: The Japanese

exploring the data should be recognized for what it is—an identity. Numbers balance in these accounts because the identity defines them as balancing. Ex ante perhaps they would not balance, but a variety of economic factors act in such a way as to bring about the necessary equalities in the ex post data. The field of macroeconomic theory is devoted basically to developing the understanding of how economic forces actually bring about this ex post equilibrium, given a set of exogenous factors or assumptions from which to begin. The identity does not explain the causality involved, but based on what actually happened, reasonable statements can be made about the route of causality.

Gross national product, the total of all goods and services produced by a country, can be defined as the sum of private-sector consumption, C, private-sector investment, I, government spending, G, at all levels, and net exports (gross exports, X, minus gross imports, M) of goods and services:

$$GNP = C + I + G + (X - M).$$

Because this is gross national product, all figures are gross of depreciation, meaning that output used for replacement of worn or obsolete assets is included. This definition of GNP is basically a description of what happens to the real goods and services produced by economic activity.

Another way to define GNP is to look at the income produced by economic activity and how that income is spent:

$$GNP = C + S + T.$$

That is, the income produced by economic activity can either be consumed, C, saved, S, or paid to the government in taxes, T.

Since these two definitions describe the same total, they can be equated:

$$C + I + G + (X - M) = C + S + T.$$

Economy Coping with the New Internationalization) (Tokyo: Ministry of Finance, 1984). The facts the paper concentrates on are the ones also discussed in this chapter, but the interpretations differ. The EPA's analysis attempted to explain why Japan would continue to have large current-account surpluses, why the government could do very little about them, and why the rest of the world should accept them without complaint.

Simple algebraic rearrangement yields the following fundamental macro-economic identity:

$$(S - I) = (G - T) + (X - M),$$

which says that whatever ex post imbalance exists between private-sector savings and investment is offset by surpluses or deficits either in the government sector or in net exports of goods and services (the current-account balance) or in both. If a country has more private-sector invest-ment than savings $(S - I < 0)$, then the deficit would be offset by a government surplus $(G - T < 0)$ or a current-account deficit $(X - M < 0)$ or both. If a country has more savings than investment in the private sec-tor $(S - I > 0)$, then the surplus must be offset by a government deficit $(G - T > 0)$ or a current-account surplus $(X - M > 0)$ or both.

Because of the way the relationships have just been described, one could get the impression that the balance on private-sector savings and investment is an exogenous variable to which the other two balances must adjust. As stated above, though, the identity does not imply causality; all six variables and the three balances are affected by both exogenous and endogenous elements to produce the observed ex post equilibrium. How-ever, the following discussion focuses on the movement in Japan's private-sector savings and investment balance because the slowdown in economic growth subjected it to a strong exogenous shift. The actual record of the years since the 1973 oil shock includes a large element of the government deficit and current-account balance adjusting to this fundamental change in the private-sector balance.

A final point concerning the macroeconomic identity is that the private-sector balance between savings and investment can be further disaggre-gated into households and corporations. This is a useful distinction since the savings and investment behavior of the two can be quite different, as will be evident. Although government savings and investment are often aggregated with the private-sector totals in order to speak of the total savings and investment in an economy, this study keeps the government balance separate because the distinction between public and private is key to understanding developments in Japan since 1973.

Savings-Investment Balance

Data from Japan's national income accounts indicate that in the 1960s private-sector investment regularly exceeded savings $(S - I < 0)$, an

Table 3-1. *Sectoral Savings-Investment Balances, Fiscal Years 1960–69*[a]
Percent of GNP at current prices

Sector	1960	1961	1962	1963	1964	1965	1966	1967	1968	1969
Private										
Savings	28.2	28.6	27.9	27.5	27.2	27.4	29.4	31.4	32.9	32.6
Investment	31.1	36.0	28.4	30.7	29.2	27.5	28.7	32.7	33.0	34.5
Savings less investment	-2.9	-7.5	-0.5	-3.3	-2.0	-0.1	0.7	-1.3	-0.1	-1.9
Corporations[b]										
Savings	16.5	16.5	15.6	15.9	16.0	15.8	17.5	18.4	19.7	19.8
Investment	24.6	29.9	21.8	23.7	21.9	19.1	20.4	23.8	24.1	25.3
Savings less investment	-8.1	-13.4	-6.2	-7.8	-5.9	-3.3	-2.8	-5.4	-4.4	-5.5
Households[c]										
Savings	11.8	12.0	12.3	11.6	11.2	11.6	11.9	13.0	13.2	12.7
Investment	6.6	6.1	6.7	7.1	7.3	8.4	8.3	8.9	8.9	9.2
Savings less investment	5.2	5.9	5.7	4.5	3.9	3.2	3.6	4.1	4.3	3.6
Government										
Savings	7.7	8.5	8.2	7.5	6.8	6.0	5.6	6.3	6.9	7.5
Investment	4.7	4.8	5.7	5.3	5.3	5.4	5.4	5.1	5.1	5.0
Savings less investment	3.0	3.7	2.5	2.2	1.5	0.6	0.2	1.2	1.8	2.5
Current account	0	-1.8	0	-1.5	0	1.2	0.9	-0.3	1.0	1.2
Discrepancy[d]	0.1	-1.9	2.0	0.5	-0.5	-0.7	0	0.2	0.7	-0.6

Sources: Economic Planning Agency, *Annual Report on National Income Statistics, 1970* (Tokyo: EPA, 1970), pp. 34–35, 38–39, 40–45, 242–43; *1971*, pp. 6–7, 14–17, 62–69, 222–23.
a. Table 3-1 presents data for the 1960s and table 3-2 for the 1970s and 1980s. When Japan revised its national income accounting procedures in 1980, revised data were provided back only to 1965 (and some details only to 1970). While the data in these two tables are not strictly comparable, they are basically consistent. Percentages are rounded.
b. Includes financial and nonfinancial corporations.
c. Includes nonprofit organizations.
d. Difference between actual data and macroeconomic accounting identity.

imbalance offset by both government surpluses $(G - T \leq 0)$ and a tendency toward current-account deficits $(X - M \leq 0)$ until late in the decade. Savings in the private sector were high and rising, but investment demand was so strong that it absorbed all the savings available. (As percentages of GNP, both savings and investment levels in the private sector were double those in the United States.)[2] Investment demand was fueled by the conditions discussed in chapter 2 that led to the extremely high economic growth rates of the 1950s and 1960s.

As shown in table 3-1, private-sector savings exceeded investment in only one year (fiscal 1966). The average private-sector balance for the entire decade shows an excess of investment over savings of 1.9 percent of GNP. Furthermore, the household sector was a consistent net saver, averaging 4.4 percent of GNP, while the corporate sector was a consistent net investor, averaging 6.3 percent of GNP. These figures not only imply a net flow of savings from households to corporations, but also a corporate demand for investment so voracious that it could not be met entirely through the transfer of surplus savings from households.[3]

Because the private sector as a whole was thus a net investor, the funds had to come from somewhere other than households. That source was the net savings of government, rather than capital inflow from abroad, which is another way of saying that tax revenues exceeded government expenditures. For the decade as a whole these net savings averaged 1.9 percent of GNP. (Although the central government went into deficit officially in 1966, the national income accounts show the consolidated results of all levels of government—central, prefectural, and municipal.) Avoiding government deficits was a deliberate policy, firmly embraced from the time of the occupation, when the desirability of balanced budgets was impressed upon the Japanese government by the Dodge Mission, which was sent to Tokyo in 1949 to advise on policies for reducing rampant inflation. In fact, the belief in balanced budgets was so strong that when central government

2. Total private-sector investment in the United States during the 1960s varied from 14 to 17 percent of GNP; savings varied between 15 and 17 percent. U.S. Bureau of Economic Analysis, *Long Term Economic Growth, 1860–1970* (GPO, 1973), pp. 183, 187, 227.

3. Kazuo Satō, "Japan's Savings and Internal and External Macroeconomic Balance," in Kōzo Yamamura, ed., *Policy and Trade Issues of the Japanese Economy: American and Japanese Perspectives* (Seattle: University of Washington Press, 1982), pp. 143–72, presents his analysis in this way, evaluating savings-investment balances separately for households and corporations. Satō has emphasized macroeconomic balances in the analysis of Japan's economy for a long time, and the approach taken in this book owes a great deal to him.

deficits were officially condoned in 1966, an artificial distinction between "construction" bonds and "deficit" bonds was concocted. The government's position was that bonds issued to cover public works expenditures were acceptable but that it would continue to avoid deficits on general expenditures.[4] Although the distinction was artificial, since the construction supported by bonds did not generate revenue and did not represent collateral in the same sense as in private-sector transactions, it has continued to the present.

The other potential source of private-sector investment would have been funds from abroad, but the data show that for the decade as a whole the current account was essentially in balance (with an average surplus of 0.07 percent of GNP), shifting gradually from deficits in the first half of the decade to surpluses in the second half. As with government deficits, avoiding current-account deficits was a matter of government policy. In 1949 under the new Bretton Woods system of fixed exchange rates, Japan's exchange rate was set at 360 yen to the dollar. That rate was overvalued, meaning that Japan tended to have trouble exporting enough to pay for its imports. But under the Bretton Woods system, all adjustments had to be borne by deficit countries, which were expected to follow policies to reduce their current-account deficits (thereby defending their fixed exchange rates) or, as a last resort, to devalue their currencies. Japan was firmly committed to the system and to its obligations to defend the established exchange rate. To have devalued the yen would have been internationally humiliating and would have hurt efforts to prove to the world that it was a responsible, stable, productive member of the world economy. Thus the government instituted a variety of policies to prevent serious current-account deficits, including high tariffs and widespread import quotas, strict controls on international capital movements (essentially preventing Japanese corporations from borrowing or lending abroad), and periodic tightening of monetary policy to slow the economy and thereby reduce the growth of imports. In this way the imperatives of exchange rate policy strongly discouraged borrowing overseas to accommodate the private sector's demand for investment funds.

The strict control of imports and capital flow was also strongly influenced by economic xenophobia. Since it began to develop as a modern

4. Shinichi Gotō, *Kokusai 100 Cho: Infure Keizai e no Keishō* (¥100 Trillion in Government Bonds: An Alarm for Inflation) (Tokyo: Tōyō Keizai Shimpōsha, 1980), pp. 133–45, discusses the Diet debates at the time of the initial issuing of central government bonds and the distinction made between construction bonds and deficit bonds.

economy in the late nineteenth century, Japan has striven for an economy owned, operated, and supplied by Japanese firms. Policies to that effect proliferated in the 1930s, and postwar policies continued and strengthened the tendency. Xenophobia was given additional impetus in the 1950s by the fear that in the absence of strict controls war-weakened Japanese companies would be quickly overrun by foreign competition.

As a net saver, the government's contribution to Japan's growth strategy or industrial policy in the 1950s and 1960s is often overlooked. Given the refusal to allow extensive borrowing from abroad, had the government not acted as net saver, its deficit financing needs would have competed with and crowded out the demand for domestic investment. The corporate sector's ability to invest in productive plant and equipment would have been impaired, constraining economic growth. Had the government chosen to allow corporations to borrow freely from abroad, Japan might have grown faster, but it could easily have run into international debt problems of the sort faced by many developing countries in the 1980s. Therefore, the fiscal policies of the government in the 1950s and 1960s were consistent both with the desire to maintain the value of the yen and with the high private-sector investment demand; fiscal stimulus was essentially unneeded because of that strong demand.

With the advent of the 1970s, however, this macroeconomic balance began what was to be a fundamental long-term change of epic proportions. As table 3-2 shows, the private sector became a net saver ($S - I > 0$), with the decline in investment offset at first by government deficits ($G - T > 0$) and then by rising current-account surpluses ($X - M > 0$). This pattern emerged most strongly after 1974, but already between 1970 and 1973 the private sector showed an average surplus of savings over investment of 0.9 percent of GNP. From 1974 to 1978 the net surplus rose rapidly, yielding an annual average of 3.8 percent of GNP and reaching a peak of 6.8 percent in 1978. The average for the period is lower than it would otherwise be because of short-term developments in the corporate sector in 1974. If 1974 were taken as the dividing point rather than 1973, then the average net savings in the 1970–74 period become only 0.5 percent of GNP but rise to 4.2 percent from 1975 to 1978.

Corporate-sector savings (consisting of depreciation allowances and retained earnings) dropped somewhat, from annual averages of 16 to 20 percent of GNP that had prevailed throughout the 1960s and early 1970s to levels of 8 to 12 percent after 1974. Meanwhile, corporate investment dropped even more, from levels of 22 to 30 percent of GNP in most years

Table 3-2. *Sectoral Savings-Investment Balances, Fiscal Years 1970–85*[a]
Percent of GNP at current prices

Sector	1970	1971	1972	1973	1974	1975	1976	1977
Private								
Savings	33.3	31.0	32.0	32.3	30.0	29.0	30.4	29.5
Investment	34.0	30.0	29.2	31.7	31.4	26.8	26.0	24.6
Savings less investment	−0.7	1.0	2.8	0.6	−1.4	2.2	4.4	5.0
Corporations[b]								
Savings	18.7	16.1	16.9	15.4	10.3	8.4	9.1	9.5
Investment	27.5	24.8	23.9	26.2	23.1	17.9	16.2	15.2
Savings less investment	−8.8	−8.7	−7.0	−10.8	−12.9	−9.5	−7.0	−5.6
Households[c]								
Savings	14.6	14.9	15.1	16.9	19.7	20.6	21.3	20.0
Investment	6.5	5.2	5.3	5.4	8.3	8.9	9.8	9.4
Savings less investment	8.1	9.7	9.8	11.5	11.5	11.7	11.4	10.6
Government								
Savings	6.8	7.0	6.2	6.9	6.3	3.3	2.1	2.5
Investment	5.1	5.8	6.3	6.4	6.0	6.0	5.8	6.3
Savings less investment	1.7	1.2	−0.1	0.5	0.4	−2.8	−3.7	−3.8
Current account	1.0	2.5	2.2	0	−1.0	−0.1	0.7	1.5
Discrepancy[d]	0	−0.3	0.4	1.1	−0.1	−0.4	0	−0.4

Sources: Economic Planning Agency, *Annual Report on National Accounts, 1987* (Tokyo: EPA, 1987), pp. 82–83, 94–103, 106–09; *1984*, pp. 58, 70, 72, 74, 76.
a. See table 3-1, note a.
b. Includes financial and nonfinancial corporations.
c. Includes nonprofit organizations.
d. Difference between actual data and macroeconomic accounting identity.

between 1960 and 1974 to only 14 to 18 percent afterwards, about a one-third decline. The combined result was that the net demand by the corporate sector on other sectors of the economy for investment funds dropped significantly. Net borrowing averaged almost 10 percent of GNP between 1970 and 1974 but less than 6 percent between 1975 and 1985. The year 1974 is a better dividing year for showing this particular adjustment because investment activity reacted slowly to the 1973 oil price hikes. Corporate investment remained at a very high level in 1974 despite a sharp drop in corporate savings.

The household sector continued to be a large net supplier of funds after the slowdown. From an average of just over 15 percent of GNP in 1970–73, household savings rose to an average of 18 percent in 1974–85 (peaking in 1976 at 21.3 percent and then slowly declining toward 15 percent again by the mid-1980s). Household investment was also up a bit, from 5.6 percent in 1970–73, to an average of just over 8 percent for 1974–85.

1978	1979	1980	1981	1982	1983	1984	1985
30.7	29.0	28.4	27.9	27.2	26.9	26.7	26.8
23.9	25.2	25.1	24.2	23.3	21.9	22.3	22.8
6.8	3.8	3.2	3.7	3.9	5.0	4.5	4.0
11.4	11.7	11.3	10.6	11.2	11.0	11.4	11.8
13.9	16.1	17.0	16.9	16.2	15.3	15.9	17.2
−2.5	−4.3	−5.7	−6.3	−4.9	−4.2	−4.5	−5.4
19.4	17.3	17.1	17.3	16.0	15.9	15.3	15.0
10.0	9.2	8.1	7.3	7.1	6.6	6.4	5.6
9.3	8.1	9.0	10.0	8.8	9.3	9.0	9.4
1.5	2.5	2.7	3.3	3.2	2.8	3.9	4.8
7.0	7.2	7.1	7.1	6.8	6.4	6.0	5.6
−5.5	−4.7	−4.4	−3.8	−3.6	−3.7	−2.1	−0.8
1.7	−0.9	−1.0	0.5	0.7	1.8	2.8	3.7
−0.4	−0.1	−0.1	−0.6	−0.4	−0.4	−0.5	−0.5

Household investment, however, declined as a share of GNP after 1978. The combined result of the movements in household savings and investment was virtually no change in the sector's position as a net saver, at an average of almost 10 percent of GNP both before and after 1973.

Continued High Savings

Why did private-sector savings rates decline so little after economic growth rates fell? Corporate saving did fall because of lower profitability after 1973. Therefore, the main question is what happened to household savings rates, which declined from a historic peak in 1976 but did not return even to the level of the early 1970s until the mid-1980s. Unfortunately, the reason Japanese households save considerably more as a percentage of their disposable income than is the case in other industrial countries remains poorly understood, though progress is being made in research. The most successful attempts to explain savings behavior have focused on the life-cycle hypothesis, in which people base saving and consumption patterns on assumptions about their lifetime earnings, and various target-motive models, in which individuals save for specific goals such as buying a house.[5]

In looking at the period immediately after the first oil shock, one feature stands out: high inflation in 1973–74. The Japanese rely heavily on bank time deposits in their portfolios of financial assets, a trait that will be considered in more detail in chapter 4. The interest rates on those deposits were and still are controlled, and in 1973–74 the rates were kept far below the level of inflation. The loss in the real value of savings in this two-year period was greater than 20 percent. If people save with some goal of real accumulated savings to meet anticipated expenditures, such as the down payment on a house, then the loss in the real value of savings in those years implies a need to increase temporarily the annual rate of saving to replace the losses. The anxiety pervading Japan in the wake of the oil crisis was another incentive to save more as a hedge against a future that seemed less certain and less optimistic. Measured as a percentage of personal disposable income, the savings rate has been trending down since the mid-1970s as this temporary factor came to an end.

Other factors often cited as reasons for high rates of savings include low levels of social security benefits, privately borne educational costs, a lack of consumer credit, the bonuses paid twice a year by corporations to their employees, and the high cost of housing (and the relatively high down payments required). Some of these explanations, such as the small social security benefits, could have been important in the 1950s, but were less and less applicable by the 1970s. Others, including the high cost of housing relative to annual personal income and the resulting high down payments, have remained valid. In the case of social security, the increased levels of benefits in the 1970s may have lessened the need to save for retirement, but the availability of jobs to supplement social security and pension benefits deteriorated, so that the net effect could have been close to zero.

5. Recent studies of household saving behavior include an excellent review article by Marcus Noland, "Saving in Japan: A Critical Survey" (revised draft, October 1986). See also Kazuo Satō, "Saving and Investment in Japan," in Yasusuke Murakami and Hugh T. Patrick, eds., *The Political Economy of Japan*, vol. 1: *The Domestic Transformation* (Stanford University Press, 1987); and Charles Yūji Horioka, "Household Saving in Japan: The Importance of Target Saving for Education and Housing," paper prepared for the Japan Economic Seminar, Washington, D.C., September 21, 1985.

The most important determinant of the trend in personal savings is probably the aging of the population. Statistics for personal savings represent the net savings of those who add to their savings and those who withdraw money from their savings. As the population ages, the proportion that is retired and either is not adding to savings or is actually drawing them down has been increasing, and will continue to increase for a number of years. During the 1970s the rising proportion of elderly in the population was offset by a decline in the proportion of children, so the proportion of working-age adults remained constant, keeping savings high. Because the ratio of working-age adults to total population was dropping by the 1980s, personal savings as a share of GNP might continue its recent decline, but the picture is not very clear.[6]

At one extreme, some economists in Japan have argued that the age distribution of the population explains the very high levels of savings until the 1980s and implies a rapid fall in future savings rates. Professor Yukio Noguchi of Hitotsubashi University, for example, suggests that Japan will have rates much more in line with other countries in the future. But his own international comparison showing personal savings against an indicator of population age (the ratio of population aged sixty-five and older to those aged twenty to sixty-four) shows a wide variation among countries. Japan's savings rates would not have to fall very far to match the performance of some other countries with older populations.[7] At the other extreme, in its official long-term forecast the Economic Planning Agency has estimated the size of household savings in the year 2000 with and without changes in demographic structure, finding that average savings as a share of GNP will be only 2 percentage points lower as a result of the aging of the population.[8] Both these estimates are speculative since the savings behavior of different age groups within society could change. But any projection of large declines in the savings rate appears suspect; even though demographics are important, there are too many other factors that may offset the effects of an aging population.

What are some of these factors? Noguchi has acknowledged that uncertainty of the future may help keep savings high.[9] Slower economic growth

6. Economic Planning Agency, *Keizai Hakusho, 1984*, pp. 115–16.
7. "Naze Takai Nihon no Chochikuritsu?" (Why Japan's High Savings Rates?), *Nihon Keizai Shimbun*, December 23, 1984.
8. Economic Planning Agency, *Keizai Hakusho, 1984*, p. 115.
9. Yukio Noguchi, *Zaisei Kiki no Kōzō* (The Structure of Fiscal Crisis) (Tokyo: Tōyō Keizai Shimpōsha, 1980), pp. 113–14.

has brought higher unemployment and less rapidly rising real incomes. Both developments could encourage higher savings. Higher unemployment affects those people of mandatory retirement age at large corporations who are seeking postretirement jobs. Even with the improvements in social security and pensions, many people find it necessary to continue working. Those in younger age groups will save more out of their current income if they believe that their own chances of such employment in the future are worsened. The slower growth in income also means that individuals cannot rely on expectations of higher future real income to boost their savings (by setting aside a fixed proportion of their income each year), which could cause them to save more out of current income. Slower growth has resulted in expectations of the future that are less bright and less certain, even after the extreme anxiety of the years immediately following the oil shock had passed, and the cautious response would be to save more. Professor Kazuo Kinoshita of Osaka University reinforces these points by adding that people were living longer after retirement, which raised the amount of savings desirable to finance those years.[10]

A further factor could be a rising proportion of working elderly, another possibility suggested by Kinoshita. Despite the higher unemployment levels, there could be such a trend, which would also help maintain relatively high savings levels. But by the mid-1980s there was little evidence of the trend, as overall labor force participation rates for those sixty-five and older continued to drift slowly downward. However, while male participation was still dropping, female participation for this age group stabilized after the mid-1970s.

Although personal saving and its likely future trend are important considerations for understanding total savings behavior, corporate savings are one-third of the total and must be considered as well. As table 3-2 indicates, during the years after 1973 personal savings ranged from 15 to 21 percent of GNP while corporate savings were 8 to 12 percent. Corporate savings in this table are shown as gross savings, meaning that they include depreciation in addition to retained earnings. The advent of slower economic growth brought with it a drop in corporate profits, for the reasons discussed in chapter 2. But the fall in profits had only a modest impact on total corporate savings because of the large share of savings represented by depreciation. Data on the corporate sector show, for example, that in 1984

10. Kazuo Kinoshita, "Chochiku Shōrei Sochi wa Gimon" (Doubts about Savings Promotion Measures), *Nihon Keizai Shimbun*, November 22, 1984.

incorporated businesses set aside ¥19.2 trillion in depreciation allowances, whereas retained earnings were only ¥5.6 trillion.[11] There is no reason to expect that corporate savings will decline much further as a share of GNP.

Falling Investment Demand

The other half of the explanation of changes in the savings-investment balance in the private sector concerns declining investment. In the corporate sector this decline occurred after 1973. In the household sector investment rose as a share of GNP until 1978 but has been falling since.

For corporations, the explanation lies in a number of factors: the acceleration principle, lower profits, lower capacity utilization, and the shifting industrial structure of the economy. The acceleration principle is a basic economic observation that says the level of plant and equipment investment is sensitive to changes in the growth of demand for goods and services (rather than to the level of demand). Even without growth, some investment is always necessary to replace the depreciation of existing capital stock. But to provide increased output requires more capital stock, which requires increased investment. The same is true in reverse: a fall in economic growth leads to smaller investment requirements. This is what happened to Japan after 1973. Total GNP grew at an average annual real rate of 9.4 percent from 1966 through 1973, while corporate fixed investment expanded at an extremely high 15.0 percent rate to provide the necessary increase in capital stock to enable increased production. However, GNP growth averaged 3.8 percent from 1974 to 1985, while corporate fixed investment grew at almost the same rate (3.9 percent).[12] Not only was the long-term need for capital less, but in the short run the transition to slower growth implied that the previous high rates of investment left Japanese industry with excess capacity that depressed investment further. The outcome was an absolute drop in the level of investment in

11. Management and Coordination Agency, *Japan Statistical Yearbook, 1986* (Tokyo: Statistics Bureau, 1986), pp. 368–69. These data on corporate accounts differ somewhat from the national income accounts, which show an even larger percentage of corporate gross saving in the form of depreciation. Retained earnings are only a small portion of total corporate profits. For 1984, pretax profits in Japan were ¥21.1 trillion, of which ¥12.4 trillion went to taxes and ¥3.1 trillion to stockholders as dividends and to directors as bonuses.

12. Economic Planning Agency, *Annual Report on National Accounts, 1987* (Tokyo: EPA, 1987), pp. 118–21.

1974 and 1975, and a continuous decline in the ratio of corporate investment to GNP through 1978.

From the standpoint of corporate management, the decline in investment ought to have been motivated by lower corporate profits and lower
capacity utilization. Profits were lower because of both the long-term
decline in profitability caused by the end of technological catch-up and the
overhang of excess capacity. Table 3-3 provides data on profits in the
corporate sector as a whole. The measure of profits most commonly used
in Japan is *keijō rieki,* translated as "recurring profits." This is a before-tax
measure that includes nonoperating income and expenses, but excludes
certain extraordinary gains and losses. In nominal terms this measure
peaked in 1973 at almost ¥13 trillion, and then dropped by more than half
to under ¥6 trillion in 1975. Thereafter, profits expanded rapidly, surpass-
ing the ¥13 trillion level by 1978, and fluctuating between ¥16 trillion
and ¥20 trillion in the early 1980s. Because of rising tax rates during this
period, net (after-tax) profits did not stage as much of a recovery as the
recurring profit measure.

If profit figures are deflated by price changes, the drop is even more
evident. According to these data, recurring profits finally came close to
1973 levels in 1979 and 1980, but failed to surpass the earlier figure until
1984. After-tax profits show the same progression, as do retained earnings. All these data are for the absolute yen amount of profits, but the
economy—and the corporate sector—were growing, so that these numbers
imply decreased profitability. The ratio of recurring profits to net worth
provided in table 3-3 shows that 1973 was a year of extraordinary profitability for the corporate sector, a level not reached thereafter. Even if the
comparison is made with other less unusual years before the oil shock,
profitability dropped by half in 1975 and did not recover to earlier levels
until 1979. And this return to profitability was brief, with another decline
setting in after 1979. The average ratio of recurring profits to net worth
from 1965 to 1972 was 25.6 percent, a level that drops to 21.7 percent
from 1974 to 1984.[13]

Professor Kimio Uno of Tsukuba University has argued that profits are

13. These rates of return are high by U.S. standards, where before-tax ratios of profits
to net worth varied between 11 and 13 percent in the 1970s. However, net worth figures are
generally acknowledged in Japan to be seriously undervalued, mainly because land is
carried at purchase cost on corporate books. Net worth is the difference between assets and
liabilities, and an upward revision of assets to reflect market values of land would thereby
increase net worth. A larger value for net worth would decrease the ratio of profits to net

Table 3-3. *Nominal and Real Corporate-Sector Profits,*
Fiscal Years 1965–84
Billions of yen unless otherwise specified

	Nominal profits			Real profits[a]			Recurring profits/
Fiscal year	Recurring[b] profits	Net profits	Retained earnings	Recurring[b] profits	Net profits	Retained earnings	net worth (percent)
1965	1,916	1,069	387	4,034	2,251	815	17.4
1966	2,617	1,569	800	4,468	3,235	1,649	21.6
1967	3,774	2,050	1,114	7,718	4,192	2,278	27.2
1968	4,512	2,547	1,467	9,189	5,187	2,988	28.5
1969	6,128	3,437	2,128	12,111	6,792	4,206	32.0
1970	6,578	3,566	2,124	12,674	6,871	4,092	29.4
1971	5,619	3,010	1,536	10,911	5,845	2,983	22.5
1972	7,449	3,987	2,347	13,923	7,452	4,387	26.2
1973	12,799	6,624	4,480	19,782	10,238	6,924	37.7
1974	11,014	4,978	2,788	14,121	6,382	3,574	27.8
1975	5,956	2,202	157	7,549	2,791	199	13.5
1976	9,649	4,085	1,921	11,653	4,934	2,320	20.6
1977	10,164	4,441	2,273	12,202	5,331	2,729	20.3
1978	13,030	6,178	3,797	15,871	7,525	4,625	23.9
1979	17,722	8,670	6,030	19,518	9,548	6,641	28.4
1980	19,704	9,215	6,294	19,586	9,160	6,256	27.4
1981	17,174	7,276	4,249	16,954	7,183	4,194	21.1
1982	16,132	6,962	4,074	15,847	6,839	4,002	18.4
1983	16,924	7,044	4,083	16,890	7,030	4,075	17.6
1984	20,618	8,684	5,563	20,515	8,641	5,535	19.6

Sources: Management and Coordination Agency, *Japan Statistical Yearbook, 1970* (Tokyo: Statistics Bureau, 1970), pp. 312–14; *1973–74*, pp. 312–14; *1978*, p. 312; *1980*, pp. 318–20; *1984*, pp. 368–70; *1986*, pp. 368–70.

a. Obtained by deflating nominal profits by the overall wholesale price index for manufactured goods, including domestic and internationally traded goods.

b. Before-tax figures that exclude certain types of nonrecurring profits and losses.

not a very good indicator of corporate demand for new investment because competition for market share drives Japanese firms to increase investment in plant and equipment whenever capacity utilization is tight, regardless of profit levels. This behavior is, he contends, reinforced by a belief that government industrial policy will act in such a way as to protect some acceptable level of profitability for industries and individual firms. Whether or not one accepts his reasoning (and the point about industrial policy is suspect after the 1960s), his regressions indicate that capacity

worth. This problem with the Japanese data makes comparison with the United States difficult but should not affect the validity of the point that profitability declined. See Bureau of the Census, *Statistical Abstract of the United States, 1984* (GPO, 1986), pp. 538, 548.

utilization is a significant explanatory variable in analyzing investment behavior.[14] One might add, though, that profits and capacity utilization ought to be highly correlated, so that either indicator should show a significant relationship.

The indicator for capacity utilization that is used in Japan is not the same as the one used in the United States. Called the *kadō ritsu,* or "operation rate," it is the production index divided by the capacity index; therefore, the data cannot be presented as a percentage of full capacity, but rather as an index with a base year. According to this measure, the level of capacity utilization since 1973 has generally been lower than in earlier years. Taking 1980 as 100, the average for the index from 1965 to 1973 was 106, while from 1974 to 1984 it was only 96. Since 1973 the index has risen and fallen with the business cycle but has failed to return to the pre-1973 average in any single year.[15]

Even though profit levels recovered to some extent, the trend in capacity utilization provides a strong explanation of why investment remained below earlier levels as a share of GNP. With lower utilization levels industries had more room to expand production without additional plant and equipment, and the continuation of these lower levels made firms more cautious about adding additional capacity.

Another factor that played a small role in reducing the amount of investment was structural change in the economy. During the 1950s and 1960s, the share of gross domestic product originating in agriculture steadily dropped while both the manufacturing and service and government sectors gained (table 3-4). After 1973, however, movement out of the primary sector slowed, and the secondary sector began to lose share as the tertiary sector continued to gain. From 1970 to 1985 the share of construction, mining, and manufacturing in GDP dropped by 4.6 percentage points. If the value of output in each sector is presented in constant prices, it is clear that the changes are due to relative price movements: the share of the secondary sector continued to rise in the 1970s and 1980s. Because productivity growth has been higher in the secondary sector (primarily in manufacturing), price inflation has been lower than in the service sector.

The shifts in structure indicated by the nominal-price data provide modest evidence of reduced investment needs. Japan collects data on the

14. Kimio Uno, "Investment Trends by Industry: An Industry Analysis (2)," unpublished paper (Ibaraki, Japan: Tsukuba University, 1984), pp. 37–38, 91–93.

15. Management and Coordination Agency, *Japan Statistical Yearbook, 1970,* p. 246; *1973–74,* p. 244; *1984,* p. 259; *1986,* p. 259.

Table 3-4. *Output as Share of GDP, by Sector, Selected Years, 1950–85*
Percent

| | | Sector | | |
| | | Secondary[b] | | |
Year	Primary[a]	Total	Manufacturing	Tertiary[c]
		Current prices		
1950[d]	26.0	31.8	24.8	42.2
1960	12.9	38.9	31.9	48.1
1970	6.0	43.5	35.2	50.5
1973	5.7	43.0	33.9	51.3
1980	3.6	38.4	28.7	57.9
1985	3.1	36.8	29.3	60.1
		Constant 1980 prices		
1970	6.1	38.7	26.6	55.2
1973	5.5	39.6	27.7	54.9
1980	3.6	38.4	28.7	57.9
1985	3.1	40.3	33.5	56.6

Sources: Bank of Japan, *Economic Statistics Annual, 1971* (Tokyo: BOJ, 1971), p. 290; *1959*, pp. 293–94; and Economic Planning Agency, *Annual Report on National Accounts, 1987*, pp. 150–53, 158–61.
a. Includes agriculture, forestry, and fisheries.
b. Includes mining, construction, and manufacturing.
c. Includes service industries and government.
d. Share of national income rather than GDP.

stock of capital in different sectors and industries, and those industries whose share of GDP has been gaining tend to require less capital per unit of output than those industries whose share has been falling. Table 3-5 presents data on the capital-to-output ratios in a number of Japanese industries. From 1970 to 1985 the share of GDP originating in manufacturing, which has a high ratio of capital to output, dropped by 6.2 percentage points, while the share held by miscellaneous services, which has a very low capital-to-output ratio, rose by 4.6 percentage points, and other sectors of low capital intensity, finance and insurance, and real estate, rose by 1.3 and 1.8 points respectively. However, this observation about shifting structure should be tempered by the realization that the 1950s and 1960s were also a time of major structural shift away from agriculture, which is the most capital-intensive industry in Japan according to these data.

Households are the source of a smaller but significant portion of private-sector investment as measured in the national income accounts, averaging a little less than one-half that of corporate investment. Household investment activity peaked in 1976–78 at 9 to 10 percent of GNP (see table 3-2). Since that time the share of household investment in GNP has been declining, reaching only 5.6 percent in 1985. The main explanation

Table 3-5. *Capital-to-Output Ratios, by Industry Group, Fiscal Year 1984*
Billions of yen unless otherwise specified

Industry group	Gross capital	GDP	Capital-to-output ratio	Percentage point change in share of GDP originating in each industry, 1970–85
Agriculture	73,131	9,655	7.6	−3.0
Mining	2,026	1,195	1.7	−0.4
Construction	18,697	22,219	0.8	−0.4
Manufacturing	171,181	88,700	1.9	−6.2
Wholesale and retail trade	50,924	42,685	1.2	−0.7
Finance and insurance	10,564	16,138	0.7	1.3
Real estate	10,842	29,203	0.4	1.8
Transportation and communication	27,124	18,756	1.4	−0.7
Electricity, gas, water	37,079	10,431	3.6	1.2
Services	37,730	55,843	0.7	4.6

Sources: Management and Coordination Agency, *Japan Statistical Yearbook, 1986*, pp. 380, 561; and Economic Planning Agency, *Annual Report on National Accounts, 1987*, pp. 154–57.

may lie in the factors discussed previously, because the household sector in the national income accounts includes unincorporated businesses. Small "mom and pop" operations are far more prevalent in Japan than in the United States, and their investment in plant and equipment could form a large share of total household investment.

Nevertheless, the trend in housing also explains the downward trend in household investment since 1978. Table 3-6 shows that after a postwar peak of 2 million housing starts in 1973, there was a sharp drop in 1974 when the general recession arrived, followed by a recovery to another peak of 1.75 million starts in 1978. This recovery was caused in part by the expansion of government programs to encourage housing investment. However, after 1978, housing starts dropped consistently every year to reach only 1.33 million in 1983, followed by only a small increase to 1.37 million in 1984.

Data on housing starts can be misleading or poorly correlated with actual housing investment because of changes in the size or quality of housing. But the data on the total floor area of new housing indicate a similar pattern. From a peak of 152 million square meters in 1973, the area of new housing dropped sharply and then recovered to a second peak

Table 3-6. *Housing Starts and Total Floor Area, 1970–84*

Year	Housing starts (millions)	Total floor area (millions of square meters)
1970	1.566	104.7
1971	1.559	105.8
1972	1.920	133.9
1973	2.030	152.4
1974	1.472	114.1
1975	1.539	120.4
1976	1.719	134.1
1977	1.702	135.6
1978	1.754	145.9
1979	1.707	146.8
1980	1.483	129.1
1981	1.359	117.2
1982	1.345	116.7
1983	1.331	108.6
1984	1.367	108.8

Sources: Management and Coordination Agency, *Japan Statistical Yearbook, 1986*, p. 268; *1980*, p. 216; *1978*, p. 216; *1973–74*, p. 224.

of 147 million square meters in 1979, followed by a consistent decline to less than 109 million square meters by 1984. From 1979 the reduction in area has been 26 percent.

The Japanese are often criticized for the poor quality of their housing: chapter 2 pointed out that the size of dwelling units remained about half that in the United States by the early 1980s. Why didn't housing investment continue to expand as the Japanese used their newfound wealth to improve their personal well-being? The Japanese response is to point out that housing quality improved sharply, that the size of dwelling units increased, and that the absolute shortage of housing disappeared by the 1980s. To them the problem of housing has been solved, and they expect housing investment to proceed at a slower pace in the future as replacement of old dwelling units becomes the major focus of activity. In addition, the baby-boom generation was married and housed by the 1980s, so that the smaller numbers of new households being formed will continue to reduce the additional housing needed. Finally, the great migration of population from the farms to the cities, creating a need for rapid investment in urban and suburban housing, was largely over by the 1970s. As a result of such factors, forecasts tend to show housing investment continuing to grow at a pace slower than total GNP.[16]

The characterization of housing demand as largely satisfied is only partially true. While quality and quantity have improved, housing remains less spacious and less comfortable than what a Westerner would expect, given the level of per capita income. But throughout the postwar period, the price of housing has risen faster than household income. As table 3-7 shows, from 2.3 times annual household income in 1955, the average price of a new house rose to 4.4 times by 1965 and 6.7 times in 1983. For the Tokyo metropolitan area the climb was even steeper, from 1.8 times in 1955 to 7.9 times by 1983.[17]

One reason the ratio increased is that the Japanese have purchased larger houses. But even if adjusted for the change in size, the results are not encouraging. As table 3-7 shows, the ratio of the price per square meter of land to annual household income more than doubled from 1955 to 1965, and then rose more slowly until it stabilized after 1975. In the Tokyo metropolitan area the ratio continued to climb even after 1975. For structures, the cost per square meter of space relative to annual income has been roughly constant from 1955 through 1983. These trends mean that the Japanese purchased larger homes because they were willing to devote a large share of their income to housing and not because income growth made each unit of space relatively less expensive.

With people desiring larger houses but facing rising costs per unit of space relative to income, the average cost of new homes may have become too high relative to incomes by the 1980s, contributing to the decline in housing starts. A higher price-income ratio meant that a smaller proportion of households desiring to buy a new home would have sufficient income to do so.[18]

16. The Japan Economic Research Center, for example, in 1985 projected that private housing investment would expand at a 2.8 percent average real rate from 1984 to 1989, while GNP was anticipated to rise at a 4.3 percent rate. Japan Economic Research Center, *Gokanen Keizai Yosoku, Showa 60 nen–64 nen* (Five-Year Economic Forecast, 1985–89) (Tokyo: JERC, 1985), pp. 16–17.

17. Data on housing costs can vary widely from one survey to another in Japan. However, even if the level of prices is in dispute, the changes in price over time are more important here. Note also that the ratio of prices of new homes to average household income does not mean that the ratio of price to income for households actually purchasing those homes is so high. It does mean that a smaller share of households is likely to have sufficient income to afford new homes.

18. That the ratio of new home prices to income has risen implies an income-elastic demand for housing. An affluent family of the 1980s can devote a larger share of its income

Table 3-7. *Cost of New Housing, Selected Years, 1955–83*

Ratios	1955	1965	1975	1983
Price of land and house to annual household income				
Nationwide	2.3	4.4	6.2	6.7
Tokyo metropolitan area[a]	1.8	5.0	6.6	7.9
Price of land per square meter to annual household income				
Nationwide	0.006	0.016	0.019	0.019
Tokyo metropolitan area[a]	0.006	0.027	0.031	0.035
Price of house per square meter to annual household income				
Nationwide	0.024	0.025	0.026	0.023
Tokyo metropolitan area[a]	0.023	0.025	0.029	0.027

Source: Economic Planning Agency, *Kokumin Seikatsu Hakusho, 1985: Sengo 40 Nen: Seijuku no Jidai ni Mekate* (White Paper on the People's Life, 1985: 40 Years After the War: Facing an Age of Maturity) (Tokyo: MOF, 1985), p. 163.

a. Tokyo metropolitan area inlcudes the city of Tokyo and the prefectures of Saitama, Chiba, and Kanagawa.

Implications

The macroeconomic shifts detailed in tables 3-1 and 3-2 are summarized in the chart on page 90, which shows the balances of the high-growth era and the phases of adjustment to slower growth since the early 1970s. The discussion so far has focused on the switch from deficit to surplus in the private-sector savings-investment balance. The reasons for that shift are largely unrelated to the size of government deficits or influences from abroad. The imbalances emerged from private-sector responses to the reality of slower economic growth. The private sector desired to save more than it desired to invest, and would do so if the rest of the economic system could accommodate its excess savings. The ending of the technology gap, the acceleration-principle response to slower growth, and the changing structure of the economy all implied that business-related investment growth would moderate. Housing investment was affected by demographics and slower household income growth coupled with continued inflation of housing prices. Meanwhile, savings remained relatively high because of inflation-caused losses in the real value of savings accounts, increased uncertainty about the future, and other factors relatively unrelated to movements in government deficits and current-account surpluses. Both government fiscal policy and the current-account surplus have had

---

to housing than a poor family of the 1950s, which needed to spend more of its income on daily necessities. However, the levels that the price-to-income ratio reached by the 1980s may have moved beyond what is desirable.

Summary of Japan's Macroeconomic Balances			
Period	Private-sector savings-investment balance	Government surplus or deficit	Current-account surplus or deficit
High-growth era 1950–73	deficit	surplus	close to zero
Low-growth era 1974–79	surplus	rising deficit	small surplus
1980–85	surplus	falling deficit	rising surplus
1986–	?	?	falling surplus

some impact on the trend in savings and investment, but there has been a large exogenous element in the emergence of surplus savings in the private sector. Movements in the government deficit and the current account, the other two elements of the macroeconomic accounting identity, are better seen as adjusting to or accommodating this fundamental shift in the private sector, at least until the mid-1980s.

What Japan exhibits is the archetypical Keynesian dilemma. In the explanation of the Great Depression, the tendency of mature economies to underconsume was a central feature, so that the supply of savings would, ex ante, exceed investment. One of the more ironic aspects of the situation is that much of the Japanese economics profession in the 1980s has proclaimed itself monetarist or post-Keynesian precisely at a time the Japanese economy has come to fit rather well the conditions that originally generated Keynesian theory.

It is worth remembering that Keynes was trying to explain why the depression occurred. In the absence of any government policy to absorb the surplus of private-sector savings (and ignoring international trade), any ex ante surplus of savings over investment would simply lead the economy to contract until balance was restored (by lowering savings). That was the insight that led to the suggestion that government deficits be used to absorb those excess savings and allow the economy to escape from the depression trap.

Japan obviously did not sink into a depression in the 1970s, despite the fears of some in the cold winter of 1973–74. Since the economy slowed but did not stagnate, and since the ex post data show the existence of surplus savings in the private sector, it follows that either the government deficit or the current account or both must have adjusted to accommodate that surplus. Japan has undergone two phases of accommodation to the surplus private-sector savings that emerged in the 1970s. From 1974 to 1980 fiscal policy rapidly expanded government deficits, while current-account balances were constrained by the two oil shocks. But from 1980 to 1985 government deficits contracted while the current-account surplus expanded sharply. This chapter explores why fiscal policy expanded and then contracted, while chapter 5 considers the movement in the current account. The latest phase, beginning in 1986, is being driven by the external constraint imposed by the strong appreciation of the yen, with the adjustment of government deficit or private-sector savings-investment balance as yet unclear. Chapter 6 delves further into the problems of this phase.

Fiscal Policy Response

How was it that the Japanese government acted quickly to expand government deficits in the 1970s to offset the excess of savings over investment in the private sector? This behavior seems especially puzzling given the adamant refusal to allow any deficit spending at all until 1966. While it would be comforting to believe that the altered policy response resulted from some sophisticated understanding of the economic problems facing the economy, the reality is that this policy was only partly deliberate. Chapter 2 underscored the intention of the Japanese government to provide increased support for social infrastructure and its realization that this action would involve some deficit spending. To that extent the policies were deliberate. But the slowdown in economic growth came just as this new policy direction was getting under way, and the resulting deficits turned out to be much larger than anticipated because of the failure of tax revenues to grow as originally predicted. Therefore, the amount of fiscal stimulus provided was partly accidental.

The policy of expanding government deficits to handle the surplus of private-sector savings came to an end in 1979. Fearful of the purported consequences of large fiscal deficits, the government thereafter focused almost single-mindedly on deficit reduction. The reason for this sustained effort comes from a combination of the emergence of anti-Keynesian theory, bureaucratic struggles, politics within the Liberal Democratic party, and pressure for administrative reform from the corporate sector.

For local government, the picture is somewhat different—with neither as large a rise in deficits nor as strong a contraction after 1979.

The Widening Deficit

Table 3-8 shows the trend in final expenditures and revenues of the central government for fiscal years 1960 to 1984. The central government moved from very small deficits as a ratio to total government expenditures in the second half of the 1960s to somewhat larger ones (11 to 16 percent of total expenditures) until fiscal 1975, followed by a very rapid buildup in deficits to a peak of 35 percent in fiscal 1979. Although the degree of dependence on deficits declined somewhat after that, it has remained close to 30 percent. Expressed as percentages of GNP, the size of the deficits rose from levels of 1 to 2 percent of GNP in the early 1970s to peak at 6.1 percent in 1979, followed by a decline back to 4.3 percent by 1984. These figures are different from the national income figures in table 3-2 because that table includes prefectural and municipal governments. When combined with prefectural and municipal changes, the contraction is much sharper—from 5.5 percent of GNP in 1978 to 0.8 percent in 1985.

Since 1974 was the first postwar recession year and marked the beginning of the era of slower growth, one might expect that fiscal stimulus would have begun then. However, government policy was firmly set against inflation, even at the cost of recession. A change in policy did not really appear until the fiscal 1975 budget, which was drawn up in the summer and fall of 1974 as inflation was subsiding and the stagnation in economic growth was becoming apparent. Since the government maintained the distinction between construction bonds and deficit bonds, the real beginning of the buildup in deficit spending from the Japanese perspective comes in 1975 with the official issuance of deficit bonds.

The rapid rise in deficits was caused by continued increases in government spending and lagging tax revenues. Actual expenditures rose at a nominal annual rate of 17.9 percent from 1961 until 1973 and continued to expand at almost the identical pace from 1974 to 1979, on average by 17.4 percent (see table 3-8). The consistency in the spending increases is remarkable. In real terms, of course, spending in this second period rose less rapidly because of higher average inflation, but the nominal data suffice here for the comparison with revenues. Central government revenue had largely kept pace with spending during the high-growth era, increasing on average by 15.7 percent annually from 1961 to 1973, but from 1974 to

Table 3-8. *General Account of the Central Government,*
Final Settlement Figures, Selected Fiscal Years, 1960–84
Billions of yen unless otherwise specified

Fiscal year	Expenditures	Revenue	Balance	Ratio of deficit to expenditures (percent)	Ratio of deficit to GNP (percent)
1960	1,743	1,961	218	0	...
1965	3,723	3,526	−197	5.3	0.6
1970	8,188	7,841	−347	4.2	0.5
1971	9,561	8,374	−1,187	12.4	1.5
1972	11,932	9,982	−1,950	16.3	2.1
1973	14,778	13,012	−1,766	12.0	1.6
1974	19,100	16,940	−2,160	11.3	1.6
1975	20,861	15,580	−5,281	25.3	3.6
1976	24,468	17,270	−7,198	29.4	4.3
1977	29,060	19,499	−9,561	32.9	5.2
1978	34,096	23,422	−10,674	31.3	5.2
1979	38,790	25,318	−13,472	34.7	6.1
1980	43,405	29,235	−14,170	32.6	5.9
1981	46,921	34,021	−12,900	27.5	5.0
1982	47,245	33,200	−14,045	29.7	5.2
1983	50,635	37,149	−13,486	26.6	4.8
1984	51,481	38,700	−12,781	24.8	4.3

Sources: Ministry of Finance, *Zaisei Tōkei, 1986* (Fiscal Statistics, 1986), (Tokyo: MOF, 1986), pp. 63, 72–75; and Economic Planning Agency, *Annual Report on National Accounts, 1987,* pp. 106–09.

1979 the annual growth in tax revenue slowed sharply to 11.7 percent because of the slower growth of the economy.

Once the data on spending are deflated using the consumer price index for price changes, the picture of what happened to central government expenditures alters. The average annual increase in general account spending dropped from 11.0 percent between 1961 and 1973 to 6.8 percent from 1974 to 1979. The boom years were at the beginning of the 1970s, with the average real increase in spending from 1971 to 1973 running at 13.4 percent, followed by only a small increase in fiscal 1974 and a real drop in fiscal 1975 when the burst of inflation outpaced the rise in government spending.

How did the government allocate this continued rise in spending? Table 3-9 provides a breakdown of the general account budget by category. For understanding what the government intended to do, the budgets (including

Table 3-9. *Growth of Budgeted Government Spending, by Category, Fiscal Years 1970–86*
Percent change from previous fiscal year unless otherwise specified

Category	1970	1971	1972	1973	1974	1975	1976	1977	1978
Social welfare	18.8	17.7	23.5	32.0	40.9	28.8	19.8	18.3	18.8
Social security	19.8	18.9	22.3	35.4	52.3	32.0	21.5	19.8	21.8
Health	16.1	15.3	17.5	9.7	18.7	10.2	7.1	10.0	9.4
Education, science, and culture	17.7	17.2	20.4	21.7	39.3	16.9	13.3	14.3	10.8
Government pensions	12.4	12.0	9.9	28.3	26.5	26.6	30.7	17.6	14.4
Defense	19.2	17.6	18.3	19.2	25.2	11.5	11.4	11.6	10.3
Public works	17.2	33.6	40.2	7.9	4.1	11.8	14.4	31.5	16.4
Roads	17.9	29.3	31.8	4.3	−0.6	0.1	10.5	28.2	20.1
Housing	20.3	34.7	29.7	22.3	29.6	19.4	23.2	22.2	24.9
Sewers	31.3	92.1	66.9	12.4	22.5	16.2	20.7	61.0	27.7
Harbors and other	19.4	35.0	36.1	9.3	2.6	7.1	9.3	27.7	23.1
Foreign aid	−3.2	8.7	18.0	17.8	19.4	5.4	4.0	13.2	35.9
Small business	16.3	30.0	6.2	15.9	30.0	23.1	15.6	31.8	17.9
Energy	. . .	. . .	. . .	. . .	. . .	. . .	. . .	. . .	. . .
Foodstuff control	29.2	4.6	11.1	54.0	22.3	−8.1	−1.6	−8.4	13.3
Other	23.1	20.5	31.1	33.5	23.3	11.5	15.4	16.1	4.3
Revenue sharing	23.7	11.7	21.4	35.0	29.4	−20.2	17.6	22.5	19.0
Debt service	4.3	11.8	41.6	50.9	23.7	29.5	67.2	25.6	39.6
Total	18.5	17.6	25.5	26.0	25.7	8.5	18.3	19.1	17.4

Source: Ministry of Finance, *Zaisei Tōkei, 1986*, pp. 199–211.
a. The total budget for fiscal 1983 includes an extra expenditure to cover the settlement of deficits from fiscal 1981, causing a one-time jump in expenditures followed by a drop in fiscal 1984.
b. Fiscal 1986 data reflect the initial budget and exclude adjustments made later in the year. Growth rates for fiscal 1986 are based on a comparison with the initial fiscal 1985 budget.

any supplementary budget legislation passed later in the year) provide a better picture than the final settlement figures, though the two are close.

If the 1970s brought a shift in government thinking toward a broader concern with social welfare, then this ought to be reflected in these budget data. To some extent it is. Contributions from the general account budget to the special account for social security tended to set the pace among domestic programs.[19] For the whole decade of the 1970s the annual in-

19. There are two main parts to the social security system in Japan: the *kokumin nenkin* (national pension fund) and the *kōsei nenkin hoken* (welfare annuity insurance). Both work with trust funds that are separate from the government's general account budget. However, the laws stipulate that the government make a contribution to those funds from its budget each year. Roughly half the annual receipts of the kokumin nenkin come from the govern-

1979	1980	1981	1982	1983[a]	1984	1985	1986[b]	1986 expenditures[b] (¥ billions)
12.6	8.1	7.3	3.1	1.0	4.9	1.5	2.7	9,835
13.6	8.7	8.5	1.6	−4.9	−4.5	4.1	5.4	5,964
8.3	4.9	2.0	1.9	2.1	11.7	4.5	7.4	496
11.7	6.4	4.8	0.2	0	2.5	−1.0	0.1	4,845
12.9	9.3	9.9	4.9	−0.1	−0.2	−1.2	−0.8	1,850
11.7	8.3	7.1	5.7	7.6	7.3	7.0	6.6	3,344
14.7	2.2	2.9	4.0	−0.8	−4.7	0.6	−2.3	6,923
10.7	−1.8	−0.9	−0.5	0.1	−0.4	−2.3	−2.1	1,788
21.0	12.2	5.1	4.2	1.8	2.2	1.5	−0.1	757
18.7	1.6	2.0	0.1	0.1	−0.8	1.0	−0.6	964
19.0	0.4	−0.9	−0.2	0.2	−0.8	−1.5	−1.2	506
20.7	13.0	11.3	11.8	4.8	8.6	7.4	6.3	623
0.4	5.2	2.1	−1.6	−2.0	−3.8	−7.8	−5.1	205
17.5	32.0	16.7	12.7	−0.4	9.5	2.6	0.2	630
4.9	−2.6	6.1	−0.8	−8.8	11.8	−14.1	−14.2	596
9.5	5.9	1.0	−0.6	−1.5	−1.1	0.3	−5.6	4,084
16.0	17.5	11.4	−8.6	−3.8	20.1	5.1	5.1	10,185
35.4	25.5	21.2	3.8	18.3	13.0	10.3	10.7	11,320
15.2	10.1	7.9	0.9	6.9	1.3	3.3	3.0	54,089

crease in these social security contributions averaged 25.7 percent, compared with an average increase of 19.2 percent for the entire general account budget. Expenditures on education and science rose at a somewhat more modest 18.3 percent rate. Defense rose at only 15.6 percent and foreign aid at an even lower 14.0 percent (pulled up somewhat by the expansion of foreign aid that began in fiscal 1978). However, small business, a category more closely related to conventional economic goals, rose at 18.7 percent, casting some doubt on a major structural shift in govern-

ment, as do about 10 percent of kōsei nenkin hoken receipts. Therefore, the figures for the general account budget do not represent the programs in their entirety but just these annual defined contributions.

ment spending goals. The biggest growth came in debt-servicing costs, which registered a 33.0 percent average annual growth during the 1970s, rising from a minor amount to the largest single line item in the budget.

What do these numbers imply about fiscal policy? There was a moderate shift toward greater concern with broadly defined social welfare—spending for social security, housing, and sewers rose at above-average rates. But inflation meant that even social spending was growing more slowly in real terms than it had in the 1960s. The most striking feature, in fact, is that *all* categories of expenditures continued to rise relatively rapidly in nominal terms, while taxes were allowed to lag behind. Thus Japan did not get itself into large deficits because of a major burst of new spending so much as from a lack of revenue to support its relatively modest real increases in spending.

That the shift toward social spending was unremarkable is borne out by international comparison. According to data published by the Organization for Economic Cooperation and Development, Japan's ranking among OECD members on the ratio of government spending to GDP has slipped over time. Among the twenty-two nations with data available, Japan's rank dropped from nineteenth in 1960 to twentieth in 1982.[20] All OECD member countries experienced a rising share of government spending in GDP, but Japan's record turned out to be less dramatic than most others.

The same study indicates that in recent years, for the eleven largest OECD members, Japan was below the sample mean for spending as a share of GDP on defense, education, health, social security, and general administration. It was above the mean only on a category labeled "economic services." In fact, for defense, education, and social security, Japan was the farthest below the sample mean. It would be tempting to dismiss the political rhetoric about improved social welfare in Japan on the basis of these data, but the actual picture is more complex. The growth of social security spending for 1970–81, for example, was much higher than the mean for the fifteen largest OECD countries, and if the causes of change in spending are decomposed into demographics (the aging population), the percentage of the population included in the system, and the generosity of the benefits, Japan stands out on the last two items. It lagged behind these other countries in the growth of social security spending in the 1960s, but

20. Organization for Economic Cooperation and Development, *OECD Economic Studies: The Role of the Public Sector, Causes and Consequences of the Growth of Government* (Paris: OECD, 1985), p. 29.

the spread of coverage and the generosity of benefits increased at a much more rapid pace than in other countries during the 1970s.[21]

These comparisons leave a mixed picture. Clearly there was some increase in social welfare spending, and the increase in spending on some items (such as social security) was more dramatic than it was in other countries. However, the net result of these changes was an overall level of government spending that remained lower than for other countries and a structure that could hardly be labeled a welfare state.

The other half of the explanation of increased government deficits is lagging revenues. Why did tax revenues lag behind spending? During the high-growth era, government forecasts consistently underestimated the actual rate of GNP growth, and annual tax revenue estimates based on those forecasts tended to be too low. Underestimating revenue helped keep the budget in balance, since tax revenues were highly elastic with respect to economic growth. But once the growth of the economy slowed, the situation was reversed: official forecasts tended to overestimate GNP growth, leading to overly optimistic expectations about tax revenues. By 1977 a government report warned that Japan would not return to the levels of economic growth necessary to make tax revenues rise fast enough to match spending increases.[22]

Exacerbating the slower growth in tax revenues, the Japanese public had become accustomed to annual reductions in income taxes to offset the bracket creep that resulted from rapid economic growth, and politicians had become accustomed to using this annual event to boost their public support. These cuts petered out after 1977, with no significant alteration in personal income taxes until 1984. Had the cuts in 1974, 1975, and 1977 not taken place, tax revenues would have risen faster. But through a combination of lagging official perceptions of the situation, public expectations of annual cuts, and possibly some willingness on the part of the Ministry of Finance in response to domestic and international pressure to allow taxes to fall behind spending, the tax cuts simply were not ended earlier.

External pressure concerning Japan's macroeconomic policy in 1977 and 1978 further complicated fiscal policy. As economic growth in the industrial countries appeared to falter in 1976 and 1977, the "locomotive

21. Ibid., pp. 47, 104. These figures are based on an average of the latest available five years of data, which for Japan is 1978–82.

22. Zeisei Chōsakai (Tax System Council), *Kongo no Zeisei no Arikata ni Tsuite no Tōshin, 1977* (Report on Future Tax Policy, 1977) (Tokyo: MOF, 1977), p. 4.

theory" came into existence, postulating that world economic growth
could be raised if only the United States, West Germany, and Japan could
coordinate their macroeconomic policies and simultaneously stimulate
their economies. These three countries would then act as the locomotive to
pull along the rest of the world. Based on this thinking, the United States
set about to obtain that cooperation from West Germany and Japan.

In the fall of 1977 the United States and Japan held a series of bilateral
negotiations that resulted in Japan's "promise" in the Strauss-Ushiba
agreement of January 1978 to pursue policies that would lead to a 7
percent real GNP growth rate in fiscal 1978.[23] The international pressure
meshed with domestic voices for additional economic stimulus (principally those of Toshio Komoto and Kiichi Miyazawa, who were both given
important economic posts when Prime Minister Takeo Fukuda rearranged
his cabinet in November 1977). Whatever opposition the Ministry of
Finance may have raised was quelled by this combination of domestic and
international pressure. Therefore, spending was deliberately allowed to
outdistance revenues by a wider margin. When the dust settled, the nominal increase in spending for the fiscal year was 17.3 percent, very close to
the long-term average. But since inflation had been low—wholesale prices
actually dropped and consumer prices rose less than 4 percent—the real
increase was high. Taxes in fiscal 1978 rose by an even larger nominal
26.5 percent, but because of their smaller base, the size of the deficit
increased.[24]

Local Government Policy

To this picture of rising central government deficits should be added
some comment on expenditures of prefectural and local governments,
which together are larger than central government spending. Net total
government spending at all levels showed government deficits rising as a
share of GNP (tables 3-1 and 3-2), but the trends in central government
spending discussed in the preceding section need not have necessarily

---

23. I. M. Destler, "U.S.-Japanese Relations and the American Trade Initiative of 1977:
Was This Trip Necessary?" in William J. Barnds, ed., *Japan and the United States:
Challenges and Opportunities* (New York University Press, 1979), pp. 203–15, discusses
this series of negotiations. The initial U.S. request was for a promise of 8 percent growth.

24. Ministry of Finance, *Zaisei Tōkei, 1986* (Fiscal Statistics, 1986) (Tokyo: MOF,
1986), pp. 62–63, 229–30; and "Main Economic Indicators of Japan," MOF *Monthly
Finance Review* (August 1986).

characterized local trends. Compared with the situation in the United States, however, local fiscal policies are more dependent on the central government because a large share of local revenues comes from revenue sharing and other grants. In fiscal 1984, for example, 38 percent of total prefectural and municipal revenue came from the central government.[25]

Table 3-10 shows that from 1961 to 1973 nominal local government expenditures grew at an average annual rate of 18.5 percent, slightly higher than that for the central government. This growth dropped a bit to 17.0 percent from 1974 to 1978, whereas central government spending growth did not. Nevertheless, spending growth does roughly parallel that of the central government.

The picture of local government deficits does, however, provide some contrast. The percentage of local government expenditures that were deficit-financed expanded from a level of 5 to 7 percent of total spending in the 1960s to roughly 10 percent in the years 1971 to 1974. Afterward, deficits expanded modestly again, reaching a peak of 13.2 percent of expenditures in fiscal 1978. This rise stands in clear contrast to the rapid buildup of central government deficits. The large deficits of the 1970s remain the responsibility of the central government.

Economic Dangers of the Deficits?

By the end of 1978, the Ministry of Finance had become increasingly concerned about the rising deficits and was poised to reassert its voice against those who favored continued expansionary policies. An MOF document issued in 1979 identified four problems with deficit spending.[26]

First, the ministry was concerned that debt service and redemption

---

25. Ministry of Finance, *Zaisei Tōkei, 1986,* p. 321. Revenue sharing and other grants are 38 percent of the total, local taxes 37 percent, borrowing 9 percent, and miscellaneous income (fees for services and so forth) 16 percent. Steven R. Reed, *Japanese Prefectures and Policymaking* (University of Pittsburgh Press, 1986), finds a complex interaction between the central government and the prefectures in which extensive central-local bargaining implies that the central government by no means dominates decisions on specific local government policies. However, he does agree that financial autonomy is limited. The central government sets uniform nationwide tax rates for local taxes, approves all borrowing by local governments, and provides a variety of grants for specific services. The Ministry of Home Affairs is responsible for overseeing local governments, but no decision about finances can be made by the MOHA (or any other ministry) without consultations and approval from the Ministry of Finance. While this system is much more centralized than is the case in the United States, it is not very different from what prevails in Europe.

26. Noguchi, *Zaisei Kiki no Kōzō,* pp. 18–20.

Table 3-10. *Local Government Spending and Deficits,*
Selected Fiscal Years, 1960–84
Billions of yen unless otherwise specified

Year	Total expenditures[a]	Deficit	Ratio of deficit to expenditures (percent)	Ratio of deficit to GNP (percent)
1960	1,925	96	5.0	0.6
1965	4,365	321	7.4	1.0
1970	9,815	684	7.0	0.9
1971	11,910	1,175	9.9	1.5
1972	14,618	1,698	11.6	1.8
1973	17,474	1,713	9.8	1.5
1974	22,888	2,012	8.8	1.5
1975	25,654	3,260	12.7	2.2
1976	28,907	3,744	13.0	2.2
1977	33,362	4,372	13.1	2.4
1978	38,347	5,070	13.2	2.5
1979	42,078	5,193	12.3	2.3
1980	45,781	4,838	10.6	2.0
1981	49,165	5,020	10.2	2.0
1982	51,133	5,029	9.8	1.9
1983	52,307	5,338	10.2	1.9
1984	53,870	5,118	9.5	1.7

Source: Bank of Japan, *Economic Statistics Annual, 1986,* pp. 238–39.
a. Net figures, eliminating double counting of transfer payments among different levels of local government.

expenditures would eliminate the ability to use fiscal policy in a flexible and timely manner because debt-related costs are nondiscretionary items in the budget. In 1979 debt service costs were 11 percent of total general account expenditures, rising to 19 percent by fiscal 1985. One reason the growth was so rapid was that the effort to reduce deficits after 1979 relied more heavily on holding down discretionary spending than on raising taxes, so that the rising debt service costs took place in an environment of overall budget austerity, which helped push up their share in total spending. Had that share risen to sharply higher levels, the Ministry of Finance's concern would certainly have been legitimate, but no one was suggesting deficits (and thereby debt service costs) should increase completely unconstrained. The rise in the late 1970s and 1980s was largely a product of the shift from very low deficits to a higher plateau. Some Japanese critics of government policy disagreed with the ministry's fear that deficits were out of control and impinging on future fiscal policy. They argued that efforts to reduce deficits would result in cutting expenditures in areas important for government's role in society.[27]

Second, the Ministry of Finance argued that the borrowing demands caused by large deficits would crowd private corporations out of capital markets and thereby hurt economic growth. The competition between government and corporations for capital, it maintained, would drive up interest rates and result in inflation. But those concerns were very unlikely to materialize. Even the high levels of government deficits in the late 1970s and 1980s failed to absorb the surplus savings generated by the private sector. Far from crowding out private investment, the excess of savings put downward pressure on interest rates, and savings were invested abroad in increasing amounts in the absence of sufficient demand for them at home.

Third, there was concern that the deficit and debt service costs would push the debt burden onto future generations. This is an old argument against deficit spending that ignores the benefit for future generations from the larger economic base that would presumably be created for them by the increased economic activity generated through use of those deficits, especially if the deficits were created through increased government investment in social infrastructure.

Finally, the ministry argued that allowing deficit spending would remove the constraint on spending naturally imposed by the availability of tax revenues. One can sympathize to some extent with this view, but the existence of deficit spending does not imply by any means that all increases in spending would be accepted. The ministry was not about to lose its budgeting function, since within the confines of revenues plus planned borrowings there remained the same need to make choices among the many programs on which government ministries could spend money. In arguments against those ministries the backup constraint on available tax revenues might be a handy club to wield but one that was not entirely necessary.

A more sophisticated argument sometimes made in Japan is that if an expenditure is worthwhile, people ought to be willing to pay the taxes to support it. Deficit spending implies that the government is spending money on activities for which people are not willing to pay. Therefore, deficits are unfair in a democratic society and should not be allowed.[28]

27. Ibid., pp. 18–35, 110–56.
28. Based on interviews in Japan, April 1985.

While this very conservative interpretation of the evil of deficits does not appear widespread, vague notions along these lines may well have contributed to the popularity or acceptance of the efforts since 1979 to reduce deficit spending.

Another report from the Zeisei Chōsakai (the Tax System Council, an advisory body attached to the Ministry of Finance) in 1983 added two more reasons to fear deficits. One was that the rapid rise of debt service costs in the budget imperiled spending on essential government social services. This problem was true only because of the strong attempt to reduce the size of the deficit, and to do so through cutbacks in discretionary spending rather than increases in taxes. The report also argued that the increased issuance of government bonds would lead to an undesirable redistribution of income, widening the gap between rich and poor. Considering that a large proportion of these bonds were held by banks in which small savers kept their money, this accusation appears particularly weak.[29] The council presented these fears, and reiterated the four problems covered above, not as hypotheses but as a litany of accepted facts that necessitated action.[30]

One final concern unvoiced in these reports but evident in the shift of attitudes toward monetarism among officials was that budget deficits can cause inflation. If the debt is monetized by the Bank of Japan (purchasing bonds from the private sector), the money supply increases and could bring higher inflation. However, this was unlikely to happen. With its strong beliefs about the need to control inflation, beliefs reinforced by the problems of 1973–74, the Bank of Japan was not likely to monetize government debt so rapidly as to cause a significant rise in inflation.

Before moving on to discuss the resurgence of fiscal austerity, a brief comparison of Japan and the United States is in order. During the 1970s U.S. deficits ranged from 1.4 percent to 19.8 percent of total federal expenditures, followed by a steady expansion during the Reagan administration to a peak of 25.7 percent in fiscal 1983. Interest payments on outstanding debt as a share of total spending remained 8 to 12 percent through most of the 1960s and 1970s, rising to 18.9 percent in fiscal

29. In 1984, 42 percent of all central government bonds outstanding (excluding those held by the Bank of Japan or other government agencies) were held by financial institutions. Bank of Japan, *Economic Statistics Annual, 1985* (Tokyo: BOJ, 1985), p. 201.

30. Zeisei Chōsakai, *Kongo no Zeisei no Arikata ni Tsuite no Tōshin, 1983* (Report on Future Tax Policy, 1983) (Tokyo: MOF, 1983), p. 3.

1985.[31] Thus the combination of U.S. fiscal expansion and Japanese austerity in the 1980s moved the two countries closer together. Debt service costs as a share of total expenditures were essentially the same in the two by the mid-1980s. U.S. deficits generated a tremendous amount of legitimate concern about their negative economic effects, so that the emergence of an antideficit mood in Japan is perhaps not surprising. But Japan was awash in surplus savings while the United States was not; the very legitimate concerns about government deficits in the United States simply cannot be applied directly to Japan.

The Ministry of Finance Resurgence: Tax Policy

Never entirely happy with the direction fiscal policy had taken since 1973, the Ministry of Finance began seriously to reassert its preference for a balanced budget in 1979. Since then it has consistently fought to reduce deficits through a combination of tax increases and spending cuts. The emphasis has shifted back and forth between the two depending on the path of least resistance. Technically, the goal of austerity was stated in terms of eliminating deficit bond issues, but not construction bonds, which accounted for roughly half of deficit financing. The ministry's desire to reduce the budget deficits has had considerable private-sector support, but there has been opposition as well, and that opposition has tempered the ministry's ability to have its way in designing policies. Nevertheless, the MOF's resurgence led to the second phase of adjusting to surplus savings, in which the government deficit fell and the current-account surplus rose.

The initial effort to reduce deficits focused on increasing tax revenues. Goals included such bold changes as the introduction of a value-added tax, but in the end the ministry had to settle for eliminating the annual income tax cuts and for various small changes or increases in existing taxes.

In 1977 the Tax System Council completed a final report in response to a request by the MOF in late 1974 to study the future direction of the tax system. The report discussed the emergence of a fundamental structural gap between government spending and revenues and laid out three choices for solving the problem: increase personal income taxes, increase corporate income taxes, or introduce a new general consumption tax. The first

---

31. Bureau of the Census, *Statistical Abstract of the United States, 1987*, pp. 292, 298; *1970*, p. 392. Data in these two sources are similar but not completely consistent.

two were considered out of the question. Neither individuals nor corporations wanted tax rates to increase. Therefore, the primary conclusion of the report was that Japan should adopt a general consumption or value-added tax.[32]

Once the commission had made the general argument in support of the tax, the Ministry of Finance proceeded with a more concrete proposal calling for a uniform 5 percent tax on value added for all firms whose sales volume exceeded ¥20 million, which would have produced an estimated ¥3 trillion in tax revenue in fiscal 1980 (covering about 21 percent of the deficit that occurred in the year). Prime Minister Masayoshi Ohira, who had replaced Takeo Fukuda, supported the new indirect tax. However, the proposal sparked a great deal of opposition, especially from the wholesale and retail trade industry. Many small family businesses existed partly because of the opportunities to evade income taxes, and a sales tax would have removed the tax advantages. These small businessmen tend to be strong supporters of the Liberal Democratic party.[33]

Opposition was so vigorous that in the election campaign for the lower house of the Diet in October 1979, the LDP was forced to state that it would not introduce such a tax. But opposition parties accused the Liberal Democrats of a hidden plan to introduce the tax legislation after the election. Partly as a result of this fear, Liberal Democratic strength in the lower house dropped by one seat, shattering predictions that it would regain a comfortable majority. At 248 seats the party was below a majority, but managed to continue in power because a number of independents joined its ranks after the election. Whether the tax proposal was really responsible for the poor showing of the LDP is less important than the fact that people believed it was responsible. The subject of a broad new indirect tax became taboo for a number of years.

Stung by the defeat on indirect taxes and the general opposition to tax increases, the Ministry of Finance adopted a less sweeping approach to raising revenues. Not until after 1985, when overall tax reform became an issue, did the indirect tax resurface. But when it did, the new proposal was virtually identical to the one considered in 1979.

As a first step the ministry's emphasis on tax reform focused on what became known as the green card system. In Japan individuals were al-

---

32. Zeisei Chōsakai, *Kongo no Zeisei no Arikata ni Tsuite no Tōshin, 1977*, pp. 7–26.
33. Edward J. Lincoln, "Whither the General Excise Tax?" *Trade Roundup*, no. 24 (August 1979), pp. 6–7.

lowed to keep up to ¥3 million ($18,750 at 160 yen to the dollar) in certain forms of savings accounts without paying taxes on the interest income. Sums up to this amount were allowed in a commercial bank savings account, a postal savings account, and in government bonds (for a total of ¥9 million). Commercial banks had to file information on all qualified accounts with tax authorities so that an individual's accounts in different banks could be totaled to determine if he surpassed the ¥3 million limit. But the postal savings system did not have to file a report unless an account actually exceeded the limit. This situation provided easy opportunities for cheating by enabling depositors to open multiple accounts in the names of various family members or totally fictitious persons. The Japan Bankers' Association implicitly noted the cheating when it complained that postal savings deposits rose at the expense of commercial bank deposits after withholding rates on deposits in excess of the limit were raised in 1981.[34] The number of depositors in postal savings is widely reported to exceed the population of Japan.

The Ministry of Finance decided that this problem of blatant cheating and the problem of how to raise tax revenues without having to raise tax rates could be resolved simply by enforcing existing law. It proposed a system whereby all savers would be issued a green identity card with a unique identity number that must be produced whenever opening a new, tax-qualified savings account. The tax authorities could thus easily check the total deposits for any household unit in the postal savings system.

The proposal was drawn up in 1979 (as the indirect tax was going down to defeat), and the necessary legislation was included as part of the tax reform law passed in March 1980—a hastiness that meant politicians had acted without adequately consulting or winning over potential opponents to the concept. The use of the green card as the device to check on accounts was actually settled after the law was passed, through negotiations between the Ministry of Finance and the Ministry of Posts and Telecommunications (which administers the postal savings system). The new system was not to go into effect until January 1, 1984, but opposition sprang forth as soon as the law was passed and the method of enforcing it was settled. After two years of strong criticism, implementation of the law was postponed in 1983 by three years (to January 1, 1987), and the system was completely eliminated in the tax reform law passed in 1985. Although

34. Yoshio Nakamura, "Japan's Postal Savings System," *JEI Report,* no. 2 (January 1982), pp. 1–5.

it lingered through this protracted operatic death, the idea had essentially been dropped by 1982.

Why did this effort meet with such opposition? Essentially every party concerned could find objections. The commercial banks had heartily endorsed the proposal because they felt that they were losing deposits to the postal savings system. But they became convinced that the resulting law had too many loopholes. Cheating would continue within the postal savings system while the commercial banks would face greater government scrutiny. They therefore withdrew their support.

The postal savings system had very strong objections because it was under attack. Even though the Ministry of Finance has general supervisory authority over financial institutions in Japan, it has no official control whatsoever over postal savings (despite the fact that most of those deposits are turned over to the MOF for investment in public policy projects), and the Ministry of Posts and Telecommunications jealously guards its independence. The MPT may have been forced into accepting the green card format once the legislation was passed, but it remained firmly opposed. In addition, most post offices are run as small businesses under franchise from the MPT, and the proposed changes would have hurt them.

Through their representatives in the Diet, voters expressed fear that the new system represented an unfair, unwarranted intrusion into their personal lives. This criticism was not entirely hypocritical, since older Japanese still harbored a great deal of repugnance for the heavy hand of the state that they remembered from the 1930s and 1940s. But their main concern was obviously that they would have to pay more taxes. Unincorporated small businesses also objected because better information on the size of their deposits could lead tax authorities to challenge their income tax returns (lax accounting rules for small businesses in Japan are believed to result in large-scale income tax evasion).

The strength of this concern was evidenced by large transfers of funds out of postal savings accounts into other tax-free assets, such as foreign zero-coupon bonds advertised by securities firms. These discount bonds accrue interest in the form of appreciation of the value of the bond itself. In the United States the Internal Revenue Service has rules for calculating the implicit interest income and separating it from capital gains if the bonds are resold before maturity. Tax authorities in Japan, however, had no such rules, and capital gains on long-term financial assets held by individuals are not taxed at all. The flow of funds into these bonds quickly became so large that the Ministry of Finance had to ban their sale in March

1982. The ministry estimated that as much as $1.5 billion had gone into these instruments in January and February 1982 alone.[35]

What started out as a seemingly simple and fair argument for enforcing the existing tax law had quickly become a major problem. The Ministry of Finance faced serious opposition to what was perceived as an increase in taxes that would also affect the competitive balance within the financial sector. The history of this fiasco demonstrates that the Japanese bureaucracy is sometimes far from in control of policy outcomes, contrary to the customary perception by Americans.[36]

Despite the collapse of the green card proposal, the Ministry of Finance did not give up its efforts to enforce the limits on savings accounts. In the tax reform law of 1985 it included a watered-down version of the concept, but the changes were weak enough that most observers believed they would not make much difference. This modest change in the tax-free savings system was actually part of a broader discussion of the merits of the system as a whole. In the fall of 1984 the ministry proposed two alternatives: a low tax rate on all savings income or stronger enforcement of the existing tax-free limit. It favored the former, which obviously left open the possibility of raising tax rates to higher levels in the future, and the Liberal Democrats favored the latter. After much haggling in the advisory commissions and party and Diet committees, provisions for stronger enforcement were incorporated in the tax reform law of 1985. Not until the tax reform of 1987 did the MOF finally succeed in imposing a tax on all interest income.

With both the indirect tax and the green card system falling by the wayside, the Ministry of Finance resorted to various small measures to increase tax revenues. The first was to stop annual personal income tax cuts. A small reduction had been passed in 1977, but no further ones of any consequence were enacted until 1983. A second approach was to increase corporate income taxes through a variety of minor adjustments so that the official façade of promoting fiscal reconstruction without tax increases could be maintained. Even this action prompted strong opposition from business organizations such as Keidanren. The manner in which

35. Edward J. Lincoln, "Zero-Coupon Bond Brouhaha," *JEI Report,* no. 11B (March 1982), p. 7.

36. James Horne, *Japan's Financial Markets: Conflict and Consensus in Policymaking* (George Allen & Unwin, 1985), esp. pp. 118–41, considers intra- and interministerial conflicts in depth. Although he does not focus on the green card system, he discusses the broader problem of setting interest rates on postal savings accounts.

this policy has been carried out is well illustrated by the fiscal 1985 tax reform law, which made five small changes in the rules for taxing corporations:

—The allowable size of tax-free reserves for bad debts was reduced. This was expected to yield ¥200 billion in additional revenues ($838 million at average 1985 exchange rates).

—The tax rate levied on certain cooperatives and public interest corporations that pay reduced taxes was increased by 2 percentage points to provide an estimated ¥32 billion ($134 million) in additional revenues.

—A measure allowing some delay in the refund of excess tax payments was changed (covered in greater detail below). This was expected to yield ¥84 billion ($352 million).

—Special depreciation allowances on investment in machinery by small and medium-sized businesses were abolished. This was to yield ¥17 billion ($71 million).

—Some other special depreciation allowances were reduced in scope. The expected tax yield was ¥10 billion ($41 million).[37]

These increases were partially offset by a variety of small tax cuts that were expected to reduce revenues by ¥27 billion ($113 million). The net gain in corporate tax revenues was anticipated to be ¥316 billion ($1.3 billion), equal to 2.8 percent of actual corporate tax revenues in the previous fiscal year.[38]

The measure allowing delays in refunds of excess tax payments deserves special mention because it demonstrates how far the Ministry of Finance has been willing to go in its zeal to increase revenues. The ministry proposed a plan in November 1984 to tax corporations that failed to show a profit. The official philosophy behind the proposal was that even if they do not earn a profit, corporations are the beneficiaries of government services and should therefore pay taxes. A more realistic interpretation is that the plan was a way to deal with tax evasion by small businesses without directly facing the confrontational issue of evasion and enforcement. The ministry even pushed to the point of suggesting two ways in which the system could be organized: a tax could either be levied on corporate assets or it could be based on total personnel costs. When the

37. Data provided by the Embassy of Japan, Washington, D.C., January 1985.
38. Based on preliminary figures for fiscal 1984 tax revenue in Ministry of Finance, *Zaisei Tōkei, 1986*, p. 311.

proposal was submitted to the ministry's own advisory commission on taxes and the LDP tax committee, it was quickly scuttled.[39]

The ministry then suggested that at least it be permitted to limit the reimbursement of excess tax payments made by corporations, a proposal that was accepted. Under the tax revisions of fiscal 1985, corporations are subject to a 20 percent withholding tax on dividends and interest received, which they normally get back if they end the year with no tax liabilities. With the change, the ministry can hold the money until such corporations have tax liabilities against which to credit the payments. If any corporation fails to owe taxes for four consecutive years, the withholding will be refunded.[40] In the fiscal 1986 tax revision, a further change eliminated a provision whereby corporations could carry forward their losses and apply them against profits over a succeeding five-year period. These changes were typical of the entire effort to increase taxes during the first half of the 1980s: broad new concepts like the consumption tax or the tax on unprofitable corporations failed, and the Ministry of Finance was reduced to minor tinkering with the existing tax structure.

Besides personal and corporate income taxes, various excise taxes were also increased. In fiscal 1981, taxes on liquor, official stamps, and some other commodities (including automobiles) were raised to bring in an estimated additional ¥904 billion ($4.1 billion). In 1984 the MOF proposed a tax on various types of office equipment, but the proposal failed because of vigorous opposition from the Ministry of International Trade and Industry and the industries involved. In the fiscal 1986 tax revision, excise taxes on cigarettes were raised by 80 percent (from ¥1.13 to ¥2.03 a cigarette).[41]

---

39. "Akaji Kigyo ni mo Hōjin Kazei" (Corporate Taxes Even for Deficit Corporations), *Nihon Keizai Shimbun*, November 26, 1984; and "Akaji Hōjin Kazei Miokuri" (So Long to Taxation of Deficit Corporations), *Nihon Keizai Shimbun*, December 8, 1984. Such a tax would be similar in concept to the value-added tax proposed in 1979 and 1987, though it would differ in calculation and incidence among corporations.

40. Data provided by the Embassy of Japan, Washington, D.C.; interviews in Tokyo; and "Step Toward Taxation on Firms in the Red," *Japan Economic Journal*, December 25, 1984.

41. Data provided by the Embassy of Japan, Washington, D.C., attaché from the Ministry of Finance, December 1985, and by the Institute of Fiscal and Monetary Policy, MOF, February 1987; "OA Kazei Miokuri" (Farewell to the Office Automation Tax), *Nihon Keizai Shimbun*, December 15, 1984; and Yuji Gomi, *Guide to Japanese Taxes, 1981–82* (Tokyo: Zaikei Shōhōsha, 1983), p. i.

The changes in these taxes were believed by some to have led to distortions in consumer behavior: for instance, the changes increased the price of scotch-type whiskey compared with the price of a sweet-potato-based hard liquor called *shōchū*. The resulting shōchū boom reached such proportions that the mass psychology of fads would seem to be a better explanation than relative cost, but it provided an argument for those who wanted to move once again in the direction of a broad-based consumption tax.

Where did all this tinkering leave the discussion of taxes? By 1984 it was becoming evident that efforts to hold down spending could not be pushed much further. This growing belief led to renewed interest in a general overhaul of the tax system, including the introduction of new forms of taxation, since the effective increase in individual and corporate income taxes resulting from the years of minor tinkering had left individuals and corporations disgruntled. The Tax Council produced another long-term consideration of tax structure in November 1983 that reached conclusions similar to those of 1977. Citing the need for a better balance between direct and indirect taxes, the low level of indirect taxes in Japan relative to other countries, and difficulties in raising direct taxes, it called for renewed study of a broad indirect tax.[42] Japan's tax structure was indeed different from most other industrial countries. According to comparative OECD data, the ratio of indirect taxes to GDP was only 7.7 percent in Japan, compared with an average of 13.6 percent for all OECD member countries. In fact, only Spain (7.1 percent) and the United States (8.5 percent) joined Japan in being below the 10 percent level.[43] Foreign experience is often used to justify or motivate policy changes in Japan and was frequently cited in the discussion of taxes.

Japan had not always had such a high proportion of direct taxes. At the beginning of the 1960s they constituted 50 percent of tax revenues; but by the 1980s they represented more than 70 percent.[44] Concern about the high share of direct taxes in total government tax revenues became widespread by 1985 under the catchphrase *chokkan no zesei* (correction of direct-indirect). Typically, a former Ministry of Finance official published a book late in 1984 on the general theory of taxation and its function in

42. Zeisei Chōsakai, *Kongo no Zeisei no Arikata ni Tsuite no Tōshin, 1983*, pp. 6–10.

43. OECD, *Role of the Public Sector*, p. 69.

44. Ministry of Finance, *Zaisei Tōkei, 1984*, p. 311. The share of direct taxes actually peaked at 73.9 percent in 1974 and then receded a bit, but it was moving beyond the 70 percent level again in the 1980s.

democratic society that concluded the time had come to address the unfairness of the income tax system and to correct the chokkan imbalance.[45] However, economic theory provides no justification at all for the conclusion that the share of direct taxes was too high in Japan.

The other current in tax discussions by 1985 was a growing belief that the existing income tax structure was unfair. The top marginal tax rate was 70 percent (and higher when local taxes were included). Concern over high marginal tax rates was exacerbated by a strong belief that only individuals whose incomes were from wages and salaries paid these rates; farmers and owners of small, unincorporated businesses were assumed to cheat heavily. This belief is captured in the phrase *ku-ro-yon* (9-6-4), implying that wage earners pay tax on 90 percent of their income (the rest taking the form of tax-free interest and other nontaxable sources), while small businesses pay taxes on 60 percent and farmers only 40 percent.[46] The Ministry of Finance wanted to tie wage earners' opposition to tax evasion by other groups into its desire to introduce an indirect tax, since it believed that imposing a sales tax or value-added tax would be a way around the assumed widespread noncompliance with the income tax by small businesses. Not only would an indirect tax raise tax revenues from these companies, but it might also force them into stricter bookkeeping, reducing their ability to cheat on income taxes as well.

With the expressions of concern over unfairness and the renewed discussion of an indirect tax, both the Liberal Democratic tax committee and the Ministry of Finance's advisory Tax Council were charged early in 1985 with a broad reconsideration of tax policy. When the groups issued their reports near the end of 1986, they recommended similar measures, addressing the major concerns of recent years: reduction of marginal individual and corporate income tax rates, implementation of a broad indirect

45. Yukihiro Fukuda, *Zei to Demokurashii* (Tax and Democracy) (Tokyo: Tōyō Keizai Shimpōsha, 1984).

46. Another version of this concept goes by the slogan *to-go-san-pin* (10-5-3-1): wage earners reporting 100 percent of income, small business 50 percent, farmers 30 percent, and politicians 1 percent. There has been some research on this question, although disagreements exist as to the degree of tax evasion. Hiromitsu Ishi originally put the ratio of reported taxable income to true income among workers, small businesses, and farmers at 90–100 percent, 60–70 percent, and 20–30 percent, respectively. Homma, Atoda, Ihori, and Murayama find less evasion, putting the ratios at 100 percent, 70 percent, and 50 percent. Since the essence of evasion is secrecy, no one can measure this problem with any accuracy, but all observers believe evasion exists and that agriculture is an even bigger offender than small business. See discussion in M. Homma, T. Maeda, and K. Hashimoto, "The Japanese Tax System," Brookings Discussion Papers in Economics (June 1986), pp. 25–26.

tax, and elimination of tax-free savings for individuals (substituting a flat 20 percent tax on all interest income).

Legislation based on these proposals was introduced in 1987 but faced intense opposition on the floor of the Diet and was ultimately defeated, despite the efforts of the Ministry of Finance to compromise by tying the indirect tax to reductions of marginal income tax rates so that the overall package would be officially revenue neutral (a blow to goals of increasing taxes to reduce government deficits). The MOF also compromised by increasing the minimum firm size for inclusion in the new indirect tax from ¥20 million in sales ($125,000 at 160 yen to the dollar) to ¥100 million ($625,000), so that more small businesses would be excluded from the new tax.[47]

These compromises, plus the ten years that had elapsed since the indirect tax had first been proposed and the psychological boost from recent tax reforms in the United States, ought to have made it easier for the ministry to maneuver its reform proposal through the political process. However, once the legislation reached the Diet, opposition surged, and Prime Minister Yasuhiro Nakasone, who had hoped that tax reform would become a final major success for his administration, was forced to withdraw the bills at the end of April 1987. No one objected to the lower marginal income tax rates, but once again the value-added tax proved as unpopular as in 1979.

Why did this effort fail? One key political mistake was Nakasone's repeated and firm promises in 1985 and 1986 that the tax reform proposals would include no major new indirect tax. Politicians, including his colleagues in the LDP as well as groups of key supporters for the party, felt betrayed. Another fatal problem was a widespread conviction that once a value-added tax was implemented, the Ministry of Finance would begin raising the tax rate, so that it would become a vehicle for increasing total revenues. Given the confirmed dedication of the MOF to raising tax revenues, that conviction was probably correct.

Tax reform was not entirely dead after the withdrawal of the legislation, but its potential as a vehicle for raising overall tax revenues was gone. Over the summer a revised bill, stripped of the value-added tax and somewhat more modest than the original proposals to lower marginal rates was resubmitted. This bill was finally passed in the fall of 1987, but rather than furthering the ministry's goal of raising revenue, it was an overall tax cut,

47. Susan MacKnight, "Tax Reform Plan Clears Another Hurdle," *JEI Report*, no. 1B (January 1987), p. 6.

expected to reduce revenues by ¥2 trillion. The only important structural gain from the ministry's standpoint was elimination of the system of tax-free savings accounts.

The Ministry of Finance Resurgence: Spending Policy

Because major increases in taxes proved unacceptable, and because tinkering provided only modest increases in revenues, the Ministry of Finance also tried to reduce deficit spending by slowing the growth of expenditures. From the summer of 1979, when it began work on the fiscal 1980 budget, until 1986, the MOF's pressure to hold down discretionary spending remained strong. Initial budget guidelines issued for ministries to use in developing their budget requests provide vivid evidence of this determination. The limits applied to discretionary spending, exclusive of ministry personnel costs, capital expenditures, and certain other items. In the 1960s these guidelines had routinely been set higher than 20 percent. From 10 percent in 1980 they were brought to zero by 1982 and below zero in the five following years (−5 percent in fiscal 1983 and −10 percent in the succeeding years). From fiscal 1984 to fiscal 1987, capital expenditures were treated separately and subjected to a slightly less oner-ous ceiling of −5 percent.[48]

The results of increasing fiscal austerity are evident in table 3-9. The rise in nominal spending was 15.2 percent in fiscal 1979 but averaged less than 3 percent for fiscal years 1982 to 1986. Two-thirds of expenditures in the budget are not discretionary, including debt service, revenue sharing, and (in the short run) social security. In addition, personnel costs associ-ated with government programs are not discretionary in the short run because wages are subject to annual arbitration. However, some altera-tions have been made to all but debt service costs since 1979. If revenue sharing and debt service are excluded, the average annual increase in budgeted expenditures from fiscal years 1980 to 1986 was only 1.4 per-cent.

Virtually all programs were affected, a pattern common for the budget-ing process in Japan and labeled "budget balance" by John Campbell.[49]

---

48. Data provided by MOF, Institute of Fiscal and Monetary Policy, February 1987; and "Inside the LDP: FY 1987 Budget Guidelines," *Liberal Star,* August 10, 1986.

49. John C. Campbell, *Contemporary Japanese Budget Politics* (Berkeley: University of California Press, 1977), and discussions with John Campbell. Japanese analysts agree with Campbell's analysis; see Seiichirō Saitō and Osamu Shimomura, "Setting Priorities for Asset Accumulation," *Japan Echo,* vol. 11 (Winter 1984), pp. 13–14.

Exemptions from guidelines issued by the Ministry of Finance were granted only to defense, foreign aid, and energy countermeasures, but even these programs were not immune to the slowdown. From fiscal years 1980 to 1986 the annual budgeted increase in defense spending averaged 6.9 percent, in foreign aid 9.2 percent, and in energy countermeasures 10.5 percent. On average, defense spending had increased at more than 15 percent annually in nominal terms from 1970 to 1979. In real terms the increases shrank from 5.4 percent annually in the 1970s to 3.7 percent in the 1980s. This slowdown came despite perceptions of an increased threat from the Soviet Union, the public's greater acceptance of the self-defense forces and of military spending, and the presence of Prime Minister Nakasone, who favored defense spending. Nominal increases in foreign aid were also smaller, although the real increases were virtually the same in the 1980s. The energy budget did not exist before 1978, so no comparison is possible.

Budget items that were not exempted from the guidelines also show some deviation from the Japanese ideal of evenness and balance. In particular, from fiscal years 1982 to 1986, social welfare expenditures continued to grow at a very low level, while public works and education and science expenditures remained flat and support for small business fell 6 percent over the period.[50]

Because programs related to the social functions of government, including social security, housing, and roads, stagnated or were cut while modest increases continued in defense, the Japanese government bore the brunt of the same sort of accusations that were leveled at the Reagan administration during the same years. Cutting programs that directly affected the public ought to have been very difficult and raises the question of how the Ministry of Finance managed to garner such support for its austerity program.

To some extent, the answer may lie in the revision of public expectations. With an unsettled international environment and slower economic growth at home, people accepted the proposition that expectations of what government could provide ought to be lower.[51] Such a shift would appear to lie behind the swing in local elections away from the opposition parties back to the Liberal Democratic party in the late 1970s and 1980s that was

50. Calculations based on fiscal 1986 amounts, including the supplementary budget.
51. Seizaburō Satō, "The Shifting Political Spectrum," *Japan Echo,* vol. 11 (Summer 1984), p. 33.

discussed in chapter 2. Nevertheless, it is surprising that the public accepted stagnation in social spending without putting up more vigorous opposition.

Local Government Policy

Lowered expectations appear to have applied to local governments as well. Had the public insisted on the continued rapid growth of services, local governments could have filled the gap, increasing their expenditures and deficits as the central government slowed spending and contracted its deficit. This did not happen. Instead the growth of local spending decelerated in tandem with that of the central government (see table 3-10). Beginning in fiscal 1979, expenditures grew by less than 10 percent in nominal terms, and growth in each succeeding year was slower still, actually falling more quickly than at the central government level and reaching only 3 percent in 1984. Having never pushed deficits as a share of total expenditures to as high a level as the central government, local governments' contraction of those deficits was also more modest. From a peak of 13.2 percent, local deficits as a share of expenditures dropped to 10.0 percent by 1981 and slightly below that by 1984; as a share of GNP, they peaked at 2.5 percent in fiscal 1978, fell to 2.0 percent by 1980, and dropped to 1.7 percent by 1984.

Local government could, of course, mask its true fiscal policy by pushing expenditures onto local public enterprises, which include water supply, sewage plants, hospitals, and lotteries and other forms of controlled gambling. These activities are run off-budget as individual enterprises and could form a basis for fiscal expansion by increasing expenditures and debt. Statistical data, though, indicate that public enterprises have expanded less rapidly in the late 1970s or 1980s than before. After growing at an annual rate of 17.1 percent from 1961 to 1973, their expenditures grew at a 13.0 percent rate from 1974 to 1978 and then dropped to 5.1 percent from 1979 to 1983.[52] This pattern closely follows that of the budgets of local governments.

52. Management and Coordination Agency, *Japan Statistical Yearbook, 1986,* pp. 470–72; *1982,* pp. 528–29; *1980,* pp. 490–91; *1967,* pp. 498–99. Growth rates for expenditures of local public enterprises are based on data for several subcategories. One of these, "public enterprises not under the local public enterprise law," shows a major discrepancy due to an unexplained change in accounting procedures. Therefore the 1983 level of expenditures is estimated by adding current and capital expenditures plus a 4 percent adjustment representing the size of the discrepancy between the old and new numbers reported for earlier years.

Because local government shows a smaller shift from expansionary to contractionary fiscal policies after 1979, focusing on the Ministry of Finance and central government policy to explain fiscal trends is entirely appropriate. What shifts did take place at the local level were broadly consistent with central government trends, whether because of local concerns over the role of government and government deficits or pressure from the Ministry of Home Affairs and the Ministry of Finance to keep from heading too far down a separate path.

The Administrative Reform Movement

The main public support for the Ministry of Finance's desire to reduce government deficits came from the administrative reform movement, primarily initiated by big business. Behind the movement lay real concern that unless programs were cut back, the government's involvement in the economy would reach intolerable levels. One projection, for example, anticipated that government spending would reach 60 percent of GNP by 2010 because of increased social security payments to the aging population.[53] But the movement's main justification was a deep-seated belief that the government was inefficient and wasteful. One example frequently cited was the Japanese National Railways with its large annual operating deficit ($7.2 billion in fiscal 1983). Hiroshi Kato, a participant in the administrative reform commission, mentions other examples, focusing on the excessive costs of government-run services when they can be compared with similar private-sector operations.[54]

Government waste is hardly a new development, and one wonders why the Japanese should so suddenly have become concerned about it, especially considering that even with the increases in government activity during the 1970s, Japan continued to have a rather lean administrative structure. One interpretation is that in the years after the first oil shock the mass media compared government unfavorably with the private sector, which was portrayed as making great efforts to hold down unit costs to preserve profitability. As Shumpei Kumon, another professor on the administrative reform commission, asked, "What were the government and

53. Shumpei Kumon, "Japan Faces Its Future: The Political Economics of Administrative Reform," *Journal of Japanese Studies*, vol. 10 (Winter 1984), p. 155.

54. Japanese National Railways, *Kokutetsu Tōkei Daijiesuto: Tetsudō Yōran, 1984* (National Railways Statistical Digest: Railways Survey, 1984) (Tokyo: JNR, 1984), p. 123; and Hiroshi Kato, "Fiscal Reform Comes First," *Japan Echo*, vol. 11 (Winter 1984), p. 21.

public corporations doing? Instead of reducing their weight, had they not been even more hypertrophous than ever, accumulating both deficits and liabilities, and maintaining excess personnel and departments?"[55] The time had come, these analysts argued, for the government to be exposed to an equivalent soul-searching about costs.

For big business to support austere fiscal policies was an unusual development—it had in the past been more likely to support policies bene-fiting economic growth. However, self-interest provided a cogent reason to support administrative reform. Big business could not effectively dis-agree with the MOF's desire to reduce government deficits, but it re-mained adamantly opposed to higher marginal tax rates and the value-added tax proposed by the ministry. Reducing expenditures through a vigorous administrative reform campaign was the only other possibility, so corporations emphasized reform to pressure the Ministry of Finance to turn from its concentration on raising revenues to reducing expenditures.

The corporate sector still bore much of the burden of the modest rise in taxes after 1979, but the increases might have been much larger had the administrative reform movement not existed. Finally, it is worth noting that in the complex relations between government and business in Japan, business was eager to exercise some influence over the structure of gov-ernment, reversing the usual roles.

The impetus for the administrative reform movement came from Keidanren, the federation of economic organizations, which is the voice of big business in Japan. In particular, the idea was championed by Toshio Doko, an elderly business leader just retiring as chairman of Keidanren. It was also supported by Yasuhiro Nakasone, at that time a contender for prime minister who had just become head of the obscure Administrative Management Agency. Although this cabinet appointment appeared to be an attempt to shuffle him off the center stage of political action or saddle him with difficult problems where the possibility of failure would be high, Nakasone seemed to welcome the post and became a champion of reform. With his support, legislation was approved by October 1980 to establish the Rinji Gyōsei Chōsakai (Provisional Commission for Administrative Reform, most commonly referred to in Japan as the Rinchō).[56]

---

55. Kumon, "Japan Faces Its Future," p. 152.

56. This commission was actually the second in the postwar period to address general administrative reform. The first one, in the early 1960s, made recommendations, but few changes in government organization resulted. Ibid., pp. 145–47.

Doko was appointed head of the Rinchō early in 1981. He asserted that administrative reform should proceed without tax increases so that the burden of reducing government deficits would depend entirely on reducing expenditures. From this fundamental position, and with the assumption that the deficits evidenced the need for reform, the commission set about its work. Between July 1981 and March 1983 it issued five reports, recommending, among other reforms, absolute cuts in public works spending, reducing the number of government employees by 5 percent over five years, curbing social security benefits, reforming and simplifying certification and inspection procedures for manufactured goods, reshuffling some government agencies, privatizing the three major government-owned corporations (Nippon Telegraph and Telephone, the Japanese National Railways, and Japan Tobacco and Salt), and restricting government support for education. In addition to the formal reports, the Rinchō offered its opinion on the budget process each year, pressing again for fiscal reform without tax increases. By the mid-1980s virtually all of its major proposals had been implemented. Public works spending had at least been held constant (with some items cut), the number of government employees was down, social security benefits were curbed, some certification and inspection procedures were simplified, some agencies were consolidated, and the three big government corporations were privatized.

Once the Rinchō had completed its task, its voice was continued for an additional three years through the Rinji Gyōsei Kaikaku Suishin Shingikai (Advisory Council on Enforcement of Administrative Reform), also headed by Doko. The council critiqued the annual budget guidelines and issued three more reports, generally reiterating the positions of the Rinchō. In all, the Rinchō and the follow-up commission commented on and influenced six consecutive government budgets as they were formulated. As one Rinchō member put it, the rather lengthy period during which the commission was active resulted in a "starving out" process on government expenditures.[57]

The five Rinchō reports tended to be repetitive and vague on how the desired policies were to be accomplished, which is common for documents of this type in Japan. Despite their seeming shortcomings, however, it would be a mistake to believe the reports were not important. They established broad agendas, and their repetitiveness helped keep the issues to the fore long enough to accomplish most of the goals. And the Rinchō

57. Ibid., pp. 143–65.

History of the Administrative Reform Process

1980

July 22   Yasuhiro Nakasone, director general of the Administrative Management Agency, presents plan to Prime Minister Zenkō Suzuki for a special commission on administrative reform

October 24   Cabinet finalizes bill to create Rinji Gyōsei Chōsakai (Provisional Commission for Administrative Reform)

1981

January 21   Toshio Doko, former chairman of Keidanren, named chairman of commission

March 11   Doko calls for "administrative reform without tax increases"

March 16   First meeting of commission

March 25   Liberal Democratic party sets up special office to promote administrative reform

July 10   First report issued by commission

November 27   Diet passes bill incorporating some ideas in the first report

1982

February 10   Second report issued

March 19   Cabinet approves bill to streamline administrative structure

July 30   Third report issued, covering basic philosophy and privatization of government enterprises

1983

February 28   Fourth report issued

March 14   Fifth report issued

March 15   Commission disbanded

July 4   Commission replaced by the Rinji Gyōsei Kaikaku Suishin Shingikai (Advisory Council on Enforcement of Administrative Reform), also headed by Doko

1984

July 25   Council presents desired budget policy for fiscal 1985

August 4   First report (on urgent administrative reform issues)

1985

July 22   Second report issued

1986

June 10   Report on future administrative and fiscal reform

June 27   Council disbanded

Sources: Foreign Press Center/Japan, *Administrative Reform in Japan* (Tokyo: Foreign Press Center/Japan, 1984), esp. pp. 35–36; "An Anatomy of the Japanese Economy: Prescription for Administrative and Fiscal Reform," *KKC Brief,* no. 23 (October 1984), p. 1; and information supplied by Keidanren.

was special in another way. Many of the advisory commissions permanently attached to government ministries do little beyond perfunctorily endorsing ministry proposals, especially since the ministries choose who will serve on them. The ministries also normally provide the staff for their commissions, thus shaping the agenda, selecting most of the data, and providing the draft reports. Because the Rinchō originally grew out of pressure from the private sector and was headed by a prestigious senior business leader, it was relatively independent. Its proposals generated considerable consternation and opposition within both the government bureaucracy and the Liberal Democratic party.

Why was this particular commission so successful? One factor was the political support from both Nakasone and Zenkō Suzuki, who was prime minister when it was established. Suzuki went so far as to "stake his political life" on administrative reform, which indeed he did. His failure to make much progress helped call into question his ability to lead and contributed to his demise as prime minister. But even after departing from the post, he continued to head an important faction within the LDP, building support for later reform measures.

Doko himself was also instrumental in the success of the movement. His prestige gave administrative reform a certain cachet, and his age suggested that his positions could be taken as the sincere efforts of a man not seeking future rewards. In addition, the staff work for the Rinchō was performed largely by people at Keidanren and its member corporations, so that the government bureaucracy was denied its usual role of shaping the agenda.

Enthusiasm for administrative reform included a strange mixture of concern over both waste and government deficits. Waste and inefficiency are not connected with the size of government deficits in a theoretical sense at all; how money is spent has no intrinsic relationship with the balance between spending and revenue. An inefficient government can have a balanced budget and an efficient one can have large deficits. Some people involved with the movement recognized this distinction but felt that reform could not be achieved without an environment of fiscal austerity— it is difficult to tell officials to spend more efficiently when their budgets are rising rapidly each year.[58] Prime Minister Suzuki endorsed this pragmatic linkage, although his point of departure was deficit reduction. At the opening session of the Rinchō he stated, "Reorganization of the govern-

58. Ibid., p. 155.

ment is an urgent task from the point of view of fiscal reconstruction. Future tax increases will not be supported by the public. We must reconstruct the fiscal structure by cutting inefficient government expenditures, simplifying government machinery, and retrenching government administration."[59] Still the need to tie the issues together seemed exaggerated, and many participants appeared confused or even divided on the main purpose of the movement. Was it to eliminate inefficiency from government, aided by an environment of fiscal austerity, or was it to reduce the government deficit through a program of administrative reform? The self-interest of the corporate sector, which dominated the movement, suggests the latter was the true agenda.

The various Rinchō reports reflect this confusion. Some proposals, such as cutting social security benefits and reducing support for education, had no implications for rooting out inefficiency, while others, such as privatization of the large government-owned corporations, were consistent with efficiency goals but had little connection with deficit reduction (none of the corporations was part of the general account budget of the central government).[60]

Whatever the mixture or confusion of goals and beliefs involved in administrative reform, it did result in legislation to implement many of its objectives. After reaching a peak of 2.01 million in 1979, the number of government workers declined by 3 percent to 1.95 million by 1982 but rose again to 1.99 million by 1985.[61] Health insurance was reformed in 1984, requiring a larger share of medical costs to be borne by patients, and the social security system was reformed in 1985, reducing benefits for future recipients. Both Nippon Telegraph and Telephone and Japan To-

59. Yoshio Nakamura, "Advisory Commission to Study Japanese Government Reorganization," *Japan Insight,* no. 12 (March 1981), p. 9.

60. Their records were also diverse; Nippon Telegraph and Telephone and Japan Tobacco and Salt generated profits, while the Japanese National Railways had large deficits. Even the railroad, which has lost an increasing amount of money each year since 1964, covered its deficits mainly by borrowing from the Fiscal Investment and Loan Program (the money from postal savings and some other government-run sources). For complex reasons, subsidies from the government were couched in terms of covering part of the interest cost on that debt, rather than covering operating deficits directly. In fiscal 1983, subsidies received by the railroad amounted to ¥346 billion ($1.5 billion), only 20 percent of the total ¥1.7 trillion ($7.2 billion) deficit for JNR in that year. Therefore, privatizing the railroad will not have as much impact on the general account deficit as is often assumed. In addition, privatization was a doubtful way to reduce the need for some form of public subsidy. See Japanese National Railways, *Kokutetsu Tōkei Daijiesuto, 1984,* p. 123.

61. Management and Coordination Agency, *Japan Statistical Yearbook, 1980* p. 51; *1986,* p. 73.

bacco and Salt were privatized in April 1985 (although the government initially held all of the stock of the new corporations) with public sales of NTT shares beginning in the fall of 1986. The Japanese National Railways was privatized in the spring of 1987 and broken into several nominally independent companies.

Facing decisive opposition in its attempt to institute a major new tax in 1979, the Ministry of Finance was willing to accept the administrative reform movement's emphasis on controlling expenditures, and the high visibility of the Rinchō made the job of imposing rather severe spending constraints easier. The MOF may have preferred increases in taxes over cuts in spending, but its overarching goal was deficit reduction, and the administrative reform movement meshed well with that goal.

This rough complementarity, however, does not imply that the ministry directed the process or was entirely pleased with the outcomes. The Rinchō sometimes criticized the government severely, and proposals in the reports were not what the MOF would have made on its own. Although the ministry was reduced to tinkering with taxes rather than instituting more sweeping changes, for example, it acted inconsistently with the concept of reducing deficits without tax increases. The very existence of the Rinchō itself was something of an affront, since the MOF's budget examiners pride themselves on their careful scrutiny of the budget requests submitted by each ministry to root out waste, duplication, and irrelevant expenditures. Nevertheless, the broad goal of the ministry to reduce the size of government deficits was served rather well by the existence of the administrative reform movement in the 1980s.

A New Direction in Fiscal Policy?

The rapid rise of the yen in 1985 and 1986 ushered in the third phase of Japan's macroeconomic adjustment to slower growth. If the exchange rate movement were to push the external surplus down, then either the private-sector savings surplus would have to diminish or the government would have to abandon fiscal austerity. As the need for some adjustment became evident, a great deal of discussion was generated. But there was little real change in fiscal policy until 1987.

Just before the movement in the exchange rate, the possibility for any reversal of fiscal policy seemed unlikely. The Keidanren stuck to the position of its former chairman, and reiterated its commitment to deficit reductions without tax increases in official statements made in 1984 and

1985.[62] At the end of December 1984 a newspaper survey of business reactions to the draft fiscal 1985 budget found general satisfaction with its austerity. Although there was some grumbling about the failure to include tax cuts for high-technology industries, those interviewed expressed basic agreement with the discretionary spending cuts.[63] Within the Liberal Democratic party, Prime Minister Nakasone and Finance Minister Noboru Takeshita remained firmly committed to fiscal austerity. And although the Economic Planning Agency and the Ministry of International Trade and Industry generally supported expansionary policies in the past, in 1985 neither was led by a politician likely to speak out in favor of fiscal expansion. MITI was headed by Keijirō Murata, a relatively junior LDP member holding his first cabinet post, and the EPA was headed by Ippei Kaneko, a former employee of the Ministry of Finance who had previously served as finance minister.

The only major LDP leaders who had spoken out against austerity in the first half of the 1980s were Toshio Kōmoto and Kiichi Miyazawa. Both were unsuccessful contenders for prime minister in 1982 and 1984, and Kōmoto's position was damaged in 1985 by the collapse of Sankō Steamship, a company he had helped found earlier in his career. Miyazawa was the most articulate about using government policy to stimulate the domestic economy, although even his proposals were somewhat vague. In the summer of 1984, as an LDP presidential election was looming, he proposed a concept of "asset doubling," drawing on a catchphrase of the Ikeda cabinet at the beginning of the 1960s. As Miyazawa put it, "about 20 years have passed since our predecessors raised the banner of 'income doubling' with the aim of expanding the flow of the economy. It is our turn now, our sights set on the twenty-first century, to raise the banner of 'asset doubling' and strive to double the nation's stock of wealth, both that in the public sector and that held by individuals."[64] His plan called for a 10 percent increase in the average floor space per dwelling, elimination of substandard housing, doubling the sewer diffusion rate, a 60 percent increase in urban park area per capita, and a 46 percent increase in miles of

62. "An Anatomy of the Japanese Economy: Prescription for Administrative and Fiscal Reform," *KKC* Brief, no. 23 (October 1984), pp. 1–27; and Takuji Matsuzawa, "Keidanren's Viewpoint on Government Spending and Future Administrative and Fiscal Reform," *Keidanren Review*, no. 95 (October 1985), pp. 2–6.

63. "Keizaikai, Ichiō wa Hyōka" ([Reform] More or Less Valued in Economic Circles), *Nihon Keizai Shimbun*, December 25, 1984.

64. Kiichi Miyazawa, "A Plan for Asset Doubling," *Economic Eye*, vol. 5 (September 1984), p. 10.

expressway. The proposal was made with the twin goals of increasing domestic economic growth through expanding private-sector investment and government spending and reducing the current-account surpluses (and thereby foreign criticism of Japan).

Even Miyazawa had to be very circumspect in advancing his program, given the very strong position of the administrative reform and fiscal austerity ideologies. Therefore, he included a goal of eliminating government deficit bonds by 1995, which opened him to legitimate criticism that the plan was unrealistic and that he was trying to have his cake and eat it too.[65]

Although Miyazawa was considered a strong advocate of expansionary fiscal policies, his spending proposals were really not radical. The plan included, for example, a goal of 5,000 kilometers of expressway by 1995, but the 1966 National Development Trunk Road Construction Law had called for more than 7,500 kilometers by 1985 and the Tanaka plan had called for an even more ambitious 9,900 kilometers by 1985.[66] For Miyazawa's goal to be labeled radical or expansionary demonstrates the enormous scaling back in expectations that took place in Japan after the 1973 oil shock.

Miyazawa was a serious contender for LDP president, and the asset-doubling plan provided a way to distance himself from Prime Minister Nakasone, who chose to stick to a strong position on fiscal austerity. However, Miyazawa's challenge to Nakasone failed, and with that failure fiscal expansion was also discredited. Even though differences over macroeconomic policy were not the determining element in the power struggle, the concept of asset doubling was clearly tied to Miyazawa, and lost with him.

Once the yen began to appreciate rapidly against the dollar, the environment for the debate over domestic policy changed. Export industries began to feel the pinch and confront the government with the need to adopt some policy to stimulate domestic demand or else suffer economic stagnation or recession. The United States helped push the debate along by criticizing Japan's failure to stimulate demand in 1985, beginning with a speech by Secretary of State George Shultz in April. With the entrenched support for fiscal austerity, however, the policy debate in 1985 and 1986 resulted in a

65. Kōji Nakagawa, "Asset-Doubling Plan," *Economic Eye*, vol. 5 (September 1984), p. 11.

66. Kakuei Tanaka, *Building a New Japan: A Plan for Remodeling the Japanese Archipelago* (Tokyo: Simul Press, 1973), pp. 126–30.

rhetoric of stimulus but few meaningful policy changes. *Minkatsu* (private-sector vitality) became the rallying cry of those who favored continued austerity. By deregulating the economy, they said, a burst of private-sector investment would provide the necessary stimulus to keep economic growth from faltering and reduce the imbalance between savings and investment. But while one can point to many petty regulations in Japan that might have some inhibiting effect on investment, their overall impact on investment seems small except perhaps for tax rates and other rates affecting land use.

Enthusiasm for promoting minkatsu resulted in passage of legislation (the *minkatsu-hō*) in 1986 to promote private-sector participation in projects normally undertaken by the government. Projects to be undertaken starting in 1987 included construction of research centers related to emerging high-technology industries, international exchange facilities, and some forms of telecommunications infrastructure. These projects were to be joint ventures between prefectural or municipal governments and local businesses. Approved projects were to be eligible for special depreciation allowances, reduction or exemption of local taxes, loan guarantees from the central government, and low-cost loans from the Japan Development Bank.[67]

The minkatsu-hō represented a positive step but a very small one. Some of the projects would have been undertaken in any case—either by the private sector or by the government under other programs. Even the initial projections of the total value of construction under the program were a modest ¥1.4 trillion ($8.75 billion at 160 yen to the dollar) spread over a ten-year period. The net impact, after discounting those projects that would be undertaken anyway, would be much less.

Recognizing that foreign criticism was getting stronger and that the minkatsu-hō would not provide a complete solution, the debate over domestic policy intensified. In June 1985 an advisory group to the Ministry of International Trade and Industry issued a strong repudiation of existing fiscal policy, warning that the rising current-account surpluses resulting from the effort to drive down government deficits were threatening Japan's trade relations with the rest of the world.[68] The report called for a more

67. Hirotaka Yamakawa, "Private-Sector Vitality Spurs Projects," *Journal of Japanese Trade and Industry,* no. 6 (1986), pp. 24–26. A publication of MITI, this source understandably takes an optimistic and exaggerated view of the law's impact.

68. Ministry of International Trade and Industry, Makuro Keizai Un'ei ni Tsuite no Kenkyūkai (Study Group on Japanese Macroeconomic Policy), *Hōkokusho* (Report), June 20, 1985.

expansionary fiscal policy with increased government spending on housing, sewers, roads, and parks. Although this report stemmed from an
advisory council and not from MITI itself, it can be taken as representing
the ministry's opinion, which after several years of quiet was surprisingly
critical, though it represented a fairly traditional stance for the ministry
that fiscal stimulus would be good for business and for Japan's international trade relations.

Little happened as a direct result of the MITI advisory commission
report, but another, the Maekawa report, submitted to the prime minister
in April 1986 struck a similar note and provided a stronger spur to the
policy debate. This short statement endorsed a deemphasis on increasing
exports and recommended encouraging domestic demand.[69] By the time it
was issued, the strengthening of the yen against the dollar was putting
great pressure on the profits of many export industries, making the need
for a policy change more obvious. However, the recommendations were
mild. Although the report included encouragement of housing investment,
continued import liberalization, increased local public works spending,
promotion of leisure time, economic deregulation to spur investment,
increased foreign aid spending, and tax reform, it mainly included proposals that had been made before. To achieve these goals, the report
stressed private-sector vitality and downplayed fiscal commitment by the
government, and although it referred to the need for short-term "flexibility" in fiscal policy, it did not abandon the longer-term goal of eliminating
deficit bonds.

The Maekawa report was as vague as some of the Rinchō reports, and
the commission producing it lacked both the independence and longevity
that had made the Rinchō successful. But at least the report raised the issue
of finding ways to stimulate domestic demand as foreign criticism and the
appreciation of the yen against the dollar eliminated the option of increasing exports as a source of economic growth. The lively debate it engendered over the desirability and feasibility of stimulating domestic demand
in 1986 represented a major shift from the mute acceptance of the drive for
fiscal austerity in the previous five years.

While the debate may have been lively, little action resulted from the
government other than the minkatsu-hō. MOF budget guidelines continued to aim at a 10 percent reduction in discretionary spending (and 5

---

69. *The Report of the Advisory Group on Economic Structural Adjustment for International Harmony,* submitted to Prime Minister Yasuhiro Nakasone, April 7, 1986.

percent in capital expenditures) for fiscal years 1985, 1986, and 1987. When compiled, all three budgets anticipated a reduction in the gap between spending and revenue.

Supplementary budgets adopted halfway through the fiscal year, however, provided an opportunity to modify initially austere budgets. Minor increases in spending were included in the supplementary budget passed in the fall of 1985 as part of a "stimulus package" announced by the government. Another stimulus was expected in the fall of 1986, as economic growth decelerated in the face of the stronger yen. But although public works spending was increased in the supplementary budget, other categories were cut, so that the net change was negative. The only stimulus came from automatic stabilizers; with economic growth slowing, tax revenues were falling below the forecast in the initial fiscal 1986 budget, and the fiscal deficit was widening.

That the Ministry of Finance could preside over continued austerity in the regular and supplementary budgets in spite of a weakening economy, a heated domestic debate over stimulating demand, and foreign criticism of Japan's economic policies was a clear sign that macroeconomic policy would be slow to change. The 1986 supplementary budget was enacted after Kiichi Miyazawa was appointed finance minister and after the major victory of the LDP in the July general elections. The appointment could have signaled a change in fiscal policy, but Miyazawa, who just two years earlier had pushed his asset-doubling plan, became more conservative when given the finance post. Not until the summer of 1987 did some change come. A mildly stimulative budget passed the Diet, but its fiscal impact was minor (see chapter 6).

Summary

Japan experienced a fundamental shift in the macroeconomic balances in the economy when growth slowed after 1973. From struggling to generate sufficient domestic savings (private and public) to feed the enormous appetite of private-sector investment during the 1950s and 1960s, the country began to experience excess savings in the private sector. The principal driving force for this change was the decline in investment as a share of GNP as the technological gap between Japan and other industrial nations that had made investment in new plant and equipment so profitable disappeared.

Offsetting most of the excess savings for the remainder of the 1970s was a rapid growth in government deficits, the result of alterations in spending priorities established early in the decade, and a drop in the rate of tax revenue increases caused by slower economic growth. Current-account surpluses, the other possible outlet for the excess savings, were small on average. The first half of the 1980s brought a major reversal in fiscal policy as the Ministry of Finance once more became concerned about deficit spending. While the government deficit dropped by more than four-fifths as a percentage of GNP, the current-account surplus rose rapidly to absorb the savings surpluses in the private sector.

That phase of adjustment ended in 1986 as the appreciation of the yen began to drive down the current-account surplus. The direction of the domestic response to this new development is as yet unclear. The government moved very slowly to increase spending, despite the rhetoric urging that domestic demand be stimulated. The alternative was for the excess private-sector savings to shrink through recession or for tax reform and deregulation to bring greater investment and less saving. However, deliberate government action to reduce savings or increase investment was unlikely to be strong enough to have much impact. In fact, despite the official commitment to revenue neutrality, the initial tax reform bills that failed the Diet in 1987 could easily have become a vehicle for increasing taxes to continue the drive for fiscal austerity.

The economic forces in the Japanese economy that led to the surplus of savings over investment will continue. The aging of the population may result in some decline of personal savings, but there is no agreement on how much that drop will be. Private-sector investment will not rebound to earlier levels. Corporate investment will fluctuate over the business cycle, but the permanent end to the technology gap has lowered potential profits from new investment. And because of the lackluster performance of housing starts, individual investment has not made up for the decline in corporate investment. Unless the government provides some strong incentives for housing investment, that pattern is unlikely to change.

These trends imply that the existence of surplus private-sector savings will continue for some time. Even in 1984, which was characterized by a cyclical upturn in economic growth caused by the strength of exports, the rise in private-sector investment was fueled largely by higher corporate savings, so that the surplus of savings over investment was just as large or larger than in earlier years. If the technological revolution in areas such as computers, new materials, and biotechnology brings about an increase in the profitability of investment, the ratio of corporate investment to GNP could rise, but the impact could be muted for the next few years because these industries are not very large.

Just as the private sector is likely to continue to generate surplus savings, government may continue to refuse to generate deficits large enough to absorb those surpluses. The government did very little to change its proclivity for fiscal conservatism through 1986 (and even the efforts to stimulate the economy in 1987 were weak). That stance could change as the economy slows, but a return to the high deficit levels of the late 1970s appears unlikely.

Continued surplus savings in the private sector, fiscal austerity, and a falling current-account surplus cannot coexist. One or more of these tendencies will have to give way. The strongest constraint appears to be the external one imposed by the strengthening of the yen. If the current account falls as a result, domestic adjustment must occur.

These conditions present a serious dilemma and a real puzzle. Will fiscal policy become more expansionary? Will tax changes to reduce saving and increase investment be approved? Will slow growth or stagnation impose the adjustment if deliberate policy moves fail? Any of these outcomes is possible, but the slowness of the policy response from 1985 to 1987 strongly suggests that disappointingly weak economic performance in Japan will be a major element of adjustment.

CHAPTER FOUR

Financial Restructuring

SURPLUS SAVINGS, government deficits, and capital outflows represented a massive reorientation of financial movements within the Japanese economy after 1973 and necessitated extensive changes in the regulations and institutions governing them. In simple terms, from the 1950s to the early 1970s Japan's investors, both individuals and corporations, held most of their financial assets in deposits at heavily regulated and highly specialized banks that in turn lent the funds to domestic industry. Since then Japan has been moving toward a more diverse, less tightly controlled system offering investors and borrowers a broader range of options. Interest rates on many forms of investment have been deregulated, many more types of financial instruments have become available, and the strict differentiation or segmentation of roles and responsibilities among the various financial institutions has weakened. Awash with funds to invest and freed from the stringent regulations of the past, Tokyo has emerged as one of the largest and most important financial centers in the world.

Japan is by no means the only industrial country to have experienced such rapid change in its financial system, but both the process of adjustment and the motivations for it have been very different from those in the United States or Western Europe. Japan started with a more tightly controlled system, one that had served the country well in the era of high growth, and changes, while necessary and in hindsight unavoidable, have not come easily. Government decisions to deregulate have been cautiously incremental, characterized by an extreme aversion to risk, the need to proceed on the basis of consensus, and the desire to distribute both the benefits and burdens of liberalization fairly among all segments of the industry. Although Japanese financial markets still do not have the breadth, flexibility, or freedom of those in the United States, that does not detract from the importance or extent of the continuing rapid evolution.

Capital Markets in the High-Growth Era

To understand what happened to Japan's financial sector after 1973, it is necessary to have some grasp of the earlier structure of financial markets. A complete description is not needed here, but discussion of three aspects—the role of government finance, the preference for indirect finance, and the preference for direct controls in monetary policy—provides important background.

Government Finance

Because the central government avoided deficit spending, almost no market for government bonds existed in the 1950s and early 1960s. The government did issue several types of short-term bills for particular seasonal needs, but they carried unattractively low interest rates. Virtually all were purchased by the Bank of Japan and thus did not figure in financial markets. Even when the government did begin to issue long-term bonds in 1966, they were carefully controlled: only one maturity was used (ten years), and initially all were purchased by financial institutions at interest rates decided by the government. Banks were willing to purchase the bonds for two reasons: in the highly regulated financial system of the day, refusal could bring reprisal from financial authorities, and the Bank of Japan implicitly agreed to repurchase any unwanted bonds from the commercial banks one year after issuance.[1] Given the relatively small amounts being offered until well into the 1970s, this system worked smoothly.

An equally important feature of the government's financial role was state-owned financial institutions. Japan had and continues to have a postal savings system in which most post offices also act as savings banks. The deposits, and certain other funds such as postal life insurance premiums, are turned over to the Ministry of Finance, which lends them through the Fiscal Investment and Loan Program. Some of the money goes to government-owned financial institutions, including the Japan Development Bank and the Export-Import Bank; the rest goes to a variety of policy-related projects—highway and school construction, airport expan-

---

1. Virtually all bonds (98 percent) were repurchased by the Bank of Japan, making this a very strong implicit guarantee. See Eisuke Sakakibara and Yoriyuki Nagao, eds., *Study on the Tokyo Capital Markets*, JCIF Policy Studies Series, 2 (Tokyo: Japan Center for International Finance, 1985), p. 40.

sion, and so forth. The concept behind the entire program is to give the government an opportunity to control part of the flow of financial resources in the economy and to do so at interest rates lower than those in the private sector. Depositors in the postal savings system receive interest rates equal to or higher than those available at commercial banks, but because the government is required only to break even on its loans, rates for borrowers are below those of the private sector. A good deal of controversy has surrounded the economic role of this program in the postwar growth of Japan, but that is not important to the present discussion.[2] What does matter is that the postal savings system has long competed with private-sector financial institutions in the market for individual deposits.

Preference for Indirect Finance

Savers and investors in a society can be connected either directly through financial instruments issued by the investors and purchased by the savers, such as corporate equity, or indirectly through financial intermediaries, at which savers have deposits and from which investors borrow. Japan has been characterized by a very high incidence of indirect finance.

During the rapid growth of the 1960s, corporations could finance relatively little of their expansion out of internal funds, even though a high proportion of profits were reinvested: retained profits and depreciation allowances were simply too limited, given the enormous appetite for investment in plant and equipment, and new stock issues were unattractive because new stock was traditionally issued at par value, which was usually well below the market value of existing shares. Therefore, corporations depended more on borrowing than did their counterparts in the United States. Although borrowing could rely either on bonds or bank loans, for a variety of reasons, some related to risk aversion and others to regulatory controls on bonds, Japanese corporations depended mostly on bank loans.

From 1965 to 1969 corporations raised only 57 percent of their investment funds from depreciation and retained earnings. Less than 2 percent came from new equity issues and less than 2 percent from bonds; bank loans supplied the remaining 39 percent. In contrast, American firms in

2. For a discussion of the implications of the program for industrial policy, see Edward J. Lincoln, *Japan's Industrial Policies: What Are They, Do They Matter, and Are They Different from Those in the United States?* (Washington, D.C.: Japan Economic Institute, 1984).

these years raised 13 percent of their funds from corporate bonds and only 16 percent from bank loans.[3]

The Japanese people preferred to deposit savings in banks instead of purchasing corporate stocks and bonds directly. In 1965 they held an overwhelming 93 percent of their financial portfolios in the form of cash, demand deposits, and time deposits; only 7 percent was held in securities.[4] Why would people choose to keep such an extraordinarily high proportion of their assets in low-yield deposits? Statements about national character can often be so broad as to be meaningless, but a strong case can be made that the Japanese tend to avoid taking risks. How else, for example, can one explain the fact that the share of corporate equity held by individual Japanese investors has steadily declined despite the very strong long-term performance of the stock market (where the indexes of stock prices show much higher growth than in the United States) and the absence of a capital gains tax? When asked, Japanese tend to respond that the stock market is too volatile and frequently cite the experience of the mid-1960s when stocks briefly went into a steep decline. That they would remember the short-term market decline of twenty years earlier and ignore the very strong gains of the whole postwar period contrasts sharply with the attitudes and behavior of Americans.[5]

The Japanese preference for bank deposits was reinforced by the lack of alternative financial instruments into which they could place their money. There were no government bonds; there were few corporate bonds and these were purchased primarily by banks; short-term government securities did not exist; and there were no commercial paper, banker's acceptances, or negotiable certificates of deposit. Essentially, investors could choose only between bank deposits and corporate equity. They overwhelmingly chose low-risk but low-return bank deposits over high-risk but high-return corporate equity.

With both preference and limited alternatives pushing individual and corporate investors toward the use of banks as intermediaries, the govern-

3. Edward J. Lincoln, "Corporate Financing in Japan," *JEI Report,* no. 38 (October 1981), p. 8.

4. Ryōichi Mikitani, "Monetary Policy in Japan," in Karel Holbik, ed., *Monetary Policy in Twelve Industrial Countries* (Federal Reserve Bank of Boston, 1973), p. 256.

5. While the share of equity held by individuals fell, the share held by the corporate sector rose. Corporations may have purchased equity because they saw a need for mutual stockholding (*kabushiki-mochiai*) to confirm business ties among firms or as insurance against takeovers. Nevertheless, the fact remains that individuals let corporations outbid them for purchases of shares.

ment carefully regulated the industry. Banks had suffered periodic crises in the 1920s, marked by waves of bankruptcies and consolidations, an experience that the government was determined not to see repeated.[6] The end of World War II also brought financial confusion, with rampant inflation and a reorganization of the banking industry. Therefore, Tokyo carefully compartmentalized the private financial sector, not only separating banking from the securities business but also finely subdividing the responsibilities and allowed services of the banking industry itself (table 4-1). To preserve the distinctions, many aspects of business—deposit and loan interest rates, other forms of nonprice competition such as presents to depositors, and access to the Bank of Japan discount window—were closely regulated. Regional banks were restricted primarily to their local areas, establishment of new branches by city banks was controlled to avoid crowding out regional banks, and both types of banks were limited in principle to short-term loans. Long-term credit banks and trust banks specialized in long-term loans; only long-term credit banks could issue bonds; only trust banks (with one exception) operated trust accounts; and the big banks avoided loans to small business and agriculture. Even the insurance business was strictly divided into those companies issuing life insurance policies and those dealing with other forms of insurance.

Behind this system, and supporting it, lay the dependence of financial institutions on the government. They might complain about government decisions, but regulation gave them a very secure portion of a rapidly growing business. If an institution did choose to balk at regulation, the government could take various retaliatory measures, including refusal to allow some transactions for which its prior notification or approval was necessary. While such a system would appear inefficient by definition, resulting in obstacles to the smooth flow of capital to the most productive uses, many officials and academic analysts believe it worked well. To attribute Japan's economic success to the financial system would be a clear exaggeration, but the system did transfer capital from savers to investors in such a way that rapid growth took place without severe bottlenecks. Nor was the economy plagued with financial crises. Protected niches and restraints on competition prevented any serious failures among financial institutions. The only disruption was the near failure of Yamaichi Securi-

6. For an analysis of the financial problems of the 1920s, see Hugh T. Patrick, "The Economic Muddle of the 1920s," in James W. Morley, ed., *Dilemmas of Growth in Prewar Japan* (Princeton University Press, 1971), esp. pp. 239–49.

Table 4-1. *Private-Sector Banks, by Type, December 1985*

Institution	Characteristic	Number
City banks	Nationwide service	13
Regional banks	Regional service	64
Long-term credit banks	Long-term loans with funds raised from bank debentures	3
Trust banks	Long-term loans with funds raised from trust certificates	7
Sōgo banks (mutual savings and loan banks)	Small business loans	69
Shinkin banks (credit associations)	Small business loans	456[a]
Credit cooperatives	Small business loans	448[a]
Shōkōchūkin Bank	Servicing small business lenders	1
Labor credit associations	Personal loans	47[a]
Nōrinchūkin (Central Cooperative Bank of Agriculture and Forestry)	Servicing agricultural lenders	1
Agricultural cooperatives	Agricultural loans	4,096[a,b]
Fisheries cooperatives	Fishery loans	1,692[a]

Sources: Bank of Japan, *Economic Statistics Annual, 1985* (Tokyo: BOJ, 1985), p. 156; and Ministry of Finance, *Ginkōkyoku Kin'yū Nempō, 1984* (Annual Report of the Banking Bureau, 1984) (Tokyo: Kin'yū Zaisei Jijō Kenkyūkai [Fiscal and Monetary Research Group], 1984), p. 180.
a. Does not include regional and national federations of these organizations.
b. In 1984.

ties in 1965 during the drop in the stock market, but actions were taken to prevent its bankruptcy, and it remains one of the largest securities companies.

Monetary Policy

Given a financial system in which so much was regulated by the government, the tools of monetary policy during the high-growth era were very different from those used in the United States. Without a market for government bonds or a broad market for any form of short-term securities, the Bank of Japan could not use the purchase and sale of government securities to influence money supply and interest rates. It could, however, affect interest rates through alterations in the discount rate, the rate at which it lent to city banks. Since the prime rate for short-term loans by the city banks was automatically tied to the discount rate, such a policy had an immediate impact on posted loan rates. But the actual impact of changes in the discount rate on commercial loan rates was by no means as clear as the connection with the prime rate would imply. Banks faced with excess demand for loans practiced a policy known as compensating balances, by which a borrower was required to keep part of his loan on deposit at the bank, thus denying him use of the funds and raising the effective interest rate. In any case, changes in the discount rate were rare: during the entire decade of the 1960s the rate varied from a low of 5.48 percent to a high of 7.30 percent and was changed only sixteen times, at one point remaining the same for two years.[7]

The Bank of Japan could also manipulate monetary policy by altering reserve requirements—as in the United States, banks in Japan are required to keep a percentage of total deposits in reserve, although the percentage is much smaller. But this percentage was changed only rarely during the 1960s. The reserve requirement for banks with time deposits of less than ¥20 billion, for example, remained at 0.25 percent for the entire decade, while for other deposits the rate was changed only four times.

In the absence of extensive use of either the discount rate or reserve requirements, the Bank of Japan relied primarily on "window guidance," announcements of the maximum allowable increase in lending by the city banks. Window guidance was not legally binding, falling in the amorphous category of what is known as administrative guidance in Japan, but it was effective. City banks were continuously faced with excess demand for their funds during the 1950s and 1960s, and they coped by borrowing from two sources: the regional banks and other small institutions such as the sōgo banks, and the Bank of Japan discount window. Any city bank violating the Bank of Japan's guidance could be penalized at the discount window. And although for short periods banks could replace Bank of Japan loans with increased borrowing from the interbank market (named the call market in Japan, corresponding to the federal funds market in the United States), interest rates in that market were freely determined, and increased demand would drive them up.

Window guidance worked well in the 1950s and 1960s. In times of monetary restraint the limits were tightened and city banks turned more heavily to the call market, which acted as a transmission mechanism to spread the effects of restraint more generally through the banking industry. Since the corporate sector was so heavily dependent on bank loans to finance its investment in plant and equipment, window guidance could have a very quick impact on corporate investment, which would then affect overall economic growth.[8]

---

7. Bank of Japan, *Economic Statistics Annual, 1985* (Tokyo: BOJ, 1986), pp. 25–26. This is the rate applicable to commercial bills (one of several separate discount rates used by the Bank of Japan at that time).

8. Yoshio Suzuki, *Money and Banking in Contemporary Japan* (Yale University Press, 1980), provides an elegant theoretical model of how the transmission process in monetary

Until the mid-1960s, Japan periodically had to use macroeconomic policies to slow the economy (and thereby the growth of imports) to prevent current-account deficits from becoming so serious that a devaluation of the currency would be necessary. In each of these episodes monetary policy bore the brunt of the responsibility, and window guidance was the main policy tool. The sharp reductions in economic growth in the periods of restraint demonstrated the policy's effectiveness.

Changes of the 1970s

The tightly controlled financial system that seems to have worked efficiently in the 1950s and 1960s underwent substantial alteration at the hands of the government in the 1970s and is still changing. Why tamper with a structure officials once considered so successful? Important factors underlying the system's creation and success began to change. Figure 4-1 identifies five main sources of pressure: slower economic growth, continued high savings, an aging population, technological change, and foreign pressures. This chapter focuses mainly on the impact of slower growth, high savings, the aging population, and foreign pressures. The discussion is divided into domestic financial deregulation and international liberalization (chapter 5), a somewhat artificial distinction since much of the foreign pressure has been directed toward effecting changes in domestic markets (deregulation of interest rates and creation of new financial instruments) rather than simply toward achieving freer access to existing markets.

Technological innovation has also been significant, but it is not discussed in depth in either chapter. Although some Japanese analysts place heavy emphasis on its role in modernizing the financial sector, what matters for the purposes of this study is that innovation facilitated the desire and ability of the financial sector to respond to changing economic conditions. Computerization, for instance, was a necessary ingredient for some financial innovations such as the automatic transfer of funds between accounts. Beyond this, new technology represented no unusual influence. The changes were no different than those experienced in the United States or elsewhere. And the impact of changing technological capabilities has

---

policy worked in the 1960s. See also Gardner Ackley and Hiromitsu Ishi, "Fiscal, Monetary, and Related Policies," in Hugh Patrick and Henry Rosovsky, eds., *Asia's New Giant: How the Japanese Economy Works* (Brookings, 1976), pp. 153–248.

Figure 4-1. *Process of Change in the Japanese Financial System*

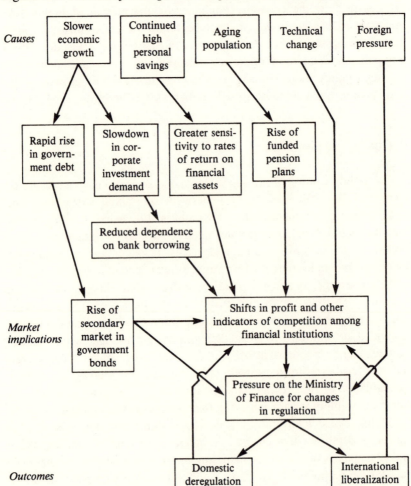

been surprisingly slow: American banks, for example, have compounded interest on a daily basis as part of their competitive strategy for many years, but Japanese banks have been held in check by regulation—the postal savings system compounds semiannually and commercial banks only annually. Thus technological innovation has facilitated the changes discussed in this chapter but has hardly driven the process of change.

Figure 4-1 shows another important feature of developments in the the financial sector. Once the process began, it became self-sustaining; change begat change. Each decision by the Ministry of Finance to make a marginal alteration in an activity permissible for a particular type of financial institution affected the competitive balance and led to demands from other institutions for additional changes in their favor. How to balance these demands has been a key concern of the ministry, pervading many of the decisions during the past decade.

One of the problems with current discussions of changes in the Japanese financial sector is their tendency to focus on only one causal factor or to ignore the complex economic, social, and political interrelationships involved in bringing about deregulation and international liberalization.[9] Using figure 4-1 as an organizing principle, the following sections consider these complexities.

The Rise of Government Debt

Ballooning fiscal deficits in the 1970s put great stress on the system under which new government bonds were issued. As the pool of bonds outstanding increased, a secondary market with freely determined interest rates arose, creating problems in selling the new issues, whose interest rates were set administratively. The immediate outcome was that the Ministry of Finance approved piecemeal changes that brought interest rates on the new bonds closer to market rates without destroying the system of placing new issues through a syndicate of financial institutions at a negotiated rate. In addition, new maturities were also created and sold through tender offer, so that part of the government debt was actually financed at market rates. The broader implication of these adjustments was that the entire system of administratively set interest rates was challenged. And as the range of transactions at market rates increased, pressure grew for changes in other parts of the system as well.

The bulk of government debt has been issued in the form of bonds (table 4-2), most of which until recent years carried ten-year maturities. Short-term securities were of little significance to the financial system, since most were held by the Bank of Japan or other government-owned institutions, as noted earlier. Before 1966 the government was not supposed to be operating at a deficit, so bonds constituted a small share of

9. See, for example, Geoffrey W. Picard, "Liberalization of the Japanese Financial Markets," speech delivered at the Asia-Pacific Conference, 1984, which emphasizes the rise in government debt.

Table 4-2. *Central Government Debts Outstanding, by Type, 1965–86*[a]

End of calendar year	Total (billions of yen)	Bonds		Short-term securities		Borrowings	
		Billions of yen	Percent of total	Billions of yen	Percent of total	Billions of yen	Percent of total
1965	1,887	467	25	1,147	61	272	14
1966	2,886	1,395	48	1,164	40	327	11
1967	3,895	2,049	53	1,467	38	379	10
1968	4,909	2,688	55	1,804	37	418	9
1969	5,749	3,081	54	2,182	38	486	8
1970	6,508	3,550	55	2,374	36	584	9
1971	7,426	4,293	58	2,459	33	674	9
1972	10,632	6,430	60	3,489	33	713	7
1973	11,587	8,034	69	2,786	24	767	7
1974	14,254	9,999	70	3,312	23	943	7
1975	20,862	13,946	67	4,657	22	2,259	11
1976	30,699	21,750	71	4,722	15	4,227	14
1977	42,825	30,377	71	6,789	16	5,659	13
1978	62,254	42,165	68	12,391	20	7,698	12
1979	76,196	53,652	70	12,386	16	10,158	13
1980	92,562	67,354	73	13,957	15	11,251	12
1981	108,753	81,189	75	16,078	15	11,486	11
1982	122,107	93,523	77	15,154	12	13,429	11
1983	140,176	110,010	78	14,151	10	16,016	11
1984	153,267	122,388	80	14,274	9	16,605	11
1985	165,384	135,202	82	13,659	8	16,523	10
1986	177,479	144,257	81	16,566	9	16,656	10

Sources: Bank of Japan, *Economic Statistics Monthly* (February 1987), pp. 123–24; (February 1986), pp. 123–24; (July 1985), pp. 123–24; (January 1984), pp. 125–26; (January 1983), pp. 125–26; (January 1982), pp. 125–26; (January 1981), pp. 123–24; (January 1980), pp. 123–24; (January 1979), pp. 117–18; (January 1978), pp. 115–16; (January 1977), pp. 113–14; (January 1976), pp. 113–14; (January 1975), pp. 109–10; (January 1974), pp. 109–10; (December 1973), pp. 109–10; (June 1972), pp. 103–04; (June 1971), pp. 101–02; (June 1970), pp. 99–100; (June 1969), pp. 99–100; (June 1968), pp. 101–02; (June 1967), pp. 125–26; and (June 1966), pp. 129–30.

a. Does not include debts of local governments or government-owned corporations.

total debt when they were first issued in 1965; short-term securities, used for a variety of seasonal or other temporary reasons, dominated government borrowing. But with the emergence of substantial government deficits, the share of borrowing represented by bonds rose steadily, from 60 percent in 1972 to 81 percent by the end of 1986.

Table 4-3 shows that the increased share of bonds held by the private sector in the mixture of government debt was what counted in the process of change. The government uses its own institutions to purchase a portion of its debt, mainly through the Bank of Japan or the Trust Fund Bureau of the Ministry of Finance. The Trust Fund Bureau invests the monies collected by the postal savings system and other sources that make up the Fiscal Investment and Loan Program. Debt purchased by the Trust Fund and government-owned financial institutions is labeled "government" in the table. As the data show, government-controlled institutions hold a significant share of the bonds, but the share held by the private sector has increased markedly in the past two decades. As part of the compromise to facilitate marketing them when they were first issued, the Bank of Japan informally agreed to buy unwanted bonds from the commercial banks one year after issuance, which accounts for the generally high share held by the bank in the years before the mid-1970s. However, because of changes in financial markets described later, the share of bonds held by the private sector increased from 50 percent or less in the early 1970s to a high of 70 percent in the 1980s. The private sector held only 4.6 percent of the outstanding short-term securities in 1985, however, and supported only 0.2 percent of other borrowings.

As the amounts of outstanding government bonds held by the private sector increased, a new market that traded bonds with market-determined interest rates was created. The rise of this market translated government debt into a force for change in the financial sector. The key events and decisions allowing the development of the market came in 1975, when the Bank of Japan failed to meet its implicit guarantee to repurchase bonds from financial institutions, and in 1977, when resale of bonds to a second-ary market was allowed. After 1977 the secondary market expanded rap-idly.[10] Government bonds also played a role in change through the gensaki market, a short-term market involving repurchase agreements that will be considered later. Basically, though, the rise of government debt changed the way the government issued bonds, with the result that interest rates on new issues moved closer to market-determined rates. This result led to two further outcomes: stresses in the system of issuing ten-year bonds and changes in the maturity structure of new issues.

NEW ISSUES OF TEN-YEAR BONDS. When the government first issued ten-year bonds, it expected to continue tight control over interest rates. Therefore the bonds were not issued at auction, in which prices and interest yields would adjust until the issue was completely sold. Instead,

10. Initially, financial institutions had to hold bonds for one year after issue before selling them on the market. This waiting period was shortened to six months in 1980 and to three months in 1981. Sakakibara and Nagao, eds., *Study on the Tokyo Capital Markets*, p. 40.

Table 4-3. *Government Debt by Type and Holder, Selected Years, 1965–85*[a]

Year	Total (billions of yen)	Government		Bank of Japan		Other	
		Billions of yen	Percent of total	Billions of yen	Percent of total	Billions of yen	Percent of total
Medium- and long-term bonds							
1965	467	2	0.4	207	44.3	258	55.2
1970	3,550	428	12.0	1,711	48.2	1,412	39.8
1973	8,034	4,054	50.5	741	9.2	3,239	40.3
1974	9,999	4,546	45.5	2,544	25.4	2,909	29.1
1975	13,945	2,162	15.5	6,199	44.5	5,584	40.0
1976	21,750	3,642	16.7	6,582	30.3	11,526	53.0
1977	30,377	8,480	27.9	3,587	11.8	18,310	60.3
1978	42,164	8,565	20.3	4,664	11.1	28,935	68.6
1979	53,651	13,077	24.4	3,621	6.7	36,953	68.9
1980	67,353	17,346	25.8	4,572	6.8	45,435	67.5
1981	81,190	19,809	24.4	6,239	7.7	55,142	67.9
1982	93,524	19,686	21.0	7,938	8.5	65,900	70.5
1983	110,009	24,644	22.4	7,630	6.9	77,735	70.7
1984	122,388	30,358	24.8	7,529	6.2	84,501	69.0
1985	135,202	39,139	28.9	6,055	4.5	90,008	66.6
Short-term securities							
1965	1,148	348	30.3	728	63.4	72	6.3
1970	2,374	1,565	65.9	692	29.1	117	4.9
1973	2,786	989	35.5	1,536	55.1	261	9.4
1974	3,312	393	11.9	2,797	84.5	122	3.7
1975	4,657	3,041	65.3	1,406	30.2	210	4.5
1976	4,722	2,326	49.3	2,104	44.6	292	6.2
1977	6,790	1,820	26.8	4,539	66.9	431	6.3
1978	12,391	4,897	39.5	6,647	53.6	847	6.8
1979	12,386	1,706	13.8	9,862	79.6	818	6.6
1980	13,956	1,465	10.5	11,741	84.1	750	5.4
1981	16,078	1,585	9.9	14,001	87.1	492	3.1
1982	15,154	2,601	17.2	12,030	79.4	523	3.5
1983	14,150	2,822	19.9	10,618	75.0	710	5.0
1984	14,275	705	4.9	12,915	90.5	655	4.6
1985	13,658	1,635	12.0	11,389	83.4	634	4.6

the government set the interest rate and told financial institutions how much they would be required to buy (all at face value). And because it wanted to limit the burden from its deficits, the government held interest rates down. While a comparison of bond yields with the prime lending rate shows that bond rates were higher, the real yield to banks on their loan portfolios was unlikely to be as low as indicated by the prime rate because of the practice of requiring compensating balances, discussed earlier.

Table 4-3. *(Continued)*

Year	Total (billions of yen)	Government Billions of yen	Government Percent of total	Bank of Japan Billions of yen	Bank of Japan Percent of total	Other Billions of yen	Other Percent of total
Other borrowings							
1965	272	194	71.3	...	...	78	28.7
1970	583	507	87.0	...	...	76	13.0
1973	767	726	94.7	...	...	41	5.3
1974	943	902	95.7	...	...	41	4.3
1975	2,259	2,218	98.2	...	...	41	1.8
1976	4,227	4,186	99.0	...	...	41	1.0
1977	5,659	5,618	99.3	...	...	41	0.7
1978	7,697	7,656	99.5	...	...	41	0.5
1979	10,158	10,117	99.6	...	...	41	0.4
1980	11,251	11,210	99.6	...	...	41	0.4
1981	11,486	11,445	99.6	...	...	41	0.4
1982	13,429	13,388	99.7	...	...	41	0.3
1983	16,015	15,974	99.7	...	...	41	0.3
1984	16,605	16,564	99.8	...	...	41	0.2
1985	16,522	16,481	99.8	...	...	41	0.2

Sources: Bank of Japan, *Economic Statistics Monthly* (February 1986), pp. 123–24; (July 1985), pp. 123–24; (January 1984), pp. 125–26; (January 1983), pp. 125–26; (January 1982), pp. 125–26; (January 1981), pp. 123–24; (January 1980), pp. 123–24; (January 1979), pp. 117–18; (January 1978), pp. 115–16; (January 1977), pp. 113–14; (January 1976), pp. 113–14; (January 1975), pp. 109–10; (January 1974), pp. 109–10; (June 1971), pp. 101–02; and (June 1966), pp. 129–30.

a. Values represent end of year holdings.

To simplify the selling of each new bond issue, financial institutions were formed into a syndicate. The other buyer of new issues has been the Trust Fund Bureau, using the Fiscal Investment and Loan Program funds. The share of bonds purchased by the syndicate was very high in the early 1970s and climbed to a peak of 97 percent in 1978 (table 4-4). Since then, however, its share has declined dramatically, because the number of bond issues floated outside the syndicate system through tender offer (discussed in the next section) has increased and because the Trust Fund Bureau has expanded its purchases.

Since the syndicate purchased such a large share of the government bonds, a bilateral monopsony-monopoly developed. When the bond issues were small and the banks were unwilling to oppose the government, they accepted the interest rates. But as the issues grew larger the syndicate began to exercise its power to negotiate the rates. When interest rates in the economy were declining, syndicate members would readily purchase

Table 4-4. *Sales of Government Bonds, by Purchaser,*
Fiscal Years 1971–85
Billions of yen unless otherwise specified

		Syndicate				Tender offer		Trust Fund Bureau	
Fiscal year	Total	Amount purchased	Percent of total	Amount resold	Percent of total resold	Amount purchased	Percent of total	Amount purchased	Percent of total
1971	1,209	936	77.4	98	8.1	...	...	273	22.6
1972	1,967	1,715	87.2	238	12.1	...	...	252	12.8
1973	1,800	1,500	83.3	228	12.7	...	...	300	16.7
1974	2,200	1,772	80.5	178	8.1	...	...	428	19.5
1975	5,363	4,510	84.1	306	5.7	...	...	853	15.9
1976	7,049	6,023	85.4	953	13.5	...	...	1,027	14.6
1977	9,575	8,570	89.5	2,066	21.6	...	...	1,005	10.5
1978	9,500	9,200	96.8	1,786	18.8	...	...	300	3.2
1979	12,280	9,600	78.2	1,095	8.9	...	...	2,680	21.8
1980	14,245	8,200	57.6	2,070	14.5	1,745	12.2	4,300	30.2
1981	13,569	5,539	40.8	1,125	8.3	3,443	25.4	4,587	33.8
1982	17,640	7,300	41.4	1,330	7.5	4,109	23.3	6,231	35.3
1983	17,880	5,530	30.9	2,561	14.3	6,390	35.7	5,960	33.3
1984	17,902	6,420	35.9	4,264	23.8	5,447	30.4	6,036	33.7
1985	19,910	7,029	35.3	5,151	25.9	4,968	25.0	7,914	39.7

Sources: Bank of Japan, *Economic Statistics Annual, 1986*, p. 205; *1985*, p. 205; *1979*, p. 197.

government bonds and later resell them at a profit (since falling rates imply a rise in bond prices). When rates were rising, however, these institutions faced losses if they chose to resell—losses that became more important to them as the size of bond issues rose—and therefore the syndicate used its power to negotiate higher rates.

The syndicate has also periodically refused to purchase the monthly issue from the government (table 4-5).[11] In 1981 when this first occurred, monetary policy had been eased, but market-determined rates in the secondary bond market were still rising. To support their monetary policy authorities did not raise the rate on new bond issues; by the summer of 1981 the market rate was close to 8.50 percent, while the issue rate was at

11. James Horne, *Japan's Financial Markets: Conflict and Consensus in Policymaking* (Allen & Unwin, 1985), pp. 65–70, notes that the conflicts predated 1981. He argues that the syndicate first began to challenge the Ministry of Finance over issuing conditions in 1978—a radical departure from previous norms in the MOF-syndicate relationship. And, partly because of the timing of his research, he considers the refusal to buy in 1981 as the end of the process of change rather than the beginning. From the vantage point of the mid-1980s, however, the major changes in ministry policy date from after the episodes of open opposition from the syndicate that started in 1981. Horne also notes (pp. 70–72) that syndicate members did not always have a consensus position in dealing with the MOF.

Table 4-5. *Banking Syndicate Refusals to Buy Bonds, 1981–84*

Date of refusal	Interest rates increase next month?	Increase (percent)	Market rate at the time[a]
July, August 1981	Yes	7.96 to 8.37	8.18[b]
July 1982	Yes	7.81 to 8.27	8.71
February 1983	Yes	7.76 to 7.86	7.88
July 1983	Yes[c]	7.86 to 7.99	8.03
June, July 1984	Yes	7.35 to 7.70	7.83

Sources: Bank of Japan, *Economic Statistics Annual, 1984*, pp. 195, 209; *1983*, p. 209; *1982*, p. 205; *1981*, pp. 189, 203; and Bank of Japan, *Economic Statistics Monthly* (January 1985), p. 99; (June 1983), p. 113; (June 1982), p. 113.
a. Market rates taken from Bank of Japan data for over-the-counter sales yield on interest-bearing government bonds.
b. End of June figure. By the end of July the market rate was 8.44 percent.
c. In September 1983.

7.96 percent (even after a very small increase in June). Because its members faced losses if they chose to resell, the syndicate simply refused to purchase the new issues of July and August.[12] By September the government relented, and the rate on the new issue rose to 8.37 percent.

After 1981, refusals to buy were repeated every year through 1984, usually in July. Each time, the refusal resulted in an immediate increase in the interest rate. Although the government used the Trust Fund Bureau to buy up the bonds in July and August 1981, after that it simply cancelled that month's planned issue. As with so many events in Japan, the initial unexpected shock was transformed into a ritual, but it still had a major impact on government policy.

Increasing syndicate resistance to the low rates on new bond issues caused the government to seek alternative strategies, including other maturities, increased use of the Trust Fund Bureau, and greater flexibility in setting interest rates. But use of the Trust Fund Bureau was necessarily limited because there are many claimants for its funds, and excessive purchases of government bonds would impair fulfillment of its other functions. The most important outcome has been greater flexibility of interest rates, bringing the rates negotiated with the syndicate closer to market rates. These changes were extensive enough that the syndicate has not refused to buy since 1984.

The Ministry of Finance has not taken the ultimate step of issuing ten-year bonds through tender offer, probably because negotiations with the syndicate have produced interest rates close enough to market rates that the move to tender offer could be postponed. In the negotiating process the government has also managed partially to offset the monopsony power of

12. Edward J. Lincoln, "Difficulties in Japan's Government Bond Market," *Japan Insight*, no. 29 (July 1981), pp. 3–4.

the syndicate through heavier use of the Trust Fund Bureau. Finally, the Ministry of Finance has chosen not to use short-term securities more widely nor to use other borrowings to avoid bond issues; both instruments have low nonmarket interest rates that the government has not wanted to jeopardize through an expanded public market.

WIDER RANGE OF MATURITIES. Along with efforts to come to terms with the syndicate, the Ministry of Finance widened the range of maturities of government bonds, with the new ones falling outside the negotiating arrangement. This effort began in 1976 when the first five-year discount bonds were issued. Two-, three-, and four-year maturities were introduced in several steps between 1978 and 1980 and were sold through tender offer. By the mid-1980s more than 20 percent of new bond issues fell in these shorter maturities.[13] Creating new maturities thus became a way to sidestep the problems of negotiated interest rates on ten-year bonds.[14] The negotiation scheme on the long-term bonds was not altered, but market rates could be applied to the other maturities and their share in debt structure increased. The power of the syndicate could be controlled, while government officials could pretend they were sticking to a system of floating government debt at low interest rates because the rates on the ten-year bonds were still negotiated. The success of this effort to sidestep the syndicate is shown in table 4-4: from a peak of 96.8 percent in fiscal 1978 the share of new government bonds placed through negotiated sales to the syndicate declined to only 35.9 percent by fiscal 1985.

By the mid-1980s the problem of government bond issues was taking a new turn. Since most of the increase in government deficits in the second half of the 1970s was financed by ten-year bonds, refinancing needs began to grow rapidly in 1985. As is often the case in Japan, the problem was blown out of proportion and became part of panicky appeals for the government to reduce its fiscal deficits. Behind the fear was concern that investors cashing in their matured ten-year bonds would not accept new ones (once again issued below market interest levels) and that the negoti-

13. Bank of Japan, *Economic Statistics Annual, 1986,* pp. 199–200. The share peaked at more than 25 percent in fiscal 1983 and declined to 20 percent in 1985.

14. For details on the new medium-term bonds, see Sakakibara and Nagao, eds., *Study on the Tokyo Capital Markets,* pp. 39–40. How closely this change was related to the problem of negotiations with the syndicate is indicated by the fact that eligible bidders on issues of new medium-term bonds were limited to members of the syndicate. That restriction was not removed until the end of 1986 (ostensibly to allow foreign securities firms to join the syndicate). *Japan Economic Journal,* December 27, 1986.

ated interest rate system would finally collapse, raising the interest costs on government debt. This concern was excessive. First, the negotiated rates were no longer very far below market rates. Second, the changes in the number and type of debt instruments available to the government since the late 1970s meant that a sizable portion of debt was already being raised at market rates. Finally, the refinancing bonds being issued did not represent any net increase in government demands on financial markets, so the new bonds would not drive up market rates.

Fears about the scale of the refinancing needs generated new discussion about creating a true market in short-term treasury bills to smooth out the timing between the maturation of old bonds and their refinancing through new long-term bond issues. The Ministry of Finance proposed a short-term financial instrument to be sold through tender offer and to be free of the securities transaction tax. Calls for creating a true market for short-term securities had been made for a number of years without ever having a visible impact. Modest developments finally began in 1986, with some increase in treasury bill sales to the private sector. Expanded sales to the public in April and May 1986 brought the private-sector share of short-term government securities to 26 percent of the total outstanding amount, but it remains unclear whether this signals a permanent change in policy.[15]

Corporate Financial Demands

The decline in corporate investment in plant and equipment as a ratio to GNP had consequences for financial markets and institutions almost as significant as the rise in government debts. On the one hand, banks felt the impact of the investment slowdown, the financing of which had been their bread and butter. On the other hand, some corporations began actively looking for better ways to manage their cash than simply sticking it in bank demand and time deposits. The corporate sector thus ceased to be the docile and growth-producing customer for the banking sector that it had been.

At the beginning of the 1970s the pattern of corporate financing described earlier persisted—heavy reliance on bank loans to make up for the inability of depreciation and retained earnings to provide a high share of

15. Bank of Japan, *Economic Statistics Monthly* (September 1986), pp. 123–24. By the end of the year the private-sector share was back down to 10 percent. Short-lived jumps in treasury bill sales to the private sector had occurred previously without signaling either an increased use of these instruments or a permanent increase in private-sector participation.

Table 4-6. *Sources of Corporate Investment Funds, Fiscal Years*
1970–74, 1975–79, 1980–84
Percent of total

Fiscal years	Equity	Depreciation	Retained earnings	Bank loans	Bonds	Other[a]
1970–74	1.5	35.9	12.7	46.6	1.9	1.4
1975–79	2.0	51.1	6.4	37.9	2.6	0
1980–84	2.1	45.2	13.3	34.4	1.3	3.7

Sources: Bank of Japan, *Economic Statistics Annual, 1985*, p. 216; *1984*, p. 28; *1983*, p. 28; *1982*, p. 28; *1981*, p. 28, for flow of funds tables for data on equity, bank loans, bonds, and "other"; and Economic Planning Agency, *Annual Report on National Accounts, 1986*, pp. 254, 258, for depreciation and retained earnings.

a. Includes both foreign currency bonds and net inflow of foreign trade credit. For 1975–79 these sources actually came to less than zero and are therefore set to zero for this table.

investment needs (table 4-6). By the early 1980s, however, this dependency had decreased considerably. From almost 47 percent in the first half of the 1970s, the share of corporate funds coming from bank loans dropped to under 35 percent by the first half of the 1980s. Why? Reliance on neither bonds nor equity increased appreciably.[16] Depreciation filled the gap—rising from 36 percent to 45 percent of total funds over the same time period.

Although lower rates of economic growth brought lower profits and retained earnings, they meant that depreciation allowances were able to provide a larger share of total investment needs. (Depreciation, it should be remembered, is simply a portion of corporate income set aside as tax-free under the tax laws to replace worn equipment.) These changes meant that bank lending to the corporate sector grew more slowly. Loans to the manufacturing sector, for example, grew at a nominal rate of 15.1 percent from 1960 to 1975 but dropped to 5.7 percent from 1976 to 1985. In real terms the change was from 10.8 percent to 2.9 percent—in either case a dramatic deceleration. For the corporate sector as a whole, nominal growth over the same two periods dropped from 16.5 percent to 9.4 percent, or from 12.1 percent to 6.5 percent in real terms, less dramatic than for manufacturing alone but still a major scaling back.[17]

16. The picture for bonds is confused, however. The use of foreign currency bonds has increased, but because issues were so small until recent years, the government did not list them separately (they are included under "other" in table 4-6). These bonds represented 2.2 percent of available investment funds in fiscal 1983 and 2.9 percent in fiscal 1984, larger shares than domestic bond issues in either year.

17. Bank of Japan, *Economic Statistics Annual, 1985*, pp. 130, 132; *1977*, p. 21; *1966*, p. 103. Figures represent the average annual growth of outstanding loans and discounts by all banks. Data for all industries are derived by subtracting lending overseas and to local governments and individuals from total loans and discounts outstanding. Real data are obtained by deflating by the wholesale price index.

Table 4-7. *Corporate Cash Management, by Type of Financial Instrument, End of Selected Fiscal Years 1964–85*[a]

Financial instrument	Dec. 31, 1964 Billions of yen	Percent of total	March 31, 1970 Billions of yen	Percent of total	March 31, 1975 Billions of yen	Percent of total	March 31, 1985 Billions of yen	Percent of total
Cash	274	2.2	377	1.6	915	1.6	1,921	1.2
Demand deposits	4,114	32.3	8,114	34.0	20,634	36.6	40,087	25.9
Time deposits	5,766	45.3	12,231	51.2	26,027	46.1	62,736	40.5
Certificates of deposit	...	...	...	...	...	...	6,953	4.5
Trust accounts	638	5.0	1,099	4.6	3,070	5.4	8,271	5.3
Bonds[b]	575	4.5	1,106	4.6	2,231	4.0	12,783	8.2
Securities investment trust	57	0.5	23	0.1	44	0.1	433	0.3
Other	1,306	10.3	942	3.9	3,468	6.2	21,803	14.1
Total	12,730	100.0	23,892	100.0	56,389	100.0	154,987	100.0
Ratio of managed cash to total assets	...	23.7[c]	...	16.2	...	17.6	...	23.8

Sources: Based on flow-of-funds data compiled in Bank of Japan, *Economic Statistics Annual, 1986*, pp. 219–20; *1975*, pp. 19–20; *1970*, pp. 17–18; *1965*, pp. 17–18; and Management and Coordination Agency, *Japan Statistical Yearbook, 1986*, p. 366; *1979*, p. 310; *1973–74*, p. 310; *1965*, p. 316.

a. Excludes trade credit granted and equity holdings, which are not closely related to cash management. Trade credit is part of corporate sales strategies, and much of the holding of corporate equity is stimulated by the need to cement business ties rather than the desire to diversify portfolios.

b. Includes all forms of government and private-sector issues (and both bank debentures and industrial bonds). Bonds held pursuant to gensaki transactions are also included.

c. As of March 31, 1965.

The decline in the growth of fixed investment also brought a rise in corporate financial investment (table 4-7). From levels of 16 to 18 percent in the first half of the 1970s, the ratio of financial assets to total corporate assets rose to 23.8 percent by 1985. (The high value of 23.7 percent at the end of 1964 can probably be discounted on the grounds that Japan was heading into a short-run growth recession, causing corporations to hold back temporarily on making fixed investments.) Since financial assets were becoming a larger share of corporate assets, their management became increasingly important.[18]

Formerly, the strategy had been to keep surplus cash on deposit with the major banks lending to the corporation. Part of the cash was required because of the compensating balances demanded by banks as a condition for loans. However, as corporate demand for loans slackened and banks had to compete for them, banks' demands for compensating balances diminished.[19] With less pressure to keep cash on deposit and with more

18. Not all corporations shared in this trend. The structural changes of the 1970s and 1980s meant that some industries and companies became cash-rich (leading to jokes about the Toyota Bank), while others faced hard times.

19. One official estimate of the size of the compensating balances shows them shrinking from 17.6 percent of loan amounts in 1965 to only 2.2 percent by 1985. These are average

cash to invest, corporations became increasingly active in managing their financial portfolios.

Looking for liquid, short-term investments with good rates of return, financial officers turned first to the gensaki market. This market began growing rapidly in the late 1960s and was officially recognized by the Ministry of Finance in 1976. Nonfinancial corporations represented 42 percent of the money invested in the market at the end of 1984 but only 3 percent of the money borrowed through the market. The 42 percent figure is far less than it had been, however; as recently as 1980 nonfinancial corporations supplied 68 percent of total funds invested (and 7 percent of the total borrowed).[20] Nevertheless, corporations remain major investors in the gensaki market. (The share seems to have decreased because the market has become larger and more popular.)

Corporations were also the principal potential market for negotiable certificates of deposit when they were created in 1979, since CDs initially carried a minimum denomination of ¥500 million. Before the 1970s there had been no short-term liquid financial assets other than bank deposits into which corporations could easily put their money (although the gensaki market actually had its origins about 1949),[21] because the call market was restricted to financial institutions. These new markets met the corporate need for better returns on short-term cash portfolios.

The corporate financial portfolio choices shown in table 4-7 confirm these changes. Corporations held more than one-third of their financial assets in the form of cash and demand deposits in 1964, 1970, and 1975, a share that declined sharply to 27.1 percent by 1985. Almost one-half was simply placed in time deposits in banks in the late 1960s, and that share also dropped, to 40.5 percent in 1985. Offsetting these declines was increased investment in certificates of deposit (reaching 4.5 percent of corporate financial assets by 1985), a rise in holdings of bonds (which almost doubled as a share of the total from 1964 to 1985), and the category "other." The shift in portfolios was slow to start, since the cash, demand deposit, and time deposit subtotal was even higher in 1975 than it was at

---

figures for city banks, regional banks, sōgo banks, and the shinkin banks. Large corporations, which have become the most interested in managing their financial portfolios, would have had most of their loans from the city banks. However, even here the reported drop in the ratio of compensating balances to loan amount has been substantial, from 8.9 percent in 1965 to only 1.1 percent by 1985. Data are from the Institute of Monetary and Fiscal Policy, Ministry of Finance.

20. Bank of Japan, *Economic Statistics Annual, 1985,* pp. 197–98; *1981,* pp. 195–96.

21. Robert F. Emery, *The Japanese Money Market* (D.C. Heath, 1984), pp. 17, 82–83.

the beginning of 1965, but from 1975 to 1985 it dropped by 16.8 percentage points to 67.6 percent.

Changing corporate needs were, therefore, an important ingredient in the elements altering the financial system. Banks discovered that their strong dependence on loans to corporations was becoming a liability as that market stagnated. Corporations were also a less reliable source of low-cost deposits as they demanded better investments for their short-term cash management.

Personal-Sector Finances

When economic growth decelerated in the 1970s, personal savings fell very little. Chapter 3 considered the macroeconomic problems that emerged from the combination of continued high savings and reduced investment demand, but high savings also had implications for the structure of financial markets, as indicated in figure 4-1. One would expect that the continuation of high savings rates (with an attendant increase in the stock of personal-sector savings) would cause people to be more sensitive to interest rates in making financial decisions. But while some change has taken place, it has been surprisingly slow; the amount of talk about Japanese savers' changing demands far outweighs actual rearrangement of portfolios.

People certainly ought to have had strong motivations to rearrange their portfolios to get the best rates of return. With higher income levels the absolute size of savings was larger, so that interest income was not trivial. At the same time, slower growth of income should have meant that people were more concerned with high returns on investment to reach desired levels of accumulated savings. Higher rates of return could make up for less rapidly growing additions to savings from annual income. The aging of the population, combined with greater uncertainty about the future ability of government to provide adequate social security benefits, should also have led to a change in expectations: people ought to have felt they had to rely more heavily on savings to provide retirement support and should have had a greater incentive to try to make savings grow more rapidly.

Another point, much discussed in Japan but rarely examined in any detail, is that the experience of 1973 and 1974 ought to have made individuals more sensitive about rates of return because interest rates on savings deposits at banks fell far below the level of inflation. During the 1960s, strict government regulations meant that the various types of banks paid virtually identical interest rates on deposits of the same maturity, and these rates remained almost unchanged (table 4-8). Two-year postal savings deposits, one-year commercial bank deposits, and one-year trust certificates at trust banks, for example, all paid 5.5 percent interest from 1961 to 1970 (postal savings accounts had the minor advantage of semiannual compounding). Nominal deposit rates remained roughly equal to consumer price inflation, so the real return was approximately zero: the average annual change in the consumer price index during the 1960s was 5.8 percent and the maximum paid on time deposits 5.5 percent (five-year loan trust certificates offered by the trust banks were an exception). This simple, stable world was severely rocked when consumer prices rose 11.7 percent in 1973, 24.5 percent in 1974, and 11.8 percent in 1975, while maximum interest rates on savings varied from 6 to 9 percent. Real returns were −4 to −7 percent in 1973 and 1975, and an enormous −17 percent in 1974. That the real value of deposits had plummeted was obvious to all and ought to have created strong incentives to move savings into other assets.

Negative real interest rates on savings deposits continued until 1978 (see table 4-8). Accounts yielding the maximum interest allowed lost almost 30 percent of their value from 1973 to 1978. During the second oil shock, however, interest rates managed to stay close to inflation rates and by the early 1980s were actually higher. In 1985, for example, an inflation rate of 2.1 percent meant that real interest rates ranged from 1.4 percent on three-month commercial bank time deposits to 3.6 percent on two-year bank and three-year postal savings time deposits. Five-year loan trusts at trust banks earned 4.5 percent. The years of negative real rates in the 1970s should have increased public awareness of rates of return, and indeed an annual survey of what people look for in financial assets shows that more of them are citing high rates of interest or capital gains and fewer are concerned with security or liquidity. In 1977, 23 percent of respondents emphasized return; in 1984, 32 percent. Those emphasizing security of principal were down from 42 percent to 38 percent, and those valuing liquidity down from 27 percent to 23 percent.[22]

But what has actually happened to personal financial asset portfolios, based on flow-of-funds data? Table 4-9 indicates that the percentage of total financial assets held in the most liquid, lowest-return form—cash and demand deposits—has indeed fallen. Ordinary demand deposits were pay-

22. Wakabayashi, "Naze Takai Nihon no Chochikuritsu" (Why Japan's High Savings Rate), *Nihon Keizai Shimbun*, December 16, 1984.

Table 4-8. *Time Deposit Interest Rates, by Type of Institution, 1969–85*[a]
Percent

Year	Inflation rate	Postal savings[b] Maximum (more than three years)	Minimum (less than one year)	Commercial banks Maximum (two years)	Minimum (three months)	Trust banks Maximum (five year loan trust)	Minimum (one year)
1969	5.2	5.5	4.2	5.5	4.0	7.27	5.5
1970	7.7	5.75 (4)	4.25 (4)	5.75 (4)	...	7.47 (3)	5.75 (4)
1971	6.1	6.0 (2)	...	6.0 (2)	...	7.27 (9)	...
1972	4.5	...	...	...	...	7.12 (4)	...
		5.5 (8)	4.0 (8)	5.5 (7)	3.75 (7)	6.82 (7)	5.25 (7)
1973	11.7	6.0 (4)	4.25 (4)	6.0 (4)	4.0 (4)	7.12 (4)	5.75 (4)
		6.5 (7)	...	6.5 (7)	...	7.42 (7)	6.0 (7)
		6.75 (10)	4.5 (10)	6.75 (10)	4.25 (10)	7.72 (9)	6.25 (9)
		...	...	...	...	8.52 (12)	...
1974	24.5	7.5 (1)	5.25 (1)	7.5 (1)	5.25 (1)	...	7.25 (1)
		8.0 (9)	6.0 (9)	8.0 (9)	5.5 (9)	9.02 (9)	7.75 (9)
1975	11.8	7.0 (11)	5.0 (11)	7.0 (11)	4.5 (11)	8.82 (8)	6.75 (11)
		...	...	...	...	8.32 (11)	...
1976	9.3	...	...	...	...	...	...
1977	8.1	6.0 (5)	4.25 (5)	6.0 (5)	3.75 (5)	7.52 (5)	5.75 (5)
		5.5 (9)	3.75 (9)	5.5 (9)	3.25 (9)	6.72 (9)	5.25 (9)
1978	3.8	4.75 (4)	3.0 (4)	4.75 (4)	2.5 (4)	6.22 (4)	4.5 (3)
1979	3.6	5.5 (5)	3.75 (5)	5.5 (5)	3.25 (5)	6.82 (5)	5.25 (5)
		6.25 (8)	4.5 (8)	6.25 (8)	4.0 (8)	7.32 (8)	6.0 (8)
1980	8.0	7.25 (3)	5.5 (3)	7.25 (3)	5.0 (3)	7.92 (2)	7.0 (3)
		8.0 (4)	6.5 (4)	8.0 (4)	6.0 (4)	8.62 (3)	7.75 (4)
		7.25 (12)	5.5 (12)	7.25 (12)	5.0 (12)	7.92 (12)	7.0 (12)
1981	4.9	6.5 (4)	4.75 (4)	6.5 (4)	4.25 (4)	7.62 (5)	6.25 (4)
		...	...	...	...	8.02 (11)	...
1982	2.7	6.0 (1)	4.25 (1)	6.0 (1)	3.75 (1)	7.72 (1)	5.75 (1)
		...	...	...	...	7.52 (4)	...
		...	...	...	...	8.02 (9)	...
1983	1.9	...	...	...	...	7.72 (1)	...
		...	...	...	...	7.52 (2)	...
		...	...	...	...	7.32 (11)	...
1984	2.2	5.75 (1)	4.0 (1)	5.75 (1)	3.5 (1)	7.02 (4)	5.5 (1)
		...	...	...	...	6.72 (11)	...
1985	2.1	...	...	...	...	6.62 (12)[c]	...

Sources: Bank of Japan, *Economic Statistics Annual, 1985*, pp. 177–78; *1979*, pp. 73–74; and "Main Economic Indicators of Japan," MOF *Monthly Finance Review* (August 1986).

a. Figures in parentheses refer to the month in which the interest rate was altered.

b. Maximum deposit rate in postal savings applied to two-year deposits in 1969, raised to two and a half years in 1971 and three years in 1973. Commercial bank maximum rates were similarly lengthened from one year to one and a half years and then two years at the same time.

c. Interest rate was altered six times during the year.

Table 4-9. *Distribution of Personal Financial Assets in Japan and the United States, by Type, 1971, 1985*[a]
Percent of total

	Japan		United States	
Type of asset	1971	1985	1971	1985
Cash and bank deposits	62.5	65.2	29.1	33.8
Cash and demand deposits	15.4	9.6	6.1	5.4
Time deposits	41.9	48.8	23.0	28.4
Trust deposits	5.2	6.8	...	...
Insurance	12.2	15.0	6.4	3.2
Securities				
Government securities	0.5	3.1	6.5	10.7
Government-owned				
corporation securities	1.5	0.9	...	...
Bank debentures	3.1	3.6	...	...
Corporate bonds	0.3	0.4	2.5	1.7
Corporate equity[b]	17.2	11.4	38.8	24.8
Other[c]	2.7	0.4	16.7	25.8

Sources: Board of Governors of the Federal Reserve System, *Flow of Funds Accounts, Financial Assets and Liabilities, Year End, 1962–85* (The Board, 1986), pp. 5–6; and Bank of Japan, *Economic Statistics Annual, 1985*, pp. 219–20; *1971*, pp. 17–18.

a. U.S. data are for the end of the calendar year; Japanese data are for March 31 of the year listed.

b. Includes mutual funds, investment trusts, and other fund arrangements investing in corporate equity. Corporate equities are valued at market prices rather than purchase cost.

c. Includes pension fund reserves, mortgages, and other miscellaneous assets for the United States.

ing only 1.5 percent interest in 1985, and as a form of investment are less useful than checking accounts in the United States because very few Japanese use checks. Most of the adjustment in personal portfolios has been to shift that money into time deposits, trust deposits, and bank debentures (the latter two closely resemble time deposits). The share of personal financial portfolios in bank time deposits, for example, increased from 42 percent to 49 percent between 1971 and 1985, despite the failure of time deposit interest rates to keep up with inflation in 1973–74. The only reasonable explanation is that time deposits at least provided a higher return than demand deposits, and people had been holding an excessively high proportion of their portfolios as cash and demand deposits.

Use of some other financial instruments also increased between 1971 and 1985, though not by as much as the use of time deposits. The share of portfolios held in the form of trust deposits was up by 1.6 percentage points; the cash value of insurance policies gained 2.8 points; bank debentures were up 0.5 point; and holdings of government bonds were up from a very minor 0.5 percent to 3.1 percent. Holdings of corporate equity, however, decreased sharply. Their share in Japanese portfolios declined by 34 percent, to only 11.4 percent in 1985.

Japanese investors still behave in ways quite different from Americans, whose portfolios depend less on cash, demand deposits, and time deposits. These categories together accounted for 58 percent of Japanese personal portfolios in 1985, but only 34 percent in the United States (see table 4-9). Instead, Americans held far more stocks and bonds. The other remarkable difference is the large proportion of U.S. personal financial assets that fall under the category of "other." A substantial share of this category consists of pension fund reserves, an item of rather recent origin not listed in Japanese flow-of-funds data as part of personal-sector assets. However, if pension funds are removed from the U.S. data for the sake of comparison, the picture presented in table 4-9 is not substantially altered; the portion of assets held in the form of cash, demand deposits, and time deposits in the United States rises somewhat to 43 percent, but so does the portion held as bonds and equity (to 34 percent).

Perhaps the most significant development in Japanese portfolios since the early 1970s is the drop in investment in corporate equities. One would expect that as incomes rose people would feel they could shift part of their financial portfolios into such higher-risk, higher-expected-return assets. Stock prices temporarily declined during the 1974 recession, but even starting from the high base year of 1973, the average annual increase to 1985 in the Nikkei–Dow Jones stock index has been 8.4 percent and in the Tokyo Stock Price Index 8.8 percent. Starting from the lower prices in 1974, the average annual gain through 1985 has been 10.3 percent and 11.3 percent, respectively. Considering that capital gains on long-term financial assets are not taxed, corporate equities have been a lucrative investment relative to bank deposits. Why then has the share of equities in personal portfolios nosedived?

One answer is that the Japanese tend to perceive the stock market as requiring specialized knowledge; and they remain convinced that even with special knowledge it represents a very high risk investment. In addition, brokers' branch offices are not as conveniently located as bank branches, and restrictions on advertising hinder the ability of securities companies to woo customers from the banks.[23] Perhaps this downward trend should not be overemphasized, however, since table 4-9 indicates a

23. Hirohiko Okumura, "Kakei no Kin'yū Kōdō to Kin'yū Kikō," (Household Financial Behavior and Financial Structure), *Gendai Keizai: Rinji Zōkan* (Contemporary Economics: Special Issue), no. 45 (November 1981), pp. 95–102.

similar development in the United States, where the share of portfolios held in the form of corporate equity has slipped from almost 39 percent in 1971 to less than 25 percent in 1985.[24]

Given the sluggish economic growth that brought slower growth of personal income, the negative performance of interest rates on time deposits during the 1973–74 inflation, and heightened anxiety about post-retirement income, the changes in personal financial portfolios appear modest. People have chosen to hold less money in assets with the lowest returns but have not to any great extent moved their holdings out of assets with controlled interest rates. One of the explanations is that consumer choice remained constrained. The large minimum denominations required for most of the new financial instruments such as certificates of deposit, banker's acceptances, and money market certificates effectively precluded individuals from the market. By the 1980s, however, banks and securities firms were constructing new forms of accounts built around mutual investment funds. These have grown rapidly, but even the most popular type, a medium-term government bond fund (the *chūki kokusai* fund) offered by securities companies, has not attracted a significant portion of individual investments.

If the changes in individual portfolio behavior have been so modest, what kind of pressure for change have they placed on the financial system? With the notable exception of the competition between the postal savings system and commercial banks for individuals' time deposits (explored in the following section), not much. Most of the financial innovations considered later in this chapter have been tailored to meet the needs of corporate depositors, not those of the individual. Nevertheless, Japanese investors' increased awareness of rates of return in choosing their portfolios and the perception that their awareness was changing may have been a factor in the pressure applied by financial institutions on the Ministry of Finance for more freedom in creating instruments with market-determined interest rates.

Shifts in Financial-Sector Competition

Given the changes in the economic environment and in both corporate and individual financial behavior, narrow specialization ought to have

24. The decline in the United States may be illusory, however, since the category "other" includes pension funds—many of which are invested in the stock market. Thus individual investors have been supplanted by institutional investors acting on their behalf.

Table 4-10. *Postal Savings Deposits, Selected Years, 1965–85*[a]
Billions of yen unless otherwise specified

Year	Postal savings deposits	Total deposits[b]	Postal savings as a percent of total
1965	2,703	35,393	7.6
1970	7,744	76,675	10.1
1973	15,377	141,396	10.9
1974	19,431	160,228	12.1
1975	24,566	187,227	13.1
1976	30,525	215,335	14.2
1977	37,726	242,666	15.5
1978	44,996	277,178	16.2
1979	51,912	306,354	16.9
1980	61,954	338,770	18.3
1981	69,568	374,806	18.6
1982	78,103	407,284	19.2
1983	86,298	442,764	19.5
1984	94,042	479,689	19.6
1985	102,998	520,380	19.8

Sources: Bank of Japan, *Economic Statistics Annual, 1985*, p. 99; and Bank of Japan, *Economic Statistics Monthly* (November 1986), p. 68.

a. A slight error is introduced because data for commercial institutions are for December 31 of each year, whereas postal savings figures are for the end of the fiscal year, March 31 of the following calendar year.

b. Includes all forms of demand and time deposits, certificates of deposit, and bank debentures, but excludes trust accounts. Deposits are calculated based on types of deposit-taking institutions listed in table 4-12, leaving out the regional and national organizations for the agricultural, fishing, and labor cooperatives. These organizations receive most of their deposits from their local organizations, which would result in double counting. Commercial banks also hold some deposits at other banks, but not to such a large degree.

resulted in considerable losses of market shares for some financial institutions and considerable gains for others. There does seem to have been a sizable movement of deposits toward the postal savings system. However, among all forms of commercial banking institutions, market shares have changed very little when measured by either deposits or total assets.

POSTAL SAVINGS. The share of the postal savings system in total deposits at financial institutions increased from the 11 percent or less that characterized the second half of the 1960s and early 1970s to the nearly 20 percent of the 1980s (table 4-10). This increase could have been caused by the prevalence of postal savings branches, which greatly outnumber those of the commercial banks because most post offices act as branches. But this situation was as true in the 1960s as in the 1980s. A more convincing explanation comes from consumers' beliefs that the rate of return on long-term time deposits is considerably higher than that obtainable at commercial banks. A third possibility lay in the nature of the tax system.

Even in the 1980s, interest rates on deposits at banks have remained strictly regulated. However, the increased concerns of depositors about rates of return have led to much heavier emphasis on deposit rates in bank advertising (although even the permissible forms of advertising are regulated). If consumers rely on advertising to judge the relative merits of postal savings deposits and commercial bank deposits, then the postal savings system looks more attractive. Advertising, though, relies on claims that would be illegal in the United States. For example, the maximum interest rate available on both postal savings time deposits and commercial bank deposits in 1985 was 5.75 percent (see table 4-8) with semiannual compounding on postal savings accounts and annual compounding at commercial banks. However, advertising brochures from the postal savings system claimed that if left in for ten years, deposits would earn an effective annual yield of 7.62 percent. In the example used in the advertising flier a deposit of ¥100,000 earns ¥76,277 in interest over ten years, a gain of 76.3 percent, which is declared to be a 7.63 percent annual return. The advertised yield is presented as if the interest earnings were withdrawn from the account as they accrued. But to achieve the advertised yield, semiannual interest earnings must be added to the principal as they accrue. The actual annual compound rate, the true effective yield, is 5.83 percent, which is what a bank in the United States would be allowed to advertise. Commercial banks advertise their interest rates in the same way. They have a maximum three-year time deposit and only annual compounding, but advertisements in 1985, with the same maximum 5.75 percent deposit rate as the postal savings system, claimed an effective return of 6.086 percent. In reality, the effective annual compound yield is exactly 5.75 percent because of the less frequent compounding.[25] Thus the difference between the two annual yields is 0.08 percentage point rather than the advertised difference of 1.54 percentage points.

The other major reason postal savings appeared to have gained so much

25. Some further widening of the difference could result from the timing of withdrawals. Money withdrawn from a commercial bank time deposit one day short of three years would earn only two years of interest at the lower two-year time deposit rate, a problem that is lessened in the postal savings system because of the semiannual payment of interest and because money kept in the account for as long as ten years continues to earn interest at the maximum interest rate after three years. In the commercial banks the money would have to be rolled over into another three-year account with the same problems of early withdrawal.

popularity among consumers involved after-tax rates of return. Both commercial banks and the postal savings system could offer tax-free savings deposits, but the opportunity to evade taxes by maintaining unreported accounts beyond the tax-free limit was far greater in the postal savings system. As incomes rose in the 1970s and the tax-free limit on savings stayed the same (it was last increased—to ¥3 million—in 1974), the number of investors with savings deposits over the limit ought to have increased rapidly, and thus the attractiveness of the postal savings system would have increased. That seems to have been the case. Between 1976 and 1985 the share of total deposits given tax-free treatment rose from 52.7 percent to 58.2 percent. Of the major institutions authorized to offer tax-exempt savings, the postal savings system showed the most rapid increase in assets, accounting for 35 percent of total tax-exempt savings in 1985.[26] The system was, in effect, engaging in a form of price competition, since the possibility of evading taxes meant that similar posted interest rates on commercial bank deposits and postal savings deposits would yield a considerably higher after-tax return for postal savings.

DEPOSITS. The market shares of commercial deposit-taking institutions, relative to one another, have shown suprisingly little change. Large institutions should have gained at the expense of small or specialized ones because of greater convenience and more diversified services (including credit cards). In addition, agricultural cooperatives ought to have been hurt as their membership base continued to erode. But rather than increasing their market share, city banks showed some loss (table 4-11), although most of the loss was concentrated in 1972–74. They have had a very stable position in the 1980s. The regional banks, trust banks, and long-term credit banks have shown no discernible movement in market share in either direction. The sōgo banks experienced some increase in market share in the 1970s (offsetting a previous decline), but their share declined slightly in the 1980s. Other smaller institutions—the shinkin banks, credit cooperatives, labor credit cooperatives, and agricultural cooperatives—also saw their share of the deposit market increase in the 1970s, although in some cases the changes predate 1973 and in all cases were minor. The shinkin banks and agricultural cooperatives experienced a slow decline in the 1980s, but not enough to identify any important trend.

That the larger institutions showed so few gains is perhaps due to the

26. Bank of Japan, *Economic Statistics Annual, 1985*, p. 158, provides data on the size of tax-free savings deposits.

Table 4-11. Shares of Total Bank Deposits, by Type of Financial Institution, 1965–85[a]

Percent

Year	City banks	Regional banks	Trust banks	Long-term credit banks	Sōgo banks	Shinkin banks	Credit co-ops	Labor credit co-ops	Agricultural and fisheries co-ops
1965	38.4	21.7	2.5	7.7	9.9	9.5	2.4	0.4	7.7
1966	37.4	21.9	2.4	7.9	9.8	9.7	2.5	0.4	8.1
1967	35.4	22.2	2.5	8.1	10.0	10.1	2.7	0.4	8.6
1968	35.9	22.4	2.4	8.1	8.8	10.3	2.8	0.4	8.8
1969	36.2	21.1	2.4	7.9	9.1	10.8	2.8	0.5	9.2
1970	35.4	21.0	2.5	7.9	9.2	11.2	2.9	0.5	9.3
1971	37.0	20.3	2.8	8.0	8.8	10.9	2.8	0.5	8.9
1972	37.2	20.2	2.7	8.1	8.8	11.0	2.7	0.5	8.8
1973	34.7	20.5	2.6	8.2	9.4	11.6	2.8	0.6	9.5
1974	33.3	20.7	2.5	8.2	9.9	12.0	3.0	0.7	9.8
1975	33.0	20.6	2.4	8.5	9.8	12.0	3.1	0.8	9.9
1976	32.7	20.6	2.3	8.4	9.8	12.1	3.1	0.9	10.0
1977	32.3	20.9	2.2	8.4	9.8	12.1	3.1	1.0	10.2
1978	32.3	21.3	2.1	8.2	9.9	12.1	3.0	1.0	10.1
1979	31.4	21.7	2.1	8.1	10.0	12.4	3.1	1.0	10.3
1980	31.7	21.4	2.0	7.9	9.9	12.5	3.1	1.1	10.4
1981	31.9	21.4	2.0	7.7	9.9	12.4	3.1	1.1	10.4
1982	31.3	21.7	2.1	7.8	10.0	12.5	3.1	1.1	10.4
1983	31.6	21.6	2.1	8.0	9.9	12.3	3.1	1.2	10.2
1984	31.6	22.2	2.1	8.4	9.3	12.2	3.1	1.2	10.1
1985	31.9	22.2	2.2	8.4	9.2	12.1	3.0	1.2	9.9

Sources: Bank of Japan, *Economic Statistics Annual, 1985*, pp. 49, 55, 61, 67, 78, 80, 83–84, 86–87; *1977*, pp. 81, 87, 93, 99, 138, 144, 153–54, 158; *1971*, pp. 134–35, 138–39.
a. Table excludes a number of regional and national institutions that primarily accept deposits from small credit associations. The institutions are: Nōrinchūkin, Shōkōchūkin, the National Federation of Credit Cooperatives, the National Federation of Labor Credit Cooperatives, the (regional) Credit Federations of Agricultural Cooperatives, and the (regional) Credit Federations of Fisheries Cooperatives. Since their deposits come mainly from the cooperatives listed in this table, their inclusion would result in double counting. Deposits include demand deposits, time deposits, certificates of deposit, and bank debentures. Trust accounts are not included.

small, specialized institutions' offsetting advantages. The smallest are allowed a minor interest rate advantage, and because they represent only one service of a broad membership organization, they have loyal depositors. Deposits might also be a poor measure of market share (although it is a measure watched very closely in Japan) because financial institutions have other ways to raise funds, including the call market and the gensaki market. During the high-growth era, for example, the call market played a major role in shifting surplus funds from the regional banks to the chronically fund-short city banks. Therefore total assets, representing the ability of institutions to find ways to invest funds acquired by deposits and other means, could be considered a better measure of what has happened since 1973.

TOTAL ASSETS. A reasonable hypothesis would be that the economic changes of the 1970s caused losses in market share of total assets for the smaller, most specialized institutions with offsetting gains for the larger, more diversified institutions. City banks and regional banks ought to have gained at the expense of the trust banks, long-term credit banks, sōgo banks, credit cooperatives, and agricultural cooperatives. The trust banks and long-term credit banks would be expected to have lost ground because they concentrated in long-term loans for such capital-intensive industries as steel, petrochemicals, and shipbuilding that were no longer growing rapidly. The sōgo banks and cooperatives specializing in loans to small business ought to have been hurt as large companies tried to push the cost of adjusting to slower growth onto their small suppliers and as large commercial banks turned to making loans to small businesses when demand from large corporations slowed.

Mortgages provide an example of shifting city bank activity. Such loans represented less than 3 percent of all commercial bank lending and just over 1 percent of city bank lending in the 1960s, but late in the decade they began to grow rapidly, reaching a peak of 9.4 percent by 1980 for all banks and 8.5 percent for the city banks. The ratio of new mortgages to total new loans was as high as 17 percent in some years during the mid to late 1970s.[27] However, since 1980 the share of mortgages in total out-

27. Ministry of Finance, *Ginkōkyoku Kin'yū Nempō, 1984* (Annual Report of the Banking Bureau, 1984) (Tokyo: Kin'yū Zaisei Jijō Kenkyūkai [Fiscal and Monetary Research Group], 1984), pp. 86–87. Regional banks, trust banks, long-term credit banks, and others also increased the share of their loan portfolios going to mortgages. Previously only the labor credit cooperatives and agricultural cooperatives had been heavily involved with mortgages (representing over half of labor credit cooperative lending and 10 to 16 percent of agricultural cooperative lending).

Table 4-12. *Shares of Total Bank Assets, by Type of Financial Institution, 1965–85*[a]
Percent

Year	City banks	Regional banks	Trust banks	Long-term credit banks	Sōgo banks	Shinkin banks	Credit co-ops	Labor credit co-ops	Agricultural and fisheries co-ops
1965	41.1	18.1	10.4	6.5	7.9	8.0	1.8	0.3	5.8
1966	39.2	18.6	10.2	6.7	8.3	8.4	1.9	0.3	6.3
1967	37.4	19.0	10.0	6.8	8.7	8.9	2.1	0.3	6.7
1968	37.8	19.1	9.9	6.8	7.6	9.2	2.2	0.4	7.0
1969	38.4	17.8	10.1	6.7	7.8	9.5	2.2	0.4	7.2
1970	37.9	17.7	10.5	6.7	7.8	9.7	2.2	0.4	7.2
1971	37.3	17.5	11.2	7.0	7.8	9.6	2.2	0.4	7.0
1972	37.1	17.2	11.7	7.1	7.8	9.7	2.1	0.4	6.9
1973	36.2	17.2	11.7	6.8	8.2	10.1	2.2	0.5	7.1
1974	35.8	17.0	11.8	6.9	8.4	10.2	2.2	0.5	7.1
1975	34.7	17.0	12.1	7.2	8.4	10.3	2.3	0.6	7.4
1976	34.1	17.0	12.6	7.2	8.3	10.3	2.3	0.7	7.5
1977	32.8	17.2	13.3	7.2	8.4	10.3	2.3	0.7	7.7
1978	32.0	17.5	14.0	7.0	8.4	10.2	2.4	0.7	7.8
1979	31.1	17.8	14.3	6.9	8.6	10.5	2.4	0.7	7.8
1980	31.4	17.6	14.2	6.9	8.4	10.4	2.4	0.7	7.9
1981	31.2	18.0	13.4	6.9	8.5	10.6	2.4	0.8	8.1
1982	30.8	17.8	14.5	6.9	8.3	10.4	2.4	0.8	8.0
1983	30.6	17.5	15.8	6.9	8.0	10.1	2.4	0.8	7.8
1984	30.3	17.6	17.1	7.0	7.4	9.9	2.3	0.8	7.5
1985	30.9	17.2	18.1	7.1	7.0	9.4	2.2	0.8	7.1

Sources: Bank of Japan, *Economic Statistics Annual, 1985*, pp. 50, 56, 62, 68, 72, 78, 80, 83–84, 86–87; *1977*, pp. 82, 88, 94, 100, 104, 138, 144, 153–54, 158; *1971*, pp. 134–35, 138–39.
a. Excludes same institutions as table 4-11.

standing bank loans has been declining somewhat, both for all banks and the city banks. This suggests that even though the banks cultivated the consumer market when corporate demand slipped, they still preferred corporate clients. In addition, the mortgage market turned out to be rather weak after the late 1970s (see chapter 3).

The large banks also became much more active in lending to small businesses, the traditional realm of the sōgo banks, shinkin banks, and credit cooperatives. For individual city banks the share of loans to medium and small businesses in their portfolios increased from levels of 27 to 37 percent in 1973 to levels of 48 to 52 percent by 1983.[28] The city banks were not legally restricted to large corporate customers during the high-growth era, but they did concentrate on them as being most appropriate, or less risky, or more in line with Ministry of Finance wishes. When the economy slowed, however, the city banks were not averse to finding new outlets for their money. Lending to small businesses should have been a direct threat to the specialized institutions catering to that sector.

Table 4-12, showing shares in total assets for the same types of commercial financial institutions covered in table 4-11, indicates that, as with deposit shares, the relative position of the city banks has actually eroded somewhat, and the shares of credit cooperatives and agricultural cooperatives have increased until recently. The major difference from deposit data is that the share of the trust banks (plus the trust assets of Daiwa Bank—a large city bank—the data for which are not separated from those on the pure trust banks) has increased since 1973 to represent more than 18 percent of total assets, and the increase accelerated after 1980. The acceleration stems from the expanding pension business as Japanese corporations began to move from lump-sum retirement settlements paid out of operating expenses to funded pension plans.

Other types of banks have experienced little change in shares. The long-term credit banks, sōgo banks, shinkin banks, credit cooperatives, labor credit cooperatives, and agricultural cooperatives all maintained their market shares until 1980. Since then the shares of the sōgo banks, shinkin banks, and agricultural cooperatives have decreased, but the changes are still too small and short-term to reflect any clear trend. The ability of the long-term credit banks to maintain their market share appears to depend on their ability to diversify their traditional portfolio of long-

28. Takashige Kondō, *Ginkō 10 Nengo no Hōkai Chizu: Dame ni Naru Ginkō Saiten* (A Scenario for Bank Collapse in Ten Years: Highlights of Banks That Will Fail) (Tokyo: Yell Publishing, 1984), p. 47.

Table 4-13. *Number of Financial Institutions and Branches, by Type,*
1965, 1973, 1985

	Institutions			Branches		
Type of Institution	1965	1973	1985	1965	1973	1985
City banks	13	13	13	1,978	2,397	2,766
Regional banks	63	63	64	3,936	4,428	6,120
Trust banks	7	7	7	226	268	353
Long-term credit banks	3	3	3	26	37	61
Sōgo banks	72	72	69	2,513	2,968	4,041
Shinkin banks	526	484	456	2,713	3,754	6,505
Shōkōchūkin Bank	1	1	1	63	70	86
Credit cooperatives	529	499	448	1,101	1,613	2,318
Labor credit associations	46	47	47	207	292	496
Nōrinchūkin Bank	1	1	1	26	27	28
Agricultural cooperatives	7,308	5,267	4,096[a]	10,267	12,412	12,370[a]

Sources: Bank of Japan, *Economic Statistics Annual, 1985*, p. 156; *1977*, p. 38.
a. Data are for end of 1984.

term loans to industry.[29] The decline of the sōgo banks (1.5 percentage points in the first half of the 1980s) may be related to the management problems of Heiwa Sōgo Bank, which was finally absorbed in 1986 by Sumitomo Bank, and not directly related to problems stemming from deregulation. This result is surprising; despite frequently expressed fears to the contrary, there is little evidence yet that small, specialized financial institutions are disappearing in Japan.

Data on the numbers of financial institutions does show some drop in the number of sōgo banks, shinkin banks, credit cooperatives, and agricultural cooperatives, but in most of these cases the declines are again not dramatic, generally representing a continuation of trends from the 1960s. Because the number of branches tended to increase despite the decline in the number of institutions (table 4-13), and because their share in total deposits and assets held up, the drop would appear to represent consolidations within these particular parts of the financial sector that are relatively unrelated to the economic changes that have taken place since the early 1970s.

Changing economic conditions could also have affected the competitive

29. Loans were 72 percent of total long-term credit bank assets in 1970, slipping to 64 percent by 1985. Securities made up the difference, rising from 11 percent to 19 percent of assets. Government securities were part of this change, growing from 2.1 percent to 7.3 percent of total assets. Bank of Japan, *Economic Statistics Annual, 1985*, pp. 65–70; *1971*, pp. 85–89.

Table 4-14. *Securities Companies Assets, 1970–85*[a]

Year	Total assets (trillions of yen)	Percent of combined assets of banks and securities companies
1970	1,838	1.9
1971	2,267	1.9
1972	2,841	1.9
1973	2,842	1.6
1974	2,988	1.4
1975	3,157	1.3
1976	3,607	1.3
1977	4,036	1.4
1978	4,745	1.4
1979	5,371	1.5
1980	6,096	1.5
1981	6,808	1.6
1982	6,466	1.4
1983	8,834	1.7
1984	10,869	1.9
1985	13,088	2.0

Sources: Table 4-12, plus Ministry of Finance, *Ōkurashō Shōkenkyoku Nempō, 1986* (MOF Securities Bureau Yearbook, 1986) (Tokyo: Kin'yū Zaisei Jijō Kenkyūkai, 1986), p. 447; *1985*, p. 384; *1984*, p. 386; *1983*, p. 402; *1982*, p. 382; *1981*, p. 393; *1980*, p. 375; *1979*, p. 361; *1978*, p. 359; *1977*, p. 327; *1976*, p. 335; *1975*, p. 331; *1974*, p. 339; *1973*, p. 397; *1972*, p. 393.

a. Total assets for the securities companies are measured as of the end of September (the end of their accounting year) while those of banks are as of the end of December. Since the assets of securities companies consist heavily of equity shares with market-determined values that are counted at purchase value, assets are understated.

balance between banking institutions and securities firms. Table 4-14 shows the total assets of Japanese securities firms and compares them with the total assets of the deposit-taking institutions. Assets of securities firms appear small because a large part of their business is brokerage—they buy and sell securities on behalf of clients, but ownership of the securities rests with the clients.[30] Nevertheless, the comparison is instructive. The relative size of security firms' assets declined in the mid-1970s but began to rise in the 1980s, returning them to the position of the early 1970s. Assets grew at a 15.3 percent annual rate from 1976 to 1985 while those of banks grew at 10.4 percent. Securities may have been the beneficiaries of financial deregulation during the decade, but the real differential in performance is very recent, a product of the 1980s, when security firms acceler-

30. In 1983 brokerage accounted for 51.8 percent of the income of securities firms, with an additional 14.6 percent from underwriting, while only 12.5 percent came from dealing (buying and selling securities owned by the firm) and another 21.1 percent came from other activities. Ministry of Finance, *Ōkurashō Shōkenkyoku Nempō, 1984* (MOF Securities Bureau Yearbook, 1984) (Tokyo: Kin'yū Zaisei Jijō Kenkyūkai, 1984), p. 387.

ated moderately to achieve 16.5 percent average annual growth. This could well represent the early phases of a continued gain in market share.

PROFITS. Some institutions may have struggled to maintain their market shares at the expense of profits. Since market shares are so prominently discussed and compared in Japan, market-share competition is considered by many to provide a better explanation of corporate behavior than the standard economic theory of profit maximization. For example, large banks have competed fiercely for the more slowly growing corporate loan market, leading to endless complaints from bankers about the shrinking difference between the cost of funds and interest rates on loans.

Table 4-15 shows the return on net worth reported by six types of deposit-taking institutions plus the securities companies.[31] In the early 1970s all these institutions were quite profitable, but the smaller institutions tended to be more profitable than the large ones. From 1971 to 1974, for example, the average profit rate for the sōgo banks was 32.2 percent, and for the shinkin banks, 28.4 percent, while the city banks averaged 26.5 percent and the regional banks 27.8 percent. All types of banks showed a decline in profitability in the mid to late 1970s, which corresponds to the time when plant and equipment investment by the corporate sector was weakest. It is not surprising that the trust banks (specializing in long-term loans for plant and equipment) were the most affected.

As these institutions rebounded from the slump in profits, their performances varied considerably. The city banks and trust banks came back strongly: city bank profitability in 1981–84 averaged 22.7 percent annually and the trust banks 22.5 percent. While weaker than in the early 1970s, this performance is broadly consistent with that of nonfinancial corporations (see table 3-3). The trust banks appear to have benefited from their right to manage pension funds. Their recovery in the 1980s pushed their average return on net worth higher than that of the city banks. The long-term credit banks, with much the same lending portfolio as the trust banks but without the right to manage pensions, failed to stage a similar

31. Data for this table are based on the *Ginkōkyoku Kin'yū Nempō,* as indicated. Although the Bank of Japan *Economic Statistics Annual* also contains balance-sheet profit data for banks, they are inconsistent with the data used here, mainly because the balance sheets are not complete and the profit figures are unreliable. The more complete and detailed data in the *Ginkōkyoku Kin'yū Nempō* yield more believable results, but even these data seriously understate net worth for the same reason as do data on nonfinancial companies (discussed in chapter 3)—the valuation of land and other assets (in this case, corporate stock) at purchase cost. This means that return on net worth is overstated, but this should not invalidate the comparisons among different types of institutions or changes over time.

Table 4-15. *Banking Industry Return on Net Worth,*
by Type of Institution, Fiscal Years 1971–84[a]

Fiscal year	City banks	Regional banks	Long-term credit banks	Trust banks	Sōgo banks	Shinkin banks	Securities firms
1971	30.6	29.0	24.9	34.4	30.4	29.8	30.3
1972	27.3	24.9	26.3	26.7	31.0	28.5	42.6
1973	23.8	25.8	20.1	26.5	32.1	24.1	35.0
1974	24.4	31.3	18.3	24.5	35.2	31.1	9.1
1975	20.3	21.0	19.7	19.7	24.0	27.0	17.1
1976	20.5	18.8	23.5	19.4	21.7	22.4	22.8
1977	16.3	18.7	23.9	15.2	19.9	21.8	31.2
1978	17.4	16.4	19.6	15.8	18.7	19.4	31.1
1979	13.1	14.6	16.4	14.1	17.5	14.3	21.3
1980	16.2	14.7	15.6	12.3	16.4	14.5	19.6
1981	19.7	14.1	11.9	23.2	16.1	14.1	23.2
1982	22.9	17.1	14.7	27.7	20.0	17.7	12.0
1983	24.5	18.3	20.0	16.6	20.0	17.9	27.0
1984	23.8	16.3	18.2	22.6	18.3	15.7	30.0

Sources: Ministry of Finance, *Ginkōkyoku Kin'yū Nempō, 1985* (Banking Bureau Finance Annual, 1985) (Tokyo: MOF, 1985), pp. 156, 163, 410–11, 415, 424, 427; *1984*, pp. 161, 168, 438–39, 443, 452, 455; *1983*, pp. 201, 209, 464–65, 469, 478, 481; *1982*, pp. 197, 205, 452–53, 457, 466, 469; *1981*, pp. 251, 268, 584–85, 588–89, 593, 602, 605; *1980*, pp. 182, 195, 446–47, 450–51, 455, 464, 467; *1979*, pp. 250, 263, 558–59, 562–63, 567, 576, 579; *1978*, pp. 218, 498–99, 502–03, 507, 516, 519; *1977*, pp. 187, 199, 442–43, 446–47, 451, 460, 463; *1976*, pp. 202, 219, 474–75, 478–79, 483, 492, 495; *1975*, pp. 203, 217, 466–67, 470–71, 475, 484, 487; *1974*, pp. 203, 218, 484–85, 488–89, 493, 502, 505; *1973*, pp. 179, 199, 468–69, 474–75, 486, 514, 517; *1972*, pp. 195, 212, 488–89, 492–93, 504, 534, 537; and Ministry of Finance, *Ōkurashō Shōkenkyoku Kin'yū Nempō, 1986*, pp. 447–48; *1985*, pp. 384–85; *1984*, pp. 386–87; *1983*, pp. 402–03; *1982*, pp. 382–83; *1981*, pp. 393–94; *1980*, pp. 375–76; *1979*, pp. 361–62; *1978*, pp. 359–60; *1977*, pp. 327–28; *1976*, pp. 335–36; *1975*, pp. 331–32; *1974*, pp. 339–40; *1973*, pp. 397–98; *1972*, pp. 393–94.

a. The profit measure is before-tax profits, including all operating, nonoperating, and extraordinary items. Net worth is based on reported figures for *shihon* (capital) or *jiko shihon* (own capital). For securities firms, the reporting year ends in September rather than December.

recovery, averaging only a 16.2 percent return on net worth in 1981–84. Without the advantage of pension funds, profitability at the trust banks probably would have been closer to that of the long-term credit banks. The smaller institutions did not fare as well, either. The profitability of the sōgo banks was only 18.6 percent annually and for the shinkin banks only 16.4 percent.

Profitability is rarely featured in Japanese data, but table 4-15 suggests that it should be. Some types of institutions maintained their relatively stable market shares in deposits or assets at a significant cost. In the short run the lack of emphasis on profits in Japanese data may be justified; banks may choose to compete for share without much attention to profits. Over a longer time span, profitability must matter. Unprofitable institutions simply cannot afford to continue expanding.

Tables 4-12 and 4-15 further suggest the attraction of pension funds as a factor motivating pressure for change. Not only did the market share of the trust banks expand, but the added business was very lucrative. The city banks also proved to be relatively adept at adjusting to and benefiting from the market and regulatory changes of the 1980s. But the weak profitability of the other institutions must have been of concern both to them and to the Ministry of Finance.

These data further confirm the relative success of the securities firms. They shared the decline in profitability during the 1970s (keeping in mind that profits tend to be more variable from year to year because of the short-term variability in the stock market): from an average of 35.9 percent in 1970–73, the return on net worth dropped to 21.7 percent in 1974–80. Since 1980, profits have recovered somewhat, averaging 23.1 percent from 1981 to 1984, and reaching their early 1970s level by 1984. Thus their relative success in expanding their market share did not come at the expense of lower profit rates. The combination of rapid growth and rising profits puts these firms in a strong, expanding position, and may explain the pressure from the banking sector on the government to lower the barriers between banking and dealing in securities.

SUMMARY. The rapid rise in government debt, the slowdown in the growth of corporate investment demand, and the continuation of high rates of individual saving brought important changes in corporate and household financial behavior. Weaker corporate investment demand meant less dependence on bank loans, slower growth of bank lending to the corporate sector, and changes in corporate financial portfolios as managers became more concerned with rates of return. Individuals also became concerned with returns on their investments because of the experience with negative real interest rates on savings accounts in the mid-1970s, slower growth in disposable income, and greater uncertainty over future social security benefits. Household portfolio diversification remained modest, however, represented largely by a greater preference for time deposits in the postal savings system.

These developments ought to have caused realignments of competitive positions among various types of financial institutions because of their high degree of specialization and heavy government regulation of interest rates. Four changes stand out. First, the postal savings system expanded its share of total financial-sector deposits. Second, because of an aging population and the decision of many corporations to convert to funded pensions, the relative market share of the trust banks, which shared a monopoly over this business with the life insurance companies, expanded rapidly. Third, otherwise stable market shares among types of banks belied an emerging gap in profitability, with the city banks and trust banks doing well and other types suffering. Finally, increasing awareness of higher rates of return, coupled with brokerage related to the rapidly growing pension funds, worked to benefit securities firms.

Government Policy Response

Government regulation of the financial sector has heavily influenced the portfolio choices available to corporations and individuals and affected the market shares of financial institutions. The pressure to change the regulatory framework had to be transmitted to the Ministry of Finance (mainly through the financial institutions rather than directly by depositors and borrowers) and then put through the process of government decision-making.

Many Japanese felt that the financial system of the 1950s and 1960s had worked well. Could the government have avoided change in the 1970s? No. There was a limit to the amount of new government bonds the syndicate of financial institutions could be forced to accept without the government's acceding to demands for interest rates closer to market levels. Nor could the government have held off criticisms about the unfair competition of the postal savings system and the trust banks, since the whole concept of segmentation was premised on government regulation to maintain a modicum of stability among institutions. The only way the government could have avoided change would have been to keep its own deficit spending at low levels, discourage the establishment of funded pension systems, and end the advantages of the postal savings system for individual savers by eliminating the system's tacit abetment of tax evasion. None of these alternatives seemed feasible in the 1970s.

Ministry of Finance Motivations

Since some changes in the regulation of the financial sector were inevitable, understanding the motivations of the Ministry of Finance in approaching the problem is essential for analyzing its decisions. Three overlapping factors come into play: the nature of Japanese society and behavior, the ministry's perception of its responsibilities toward the financial sector, and the tempering quality of intragovernmental organization and conflict for decisionmaking.

THE SOCIOLOGY OF JAPAN. The economic changes discussed in previous chapters can be summarized and analyzed with statistics, but the bureaucrats in the Ministry of Finance charged with regulating the financial system are Japanese. Their perceptions of the meaning of the available economic data were necessarily filtered through their cultural values, values generally different from the ones Americans hold.

First, the decisions of ministry officials have been characterized by a distinctly Japanese desire to avoid winner-take-all situations. Those on the losing side of an issue cannot be entirely ignored and left to cope with their loss; in its role as a regulator the government feels an obligation to provide some form of compensation to make the outcome more "fair." The government cannot, for example, simply exercise rights of eminent domain and force property owners to sell their land at an administratively or court-determined price; it must negotiate a compensatory package for them. The government's failure to abide sufficiently by this social doctrine was an important ingredient in the long-running conflict over the construction of the new international airport at Narita.

As a corollary, the Japanese often avoid direct confrontation with an issue or problem, preferring instead to accomplish all or part of the desired outcome without eliminating the earlier policy. As discussed previously, their solution to the negotiated interest rates on ten-year government bonds was to create a broader set of bond maturities floated through tender offers. They have also preferred to grant ever-larger quotas for imported beef (to the point that the quotas will eventually become meaningless) rather than eliminate the beef quota per se. They can thus contain the policy or institution that is the object of change and diminish its importance without entirely ignoring the concerns of those who have a vested interest in its existence.

The desire to avoid winner-take-all situations results in a propensity for consensus decisions. This does not mean that conflict and disagreement are suppressed but rather that negotiations often continue far beyond what is necessary to achieve a majority decision. In the social dynamics of this process, there comes a point when those on what is becoming the losing side will withdraw their opposition, secure in the belief that their position or welfare will not be entirely ignored. But building a consensus on such important issues as deregulation of the financial sector takes so long that once a decision is made, it is difficult to change direction. For example, it would be difficult to reimpose the rigid regulatory structures of the 1960s on the financial sector in Japan in the absence of some major new development (such as a wave of institutional bankruptcies).

When solutions must result in winners and losers, the Japanese try to find an external catalyst to force the issue. This *gaiatsu* (outside pressure) has become a standard feature of bilateral trade negotiations. Japanese officials have frequently asked their U.S. counterparts to apply pressure to help them carry out a desired policy change. Without that external threat, they fear an inability to overcome domestic opposition or reach an acceptable compromise. This tactic will show up in the discussion that follows of some situations when the needs or demands of foreign financial institutions became the motivation for creating new financial instruments that were then dominated by Japanese institutions.

The Japanese can also be characterized as having greater respect for authority than Americans. Private-sector businessmen often speak about the government and government officials with considerable contempt but remain much more willing to listen to the government and ultimately accept its guidance than is the case in the United States. As a corollary, those in authority have an obligation to use their position in a benevolent or paternalistic way so that the respect is justified. Thus financial institutions have been willing to accept heavy government regulation in exchange for greater security. This characteristic, however, tends to lead those in authority to assume that their charges are incapable of making decisions on their own; one frequently hears government officials referring to private industry in the terms of a parent talking about children.

Because of their desire to avoid risk, the Japanese especially dislike surprises and uncertainty. Of course, no one likes uncertainty, but its avoidance is a remarkably strong trait in Japan, resulting in lengthy discussions on pending policy issues so that all parties considered relevant to the decision will know in advance the likely outcome and can adapt to it. For example, far from the secrecy that surrounds the decisions of the U.S. Federal Open Market Committee, which determines Federal Reserve open market operations to control money supply, decisions on Bank of Japan discount rate changes, an important tool of monetary policy, are preceded by months of leaks to the press, official denials, and other signals, so that the changes are never a surprise. Again, an article published in January 1984 stated that the minimum denomination of certificates of deposit would drop to ¥300 million in 1984, followed by reductions to ¥100 million, and then to as low as ￥10 million within two or three years. Since the decision for even the initial reduction had not been taken at that point, it is interesting that a private-sector Japanese observer could predict the result so confidently.[32]

As a means for promoting consensus and communication with affected parties, the Japanese government makes extensive use of advisory bodies. These groups run the gamut from formal commissions (*shingikai*) established by law, and which must be consulted on particular issues, to informal study groups (*kondankai*) for considering possible policies. Membership is determined by the government and includes representatives from the relevant industry and from academe, journalism, and sometimes labor.

Another characteristic is that in all contacts the informal predominates over the formal. Just as the Japanese avoid direct confrontation with thorny issues, so they try to avoid it between individuals or organizations. Direct confrontation through the courts is frequently resorted to in the United States but not in Japan. Any Japanese organization that feels unfairly treated by a government decision would be very reluctant to use a court challenge to seek redress. To do so would be inappropriate. The government, to encourage this behavior, severely limits the number of judges, creating a very long backlog of cases. Therefore, court decisions have not been an important part of changes in the financial sector in the past decade.

Preference for informal interactions does not mean that laws are not important. All regulation of the financial sector is firmly based on law, but Japanese laws typically give government ministries broad latitude in interpretation and implementation. When, for instance, administrative decisions on deregulation had proceeded far enough to make the legal framework awkward, new legislation was written by the Ministry of Finance and enacted. The Banking Law of 1927 was replaced with a new banking law in 1981, and the Foreign Exchange Control Law of 1949 was extensively amended in 1979.[33]

Finally, the Japanese try to avoid fundamental change. Thus institutional structures that appear fragile or full of contradictions are often surprisingly stable and enduring. The entire governmental system of the

32. Hirohiko Okumura, "Financial Liberalization Gathers Pace," *Banker* (January 1984), p. 76.

33. For a review of the Banking Law, see Brian W. Semkow, "Japanese Banking Law: Current Deregulation and Liberalization of Domestic and External Financial Transactions," *Law and Policy in International Business*, vol. 17 (1985), pp. 81–155.

Tokugawa period (1600–1867), for example, involved a seemingly tenuous balance of power between the central government and the quasi-independent local domains, between long-time supporters of the Tokugawa family and those who had fought against them in 1600, and among the samurai, merchant, and peasant classes. But this balance provided stable political rule for Japan for two and a half centuries. Even the increasingly evident problems and failures of the system were not enough to bring about its overthrow until the emergence of a foreign threat galvanized domestic opposition.[34]

This tendency toward stability suggests two features of government decisionmaking on issues affecting the financial sector: a preference for marginal changes and the usefulness of a crisis atmosphere. More than in the United States, decisions in Japan involve marginal or incremental alterations, and even these seem to take an inordinate time to accomplish as the decisionmaking process considers their relationship to the overall institutional framework. To achieve substantial change, a crisis, real or manufactured, has frequently been useful. Crises provide opportunities to bring together seemingly unrelated proposals and obtain some action on all of them. For example, offering market-access packages to the United States has become almost an annual affair, carried out when the Japanese government perceives a crisis in bilateral relations. This last point is important in understanding the yen-dollar accord of 1984, which will be discussed in chapter 5.

Despite these peculiarly Japanese characteristics, Japan and the United States cannot be considered as representing opposite extremes of social behavior. People in both countries are motivated by many of the same goals and desires. Still, the patterns of reactions and decisions in the two countries do lie at different points along a spectrum. That the Japanese generally behave in ways different from Americans must be recognized in looking at financial-sector policy.

MINISTRY PERCEPTIONS OF ITS ROLE. Reflecting the general social characteristics of Japan, the Ministry of Finance has been motivated by a very

34. One of the great anomalies of postwar Japan has been the continuing propensity for risk aversion, the desire to avoid surprises, and the desire to maintain stability all existing in the presence of major and rapid economic and social changes. One explanation is that the very speed of change necessitated the social features explored here. Consensus, information exchange, avoidance of winner-take-all, and other characteristics became a way to reduce the risks and conflicts inherent in rapid change to a manageable level, thereby enabling change to proceed.

strong desire to maintain stability and balance among financial institutions, a desire to promote safety and stability for the system as a whole, a very practical desire to hold down the cost of government debt, and a natural inclination to maintain its own bureaucratic power.

The overriding factor in all MOF decisions on deregulation of the financial sector in the 1970s and 1980s was the desire to maintain the balance among the various types of institutions. Since segmentation of the market was a product of early postwar regulation, protecting the position of the institutions that had accepted and grown within that framework seemed paramount. But the very concept of deregulation implies a wider latitude for competition and competitive gains and losses, so that the goals of deregulation and maintaining balance are somewhat contradictory. Whether balance can ultimately be maintained, though, has been less important to government officials than the need to make decisions that will be accepted by the financial sector as representing a best effort toward that goal.

An excellent example of how this desire has affected decisions comes from a six-point policy announcement made by the ministry in 1985 that included three new activities in which commercial banks could engage and three for securities companies. As that decision was being made, all the press reports focused on balance—whether the MOF would be able to mediate the conflicting demands of banks and securities companies. That it had an obligation to maintain a sense of balance in working out the final decision was simply assumed to be the governing principle.[35] By so doing, neither side would feel that it had lost more than it gained in the process; losers and winners could be avoided, and the ministry could make its announcement knowing that both banks and securities companies would support it. The private sector could respect the government's decision, and the government could continue to deserve that respect within the operation of Japanese social mores.

The final announcement in this case was made on March 29, after many months of discussion and widespread advance knowledge of the outcome:

—The number of domestic and foreign banks allowed to deal in government bonds would be increased in June 1985 from the existing list of thirty-four city and regional banks plus three foreign banks to forty-four city and regional banks, one sōgo bank, and six foreign banks.

—The banks dealing in government bonds would be allowed access to

35. See, for example, *Japan Economic Journal,* January 15, 1985.

the services of Nihon Sōgo Shōken, a broker's broker for government bonds used by all the securities companies. The creation of a second bond broker would be considered.

—Banks dealing in government bonds would be allowed to participate in the soon-to-be-created bond futures market (even though they were not members of the Tokyo Stock Exchange, where the futures market would be located).

—Securities firms would be allowed to deal in certificates of deposit, an activity formerly restricted to banks.

—Securities firms would be allowed to participate in the newly created banker's acceptance market (which began in June 1985) from April 1986.

—Securities firms would be allowed to create revolving accounts combining a demand deposit and a government bond fund in which automatic loans based on the collateral in bond investments would be made to the demand deposit account whenever the balance fell below zero.[36]

The final package thus offered three gains for banks, allowing them to expand further their dealing in government bonds, an area previously reserved for securities firms, and three gains for the securities firms, allowing them to move into areas previously reserved for banks. That some of these changes seem rather minor is not important; the appearance of balance was preserved and progress in the direction of deregulation was maintained.

In addition to maintaining an acceptable balance among concessions, the Ministry of Finance has been concerned with preserving the stability and safety of the financial system as a whole. An important element of this goal is a broad requirement that financial transactions be backed by collateral, a requirement that has been applied to bank loans, call market loans, and corporate bond issues since the 1920s and 1930s in hopes that collateral would reduce the risk of default. But the mandatory collateral requirements for all transactions and the firm belief in their necessity put Japan at odds with developments in other industrial countries.

Why has the MOF adopted such a strong position on safety and security in the financial system? If a weak bank should fail because of increased competition generated by deregulation, people would blame the government for allowing the situation to develop, a strong contrast with the United States, where the runs on savings banks in Ohio and Maryland in

36. Ministry of Finance, "Kōkyōsai Shijō Oyobi Tanki Kin'yū Shijō no Seibi Kakujū ni Tsuite" (Concerning the Expansion of Arrangements for Public Bonds and Short-term Financial Markets), mimeo, March 29, 1985.

1985 brought outrage against the poor investment decisions made by the banks involved but very little blame on the state governments for having allowed these institutions to get themselves into trouble. (Blame was attached only later for slow or ineffective state policies to solve the problems and enable depositors to regain access to their deposits.) In Japan, far more anger would be directed at the MOF for letting this situation occur. The outcome—emergency government measures to prevent losses to any depositor and arrangement of takeovers by larger, stronger institutions— might be the same in either country, but the attribution of blame would be noticeably different.

Such a situation actually developed in Japan early in 1986. The Heiwa Sōgo Bank, one of the larger sōgo banks, was rapidly approaching bankruptcy.[37] The bank was saddled with an inordinate number of nonperforming loans, a problem caused by its own management failures and not deregulation. Nevertheless, the MOF arranged several bailout measures, including assignment of some retired ministry and Bank of Japan officials to management posts, provision of emergency loans to the bank at concessionary interest rates, and arrangement of additional loans from other commercial banks. When these measures failed to solve the problem, the ministry engineered a takeover by Sumitomo Bank. All this occurred quickly and without harm or inconvenience to depositors.[38]

MOF officials frequently mention the experience of the 1920s and 1930s, when there were many bank failures in Japan, as an explanation of why the public expects them to help maintain confidence in the system and why they must proceed so carefully and slowly in carrying out deregulation. The United States has moved much more boldly in allowing the creation of new financial instruments, deregulating interest rates, and generally allowing increased competition in the financial sector, but Japanese officials watch such activities very closely (and with great skepticism). They have no desire to create problems like those experienced by the Ohio and Maryland thrift institutions.

A further motivation for the ministry is a very reasonable desire to keep the cost of government debt low. This should be evident from the earlier

37. Heiwa Sōgo Bank had assets of ¥1.4 trillion ($5.9 billion at average 1983 exchange rates), making it the fifth largest sōgo bank and considerably larger than some of the regional banks. Sumitomo Bank, which absorbed Heiwa Sōgo Bank in 1986, had ¥25.7 trillion in total assets in 1983 ($108 billion). Ministry of Finance, *Ginkōkyoku Kin'yū Nempō, 1984*, pp. 566, 638–40.

38. *Japan Times Weekly,* December 21, 1985; and *Japan Economic Journal,* February 22, 1986.

discussion of what happened to the issuance of government bonds. As late as 1984 one official was quoted as saying, "We're having trouble issuing any bonds at all. We can't get banks to buy government bonds . . . unless we raise the interest rate. The bonds would sell at a higher interest rate, but can the government afford to set such an example and initiate a high-interest policy?"[39] In a country that experienced a net capital outflow of more than $30 billion in 1984 because of a surplus of savings over private and government demands for funds, this statement appears ludicrous. In fact, by 1984 government debt issued at market rates was a substantial share of the total, and the negotiating process on ten-year bonds had brought issuing rates close to market rates. The control over interest rates that this official wished to maintain was already gone, but the desire to continue the appearance of maintaining rates below market level remained.

Finally, MOF officials are motivated by a simple desire to maintain their bureaucratic power. It would be surprising if they were not. Rarely has the ministry completely eliminated regulations that involve a role for itself. Officials would be denying their own importance or damaging their self-esteem if they wrote themselves out of active responsibility for regulating the financial sector. Even where formal approval requirements have been eliminated, informal controls remain. Few if any financial institutions would dare venture into new areas of business without first consulting with the MOF and obtaining its consent, even if formal approval is unnecessary.

INTRAGOVERNMENTAL RELATIONS. In setting new policies for the financial sector, the ministry must contend not only with the demands and expectations from financial institutions and the public but also with the internal conflicts of the bureaucracy. This constraint applies both to dealings among government ministries and those within the Ministry of Finance itself, and acts as yet another limiting influence on the decisions taken.[40]

The MOF has four bureaus that oversee the financial sector: Banking,

39. Sōichirō Tahara, "Six Views on the Asset-Doubling Plan," *Japan Echo,* vol. 11, (Winter 1984), p. 35.

40. James Horne, *Japan's Financial Markets,* focuses on the intra- and interministerial decisionmaking process in financial deregulation, as well as interaction between the bureaucracy and the politicians. He emphasizes the conflicts among bureaus within the MOF, or between the MOF and other ministries, and how these were resolved in a number of particular cases during the 1970s and early 1980s.

Securities, Insurance, and International Finance. Each concerns itself with the health and welfare of a single segment of the financial sector, and the mechanisms for overall coordination of policy are relatively weak. Thus, for example, the March 1985 decision expanding the activities permitted banks and securities companies involved not only the resolution of conflicting demands by these two types of institutions but also resolving conflicts between the Banking Bureau and the Securities Bureau. As with the general social characteristics discussed previously, bureaucratic infighting is by no means unique to Japan, but it does appear to be more serious than in the United States.[41]

The Ministry of Finance is also divided between internationalists and domestic officials (again involving separate bureaus, since the International Finance Bureau is in charge of international issues), with the internationalists often in favor of greater deregulation out of both conviction and because they personally bear the brunt of contact with foreign governments. Those in domestic divisions are less exposed and less disposed to changes demanded for purposes of international relations.

A further barrier to intragovernmental relations is the political leanings of officials. While all but the minister and the political vice minister are career employees, many important officials are known to be closely associated with one or another faction of the Liberal Democratic party or with particular politicians. These associations are known among bureaucrats and affect the support or opposition for particular policies, as well as the shifting power and prestige of individual officials. The image many Americans have of the Japanese bureaucracy—that it is largely independent of politicians—needs serious modification. Conversely, a sizable number of Diet members belonging to the Liberal Democratic party are former MOF officials, giving them another set of personal relationships and influence among their former colleagues.[42]

41. Albert M. Craig, "Functional and Dysfunctional Aspects of Government Bureaucracy," in Ezra F. Vogel, ed., *Modern Japanese Organization and Decision-Making* (University of California Press, 1975), pp. 3–32, discusses the problems within the bureaucratic structure.

42. Horne, *Japan's Financial Markets*, pp. 212–13, notes that although few of the case studies he examined involved overt participation by politicians, close communications between MOF officials and LDP Diet members resulted in implicit understanding by the officials of the political constraints involved in designing new policies. This understanding generally made direct intervention by the politicians unnecessary. However, on broader issues politicians are involved since new legislation is required; both the green card and value-added tax debates suggest that the bureaucracy does not always interact smoothly with the political process.

The most important intragovernmental division, though, is between the Ministry of Finance and the Ministry of Posts and Telecommunications. The postal savings system, under the control of the Ministry of Posts and Telecommunications, has caused serious territorial conflict, as during the green card fiasco when the MOF tried to crack down on tax evasion on large savings deposits in the postal savings system. The Ministry of Finance also lacks control over the interest rates paid on postal savings deposits, so that government discussions of whether to lower the Bank of Japan discount rate when monetary policy is being eased, which then leads to reductions in deposit rates at commercial banks, always involve heated exchanges with postal savings officials, who resist any reduction in their deposit rates.[43] The relationship is made more complex because the money raised through this savings system is turned over to the Trust Fund Bureau of the Ministry of Finance to be lent through the Fiscal Investment and Loan Program. Postal savings officials have been arguing for some autonomy in investing the money deposited in their system, since they desire a greater return than that provided by the Ministry of Finance. In particular, the Ministry of Posts and Telecommunications would like to keep part of the postal savings money so that it could be invested overseas, as is now allowed for part of the money raised through postal life insurance.

A final interministerial rift is between the Ministry of Finance and the Bank of Japan. Although the Bank of Japan is legally an independent organization somewhat along the lines of the Federal Reserve System in the United States, it is often regarded as little more than a branch of the Ministry of Finance, a reputation not helped by the fact that the president of the bank has occasionally been a retired MOF official. However, the bank is not entirely under ministry control, and attitudes on financial issues do not always coincide. For example, some bank officials would like the creation of a true market for short-term government securities so that they could use open market operations as a monetary policy tool, but that idea has run counter to ministry desires to hold down the cost of government debt.

All these divisions and conflicts put constraints on policy decisions. And the same principles of avoiding winner-take-all, avoiding the core problems, and making decisions through consensus that apply to society at large also apply within the government. These limit the speed and force of

43. Ibid., pp. 118–41, considers the conflicts involved in setting postal savings interest rates or transferring the funds to the MOF for investment.

new policy directions and may leave in place incongruous or anachronistic policies.

Private-Sector Expectations

Although the market shares of the various types of financial institutions have not undergone dramatic change in the postwar era, each type has strengths and weaknesses that have led to fears about its future viability. In general, one would expect that the smaller, more specialized institutions would be less able to adapt to the new environment because of their more limited range of experience. Despite the record of relative stability in market shares and the consistent desire of the government to maintain balance in its deregulation of the financial sector, anxiety over future winners and losers appears strong. The changes in profitability in the 1980s may be an important element in this anxiety.

Because competition could have been likely to bring a change in market shares, different kinds of financial institutions ought to have divided into two camps, supporting or resisting deregulation. Smaller institutions, including the agricultural cooperatives, sōgo banks, shinkin banks, and credit cooperatives, would appear to have chosen the side of opposition, but the opposition has been rather muted from most of them. While they may oppose deregulation that would allow other kinds of financial institutions into their territory, there has been no loud outcry against the concept of deregulation per se.

For the agricultural cooperatives, one reason may be that their deposit base has been relatively immune to deregulation. These cooperatives are much more than just financial intermediaries; they offer a wide variety of services to their members (essentially all farmers in Japan), from selling fertilizer and farm implements to making loans. They also provide a political voice on farm issues. Given these broad benefits, members are unlikely to remove money from their deposits, and if they did, the cooperatives might refuse to grant them loans. This strong membership commitment is one reason why the cooperatives have held their share in total financial deposits.

Agricultural cooperatives may also have been able to shrug at deregulation because their portfolios have diversified; they are no longer limited to making loans to the agricultural sector. These organizations exist in a hierarchy, with the individual cooperatives at the bottom, a set of credit federations of cooperatives in the middle, and the government-related Nōrin Chūo Kinko (Nōrinchūkin Bank or the Central Cooperative Bank for Agriculture and Forestry) at the top.[44] Much of the money raised through deposits at the individual cooperatives is passed upward in the form of deposits at the federations, which in turn place a significant portion of them in deposits at the Nōrinchūkin Bank.[45] In the past decade three trends are clear at all three levels: a rising share of the original deposits have been passed upward through the chain, the share of loans has fallen, and a much higher share of the portfolios has gone into holdings of securities. While no breakdown is available on securities holdings, the major increase would logically be in government bonds (and the Nōrinchūkin is a member of the syndicate that purchases the new issues of ten-year government bonds). Therefore, the rise in importance of government bonds, and the pressure it created for deregulation of interest rates, provided a new opportunity in agricultural institution portfolios. The agricultural cooperatives have also not been unduly hurt by change in the financial sector because the Ministry of Agriculture looks after their interests, and this ministry is both powerful and responsive (usually) to agricultural demands, since the Liberal Democratic party remains dependent on rural political support.

In contrast, the shinkin and credit cooperatives may be the weak links in the system. The shinkin banks suffer from low profitability, as was discussed earlier, and the credit cooperatives, unlike the agricultural cooperatives, have no *oyabun* (protector) in the central government. They fall

44. The Nōrinchūkin Bank is government-related in the sense that it is a *tokushu hōjin* (special legal entity) overseen by the Ministry of Agriculture, Forestry, and Fishery, and the Ministry of Finance. However, unlike the Japan Development Bank or the Eximbank, it has no capital participation by the government and does not borrow directly from the Fiscal Investment and Loan Program that funds most other government-related financial institutions. Administrative Management Agency, *Tokushu Hōjin Sōran, 1984* (Overview of Special Legal Entities, 1984) (Tokyo: Government Publications Center, 1984), pp. 155–56.

45. As of the end of 1985 agricultural cooperatives held 64 percent of their assets in the form of deposits with affiliated organizations (that is, the federations of agricultural cooperatives), and 30 percent in loans. In 1975 the shares had been 45 percent in deposits and 49 percent in loans. The federations held 51 percent of their assets in the form of deposits with others (that is, the Nōrinchūkin Bank) in 1985 and an additional 34 percent in securities, including government bonds, while only 13 percent went to loans. In 1975 the shares had been 37 percent in deposits, 21 percent in securities, and 41 percent in loans. Finally, the Nōrinchūkin Bank held 47 percent of its assets in 1985 in the form of securities (including government bonds), up from 22 percent in 1975. Bank of Japan, *Economic Statistics Annual, 1985*, pp. 85–87; *1984*, p. 95.

under the jurisdiction of prefectural and local governments rather than the Ministry of Finance or another central government ministry.[46] Both the shinkin banks and credit cooperatives do, however, benefit from the same type of captive membership as the agricultural cooperatives—in this case local organizations of small businesses. On the asset side, they have faced the incursion of larger financial institutions into the small business loan market, but unlike the agricultural cooperatives their portfolios show only a very modest movement away from loans. The shinkin banks had 66 percent of their asset portfolios in loans in 1973 and 62 percent in 1985. Similarly, the credit cooperatives had 77 percent of their assets in loans in 1973 and 69 percent in 1985.[47] In both cases the shifts were accounted for by greater purchases of securities. Thus even though the large commercial banks increased their lending to medium and small businesses, the fact that the shinkin banks and credit cooperatives are membership organizations appears to have helped protect their market share. The cost, as table 4-15 showed, has been declining profitability.

The postal savings system has been ambivalent about deregulation. It forcefully opposed certain changes, such as the introduction of the green card system to prevent tax evasion, but has voiced its support for liberalization of interest rates on small deposits, a move the Ministry of Finance has been conspicuously postponing into the indefinite future.[48] Whichever way the system goes on an issue, it has a powerful political voice to buttress its position. In 1983 there were 22,700 postal savings branches. Many post offices in Japan are actually small local businesses operating under a franchise granted by the Ministry of Posts and Telecommunications. According to one interpretation, these franchises are treated as local political favors by Liberal Democratic politicians. In return the owners tend to be very active politically, helping to get out the vote (and political donations) at election time.[49] They can, then, be reasonably confident that the government will protect their interests, so that changes in the regulation of bank deposits are unlikely to result in a mass exodus of funds from postal savings accounts to commercial banks. However, the Ministry of

46. Kazuo Matsumoto, *Ginkō ga Hōkai Suru Hi: Kin'yū Jiyūka no Tadashii Yomikata* (The Day Banks Collapse: Reading Financial Liberalization Correctly) (Tokyo: Nihon Bungeisha, 1985), p. 200.

47. Bank of Japan, *Economic Statistics Annual, 1985,* pp. 79–80, 83; *1980,* p. 157.

48. Matsumoto, *Ginkō ga Hōkai Suru Hi,* pp. 83–85.

49. Horne, *Japan's Financial Markets,* pp. 132–33. He also notes that a small number of former officers of the postal workers' union, representatives of both the Japan Socialist party and the LDP, are in the Diet.

Posts and Telecommunications has little interest in regulatory changes affecting assets because it invests very little of the money involved (handling only a portion of the funds collected through a postal life insurance program). It would like to control the investment of its funds, but a major change would be unlikely.[50]

Even among the city banks, a segment of the financial sector that has been pushing hard for regulatory changes, some doubts have been expressed about the viability of banks in a more competitive environment. One recent book catalogued the strengths and weaknesses of the thirteen city banks and suggested that the Kyōwa Bank ought to be merged with a stronger institution.[51] However, even it did not imply that change and deregulation should be halted because of the danger of failure.

Relative stability of market shares and the lack of any organized public opposition to the concept of deregulation does not mean that fear of failure is not strong. As indicated by the book just cited, analysts in Japan do see a distinct possibility for the failure of some institutions in a more competitive environment, even though bank failure runs counter to the Ministry of Finance's goal of preserving confidence in the entire financial system.

Such concerns prompted a report by the Kin'yū Seido Chōsakai, the Financial System Research Council, a Ministry of Finance advisory body. Again demonstrating that deregulation has achieved consensus status, the report did not advocate that deregulation be halted or reversed to prevent bankruptcies. Instead, it began by stating that a less constrained competitive environment would not necessarily imply trouble for financial institutions, since they would have more flexibility in adjusting asset and liability portfolios to produce a profit. However, acknowledging that greater competition could lead to difficulties for some institutions, the report considered in some detail (but with the vague language characteristic of such government documents in Japan) ways to prevent risk to depositors. Among the suggestions were use of administrative guidance (but carried out in a way that would not hinder competition, if one can accept that contradiction), increasing bank net worth (again using administrative

50. The elimination of tax-free savings in the tax reform bills submitted to the Diet in 1987 would seem to contradict the statement that the government would protect the position of the postal savings system. However, the Ministry of Finance obtained the acquiescence of the Ministry of Posts and Telecommunications with a promise to leave a small share of the money raised through the system in the hands of the MPT for investment. This appears to explain why elimination of tax-free savings remained in the revised tax reform bill, resubmitted to the Diet, that finally passed in 1987.

51. Kondō, *Ginkō 10 Nengo no Hōkai Chizu*, pp. 107–09.

guidance), strengthening the deposit insurance system, and encouraging mergers and other joint ventures (again with judicious use of administrative guidance).[52]

This last point is the most significant: by the mid-1980s the Ministry of Finance recognized the possibility that some financial institutions could face failure unless they were rescued through mergers. A decision to strengthen the deposit insurance system was likely as well, but in the Japanese context it is inconceivable that the Ministry of Finance would allow an institution to actually go bankrupt, its liabilities having to be met with monies from the deposit insurance fund (witness the Heiwa Sōgo case in 1986). Such failure to act would be seen as destroying confidence in the system and would be a breach of the implicit trust placed in the ministry to maintain the viability of those institutions. Even for small institutions (shinkin banks or credit cooperatives), a quick merger before actual bankruptcy is the likely outcome. The discussion in Japan over the necessity of strengthening the deposit insurance system, therefore, has been largely beside the point.

The financial sector also began to focus on the possibility of failure. After the release of the Financial System Research Council's report, Nobuya Hagura, president of the Federation of Bankers' Associations of Japan, stated publicly that mergers and acquisitions should be part of the strategy of banks in the era of liberalization and deregulation. He further stressed that such actions should be private-sector initiatives and not a result of government guidance.[53] This insistence is a long-standing one in Japan but is often ignored in times of crisis. Companies may resent or even deny the existence of government advice, but if they were faced with the prospect of bankruptcy in the financial sector, the advice would be quickly accepted.

In this context, the absorption of Heiwa Sōgo Bank by Sumitomo Bank could have important implications. Sumitomo is a large city bank and Heiwa Sōgo was one of the largest sōgo banks, so that the merger crossed boundaries between types of banks. This opened the possibility of further such mergers, pushing generally small institutions into relationships with

52. Kin'yū Seido Chōsakai (Financial System Research Council), "Kin'yū Jiyūka no Shinten to Sono Kankyō Seibi: Zenbun" (The Promotion of Financial Liberalization and Related Arrangements: Complete Text), Kin'yū Zaisei Jijō (Monetary and Fiscal Conditions) (June 1985), pp. 22–36.

53. Japan Times Weekly, July 13, 1985.

large city or regional banks rather than keeping to mergers within the same category of institution.

Financial Innovation and Change

One approach to tracing regulatory developments in the 1970s and 1980s is to provide a comprehensive list of all changes in the regulation of the financial sector. Such lists are available elsewhere, so there is little need to repeat the exercise here.[54] All these lists are subject to rapid obsolescence since Japan is changing so quickly. Just with respect to bank financial instruments, the seven years from 1979 to 1985 brought more than a dozen new products, as shown in table 4-16. The Japanese may not yet have the variety of choices for investing their money that Americans do (because of the very high minimum denominations required for instruments such as certificates of deposit and money market certificates), but the offerings proliferated rapidly.

More interesting than the number of changes is the distribution of types of institutions eligible to offer the instruments, which clearly reflects the government's desire to balance the changes. In 1981, for example, a new form of time deposit, the *kijitsu shitei teiki yokin,* was created for the city banks, regional banks, and the smaller banking institutions. At the same time, the trust banks were allowed a new account called "big" and the long-term credit banks one called "wide." The three types had similar characteristics. In addition, when commercial banks, sōgo banks, and shinkin banks were allowed over-the-counter sales of medium-term and discount government bonds in October 1983, the long-term credit banks and some others were allowed to establish discount bond funds.

The following sections consider a small subset of the many changes that have taken place, looking closely at the pressures involved in bringing about innovation.

SHORT-TERM MARKETS. During the 1950s and 1960s virtually the only short-term market was the call market (the interbank short-term loan market, equivalent to the federal funds market in the United States), which

54. See, for example, Eisuke Sakakibara and Akira Kondoh, *Study on the Internationalization of Tokyo's Money Markets,* JCIF Policy Study Series, 1 (Tokyo: Japan Center for International Finance, 1984); or Sakakibara and Nagao, eds., *Study on the Tokyo Capital Markets.*

Table 4-16. *New Financial Instruments and Eligible Issuers, 1979–85*

Instrument	Eligible issuers	Date
Certificates of deposit	All deposit-taking institutions	May 1979
Foreign currency deposits for residents	All foreign exchange banks	December 1980
Kijitsu shitei teiki yokin (specified-date time deposit)	Commercial banks, sōgo banks, shinkin banks, credit co-ops, agricultural and fisheries co-ops, labor credit co-ops	June 1981
"Big" accounts	Trust banks	June 1981
"Wide" accounts	Long-term credit banks, Nōrin-chūkin, Shōkōchūkin	October 1981
Gold sales	Commercial banks, sōgo banks, shinkin banks	April 1982
Over-the-counter government bond sales	Commercial banks, sōgo banks, shinkin banks, Nōrinchūkin	April 1983
Kokusai teiki kōza (government bond funds)	Commercial banks (except Bank of Tokyo), sōgo banks, shinkin banks	August 1983
Kokusai shintaku kōza ("double") (government bond trust fund, "double")	Trust banks	September 1983
Over-the-counter sales of medium-term and discount government bonds	Commercial banks, sōgo banks, shinkin banks	October 1983
Government discount bond funds	Long-term credit banks, Bank of Tokyo, Nōrinchūkin	October 1983
Gold investment funds	Commercial banks, trust banks, sōgo banks	December 1983
Foreign CDs and CPs	City banks, long-term credit banks, trust banks	April 1984
Money market certificates	All deposit-taking institutions	March 1985

Sources: Ministry of Finance, "Ginkō de Hanbai Shiteiru Omo na Shōhin (Yokin Nado) Gaiyō" (Overview of Principal Financial Instruments [Deposits, etc.] Sold by Banks), unpublished MOF document, August 1984; and Nihon Keizai Shimbun, *Nikkei Kin'yū Shōhinsō Gaido, 1987* (Nikkei Guide to Financial Instruments, 1987) (Tokyo: Nihon Keizai Shimbun, 1986), pp. 30, 58, 62–64, 68, 72, 80, 102, 118, 220–21.

limited participation to financial institutions. Treasury bills cannot really be counted since almost all were held by the Bank of Japan or the Trust Fund Bureau. This lack of short-term instruments suited the financial system in the era of rapid economic growth—individuals had little choice but to concentrate their savings in bank deposits, and corporations had only bank loans to cover short-term borrowing needs (commercial paper was not allowed).

During the 1970s this structure underwent considerable transformation, beginning with the creation of the gensaki market (the short-term lending market using repurchase agreements on government bonds). In the early 1970s too, the call market was split into a very short-term segment (overnight and seven-day) and a longer-term bill discount market. The next developments came with the creation of negotiable certificates of deposit in 1979 and the establishment of both banker's acceptances and money market certificates in 1985. Note, however, that these innovations were aimed at institutional participants—financial and nonfinancial corporations—rather than individuals.

The short-term money market is summarized in table 4-17, which shows the rapid rise of the new forms of instruments after they were created. Their introduction brought a considerable transfer of funds from other markets. The very rapid rise in the outstanding balance of certificates of deposit was accompanied by a stagnation in the outstanding balance of gensaki transactions, which was virtually the same in 1985 as in 1978 before rising rapidly in 1986. The fact that a securities transaction tax (*yūkō shōken torihikizei*) applies to gensaki transactions but not to CDs may account for the relative attractiveness. The bill discount market was also stagnant from 1977 until an unusual jump in 1985. The introduction of money market certificates also led to stagnation of CDs. Much of the rising relative importance of the short-term market as a whole, in fact, came before the late 1970s. In the entire period from 1972 to 1986, the total financial assets and liabilities of the nation reported in the Bank of Japan's flow-of-funds data grew at an average annual rate of 13.5 percent, while the outstanding balance in short-term money markets grew at 24.5 percent. But from 1978 to 1984 total financial assets grew at 11.6 percent, while short-term money grew at 11.4 percent. Only in 1985 and 1986 did short-term assets once again expand at an above-average rate. The introduction of certificates of deposit and acceptance of foreigners in the gensaki market did nothing to increase the relative weight of short-term instruments in the overall financial portfolio of the nation.

Japan still lacked several forms of financial instruments as of the mid-1980s, principal among which was treasury bills. There had been calls for establishing a treasury bill market for a number of years, but little happened until 1986. There was also no commercial paper market (although the government edged in that direction by allowing foreign financial institutions and Japanese securities companies to sell foreign commercial paper). Even the existing short-term markets were still affected by restrictions that limited their usefulness, such as the high minimum denominations for certificates of deposit and money market certificates.

Table 4-17. *Short-Term Money Market Yearend Balances Outstanding, by Type of Market, 1971–86*

	Call money		Bill discount		Gensaki		Certificates of deposit		Money market certificates	
Year	Billions of yen	Percent of total	Billions of yen	Percent of total	Billions of yen	Percent of total	Billions of yen	Percent of total	Billions of yen	Percent of total
1971	1,472	63	...	...	882	37	...	...	...	...
1972	1,048	46	...	...	1,224	54	...	...	...	...
1973	1,227	17	4,089	58	1,738	25	...	...	...	...
1974	2,160	24	5,207	59	1,505	17	...	...	...	...
1975	2,332	28	4,403	52	1,679	20	...	...	...	...
1976	2,567	26	5,091	52	2,217	22	...	...	...	...
1977	2,616	22	6,084	51	3,136	26	...	...	...	...
1978	2,326	18	6,590	50	4,207	32	...	...	...	...
1979	3,473	22	6,327	41	3,960	25	1,853	12	...	...
1980	4,133	25	5,738	34	4,507	27	2,323	14	...	...
1981	4,699	29	4,016	24	4,481	27	3,291	20	...	...
1982	4,494	24	5,413	29	4,304	23	4,342	23	...	...
1983	4,456	21	6,763	32	4,288	20	5,665	27	...	...
1984	5,037	20	7,998	32	3,562	14	8,461	34	...	...
1985	5,110	13	14,656	36	4,642	11	9,657	24	6,325	16
1986	10,226	21	13,544	28	7,117	14	9,926	20	8,168[a]	17

Sources: Bank of Japan, *Economic Statistics Annual, 1985*, pp. 195, 197–98; *1984*, p. 202; *1980*, pp. 193, 195–96; *1979*, pp. 45, 48; BOJ, *Economic Statistics Monthly* (February 1987), pp. 101–04; Robert F. Emery, *The Japanese Money Market* (D.C. Heath, 1984), p. 23; and data provided by Institute of Fiscal and Monetary Policy, MOF, February 1987.

a. November 1986.

Why has the movement toward greater use of short-term markets been relatively slow? One reason has been the MOF's desire to hold down debt costs; it has consistently resisted the idea of issuing a larger portion of its debt in the form of treasury bills floated at market rates. Even in 1985, when the ministry considered its first real market offer of short-term instruments, its intention was to provide temporary cushioning; it wanted to use these bills to finance the redemption of ten-year government bonds until new issues could be placed. There was no serious consideration of any important continuing role for them.

The development of short-term markets may also have been affected by the MOF's determination to protect the city banks. These banks specialize in short-term loans to large corporations, although the loans are routinely rolled over so that they become de facto long-term loans. Further development of short-term markets could threaten the banks because of disintermediation. Depositors could move to investments in treasury bills and commercial paper, hurting the deposit base of the banks. Corporate borrowers could also turn to direct credit instruments such as commercial paper in lieu of bank loans (although banks could be major holders of commercial paper). The innovations that had taken place as of the mid-

1980s, in fact, created mainly short-term instruments that did involve the banks: certificates of deposit, banker's acceptances, and money market certificates. Some intrusion came from the presence of securities companies in the gensaki market and (from 1986) in banker's acceptances, and the success of the gensaki market may have worried MOF officials concerned with preserving the position of the banks (considered further below).

CALL MARKET. The call market is the oldest of the short-term markets in Japan. Although it was useful in transferring funds from regional financial institutions (principally the regional banks) to the city banks in the 1950s and 1960s, it lost much of its importance as other short-term instruments came into being. It, too, has undergone some changes, however. The principal recent one was the removal of collateral requirements at the end of June 1985. Their removal nicely demonstrates the role of foreign institutions in Japan. In its announcement the Ministry of Finance stated that collateral requirements were being lifted in response to the needs of foreign banks. Since these banks are only branches of much larger organizations, they have fewer assets in Japan acceptable as collateral than their Japanese bank competitors. Removing the requirements supposedly meant the foreign banks would be able to raise funds more freely. There may be some truth to this statement, since foreign banks raised approximately 40 percent of their funds in Japan through the call market in 1985, but it is difficult to believe this was the main motivation. The ¥626 billion that foreign banks had outstanding in call loans at the end of 1985 represented only 12 percent of the total market.[55] The beneficiaries of the change are really the Japanese financial institutions representing the other 88 percent of the market who no longer have to tie up financial assets as collateral and are freed from the additional paperwork implied by the requirement. Nevertheless, the foreign need or demand became the official rationale for breaking a long-standing principle.

CERTIFICATES OF DEPOSIT. From its beginning in May 1979 the market in negotiable certificates of deposit included both Japanese and foreign banks. As with the lifting of collateral requirements in the call market, the rationale for creating this instrument was to allow the foreign banks a new

---

55. With respect to foreign bank call market liabilities, there is a large discrepancy between data on foreign banks (Bank of Japan, *Economic Statistics Annual, 1985*, pp. 75–76) and data on the call market (pp. 193–94). The figures used here are based on the call market data.

way of raising yen funds. Since their introduction, negotiable CDs have grown rapidly—an average annual rate of 32 percent.

However, the history of regulating CDs clearly demonstrates the MOF's avoidance of sweeping changes. When they were introduced, the minimum denomination was set at ¥500 million ($2.3 million at average 1979 exchange rates), and the maximum amount that could be issued by any single bank was set at 25 percent of net worth for Japanese banks and 10 percent of yen-denominated assets for foreign banks (which, as branches of foreign institutions, had little local net worth). These restrictions meant that the pool of potential purchasers was effectively limited to large corporations and that the total size of the market would also be limited, neither of which conditions pleased the banks.

These initial restrictions represented the ministry's caution and its desire to maintain careful control over the speed of change rather than an unalterable decision to keep the market small. The maximum amount of issue was raised to 50 percent of net worth (20 percent of yen assets for foreign banks) in 1980 and to 75 percent (30 percent of yen assets) at the beginning of 1984. A few months later the limit was moved to 100 percent of net worth or 100 percent of yen assets for foreign banks, and the minimum denomination was dropped to ¥300 million ($1.3 million at average 1984 exchange rates). The minimum denomination was lowered again in April 1985 to ¥100 million ($419,000 at average 1985 exchange rates) and the maximum amount of issue was raised in March and September 1986 (for a combined CD and MMC issue of 250 percent of net worth). There was no reason to suppose that adjustments to both the maximum amount of issue and minimum denomination would not continue. Those who think Japan encourages excessive government intervention in financial markets can point to the continuation of the limits, while those who emphasize its willingness to change can point to the successive decisions to ease them.

Certificates of deposit were initially proposed ostensibly to meet the demands of foreign banks. At that time both domestic and foreign banks were subject to limits on the amount of foreign currency they could convert into yen, which restricted the ability of the foreign banks to use funds raised elsewhere for yen-denominated lending in Japan. Foreign banks also had very limited numbers of branches in Japan, effectively restricting their yen-denominated deposit base. The creation of CDs was promoted as a way for these banks to increase their yen-denominated deposits with a financial instrument of longer maturity than the interbank call market.

Table 4-18. *Certificates of Deposit, Yearend Balances, by Type of Issuer, 1979–86*
Percent of total

Year	City banks	Regional banks	Trust banks	Long-term credit banks	Sōgo banks	Shinkin banks	Foreign banks	Other
1979	51	16	8	6	3	1	14	1
1980	45	16	13	8	5	1	11	1
1981	56	13	8	4	4	1	13	1
1982	48	17	9	8	7	1	8	1
1983	49	20	7	6	8	2	8	1
1984	54	21	6	4	6	3	5	0
1985	51	18	8	6	7	2	8	0
1986	61	12	4	7	7	6	2	1

Sources: Bank of Japan, *Economic Statistics Annual, 1985*, p. 198; *1984*, p. 202; *1982*, p. 198; and BOJ, *Economic Statistics Monthly* (February 1987), pp. 101–02.

Answering a need or demand of the foreign banks may indeed have been a consideration, but it must be noted that foreign banks never represented more than a relatively small share of the CD market (table 4-18). At the end of 1979, six months after CDs were introduced, these banks accounted for 14 percent of the market, but their share fell and stabilized around 8 percent after 1982. From 1981 to 1984 the amount of foreign bank issues stagnated at ¥400 billion ($1.8 billion at 1981 exchange rates), and in 1986 the banks actually began to withdraw from the market, bringing their total outstanding issues to less that ¥200 billion and their market share to less than 2 percent. This withdrawal was not a reaction to legal limitations—the maximum issue allowed foreign banks had risen in tandem with the changes for Japanese banks. Foreign banks may have been useful as a catalyst in getting the initial decision to allow certificates of deposit, but clearly the major beneficiaries of the change were the Japanese financial institutions that dominated the market.

A more likely cause for the introduction of CDs is the domestic banks' concern over the growth of the gensaki market and the resulting loss of large corporate deposits. In 1978 nonfinancial corporations put ¥2.5 trillion ($11.9 billion at 1978 exchange rates) into the gensaki market, 58 percent of the money invested in this market. Only 22 percent of gensaki funds went to banks in 1978, while 65 percent went to securities companies. Corporate investment in the gensaki market was still small compared with the size of their time deposits at banks (¥35 trillion in 1978), but the banks could well have been disturbed by the trend. CDs represented a means to reattract the lost deposits, and MOF officials concerned about maintaining balance readily agreed to the innovation. The stagnation of the gensaki market after 1979 suggests the effort was successful.[56]

MONEY MARKET CERTIFICATES. Introduced on March 1, 1985, money market certificates had reached a value of ¥6.3 trillion by the end of the year, representing 16 percent of all short-term financial assets (preliminary data show a rise to ¥8.2 trillion by the end of 1986). Unlike money market certificates in the United States, those in Japan are best thought of as smaller-denomination CDs. The creation of MMCs was one of the provisions included in the Yen-Dollar Agreement of May 1984 that will be discussed in chapter 5. Along with banker's acceptances, the creation of MMCs was urged by the United States out of a conviction that one of the problems for foreigners desiring to hold part of their financial portfolios in yen-dominated assets was a lack of relatively liquid, short-term instruments. The yen-dollar accord promised that consideration would be given to creating a new large-denomination deposit instrument with a market-determined interest rate, and by the end of 1984 the details were worked out for money market certificates in a process that again nicely balanced the competing interests among Japanese financial institutions.

All forms of financial institutions were invited to submit proposals to the Ministry of Finance for the rules to govern the structure of this new instrument. The final version of the rules tended to favor smaller financial institutions. As finally established, money market certificates bear maturities of one to six months, with a ¥50 million minimum denomination ($209,600 at average 1985 exchange rates) and with the total issue of CDs plus MMCs to be equal to or less than 150 percent of bank net worth. Small financial institutions had recommended this sort of limit on maximum issue amounts because the city banks were already close to their limit of CD issues (100 percent of net worth), and small institutions would thus have more leeway to expand into the new instrument.[57]

---

56. Data are from Bank of Japan, *Economic Statistics Annual, 1984,* pp. 197–98. Horne, *Japan's Financial Markets,* pp. 87–90, supports this view that the CD market was established to improve or restore the competitive balance between banks, especially the city banks, and the securities companies. He adds that competition between city banks and the postal savings system may have been a further cause, but this connection is less clear since CDs are a short-term instrument while postal savings specializes in longer-term time deposits.

57. *Nihon Keizai Shimbun,* November 15, 1984.

Small institutions were also favored by the starting date. Sōgo banks, credit cooperatives, agricultural cooperatives, and labor credit associations were allowed to begin issuing MMCs on March 1, 1985, while regional and city banks began on April 1. The argument behind the one-month offset was that among the major potential purchasers of these new instruments were local governments (presumably because their deposits were too small for them to invest in CDs), and the one-month head start would allow small local financial institutions to cultivate this market. In the long run the time differential will probably have no effect on market shares, but the important point was that these institutions believed their concerns were being addressed by the Ministry of Finance.

Interest rates on money market certificates were to be set 0.75 percentage point below CD rates. This meant that interest rates were not exactly market-determined; CD rates are reset each week, so that the MMC rate would be flexible, but the rigid formula preserved a constant differential between the two instruments, a result consistent with the entire postwar history of Ministry of Finance regulation. Since CDs have a larger minimum denomination, they ought to have a higher interest rate, and were market forces to push MMC rates closer to the CD rate, that principle would have been violated.

BANKER'S ACCEPTANCES. Provisions for creating yen-denominated banker's acceptances were also included in the May 1984 Yen-Dollar Agreement on the assumption that if a short-term, trade-related financial instrument were available, a rising portion of Japan's trade would be yen-denominated. Such a condition, it was believed, would bring about yen appreciation on foreign exchange markets. The rules for banker's acceptances were worked out by April 1985, and the instruments came into existence in June.

The biggest problem to be solved was whether securities companies would be allowed into the market. The solution was similar to that for money market certificates and the relative participation of large and small banks. On March 29, 1985, the Ministry of Finance allowed securities companies to deal in banker's acceptances beginning in April 1986, giving the banks ten months' head start in the market to assuage their feelings that the securities firms were included at all.

Early evidence suggests that the securities companies may not have missed much. The new instrument was not very popular with corporate borrowers because the Ministry of Finance was reluctant to create an instrument free of considerable red tape. In particular, a tax was imposed on banker's acceptance transactions, a requirement that did not apply to most other ways a corporation could borrow money. Major corporations that could be expected to use banker's acceptances found that straight short-term loans from commercial banks were a better bargain. As a result, the market did not expand as rapidly as had been expected.[58]

The cautious introduction of a new financial instrument was entirely in the tradition of the Ministry of Finance, but that is unlikely to be the end of the story if the banks, securities companies, and corporate borrowers show any real interest. If, however, the only true proponent of development of a banker's acceptance market remains the U.S. government, then change in the regulations would be unlikely, and the MOF would blame the lack of growth on private-sector lack of interest rather than its own rules and restrictions.

PENSION FUNDS. The talks leading up to the May 1984 Yen-Dollar Agreement also raised the issue of pension funds. Before the 1970s most corporations met their obligations to retiring employees by paying them lump sums (calculated as a multiple of monthly wages and depending on length of service and other factors), which were counted as part of current operating expenses. These payments were relatively small—a maximum of about forty months' pay for a university graduate with thirty years of service at the mandatory retirement age.[59] This represented less than four years' pay. Investing the entire sum in a savings deposit yielding the maximum interest allowed in 1985 (5.75 percent) would result in an income equal to only 19 percent of preretirement pay (or about 15 percent if one considers the large bonuses added to annual salaries).

This system offered certain advantages. The Ministry of Finance allowed corporations to establish tax-free reserves to meet the obligations, and employees were allowed to receive the retirement payment tax free up to a specified amount. However, the paltry size of the settlements meant

58. *Japan Economic Journal,* August 6, 1985. It is significant that two years after the banker's acceptance market began, the MOF had published no statistics on it (and would not supply the internal data). Either the size of the market is embarrassingly small or the ministry is uninterested, or both. The banker's acceptance market is the only short-term financial market for which no data are available, a highly unusual situation for a government that publishes an enormous volume of statistics on almost every conceivable topic.

59. Sumitomo Trust and Banking Co., *Retirement Benefits and Pension Plans in Japanese Enterprises* (Tokyo: Sumitomo Trust, 1983), p. 2.

that many employees were forced to seek postretirement employment to supplement their benefits.

During the 1970s the rapidly rising average age of the labor force implied an expanding retirement cost burden for corporations, a situation that would continue for many years until the postwar baby boom generation retires early in the twenty-first century. To offset this liability, corporations began to turn to funded pension plans to meet their obligations. Thirty-three percent of corporations with more than thirty employees had adopted pension funds (or a combination of pension fund and continued unfunded lump-sum payments) by 1975, a level that rose to 45 percent by 1981.[60] As of March 1984, 82 percent of all companies listed on the first section of the Tokyo Stock Exchange (1,471 out of approximately 1,800 large corporations) had some form of pension fund.

Companies wishing to establish a pension fund can choose among two types of legally recognized outside-managed funds and one type of self-managed fund. Of the two forms of outside funds, one is governed under rules established by the tax authorities and the other by the Ministry of Health and Welfare. The first is the *zaisei tekikaku taishoku nenkin seido* (*tekinen* for short), which translates as the "tax-qualified retirement pension system." The second is the *chōsei nenkin* (*chōnen* or "adjusted pension" for short), operated as an adjunct to the government's welfare pension fund. The rules for these two systems differ, so that the chōnen system applies mostly to corporations with more than 1,000 employees, while the tekinen system applies to any corporation with 20 or more employees. Most corporations have established pension funds under one or the other of these systems, with a few using both. Self-managed pension funds, which do not qualify for tax benefits, represent a relatively minor portion of total pension assets. They are used by only 10 percent of corporations with pension systems, mainly the very smallest.[61]

Table 4-19 shows the rapid growth of the two forms of outside-managed funds. From a mere ¥462 billion in 1971 ($1.3 billion at average 1971 exchange rates), assets rose to ¥19.5 trillion by 1986 ($115.7 billion), an average annual growth of 28 percent. Compared with the 14.1 percent growth for the nation's total financial assets over this same period, the attractiveness of this business is obvious. The trust banks have had

60. Ibid., p. 4.

61. Sumitomo Trust Bank, "Sumitomo no Nenkin" (Pensions at Sumitomo), unpublished internal document (November 1984); and Sumitomo Trust Bank, "Kōsei Nenkin Kikin no Osusume" (Progress of the Welfare Pension Fund), corporate brochure, 1981.

Table 4-19. *Pension Fund Assets, by Type of Management, 1971–86*
Billions of yen

Year	Managed by trust banks			Managed by life insurance firms			Total Tekinen	Total Chōnen	Total
	Tekinen	Chōnen	Total	Tekinen	Chōnen	Total			
1971	139	151	290	136	36	171	275	187	462
1972	190	253	443	185	61	247	375	315	690
1973	252	393	645	227	94	321	479	487	965
1974	333	575	907	281	139	420	613	714	1,327
1975	451	831	1,281	358	202	560	809	1,033	1,841
1976	585	1,152	1,737	455	286	741	1,040	1,438	2,478
1977	752	1,549	2,300	563	388	951	1,315	1,936	3,251
1978	933	2,021	2,954	700	515	1,215	1,633	2,536	4,169
1979	1,136	2,538	3,674	872	671	1,544	2,008	3,209	5,217
1980	1,377	3,131	4,508	1,101	866	1,967	2,478	3,997	6,475
1981	1,668	3,794	5,461	1,385	1,129	2,514	3,052	4,923	7,975
1982	1,984	4,564	6,548	1,723	1,467	3,189	3,707	6,031	9,738
1983	2,336	5,395	7,731	2,118	1,913	4,032	4,456[a]	7,308	11,764
1984	2,695	6,363	9,057	2,575	2,403	4,978	5,277[a]	8,766	14,043
1985	3,088	7,492	10,580	3,095	2,970	6,065	6,199[a]	10,462	16,661
1986	3,500	8,709	12,209	3,659	3,639	7,298	7,188[a]	12,348	19,536

Source: Data provided by Sumitomo Trust Bank, Pension Trust Department, April 1987.
a. Totals for 1983–86 include small amounts of tekinen funds (¥2 billion in 1983, ¥8 billion in 1984, ¥17 billion in 1985, ¥29 billion in 1986) managed by agricultural cooperatives but not shown separately.

about two-thirds of the pension fund business (divided among seven companies), with the remainder handled by twenty-three life insurance companies.

The trust banks are creatures of administrative guidance; in its zeal to segment financial markets in the 1950s, the Ministry of Finance used administrative guidance (based on no specific legislation) to force city banks to spin off their trust departments into separate, independent banks. This allowed a more finely demarcated matching of assets and liabilities, with the city banks gathering in short-term deposits and making short-term loans and the trust banks receiving longer-term deposits (trust certificates—essentially nonnegotiable certificates of deposit) and making long-term loans. Since the government was interested in promoting loans to capital-intensive industries with relatively long gestation periods for investment (such as steel and petrochemicals), this move was consistent with industrial policy goals.[62] All the banks with trust departments except

62. The distinction between long-term and short-term lending is not as important as might be assumed because the city and regional banks regularly roll over their short-term loans, making them de facto long-term loans.

Daiwa Bank followed the MOF guidance. During the 1950s and 1960s the newly created trust banks fulfilled the role envisioned by the ministry, concentrating on long-term loans to industry. But the rapid rise of pension funds in the 1970s created a regulatory dilemma as other financial institutions sought to participate.

In the early phases of the struggle to gain entry into this lucrative expanding market in late 1983, Japanese securities companies joined American banks to pressure the Ministry of Finance to liberalize regulations. The advantage of the alliance for the securities companies was that foreign pressure always improved the chances of success in such cases. American banks gained the advantage of pairing with institutions that understood the intricacies of dealing with the Japanese bureaucracy. Pairing also made American pressure more palatable to the Ministry of Finance since not just foreigners would benefit from any resulting change in the rules.[63] These alliances were put together in time to include airing the issue at the bilateral talks leading to the Yen-Dollar Agreement, and for a time pension fund management was the major concern being touted by the Treasury Department in those meetings. Nevertheless, the opposition of the trust banks and insurance companies proved to be too strong for this initial effort. The choice of the security companies as the standard-bearer also implied an internal MOF conflict between the Securities Bureau and the Banking and Insurance Bureaus.

The trust banks' resistance followed quintessentially Japanese forms. One bank president stated that allowing foreign financial institutions into the Japanese market was an excellent idea in general, but that trust banking was a special business that could not be governed by the general principle. In Japanese, there is even a convenient phrase for this type of argument—*sōron-sansei kakuron-hantai* (general agreement versus specific objections)—and it is a standard feature of virtually any argument over market access. In this case, trust banking was described as the "highest technique of financial service," involving concerns of safety and obligation that precluded getting into the business just to make money: foreign fund managers would be less averse to risk than Japanese trust banks, to the ultimate detriment of corporate pension funds. Why foreign banks would be imprudent pension fund managers or why they would be unable

63. The institutions involved at that point were Morgan Guaranty Trust, paired with Nomura Securities, BankAmerica with Nikko Securities, Chemical Bank with Yamaichi Securities, and Citicorp with Daiwa Securities. See Edward J. Lincoln, "Financial Reform Discussions Continue in Tokyo," *JEI Report,* no. 7B (February 1984), pp. 3–5.

to carry out the client-related paperwork diligently is never explained in this sort of statement.[64] But as patently ludicrous as such pronouncements may seem, they cannot be entirely dismissed by the Ministry of Finance in making its decisions. By May 1984 the issue had been resolved only to the point of a ministry promise that some form of entry for foreign banks would be allowed, but not in conjunction with Japanese securities firms.

The final resolution was to allow eight foreign banks into the trust business (five American and three European), based solely on the artificial justification that eight Japanese banks were in the business (the seven trust banks plus Daiwa Bank). The foreign banks could enter on their own or join with any one of the existing trust banks in Japan. However, nine foreign banks applied for permission, implying that one would have to be rejected. Unable to come to grips with this dilemma, and feeling substantial foreign pressure to make a decision, the MOF accepted all nine applications in June 1985.[65] Afterward the trust bankers' association offered a ritual statement of "deep regret" that the rule was broken and an additional bank accepted.

Admitting the nine foreign banks was by no means the final decision but only the first in a series that could be implemented in piecemeal fashion over a period of several years. In addition, other banks and securities companies have found alternative ways to profit from the boom in the pension business. Therefore by the summer of 1985 most of the major actors involved—the trust banks, foreign financial institutions, and the Japanese commercial banks and securities companies—had been placated to some extent.

Trust banks also benefited from another action by the Ministry of Finance that may have been related to the pension issue. In November 1984, when the decision on allowing foreign entry into trust banking was close to completion, the ministry announced that on a form of trust account called *tokutei kinsen shintaku* (specified money in trust) offered by trust banks, a requirement for advance notification on all investments made abroad would be changed to an after-the-fact reporting requirement. This was a minor change, but it did imply greater ease of investing these funds over-

64. Keiko Atsumi, "Sumitomo Trust and Banking's Sakurai Says: Nobody Is Allowed to Grab Away Only the Best Part of the Trust Business," *Japan Economic Journal*, September 11, 1984.

65. The nine banks were Citicorp (U.S.), Bankers Trust (U.S.), Morgan Guaranty Trust (U.S.), Manufacturers Hanover Trust (U.S.), Chase Manhattan Bank (U.S.), Chemical Bank (U.S.), Credit Suisse (Switzerland), Union Bank of Switzerland, and Barclays Bank (U.K.). *Japan Times Weekly*, July 13, 1985.

seas (at higher interest rates) and could be interpreted by the trust banks as a way of compensating them when they were feeling beleaguered.[66]

Foreign banks that were allowed to enter the trust business also benefited from the revision of the regulations. At the very least, they and the U.S. government could claim that movement had taken place on an issue they considered of some importance. Other foreign and domestic financial institutions were also able to get a piece of the pension fund action through the creation of investment advisory firms. For example, Prudential Insurance Corporation of America, engaged in life insurance business in Japan through a joint venture with Sony Trading Company but not licensed to handle pension funds, formed a joint venture for an investment advisory firm with Mitsui Trust and Banking Company.[67] And Jardine Fleming formed an investment advisory firm with Yasuda Trust and Banking, marking the first joint venture between a Japanese trust bank and a foreign merchant bank.[68] These agreements were announced while the trust bank issue was still awaiting resolution and represented a way around the problem. The weak point of the trust banks' management of pension funds was supposed to be the low return on their portfolios. But through joint ventures in investment advisory firms, foreigners could earn fees from advising on portfolio management, and the trust banks could feel that the pension business was still their own exclusive jurisdiction.

Domestic financial institutions, including securities companies and commercial banks, followed this same route into involvement with the pension business. Dai-Ichi Kangyō Bank strengthened its position by buying out Bank of America's share in their joint investment advisory company (Tokyo Investment Services), while other banks indicated serious intentions to create investment advisory subsidiaries (including Fuji Bank, Sumitomo Bank, Mitsubishi Bank, and Sanwa Bank).[69] Even life insurance companies were reported to be interested in moving in this direction as a way to become involved in portfolio management beyond their own pension funds. Looked at in a broader perspective, the use of investment advisory companies represented a way to get around the broad separation of securities firms and banks. The securities firms maintained their exclusive right to buy and sell corporate equity, but other financial institutions

66. *Nihon Keizai Shimbun,* November 29, 1984.
67. *Japan Economic Journal,* August 28, 1984. Prudential has since dissolved its joint venture with Sony.
68. *Japan Economic Journal,* October 9, 1984.
69. *Japan Economic Journal,* November 27, 1984.

were eagerly getting into the business of telling clients which equities to hold in their portfolios.

Although the Ministry of Finance could maintain that these innovations abided by the principle of segmentation, in reality the lines between financial institutions were being blurred. While the regulations probably kept securities firms farther from the core of the pension business or banks farther from the securities business than they desired, the new situation still represented a major change.

Closely related to the pension fund developments has been the *tokutei kinsen shintaku* (*tokkin*), portfolio management agreements in which a corporation establishes a trust account with a trust bank and enters into a contract with an investment advisory company to manage the portfolio. These agreements are for nonpension funds, although the nature of management is somewhat similar.[70]

Tokkin expanded quickly in 1985 and 1986. According to one estimate, the balance invested in them rose from ¥5 trillion in March 1985 (roughly $21 billion at 1985 exchange rates) to more than ¥15 trillion by July 1986 ($89 billion at 1986 exchange rates).[71] This placed investments in tokkin fairly close to the level of those in the gensaki market. These funds were not listed separately in table 4-8, but at the reported level in 1986 they should be approaching 10 percent of the total amounts of corporate financial asset portfolios shown there.

One reason for the popularity of these funds stems from the capital gains tax benefits made possible by separating investments in the tokkin from previous corporate investments. Another advantage is anonymity.[72]

70. *Japan Economic Journal*, June 4, 1985.

71. Michael Korver, "Developments in Japanese Finance: *Tokkin* and Fund Trusts," *Japan Economic Journal*, September 6, 1986. In a tokkin the money can be invested at the discretion of the trustor or the investment advisory company. Fund trusts are very similar, except that investments are made at the discretion of the trust bank and the redemption at the conclusion of the trust is made with the securities in the portfolio rather than in cash. The values of investment refer to the combination of tokkin and the closely related fund trusts. No official statistics are yet published on either of these financial instruments.

72. Ibid. The tax advantage arises because capital gains at time of sale are calculated as the difference between the selling price and the average purchase value of all similar equities held in the portfolio. Thus if one company has held shares in another for many years as part of a goodwill gesture related to business ties and now begins buying and selling shares of the same company for financial purposes, the low book value of the old shares would be averaged into the new when calculating capital gains for tax purposes. All shares purchased in a tokkin trust account, however, are completely separate for tax purposes because the money is technically under the control of the trust bank rather than the trustor.

Traditionally, corporate investment in equities has been mainly a means of cementing business relationships; equities were not to be bought or sold for purposes of capital gains. The tokkin provide a means to separate investment in the stock market for pure financial purposes from the more traditional behavior without revealing corporate identity to the companies whose shares are being bought or sold.

The popularity of the tokkin has worked to the advantage of the trust banks in the same way that pension funds have. However, the presence of investment advisory firms in the transactions provides room for banks and other financial institutions that establish investment advisory subsidiaries to gain as well. Both pension funds and tokkin have also worked to the advantage of securities companies, since substantial portions of these funds are invested in corporate equities purchased on the stock market through securities firms.

CORPORATE BONDS. Bonds have never represented a major form of borrowing for Japanese corporations. In fact many of the corporate bonds issued were purchased by banks, making them in effect another form of bank lending. In 1971, for example, 51 percent of new corporate bonds issued were bought by financial institutions, and 89 percent of outstanding corporate bond issues were in their hands.[73] Behind the underdevelopment of the bond market lay restrictions on interest rates, which made corporate bonds an unattractive investment. There were also complicated regulations on issuing new bonds and severe restrictions on the number of companies eligible to issue them. Among other problems, bond issues were limited to those backed by collateral. The rapid rise of government bonds in the 1970s could have been expected to increase the popularity of corporate bonds as well, especially since the effort to keep interest rates on bonds at below market levels gradually disintegrated, but they seem not to have.

What has brought about change in the corporate bond market has been heavy foreign influence. The major route for that influence was the Japanese corporations' issuance of bonds abroad in foreign currencies. Between 1976 and 1985 the ratio of bonds issued abroad to total bond issues by Japanese corporations rose from 25 percent to 56 percent (table 4-20). Thus by 1985 Japanese companies were raising more in foreign capital markets than at home. This was the product of relative stagnation in bond

73. Bank of Japan, *Economic Statistics Annual, 1971*, pp. 17–18, 161.

Table 4-20. *Japanese Domestic and Overseas Corporate Bond Issues, 1976–85*[a]

Billions of yen unless otherwise specified

Year	Domestic issues	Overseas issues[b]	Percent issued overseas
1976	1,284	428	25
1977	1,295	373	22
1978	1,622	497	23
1979	1,617	756	32
1980	1,153	685	37
1981	1,642	906	36
1982	1,638	1,131	41
1983	1,485	1,851	55
1984	2,034	2,391	54
1985	2,564	3,309	56

Sources: Ministry of Finance, *Ōkurashō Kokusai Kin'yū Kyoko Nempō, 1986* (International Finance Division Yearbook, 1986) (Tokyo: Kin'yū Zaisei Jijō Kenkyūkai, 1986), p. 148; *1982*, p. 116.
a. Bond issues include straight bonds, convertible bonds, and bonds with warrants.
b. Overseas bond issues in foreign currencies are converted to yen at average annual exchange rates.

issues at home after 1978 and a rapid expansion of foreign issues, which increased from $2.4 billion in 1978 to $13.8 billion in 1985.

The Economic Planning Agency economic white paper in 1984 acknowledged the popularity of bonds issued abroad, stating that despite higher interest rates abroad the simpler requirements (including no requirement for collateral) and procedures for issuing bonds in foreign markets were more than enough to make up for the interest-cost differential.[74] Not all these issues should be interpreted as financing corporate activity in Japan, since Japanese firms were expanding abroad during these years and foreign currency bonds would hedge the exchange risk in financing assets denominated in foreign currencies. Nevertheless, the belief that Japanese firms were deserting the domestic bond market led the Ministry of Finance to announce early in 1985 that it would study a possible relaxation of issuing conditions in the domestic market. The perceived urgent necessity for some form of change was increased by the upcoming implementation of a decision not to apply the withholding tax requirement to interest payments on Eurobonds held by nonresidents after April 1985.

Other changes in the regulations governing corporate bonds also had a foreign impetus. The requirement that all domestic corporate bonds be backed by collateral had its origins in the financial instability of the 1920s

74. Economic Planning Agency, *Keizai Hakusho: Arata na Kokusaika ni Taiō Suru Nihon Keizai, 1984* (Economic White Paper: The Japanese Economy Coping with New Internationalization, 1984) (Tokyo: EPA, 1984), p. 218.

and early 1930s. The regulation was established in 1933 to decrease the risk to investors in corporate bonds and remained unchanged until the 1980s.[75] The first crack appeared when Sears, Roebuck and Company was allowed to make an unsecured yen-denominated bond issue, an event significant not only because the issue was unsecured but because it was the first foreign corporate issue of any sort, since rules on eligible foreign issuers of yen-denominated bonds (called samurai bonds) restricted the list to foreign governments and foreign government-owned enterprises (such as electric power utilities). Theoretically this relaxation signaled a change in rules for Japanese companies as well, but the initial effect proved to be minor. Although rules were to be worked out for unsecured issues of both convertible and straight bond issues, the details for straight bonds were deliberately left incomplete so that no corporation could be approved. The incremental change, however, meant that a trickle of unsecured convertible bond issues did begin. Starting with the Matsushita Corporation in April 1979, twenty-two companies issued unsecured convertible bonds between 1979 and 1984.[76]

The next relaxation came in 1984 with completion of the rules for unsecured straight bonds, but these placed stringent balance sheet requirements that continued to severely limit the number of companies eligible to issue them. In January 1985 TDK Corporation became the first to issue an unsecured bond under these new rules, but the impact of the change was likely to remain limited. Responding to continuing pressure, the Ministry of Finance announced that a new study would be undertaken on the question of increasing the number of firms eligible to issue unsecured convertible bonds from about 100 (as of 1984) to 200 or 300.[77] The study would also consider a bond rating system to improve investor information, along with other more minor actions. After more committee reports and promises of future action came from the government in 1986,[78] the original expectation was eventually exceeded and the number of eligible companies increased to 360 in February 1987.

BANK–SECURITIES COMPANY VENTURES. The establishment of the investment advisory firms through which regular commercial banks and securities companies could gain additional business in an area technically

75. *Japan Economic Journal*, December 25, 1984.
76. *Japan Economic Journal*, November 13, 1984.
77. *Japan Economic Journal*, January 22, 1985.
78. *Japan Economic Journal*, January 25, 1986.

reserved for trust banks and life insurance companies was only one example of the gradual modification of Japan's strict segmentation of the financial sector. A rash of other actions was taking place by the mid-1980s in
which banks and securities companies created joint ventures for their
mutual benefit.

A common form of this cooperation has been the bank–security company credit cards usable for transactions with either institution. The idea
had become popular enough that in November 1984 major bankers held a
meeting to work out general rules for establishing the cards.[79] Other cooperative ventures involved foreign firms, though it would be incorrect to
identify them as the major force behind the changes. Daiwa Securities and
Citibank, for example, set up a new financial asset combining a demand
deposit at Citibank and a medium-term government bond fund at Daiwa,
with money automatically transferred to the fund when deposits in the
Citibank account exceeded a certain amount and the reverse when deposits
fell below a certain limit.[80] Daiwa Securities also established a broad
agreement with Sumitomo Bank, including a common credit card and a
securities-based collateral financing scheme in which Sumitomo would
automatically provide loans to those with securities in custody at Daiwa as
collateral, plus automatic transfer of interest payments, dividends, and
other proceeds from securities transactions to Daiwa bank accounts.[81]
Rules governing the nature of acceptable joint activities among banks and
securities firms were announced by the Ministry of Finance. Because it
preserved the official separation of banking and securities businesses, the
trend was not considered damaging.[82]

The strict separation of banking and securities within Japan does not
appear to be facing any imminent formal change as deregulation proceeds,
even though some erosion has taken place. However, the MOF has been
very flexible about allowing firms to engage in broader areas of business in
foreign countries. Sumitomo Bank's purchase of a large equity share of
Goldman Sachs in 1986 was a simple development because the Glass-
Steagall Act necessitated restrictions on the nature of Sumitomo's participation that were in keeping with MOF policy within Japan. Of greater
interest was the decision of Nomura Securities, Japan's largest securities
company, to enter banking in England. This action was approved by the

79. *Japan Times Weekly,* December 8, 1984.
80. *Japan Economic Journal,* November 20, 1984.
81. *Japan Economic Journal,* November 20, 1984.
82. Ministry of Finance, *Ginkōkyoku Kin'yū Nempō, 1984,* p. 52.

Bank of England and the MOF in 1986.[83] If this were to become a general trend, it would allow the ministry to preserve the separation of the two businesses at home while partially answering the demands from both banks and securities companies for greater flexibility.

Implications for Monetary Policy

All of the changes described here and the many other incremental adjustments in regulating the financial sector have had serious implications for Japanese monetary policy. At issue is whether, or to what extent, the government could or wanted to move away from direct controls, especially window guidance, toward indirect controls through influencing interest rates or monetary aggregates. To some extent this movement did take place, but as of the mid-1980s the final step of using operations in the open market to affect the money supply and interest rates was not yet one of the major policy tools.

Why was a change in monetary policy instruments necessary? Direct control through window guidance had provided an effective, rapid means for the government to influence economic activity in the 1950s and 1960s whenever balance-of-payments problems dictated a temporary slowing of the economy to protect the value of the yen. However, the 1970s brought developments that undermined the premises on which that control was built. With the slowdown in economic growth, the corporate sector became less dependent on bank loans as a source of investment funds, and the banks in turn became less indebted to the Bank of Japan. At the end of 1970, for example, the city banks had ¥2.1 trillion in borrowings from the Bank of Japan discount window; but by the end of 1985 this amount had climbed to only ¥3.1 trillion, so that as a proportion of banks' total liabilities, loans from the Bank of Japan dropped from 5.8 percent to 1.6 percent.[84] The connections between corporations and the city banks, and between the city banks and the Bank of Japan, were thus weaker than earlier. In addition, table 4-13 showed, the city banks' share of total financial-sector assets (the primary target of window guidance) was slipping.[85]

83. *Japan Times Weekly,* September 20, 1986.

84. Bank of Japan, *Economic Statistics Annual, 1985,* pp. 49–50.

85. Technically, window guidance limits are announced for other financial institutions as well. However, only the city banks have been major borrowers at the Bank of Japan's discount window, so that there was no effective mechanism to keep these other institutions in line.

Because of these changes, guidance to the city banks took effect more slowly and perhaps with less force. When the Bank of Japan wanted to tighten monetary policy, it could still use window guidance limits on the city banks and try to enforce those limits through its own lending policy at the discount window. But the banks felt less compulsion to obey. Restrictions could be circumvented through increased borrowing from the short-term markets, supplemented by the advent of the gensaki market. In addition, window guidance applied only to yen-denominated lending, and since 1979 Japanese banks have been allowed to make foreign currency loans within Japan. Finally, the expansion of Japanese banks overseas and the elimination in 1984 of ceilings on the conversion of foreign currency bank assets into yen meant that banks could circumvent the discount window by transferring funds from their overseas branches. Since the Bank of Japan was such a minor source of funds to the banks by the 1980s, the higher cost of other sources had relatively little effect on them. If the city banks did follow the guidance, its impact on economic activity would still be diminished because of the declining role of the city banks and the declining dependence of corporations on those loans.

Despite the decreased effectiveness of window guidance, it remained in the collection of primary monetary policy tools as late as 1979, following the second oil shock. From the first quarter of 1979, when the Bank of Japan announced that city banks should limit themselves to a 9.1 percent increase in lending over the first quarter in 1978, the guidelines were progressively tightened to a stringent 5.9 percent increase for the third quarter of 1980 (table 4-21). In most quarters the banks' actual increase in lending exceeded the recommendations, but not by much, so that the trend was for a deceleration in the growth of lending. From the first quarter of 1980 through the third quarter, the increase was above the recommended level by only 0.1 to 0.6 percentage point. Window guidance thus remained intact at the end of the 1970s, the most recent period during which monetary restraint was applied, and appears to have been effective. However, even though the city banks followed the advice, window guidance had a slower and smaller impact on the economy than it did in the 1950s and 1960s.

Realizing that guidance had begun to outlive its usefulness, the Bank of Japan increasingly used its discount rate as an instrument of monetary policy. Compared with its use in the 1950s and 1960s, the discount rate was moved flexibly up and down during the 1970s and 1980s. Inflation also gyrated more than it did during the 1960s, so that changes in the

Table 4-21. *Window Guidance and Discount Rates, Quarterly, 1979–80*
Percent growth from same period previous year unless otherwise specified

	Growth in level of outstanding loans and discounts of city banks[a]		Bank of Japan discount rate at end
Quarter	*Recommended*	*Actual*	*of period*
1979			
First	9.1	9.0	3.5
Second	8.7	8.2	4.25
Third	7.4	8.1	5.25
Fourth	6.6	6.1	6.25
1980			
First	6.4	6.7	9.0
Second	6.1	6.7	9.0
Third	5.9	6.0	8.25
Fourth	7.6	7.1	7.25

Sources: Japan Economic Institute, *Yearbook of U.S.-Japan Economic Relations, 1980* (Washington, D.C.: JEI, 1981), p. 20; *1979*, p. 36; and Bank of Japan, *Economic Statistics Annual, 1980*, pp. 36, 93; *1979*, p. 93.
a. Recommended and actual growth rates are based on end-of-quarter figures for loans and discounts outstanding.

inflation-adjusted discount rate were not as great as the nominal changes. Nevertheless, comparatively wide swings in the discount rate were a new phenomenon in Japan.

The Bank of Japan discount rate was pushed to peaks of 9.0 percent at the end of 1973 and again in 1980 as part of the tightening of monetary policy to cope with inflation. They fell to postwar lows of 3.5 percent in 1978 and 2.5 percent in 1987 as part of the effort to stimulate the economy after inflation had been brought under control. Table 4-21 shows the rate's swift rise (compared with earlier experience in Japan) during the second oil shock, jumping from the low of 3.5 percent in the first quarter of 1979 to the peak of 9.0 percent a year later. While this peak was lower than the 14 percent the Federal Reserve discount rate reached in the United States (where inflation was higher), it still represented a major change for Japan.

Changes in the discount rate are tied to other interest rates in a much more direct fashion in Japan than in the United States, since the commercial banks keep their short-term prime lending rates set at 0.5 percentage point above the discount rate. Theoretically, the banks are no longer required to follow such a rigid pattern, but in fact they have continued to do so. Thus changes in the Bank of Japan discount rate automatically affect prime lending rates (and presumably actual lending rates), which then affect economic activity by dampening or expanding the demand for loans. In addition, all deposit rates are normally adjusted when the discount rate is changed, usually within one month.

The other major indirect tool of monetary policy is alteration of the money supply and interest rates through purchases and sales of bonds, known in the United States as open-market operations. At first glance the Bank of Japan would seem to be heavily involved in open-market operations, since government bonds form a large portion of its total assets—56 percent by the end of 1985. And because Japan now has a vigorous secondary market in government bonds, it would appear the Bank of Japan could easily make open-market operations its most important means of effecting monetary policy. But much of the Bank of Japan's purchase of government bonds has been for reasons only vaguely related to monetary policy. As mentioned earlier, until the mid-1970s the bank tacitly promised to buy the bonds from the commercial banks after they had held them for at least one year from the date of issue. Later in the 1970s the bank purchased government bonds on certain occasions to reduce the interest rate differential between the secondary market and new issues so that the Ministry of Finance could avoid increasing the interest rates on the new issues. There is no reason why such purchases would necessarily be consistent with the macroeconomic goals of monetary policy.

Bank of Japan officials now attach greater importance to adjusting market interest rates, but not through purchases of government bonds. Instead, the bank has intervened in the bill discount market, one of the principal short-term markets considered earlier. By buying or selling in this market it can alter the cost at which banks borrow from one another and, by raising or lowering the cost of funds in this way, eventually affect a broader range of interest rates and lending activity. Changing the bill discount rate affects the other short-term markets (principally the call market and the gensaki market), which in turn affects other interest rates. However, the success of this strategy remains unclear. A number of key interest rates such as the prime lending rates or deposit rates are not market determined, so that transmissions of price signals from activities in short-term money markets could be muted.

One of the main hindrances to effective transmission of interest rates among markets, at least in the minds of the Japanese, is the lack of a major market in short-term government securities. The assumption is that because short-term markets are still rather thin, creation of a large short-term government securities market would remedy the problem. The 1984 economic white paper issued by the Economic Planning Agency argued that market issues of short-term government securities would deepen short-term markets in general, provide for the possibility of real open-market operations as a monetary policy tool, and generally enhance the importance of market-determined interest rates in the economy.[86] Bank of Japan officials say that they fully support the idea of short-term government securities for exactly these reasons but that the Ministry of Finance still clings to its fear that the change would increase the interest burden on government debt.

This argument over the desirability of open-market operations and of issuing larger amounts of short-term government debt at market-determined prices has been going on for some time. The calls for this change have been growing louder, though, and the increased sales of treasury bills to the private sector in 1986 may represent the beginning of a true market.[87] However, were Japan to face the necessity of severely tightening monetary policy in the very near future, it would almost certainly continue to rely most heavily on a combination of window guidance and changes in the discount rate to achieve the desired results.

Conclusion

Between the early 1970s and the mid-1980s Japan's financial markets changed significantly. Because of the nature of Japanese society, the process of adjusting to the changes assigned a great deal of importance to factors such as fairness, avoiding clear winners and losers, achieving consensus decisions, and exercising caution to avoid the possibility of instability or failures in the financial sector. While Japan will continue to act in accordance with the pressures and constraints of its society, change and deregulation will continue because a consensus agrees these changes are needed and because the fundamental economic conditions and market developments that encouraged them will not go away. Those who oppose change understand that they cannot entirely block it and are left with ensuring that their minority concerns are given sufficient consideration along the way. Deregulation appears to be accelerating as opposition weakens and as previous adjustments cause more significant shifts in the

86. Economic Planning Agency, *Keizai Hakusho, 1984*, pp. 204–05.
87. See, for example, *Japan Times Weekly*, December 29, 1984, which discusses a Bank of Japan report calling for an active short-term treasury bill market to facilitate open-market operations.

distribution of market shares and profitability among different types of financial institutions.

This process has had relatively little to do with pressure from foreign institutions or foreign governments. They have been useful at times in creating the critical mass necessary to achieve a desired reaction, but the major proponents and beneficiaries of most policy innovations have been Japanese, not foreigners. It is the existence of this strong domestic constituency that has made the process possible and guarantees that it will continue. Were foreign pressure the only voice for change, far less would have happened.

Having presided over this considerable amount of deregulation in the domestic financial markets, the government has proudly emphasized how much it has done. The 1984 economic white paper even put financial deregulation in Japan in the same category as in the United States. But believing such statements requires a leap of imagination, given the continuing restrictions on the range of financial instruments available and the strong limitations on the use of many of them.

In negotiating with Japan for further changes, the United States and other interested parties will be able to point to these continuing controls and to criticize the lack of sufficient (or sufficiently rapid) progress. Nevertheless, decisions will continue to be made in a Japanese context that emphasizes caution and incremental adjustments. Achieving an initial decision to create a new financial instrument or to allow a new form of foreign participation in the domestic market is far more important than gaining all that is demanded, because the initial opening will set the stage for a progression of further steps widening the scope of activity. That the Japanese government will move away from liberalization and decontrol is now almost inconceivable, but it is unrealistic to expect Japan to be as adventurous as the United States in the process of financial innovation or deregulation. The United States has had markets for many years in instruments such as unsecured commercial paper that still do not exist in Japan. Viewed in the context of other changes in Japanese economic regulation, the record during the past decade in the financial sector and the prospect for continued change is impressive.

CHAPTER FIVE

International Economic Transformation

THE DECLINE in economic growth, the attendant shifts in macro-economic structure, and the domestic pressures to alter financial regulations have all had important implications for Japan's international economic relations. Japan has generated enormous and unprecedented trade and current-account surpluses, extensively liberalized its international financial transactions, emerged as a major investor and lender around the world, and become embroiled in raucous disputes with many of its major trading partners over some of these developments. The same considerations are involved in looking at these international developments as were involved in the discussions of domestic changes in chapters 3 and 4. The organizing principle remains the macroeconomic identity, which summarizes what has happened to Japan's current-account and capital flow position. The same institutional pressures that led to controlled deregulation of domestic financial markets produced the international liberalization of capital flows.

Why separate out these macroeconomic and institutional issues when both are extensions of analyses in earlier chapters and could easily and logically have been incorporated there? Because the international side of the issues is the point of contact with the United States and the rest of the world. Since the United States has exerted heavy pressure on Japan to lower merchandise trade barriers and to liberalize financial transactions, the issues are worth analyzing together. Negotiations on these matters have been contentious and have seriously threatened the broad postwar movement toward more liberal trade. If a general protectionist outburst is to be avoided, policy must be grounded in a clear awareness of what is happening in Japan.

The developments covered here have their origin in the early 1970s, but the most dramatic and rapid evolution has been during the 1980s. Japan's emergence as a major creditor, in particular, could fundamentally alter its economic and political relationship with the world in the coming decade. These have been remarkable changes for a country that began the 1970s still insulated in many ways from international financial markets. Many aspects of Japan's emerging international position have been misunderstood—ranging from the meaning of capital flows in the balance of payments and the impact of deregulation on the yen-dollar exchange rate to the mistaken connection drawn between the country's trade barriers and its high trade surpluses.

Japan's International Economic Transactions

Massive current-account surpluses have been an integral part of the economic changes engendered by the permanent slowdown in economic growth after the early 1970s. This tendency toward surplus was masked in the rest of the decade by the temporary deficits caused by the two oil crises as the value of imports surged and because the first phase of the adjustment to slower growth emphasized spending and tax policies that resulted in the sharp expansion of fiscal deficits. In the 1980s, however, the tendency toward external surplus became painfully obvious and was even exacerbated by macroeconomic policy developments in the United States that resulted in external deficits which provided a ready outlet for Japan's surpluses.

Although world events clearly affected Japan's position, the domestic developments considered in chapter 3 are of critical importance. In particular, the decision of the government to pursue fiscal austerity after 1978 in the face of continued savings surpluses in the private sector was the essential cause of Japan's enormous external surpluses. From only 0.5 percent of GNP in 1981, these surpluses reached 4.4 percent by 1986, an extraordinarily high level.

Economists and government officials in Japan generally eschew responsibility for these surpluses, placing the blame on the U.S. deficits that attracted goods and capital from Japan. The role of the United States cannot be denied, but neither can the primary responsibility of Japan. Had

Japan's Balance-of-Payments Accounting Framework

Exports (f.o.b.)
− Imports (f.o.b.)
= Merchandise trade balance
+ Services exports
− Services imports
+ Unilateral transfers
= Current-account balance
+ Long-term capital balance
= Basic balance
+ Short-term capital balance
+ Errors and omissions
= Overall balance
− Official monetary movements
− Private monetary movements
= 0

the government not pursued fiscal contraction, these surpluses would not have emerged. Their accommodation by the United States and the rest of the world was a necessary condition for Japan's fiscal austerity to succeed without driving the economy into recession, but given that accommodation, Japan continued forceful pursuit of austerity.

The Balance-of-Payments Accounting Framework

The detailed picture of developments in Japan's external economic transactions can be best understood through the balance-of-payments accounting framework (see the chart above). Surprisingly few people understand the principles underlying this organization of international transactions.[1] The key feature is summarized by the word "balance" itself. What enters the country must equal what leaves; strictly speaking, there can be no such thing as a balance-of-payments surplus. Surpluses or

1. This organizational framework is somewhat different from that used in the United States, which no longer groups capital flows into long- and short-term and no longer separates out monetary movements. The change in the United States was prompted by the belief that no single partial balance (current-account, basic balance, or overall balance) really has much meaning. Japan, however, has continued to organize data in this fashion.

deficits can exist only for a subset of the accounts that make up the balance of payments.

The principal division within this framework is between trade (or current) transactions and capital movements. If the current account is in surplus (or deficit), it will necessarily be offset by an equal capital outflow (or inflow) so that the bottom line comes to zero. Many people are puzzled as to why trade and capital flows should necessarily come to a zero balance in these accounts. After all, the decisions to export, import, or invest abroad are made independently by separate economic actors. The answer is simple. Suppose the Japanese had a current-account surplus—that they received more for their exports than they paid for imports—and no one chose to invest their foreign-currency receipts in foreign equity or interest-bearing, foreign-currency-denominated financial instruments. Someone—individuals, corporations, financial institutions, or the government—must then hold the currency. This net increase of foreign currency represents a capital outflow, since currency is a non-interest-bearing debt instrument of governments. In the structure of the Japanese balance of payments this flow would show up in the category labeled "private monetary movements." In reality, of course, most foreign currency earnings are invested in other financial assets, but even though decisions to invest in foreign corporate equity or interest-bearing financial instruments are made independently of merchandise trade decisions, the flow of currency supplies the necessary balancing item.

In a practical sense, there is a problem in establishing the balance between trade and capital flows that stems from the inability to measure all transactions. Therefore, the actual balance in the statistics is provided by the category "errors and omissions." This category has tended to be very large in the United States (as high as $40 billion in some years), while it is generally small in Japan because of the more comprehensive reporting requirements resulting from the legacy of tight control over foreign exchange transactions.

While the movement of currency provides the automatic element necessary to maintain the definition of balance, some explanation is still required for why a current-account surplus is roughly offset by capital outflow. Because Japan has generated more domestic savings since the early 1970s than the society (the private sector and the government) has wanted to invest, domestic interest rates have been pushed down relative to those in other countries (such as the United States, where investment has exceeded savings in recent years). This differential in interest rates and the expectation that it will continue has led investors to buy foreign financial assets. To do so, they must exchange yen for foreign currencies. The sale of yen for other currencies depresses the value of the yen on foreign exchange markets, which in turn makes Japanese exports more price competitive and imports less price competitive, causing the current-account surplus to grow and offset the capital outflow.

This story of how trade and capital flows come into balance is oversimplified but basically represents what now underlies many economic models. Earlier economists focused more on the current account, assuming that a surplus would lead to appreciation of the currency. However, the very rapid rise of international capital flows in the 1970s and 1980s has led to revised thinking about currency markets. Even now, though, the dynamics of exchange markets remain poorly understood, especially since expectations of future interest rates, trade balances, or other factors appear to be both important and virtually impossible to predict.

The importance of capital flows in determining exchange rates implies a yen that many American businessmen considered "weak" or "undervalued" against the dollar in much of the 1970s and early 1980s. When people say that the yen is undervalued, they mean that at prevailing exchange rates the prices of Japanese products appear lower than U.S. prices (or those of other countries) for identical products. The implication of the term "undervalued" is that the yen ought to be strong enough to produce rough parity in prices of tradable goods. A whole theory called purchasing power parity has arisen around this idea.[2] However, macroeconomic conditions in Japan, coupled with the U.S. move toward international deficits, meant that Japan would generate large current-account surpluses, of which the trade surplus was the most important component. In order for this to occur it was essential that Japanese export goods have a price advantage in international markets. Given these macroeconomic conditions in the first half of the 1980s, therefore, a yen that appeared weak according to the concept of purchasing power parity was a necessary outcome.

Table 5-1 shows the movement of the yen. In 1971 it finally departed from the relation of 360 yen to the dollar that had prevailed since 1949. The fluctuations have since been very wide within the general trend of yen appreciation. In a very crude sense the concept of purchasing power parity does help explain the overall movement. Even with Japan generating large

2. See Arturo Brillembourg. "Purchasing Power Parity and the Balance of Payments: Some Empirical Evidence," *International Monetary Fund Staff Papers,* vol. 24 (March 1977), pp. 77–79, for a review of the concept.

Table 5-1. *Balance of Payments, by Type of Account, 1970–86*
Billions of dollars unless otherwise specified

Year	Merchandise trade balance	Services trade balance	Unilateral transfers	Current-account balance	Net long-term capital	Basic balance	Net short-term capital	Errors and omissions	Overall balance	Official monetary movements	Private monetary movements	Yen-dollar exchange rate (¥ per $)[a]
1970	4.0	-1.8	-0.2	2.0	-1.6	0.4	0.7	0.3	1.4	0.9	0.6	360
1971	7.8	-1.7	-0.3	5.8	-1.1	4.7	2.4	0.5	7.7	10.8	-3.0	349
1972	9.0	-1.9	-0.5	6.6	-4.5	2.1	2.0	0.6	4.7	3.1	1.8	303
1973	3.7	-3.5	-0.3	-0.1	-9.7	-9.9	2.4	-2.6	-10.0	-6.1	-4.0	272
1974	1.4	-5.8	-0.3	-4.7	-3.9	-8.6	1.8	0.0	-6.8	1.3	-8.1	292
1975	5.0	-5.4	-0.4	-0.7	-0.3	-1.0	-1.1	-0.6	-2.7	-0.7	-2.0	297
1976	9.9	-5.9	-0.3	3.7	-1.0	2.7	0.1	0.1	2.9	3.8	-0.9	297
1977	17.3	-6.0	-0.4	10.9	-3.2	7.7	-0.6	0.7	7.7	6.2	1.5	269
1978	24.6	-7.4	-0.7	16.5	-12.4	4.1	1.5	0.3	6.0	10.2	-4.2	210
1979	1.8	-9.5	-1.1	-8.8	-13.0	-21.7	2.7	2.3	-16.7	-12.7	-4.0	219
1980	2.1	-11.3	-1.5	-10.7	2.3	-8.4	3.1	-3.1	-8.4	4.9	-13.3	227
1981	20.0	-13.6	-1.6	4.8	-9.7	-4.9	2.3	0.5	-2.1	3.2	-5.3	221
1982	18.1	-9.8	-1.4	6.9	-15.0	-8.1	-1.6	4.7	-5.0	-5.1	0.2	249
1983	31.5	-9.1	-1.5	20.8	-17.7	3.1	0.0	2.1	5.2	1.2	3.9	238
1984	44.3	-7.7	-1.5	35.0	-49.7	-14.6	-4.3	3.7	-15.2	1.8	-17.0	238
1985	56.0	-5.2	-1.7	49.2	-64.5	-15.4	-1.0	4.0	-12.3	0.2	-12.5	239
1986	92.8	-4.9	-2.1	85.8	-131.5	-45.6	-1.6	2.5	-44.8	15.7	-60.5	169

Sources: Bank of Japan, *Balance of Payments Monthly* (April 1987), pp. 7–8; (November 1976), pp. 1–2; and International Monetary Fund, *International Financial Statistics Yearbook, 1986* (Washington, D.C.: IMF, 1986), pp. 418–19.
a. Annual average.

current-account surpluses in the 1980s, appreciation was necessary to prevent the price advantage of Japanese exports from becoming too large. Higher productivity growth and lower inflation in Japan than in the United States meant that at any given exchange rate Japan experienced a growing advantage in international competition.

The yen-dollar exchange rate has also been sensitive to other events. In the 1970s the two oil shocks reversed the appreciation of the yen as part of the macroeconomic adjustment made necessary by the jump in the price of oil. In 1973, 1974, 1975, 1979, and 1980 Japan experienced current-account deficits and a weakening exchange rate (see table 5-1). In these years the current-account deficits appeared to be the driving force in the exchange market, pushing down the value of the yen against the dollar. By definition, those deficits were offset by an inflow of capital, reversing the usual pattern. Table 5-1 indicates that long-term capital continued to flow out of Japan but that short-term capital flowed in and that the private sector reduced its holdings of foreign currency ("private monetary movements" in the table). However, the overall inflow of capital was not so strong as to offset the impact of the current-account deficits on the exchange rate (in contrast to the experience of the United States in the 1980s, with current-account deficits and a strengthening dollar because of strong capital inflows). What happened to produce these developments? The rising price of oil increased Japan's import bill while worldwide recession dampened the market for Japan's exports. The resulting current-account deficits pushed down the value of the yen, from an average of 272 to the dollar in 1973 to 297 in 1975.

These deficits can also be looked at in the macroeconomic accounting-identity framework. In the aftermath of the first oil shock, corporate savings dropped because of the recession and higher energy bills while corporate investment remained high, probably because it was based on decisions made before the shock. The corporate sector's net demand for investment funds from other sources thus increased, a move at odds with the drop in net corporate demands identified as part of the longer-term change discussed in chapter 3. By 1975, net corporate investment was declining, but the government began to respond to the recession by stimulating the economy, so its deficit spending increased faster than the net demand for funds by corporations decreased. The combination of private-sector and government savings and investment movements meant that in both 1974 and 1975 the demand for investment exceeded the domestic supply of savings. Capital inflow, the reverse side of the current-account deficit in those years, supplied the balance.

Once the immediate effects of the oil shock were over, Japan's current-account surplus rose rapidly, to $16.5 billion in 1978 (then a record amount) or 1.8 percent of GNP. The yen also rose rapidly, peaking at 176 to the dollar in October 1978, which reflected the fact that at its weakened level of 1974 and 1975, the prices of Japanese exports became more competitive than necessary to achieve the balance between domestic and international savings and investment once renewed world growth brought increased demand for Japan's exports. Although the current-account surpluses were, by definition, offset by capital outflows, the current account was again the dominant force in determining the exchange rate. According to table 5-1, the $16.5 billion current-account surplus in 1978 was offset by a $10.9 billion outflow of capital ($12.4 billion in long-term capital, minus a $1.5 billion inflow of short-term capital), as well as $10.2 billion in increased foreign exchange reserves (minus a $4.2 billion drop in private holdings of foreign currency).

The second oil shock checked this emerging tendency toward surpluses and a stronger yen. Once again the current account moved to deficit and the yen weakened (from an average 210 to the dollar in 1978 to 227 in 1980). Macroeconomic events were also similar to those of the first oil shock. In 1979, net investment by the corporate sector increased as improved economic growth in 1978 finally led to more optimistic corporate plans. Because household net savings had declined slightly and the government continued to run a large deficit, total domestic investment demand exceeded savings supply.

Once the immediate effects of the second oil shock passed, external surpluses returned again. This time they failed to generate a stronger yen until the sharp upturn in late 1985. Why? Unlike the experience of the 1970s, the massive net outflow of capital became the primary force in determining the exchange rate. Given the combination of continued surplus savings in the private sector and falling government deficits, money flowed out to the rest of the world, attracted by expectations of higher rates of return. This movement implied that Japanese investors were selling yen for foreign currencies (principally dollars) in order to buy foreign financial assets, thereby increasing the supply of yen and the demand for other currencies on foreign exchange markets. The size of these capital flows had become so large that they became the determining factor in the exchange market, and the rising current-account surpluses in the 1980s failed to produce a stronger yen until 1985. From 227 yen to the dollar in 1980, the exchange rate declined to an average 238 to the dollar between 1983 and 1985 (the averages mask some short-term fluctuations).

The two oil shocks demonstrate that external developments are quite capable of disrupting the normal pattern of surplus domestic savings in Japan. Although the macroeconomic balances adjusted to the external pressures in both cases, Japan experienced slower growth, including the actual recession in 1974 and the more drawn-out drop from 5 percent real growth in 1979 to just over 3 percent by 1982 and 1983. This growth was higher than that of other industrial countries, but the absolute decrease suggests that external factors disrupting the pattern of large surpluses tend to have a negative effect on the economy. However, it is also significant that both oil shocks were temporary. Once the economy adjusted to the new international environment, the primary pattern returned: people continued to save more than they invested, the government reverted to being adamant about trying to reduce fiscal deficits, and the rest of the world (principally the United States) absorbed Japan's surplus goods and capital. It all seemed permanent, but external events once again interrupted the pattern.

On September 22, 1985, the finance ministers of the five largest members of the International Monetary Fund (called the G-5) issued a statement that the dollar was overvalued. That announcement, buttressed by joint intervention in exchange markets and some tinkering with interest rates, led to a sustained fall in the value of the dollar and a strengthening of the yen.[3] From a level of 237 yen in September, the dollar fell to 203 yen by the end of the year, and near 150 yen by the summer of 1986, an appreciation of the yen of more than 50 percent. How could this happen when the basic macroeconomic situation—Japan's surplus savings and the surplus investment of the United States—had not changed? One important factor is that the exchange market is influenced heavily by expectations and interprets news in unpredictable ways. The Bank of Japan, for example, had been calling for, and intervening in favor of, a stronger yen for several years to no avail. This time the combined voice of the industrial nations convinced the market that the dollar was overvalued. These changes in the exchange rate could then force the necessary movement in macroeconomic balances. If the stronger yen were to prevail without any domestic policy changes, Japan would experience economic stagnation or

3. Technically, the appreciation of the yen began earlier in 1985. In February the yen bottomed at 260 to the dollar. This depressed value could be regarded as an unusual speculative bubble, however, and by August the yen was back to 237, a level close to its average in the previous two years. It was appreciation beyond this level that was a new development. Exchange rates here are monthly averages from the International Monetary Fund, *International Financial Statistics*.

recession and rising unemployment, which would force savings down and government deficits up (through automatic stabilizers).

The new international environment ushered in by the steep appreciation of the yen could well be the most difficult situation facing Japan since the early 1970s. Chapter 3 argued that fiscal policy has been very slow to respond to the new conditions imposed by the strong yen and a falling current-account surplus. If the yen remains strong—and there is no indication that it will not—and if the government does not offset its impact by altering domestic policy, reduced growth or recession could become the means of adjustment in the remainder of the 1980s. Not until the summer of 1987 did the Japanese government respond to this danger by modestly revising the direction of fiscal policy.

The Changing Current-Account Structure

One of the principal reasons Japan is now recognized as a world economic force has been the outpouring of capital that has accompanied its enormous current-account surpluses. By 1986 it had become the largest net investor in the world—$180 billion, a twenty-six-fold increase from $7 billion a decade earlier.[4] Even if its current-account surplus decreases as a result of the massive appreciation of the yen, the annual surpluses will likely continue on a reduced scale. This means that some capital outflow will continue, adding further to Japan's net foreign assets. Japan will be a major and highly visible participant in world markets—from stocks and bonds to real estate and art—for years to come.

This buildup of overseas assets has important implications for the structure of the country's balance of payments. Since the current account consists of merchandise and services trade and unilateral transfers (mostly foreign aid), the distribution of surpluses and deficits among these accounts is by no means fixed. In fact, a rapid change is already taking place.

The key to understanding this change is the composition of the services trade account. Many people assume that services trade is equivalent in definition to trade in service industries. But while such trade is included, the account also covers other transactions—in particular, earnings on foreign investment, which comprise profits on foreign direct investment, dividends and interest from portfolio investments, and interest from for-

4. Data on Japan's external assets and liabilities are published annually in the April issue of the Bank of Japan's *Balance of Payments Monthly.*

Table 5-2. *Investment Income in Services Trade, 1973–86*
Billions of dollars

Year	Investment income			Total balance on services	Services balance exclusive of investment income
	Received	Paid	Net		
1973	2.7	2.2	0.5	−3.5	−4.0
1974	3.6	4.0	−0.5	−5.8	−5.3
1975	3.6	3.9	−0.3	−5.4	−5.1
1976	3.5	3.7	−0.2	−5.9	−5.7
1977	3.7	3.6	0.1	−6.0	−6.1
1978	5.3	4.4	0.9	−7.4	−8.3
1979	9.0	7.0	2.0	−9.5	−11.5
1980	11.1	10.3	0.9	−11.3	−12.2
1981	15.8	16.5	−0.8	−13.6	−12.8
1982	18.3	16.6	1.7	−9.8	−11.5
1983	15.6	12.5	3.1	−9.1	−12.2
1984	18.8	14.5	4.2	−7.7	−11.9
1985	22.1	15.3	6.8	−5.2	−12.0
1986	29.1	19.6	9.5	−4.9	−14.4

Sources: Bank of Japan, *Balance of Payments Monthly* (March 1987), pp. 23, 30, 42; (July 1984), pp. 23, 30, 42.

eign loans made by banks.[5] Table 5-2 shows that in the 1970s Japan experienced increasing net surpluses on investment income, a trend interrupted by the oil shocks, because of the temporary reversal in net capital flow. Since 1981, when there was a net payment of $0.8 million because of the effect of the second oil shock, net earnings on foreign investment have been rising very rapidly, reaching $9.5 billion for 1986.

Other segments of the services account, however, have not changed very much. For many years, the net deficit on the account grew, driven in large part by increases in transportation expenses. Rising merchandise trade transactions led to larger deficits for transportation, exacerbated by an increasing dependence on foreign-flag vessels as Japanese labor costs rose (a development similar to, though not as extensive as, that in U.S. ocean shipping). As table 5-2 indicates, however, the balance on services transactions exclusive of investment earnings has changed very little since 1979. The temporary stagnation of merchandise trade in the wake of the second oil shock provides part of the explanation, but the pickup in trade volumes since 1982 has not been matched by much increase in the services

5. The money need not even be actually repatriated; earnings on foreign investment that are reinvested abroad are treated in the balance-of-payments statistics as a repatriation of earnings (a services transaction) and an equivalent outflow of capital.

deficit, at least until 1986.[6] This situation, combined with the rapidly emerging surplus on investment income, has meant the net balance on services trade contracted from a peak deficit of $13.6 billion in 1981 to only $4.9 billion in 1986.

What happens to the services account if some reasonable assumptions are made about the future course of the Japanese economy? Assume that from 1987 to 1995 GNP grows at a nominal rate of 7 percent (4 percent real growth plus 3 percent inflation), the current-account surplus averages 1.5 percent of nominal GNP (even though it has been considerably higher since 1983) and the exchange rate averages 160 yen to the dollar. Given these assumptions and actual net foreign assets of $180.4 billion in 1986 as a starting point, Japan would have net foreign assets of $578 billion by 1995 and would earn between $40 billion (assuming a 7 percent return on investment) and $58 billion (assuming a 10 percent return) annually, a dramatic increase from the $6.8 billion of net earnings in 1985. If the other segments of the services account were to grow at the average pace of 1975–85, they would expand to $28 billion by 1995; but given the relative stagnation of that part of the account since 1979, such an expansion appears unlikely (the shift away from Japanese-flag shipping may now be at an end, and other accounts such as fees and royalties will also move toward surplus because Japan is quickly becoming a net technology exporter). Therefore the rapid rise in net investment income will eliminate Japan's longstanding services deficit, turning it to a surplus of from $12 billion to $29 billion. And if annual capital outflows are higher or the yen stronger than 160 to the dollar—both of which conditions are likely—the change from deficit to surplus for the entire services account will take place by 1988 and will be billions of dollars higher by 1995.[7]

6. The deficit on transportation-related charges grew from $2.1 billion in 1975 to $4.3 billion in 1980 but improved to $2.5 billion by 1986. Another hypothesis would be that Japan's traditional deficit on patent royalties and other licensing fees reversed direction as the country moved to the forefront of technology in the 1970s and 1980s. But this has not been the case. Net payments on patent royalties continued to grow virtually every year from 1975 to 1986. The net deficit on management fees and other miscellaneous fees, however, stopped growing in the 1980s and is probably related to technology transfer in a broad sense (although miscellaneous fees include royalties on movies, printed publications, and other items not related to technology). The most that can be said about these categories is that Japan's deficit ceased growing so rapidly; for "other private transactions," which includes patent royalties, management fees, and miscellaneous fees, the country had a deficit of $2.6 billion in 1975, expanding rapidly to $7.4 billion by 1981, and then climbing slowly to $8.7 billion by 1986. Bank of Japan, *Balance of Payments Monthly* (March 1987), pp. 23–24; (April 1986), pp. 23–24.

7. At an exchange rate of 140 yen to the dollar, for example, cumulative net foreign

The other element that should be considered here is the probable course of unilateral transfers. This account has moved toward larger deficits as Japan has increased its foreign aid, and the deficits ought to continue growing slowly for the next decade.[8] Tokyo has not subjected foreign aid to the same severe constraints placed on other forms of government spending, but fiscal austerity has nevertheless limited increases. The government, for example, failed to meet the ambitious goals for foreign aid expansion mapped out in 1979 because fiscal austerity began just as the program began. New medium-term guidelines announced in the fall of 1985 called for a fairly modest expansion to double foreign aid by 1992 (a 10 percent annual growth). Therefore, the deficit on unilateral transfers appears unlikely to increase by more than $2 billion by the early 1990s (from a deficit of $1.7 billion in 1985).

What do these adjustments imply for merchandise trade surpluses? If current-account surpluses stay about the same size relative to GNP, the dramatic change in the services account suggests that merchandise trade surpluses will be smaller. This is now happening. The appreciation of the yen has been forcing a decrease in the merchandise trade surplus since the beginning of 1987, but on the current account the decline will be moderated by the increase in investment income. Growing investment earnings from abroad also imply an increase in domestic income that will go into both consumption and savings. Rising consumption ought to cause more demand for Japanese manufactured products, which could either divert goods from exports or lead to greater corporate investment to expand production.

An alternative picture is also possible in which the development of surpluses in the services account simply leads to larger current-account surpluses rather than to smaller merchandise-trade surpluses. This would result if the increase in investment earnings from abroad goes largely into savings. If, for example, the marginal propensity to save the increases in income from investment earnings abroad is 100 percent, domestic consumption would not grow, and the increase in savings would only widen

---

assets in 1995 would rise to $634 billion and annual interest to about $44 billion at a 7 percent return or $63 billion at a 10 percent return.

8. Note that only the grant portion of foreign aid appears here. A large part of Japan's foreign aid takes the form of loans (both bilateral ones and those to multilateral aid organizations such as the World Bank). In 1985 a little less than one-third of Japan's official development assistance was through bilateral grants. This proportion has been rising slowly. Eileen Marie Doherty, "Japan's Foreign Aid Policy: 1986 Update," *JEI Report*, no. 39A (October 1986), pp. 1–12.

the private-sector savings-investment imbalance, which (if the government deficit is not affected in some way) would simply push up the current-account surplus. Such a situation would result if, for example, Japanese investors reinvested all their foreign earnings abroad without actually bringing them back to Japan. The balance of payments would show a repatriation of investment earnings and an offsetting capital outflow, but no real transactions that would alter the exchange rate or domestic consumption would have taken place.

This development is unlikely since a very high proportion of reinvestment abroad may characterize direct investment (in which companies reinvest the earnings of their foreign subsidiaries in new plant and equipment in those subsidiaries rather than repatriating the money and distributing it to shareholders as dividends) but not other forms of investment. Earnings on many investments, such as the earnings of pension funds, will be repatriated and distributed to meet obligations, thus expanding domestic consumption. Only about 30 percent of Japan's net foreign assets are in the form of direct investments. While rising net investment income from abroad may not bring about a mechanistic one-for-one substitution of the services surplus for the merchandise-trade surplus, the net effect after all the complex transmissions within the economic system are worked through should be smaller merchandise-trade surpluses relative to what would have otherwise occurred.

The U.S. Role in Japan's Surpluses

From 1983 through 1986 Japan's annual current-account surplus was far higher than Japanese forecasters expected. The explanation involves Japan's surplus savings and exogenous factors such as macroeconomic developments in the United States or the beginnings of the decline in oil prices. The inclination of the Japanese is to put responsibility for the surpluses on the United States—the large U.S. budget deficits and resulting high interest rates that led to an overvalued dollar plus rapid economic growth that sucked in additional imports. The inclination of Americans is to put at least part of the responsibility on Japan by focusing on Japanese macroeconomic conditions. These differences matter greatly. If the problem lies with the United States, the solution must come from changes in U.S. policy. That is, reducing the budget deficits will reduce both the U.S. current-account deficits and Japan's surpluses. If the problem lies with the United States and Japan (plus other major industrial countries with external surpluses), the solution requires actions from both sides. Tokyo's insistence that the growth of its surpluses since the early 1980s is the fault of the United States supports the government position that fiscal policy should not be used to stimulate the economy.[9] Is this position sustainable?

Theoretically it is possible to separate the domestic effects from the external effects on Japan's current-account surplus through estimating statistical relationships. One such attempt by the Japanese government in the economic white paper for 1984 came to the conclusion that most of the $15.1 billion increase in Japan's current-account surplus from 1982 to 1983 was caused by external factors. Considering the decline in oil prices, U.S. economic conditions, and an overvaluation of the dollar as external factors, the Economic Planning Agency found that they accounted for $14.4 billion of the total increase, or 95 percent. Japan's long-term structural macroeconomic factors contributed only $0.7 billion. In the absence of the external factors, Japan's current-account surplus would have been close to 1 percent of GNP.[10]

The study concluded that $2.7 billion of the increase was due to lower oil prices, $3.8 billion to U.S. economic conditions, and $6.4 billion to the exchange rate. These are reasonable figures, although precise numbers will vary with the specification of the model. But are all three of these items truly external factors? Oil prices fit this categorization but not the others. The assumption that the exchange rate is an external factor can be questioned, and the value assigned to this factor was purely arbitrary (since their choice of an equilibrium rate against which to compare the actual exchange rate was based on arbitrary purchasing power parity criteria). The exchange rate is better explained as the result of macroeconomic developments in both Japan and the United States rather than as a true

9. This contrast in U.S.-Japanese analysis and policy prescriptions is starkly evident in several papers presented at a conference in New York cosponsored by Columbia University and the Institute of Fiscal and Monetary Policy, which is related to the Ministry of Finance, in June 1986. Masaru Yoshitomi in "Growth Gaps, Exchange Rates and Asymmetry: Is It Possible to Unwind Current-Account Imbalances Without Fiscal Expansion in Japan?" answers his question with a yes. Both Stephen Marris, in his comments on Yoshitomi's paper, and C. Fred Bergsten in "The U.S.-Japan Economic Problem: Next Steps" argue forcefully in favor of both U.S. fiscal contraction and Japanese fiscal expansion. See Hugh T. Patrick and Ryūichi Tachi, eds., *Japan and the United States Today: Exchange Rates, Macroeconomic Policies and Financial Market Innovations* (Center on Economy and Business, Columbia University, 1987).

10. Economic Planning Agency, *Keizai Hakusho, 1984: Arata na Kokusai ni Taiō Suru Nihon Keizai* (Economic White Paper, 1984: The Japanese Economy Coping with New Internationalization) (Tokyo: ETA, 1984), pp. 70–79.

Table 5-3. *Japan's Trade with the United States, 1973–86*

Year	Exports to United States (f.o.b.)		Imports from United States (c.i.f.)	
	Billions of dollars	*Percent of total*	*Billions of dollars*	*Percent of total*
1973	9.4	25.6	9.3	24.2
1974	12.8	23.0	12.7	20.4
1975	11.1	20.0	11.6	20.1
1976	15.7	23.3	11.8	18.2
1977	19.7	24.5	12.4	17.5
1978	24.9	25.5	14.8	18.6
1979	26.4	25.6	20.4	18.5
1980	31.4	24.2	24.4	17.4
1981	38.6	25.4	25.3	17.7
1982	36.3	26.2	24.2	18.3
1983	42.8	29.1	24.6	19.5
1984	59.9	35.2	26.9	19.7
1985	65.3	37.2	25.8	19.9
1986	80.5	38.5	29.1	23.0

Sources: Bank of Japan, *Balance of Payments Monthly* (January 1987), pp. 15, 19; (July 1984), pp. 15, 19.

exogenous factor. Economic conditions in the United States are also inter-connected with Japan; had Japan not been in the position to be a major creditor, the Reagan administration might not have been able to pursue fiscal expansion without driving up interest rates and creating inflation that would have forced more cautious policies. While Japan deserves no blame for U.S. developments, they cannot be viewed as completely independent. The most that can be said is that the macroeconomic policies of the Reagan administration were an important, relatively independent ingredient in the rise of Japan's external surpluses.

The importance of the United States in the buildup of Japanese surpluses is demonstrated in table 5-3. In 1981, 25.4 percent of all Japanese exports went to the United States, a level similar to those of previous years. By 1986 this share had risen to 38.5 percent. Of the $57.1 billion increase in Japan's exports from 1981 to 1986, exports to the United States increased by $41.8 billion. This stands as stark evidence of the importance of the U.S. market for Japan's overall export success at a time when rapid export growth, combined with slow import growth, was a central ingredient in Japan's total economic performance.

Casting back once again to the macroeconomic identity, what did this development imply? Increases in Japan's surplus generated by the demand from the United States and by falling oil prices meant that either the government deficit or the private-sector savings-investment balance must have adjusted. Part of the explanation lies in Japanese government fiscal policy. The pull from abroad came while the administrative reform movement was in full swing. As table 3-2 showed, from 1980 to 1985 the government deficit shrank from 4.4 percent of GNP to 0.8 percent. At the same time, the surplus of savings over investment in the private sector increased from 3.2 percent of GNP to 4.0 percent. One reason for this increase might be that corporate profits generated by rising exports were larger than the increase in corporate investment needed to produce the additional output. Another interpretation might be that the enormous appetite for foreign capital to finance the U.S. fiscal deficit kept Japanese investment at home lower than it would have been if savings had not fled abroad. There is, however, little evidence to support this claim.

While the strong dollar and the expansion of U.S. deficits did contribute to Japan's rapidly rising current-account surplus, these conditions cannot explain all of it. In their absence Japan would still have had sizable global current-account surpluses. The EPA estimates of 1 percent of GNP seem low; the long-term forecasts of Japanese growth discussed in chapter 2 suggest a level closer to 2 percent. More important, the Japanese government willingly accommodated the pressure for larger surpluses. Rather than pushing ahead vigorously with administrative reform, it could have pursued a more stringent monetary policy (higher interest rates) and a more expansionary fiscal policy to resist the foreign pull. This would have made the interest rate advantage of overseas investment smaller and provided more domestic stimulus to absorb output. Apportioning the causes for the surpluses among Japanese structural features and special external pressures is an imperfect explanation at best and can be quite misleading.

Other, more careful research supports this view. Professor Kazuo Ueda of Osaka University has extensively analyzed Japan's current account through macroeconomic econometric models, and has concluded that the primary factor responsible for the rising surplus was the divergence of U.S. and Japanese fiscal policies. He deliberately avoids laying the responsibility or blame on either country alone.[11]

If both countries are responsible for Japanese surpluses and U.S. deficits, then policies to correct the situation must necessarily involve both

11. Kazuo Ueda, "The Japanese Current-Account Surplus and Fiscal Policy in Japan and the U.S.," paper presented at the 1985 International Symposium on Current Policy Issues in the United States and Japan.

Table 5-4. *U.S.–Japanese Trade and Investment, 1973, 1985*
Percent

Component	1973	1985
Trade		
Japan's share of U.S. exports	12	11
Japan's share of U.S. imports	14	20
U.S. share of Japan's exports	26	37
U.S. share of Japan's imports (c.i.f)	24	20
Direct Investment		
Japan's share of outward U.S. investment	3	4
Japan's share of inward investment in U.S.	1	10
U.S. share of outward Japanese investment	23	33[a]
U.S. share of inward investment in Japan	66[b]	43[a]

Sources: Ministry of Finance, *Ōkurashō Kokusai Kin'yūkyoku Nempō, 1986* (International Finance Division Year-book, 1986) (Tokyo: Kin'yu Zaisei Jijō Kenkyūkai, 1986), pp. 452–53, 466; Bureau of the Census, *Statistical Abstract of the United States, 1987* (GPO, 1987), pp. 792–94; *1977*, pp. 868–70; Bank of Japan, *Balance of Payments Monthly* (November 1986), pp. 15, 19; (July 1984), pp. 15, 19; and U.S. Department of Commerce, Bureau of Economic Analysis, *Survey of Current Business*, vol. 55 (October 1975), pp. 41, 52; vol. 66 (August 1986), pp. 49, 79; Lawrence B. Krause and Sueo Sekiguchi, "Japan and the World Economy," in Hugh Patrick and Henry Rosovski, *Asia's New Giant: How the Japanese Economy Works* (Brookings, 1976), p. 446.
a. Figures are for 1984.
b. In 1972.

countries. The Japanese attribution of all blame and all responsibility to the United States is not sustainable. Tokyo has done very little to contribute to a solution.

Before leaving this topic, one other feature of Japan's external relationships should be pointed out. Table 5-3 showed the high percentage of Japan's exports that come to the U.S. market and how that percentage increased in the first half of the 1980s. In a broader context the economic ties between Japan and the United States are also asymmetrical, with Japan far more dependent on the United States than the reverse. Whereas the share of Japan's exports destined for the United States has been high and rising, the share of U.S. exports going to Japan has been stable at 11 to 12 percent (table 5-4). The same disparity is evident in foreign direct investment. In 1984, 33 percent of the accumulated value of Japan's foreign direct investment was located in the United States, but only 4 percent of U.S. foreign direct investment was located in Japan. Looked at from the perspective of the host country, 10 percent of foreign investment in the United States came from Japan, whereas 43 percent of foreign investment in Japan was from the United States.

These data suggest two points. First, given the evidence and Japan's recognition of the importance of the U.S. market, it is not at all surprising that Japan accommodated the external factors leading to a rapid expansion of the current-account surplus in the first half of the 1980s. A long history of heavy involvement with the United States and an investment in sales and service infrastructure to support that involvement meant Japanese firms were well positioned to expand their exports as the dollar rose and the U.S. economy recovered after 1982. Second, in terms of bilateral trade negotiations, Japan can ill afford a serious rupture with the United States, which may explain its willingness to offer unilateral concessions when the pressure becomes strong enough.

Summary

The macroeconomic developments in Japan discussed in chapters 2 and 3 led to a chronic oversupply of domestic savings that was passed on to the rest of the world in the form of a current-account surplus and matching capital outflow. External forces, including the oil crises of the 1970s, U.S. macroeconomic policy in the first half of the 1980s, and falling oil prices in the mid-1980s, also affected the situation, but ex ante pressure from the domestic side was quite strong. Surplus savings in the private sector, coupled with falling government deficits after 1979, must be recognized as key elements in the surpluses.

As a result Japan emerged as the largest creditor nation in the world, and the accumulation of large net external assets was rapidly changing the structure of Japan's current account by the mid-1980s, with the services account swinging from its traditional deficit toward surplus. The effect of this change should be to take some of the pressure off merchandise exports in the future, although the precise outcome would depend on complex economic interactions.

The strong rise in the value of the yen that began in 1985 interjected some uncertainty into Japan's external position. While too little time has passed to judge the outcome, the rise did represent the first downward pressure on Japan's current-account surplus since the oil shock of 1979. If it were to have a long-term effect of lowering the surplus, however, either private-sector surplus savings would have to shrink or the government deficit would have to rise. Japan could achieve that result either through deliberate government policy or passively through recession.

Problems in U.S. Perceptions of Japan's Position

All too often, U.S. politicians, government officials, and private-sector spokesmen have confused the issues between Japan and the United States by attaching too much importance to the bilateral trade imbalance and by connecting the imbalances to Japan's trade barriers. There are very serious tensions over economic issues between the United States and Japan, and this confusion has not helped.

The first problem is misplaced emphasis on bilateral balances, a mistake that has been pointed out many times. Nothing in economic theory implies that bilateral trade or current-account balances between any two countries must be zero. A country could have a zero balance on its global current account while having very large surpluses and deficits with all its individual trading partners. U.S. politicians have responded that even though economic theory sees nothing wrong with bilateral imbalances, they cannot be ignored politically, especially when they reach the size of the imbalance with Japan.[12]

That bilateral imbalances do not matter economically does not mean they should be ignored. Its deficit with Japan is symptomatic of the global deficits the United States has incurred in the 1980s. Those balances vary with macroeconomic conditions, and the conditions can be influenced or changed through policy choices. By the mid-1980s, Americans had begun to question the economic sustainability of ever-larger U.S. international debts, and loud voices expressed concern about the long-term damage to leading manufacturing industries. To put it mildly, they were not content with large current-account deficits. But trade protectionism, a frequently voiced solution, would not address the problem. The United States must deal with the federal budget deficit as the key factor that has pushed it into large external deficits.

The second problem is the irrelevance of zero global balances on the current account. This chapter and chapter 3 have shown how Japan's current-account balance has been the outcome of an interplay of domestic and international macroeconomic forces that operated to balance the internal and external supply and demand for savings. In the 1970s and 1980s Japan was in a situation in which equilibrium for its economy included a

---

12. *U.S.–Japan Trade Report, September 5, 1980*, Committee Print, Subcommittee on Trade of the House Committee on Ways and Means, 96 Cong. 2 sess. (GPO, 1980), p. 3.

sizable current-account surplus. In an economic sense there was absolutely nothing wrong with this development. Economic theory draws virtually no conclusions about the desirability of current-account surpluses or deficits. The only principle is a rather vague notion of sustainability; do the flows producing the current-account surplus or deficit appear sustainable? For example, the rapid increase in the debts of some developing countries in the late 1970s and 1980s showed signs of becoming unsustainable because the countries seemed unable to meet their external debt service obligations. Dangers for surplus countries are less clear, though the rapid climb in Japan's external surplus based largely on increased exports to the United States after 1982 showed signs of being a cyclical rather than a sustainable long-term development. But even if it were cyclical, readjustment may leave an equilibrium current-account surplus of 1.5 to 2.0 percent of GNP. There is no reason to believe that Japan could not sustain such a position for a number of years. If rates of return on investment are higher in other countries, then the movement of capital out of Japan is economically efficient, allocating scarce world capital to the most productive geographical areas.

The third point is the irrelevance of trade barriers to the size of the bilateral and global trade and current-account balances.[13] The discussion to this point has considered how macroeconomic factors have shaped the surpluses of Japan and the deficits of the United States. Trade barriers play little or no role. They would affect the macroeconomic balances only if their removal or creation had a substantial impact on private-sector savings and investment or government deficits. For example, if removing trade barriers in Japan caused people to save less and to buy imports (directly or indirectly), surplus savings would diminish, bringing some decrease in the current-account surplus. But this development is highly unlikely; Japanese consumers would indeed buy more imported products, but by reducing consumption of domestic products rather than drawing from their savings. The reduction in consumption of domestic products would presumably bring a reduction of corporate profits and corporate investment in import-

---

13. A similar point is made in C. Fred Bergsten and William R. Cline, *The United States–Japan Economic Problem*, Policy Analyses in International Economics, 13 (Washington, D.C.: Institute for International Economics, 1985). The authors emphasize macroeconomic factors in explaining changes in U.S. and Japanese trade or current-account balances. The point they make about the size of the increase in U.S. exports to Japan if all Japanese trade barriers were removed (estimated to be $5 billion to $8 billion) should not be equated with a change in the trade balance.

competing industries. If profits and investment fell by roughly equal amounts, private-sector net savings would be unaltered. Workers in import-competing industries might be adversely affected, however, bringing a decrease in their savings and perhaps an increase in government expenditures for unemployment benefits. These developments would tend to decrease the current-account surplus, but they might be offset by increased employment, income, and savings in businesses handling imports and in export industries. Finally, as imports increase, demand for foreign currency to pay for them would increase, bringing some decrease in the value of the yen. That depreciation would lead to an expansion of exports, with rising profits and employment in export industries. As these various interactions within the economy work through, the net result is likely to be negligible.

One could study these effects through a large econometric model of the Japanese economy, but the estimates for the coefficients showing the elasticity of each variable to changes in trade barriers would be very suspect because this is uncharted territory. Reducing restrictions on imported beef, for example, would clearly lead to greater beef consumption, and some estimate of the impact can be calculated from measuring the impact of past liberalizations in which the size of the beef quota has been increased. But what would be the result of complete removal of the quotas? To what extent would the Japanese continue to increase their consumption of beef? That answer depends greatly on the substitution of Western-style meals for Japanese-style meals, since meat in a Japanese meal is present in smaller quantities. Western-style meals have become increasingly popular, judging by the rapidly rising numbers of Western-style restaurants and the success of American fast-food chains. However, there will be some limit beyond which food preferences stabilize. The Japanese would not entirely abandon their national cuisine for hamburgers and steak. Therefore predicting the impact of removing an obvious trade barrier becomes a matter of great speculation despite the sophistication of statistical techniques.

Yet in 1984 and 1985 U.S. government officials announced that if Japan were to remove its trade barriers, the imbalance would shrink by about $10 billion, or just under one-third of the 1984 imbalance.[14] The United States might be able to sell $10 billion more of goods and services to Japan in the absence of import barriers, though even this estimate

14. *Japan Economic Journal*, February 5, 1985.

cannot be made with precision or certainty, but to say that the sales would reduce the bilateral imbalance by that amount is not at all justified. If the impact on Japanese savings, investment, and government fiscal policy turned out to be negligible, $10 billion in additional U.S. sales to Japan would result in $10 billion of additional Japanese exports, with some of them going to the United States. If all Japanese import barriers disappeared, the major beneficiaries might be the developing countries, who could sell products in which they have a comparative advantage because of their relatively low wage levels. If Japan tended to purchase more from developing countries and export more to the United States, the bilateral imbalance could rise rather than fall.

At times officials, politicians, and businessmen in the United States have made all three mistakes—overemphasizing the importance of the bilateral imbalance, asserting that global current-account balances should be zero, and connecting the existence of imbalances to Japan's trade barriers.[15] None of these arguments is justified, and their intrusion into bilateral discussions only confuses the issues. If the problem is the size of global and bilateral trade or current-account imbalances, then the solution is to alter the macroeconomic policies that have produced the problem. If the concern is with Japan's import barriers, pressure should be applied for their removal, without the expectation that removal will bring any major change in the imbalances. Each of these solutions is important and desirable on its own merits.

Some of the tension between the United States and Japan has been caused by the price competitiveness of Japanese products in the U.S. market, a competitiveness that was enhanced in the first half of the 1980s because of the strong dollar. To the extent that this is the problem, chapter 6 will emphasize that bilateral talks should include discussion of macroeconomic policies. Some of the tension is also caused by American exporters' belief that Japan still maintains a large number of import barriers,

---

15. The amendment offered by Richard Gephard to the 1987 trade bill being considered by Congress is a prime example. It calls for investigation of trade barriers in nations having large bilateral surpluses with the United States and imposition of punitive tariffs if the barriers are judged to have contributed to the surpluses and if the governments of the affected countries failed to reduce the barriers and thereby bring down their surpluses. While the aim of the amendment—reduction of trade barriers and moderation of the U.S. trade deficit—is admirable, the means would not achieve the intended result because the amendment fails to recognize or address the macroeconomic side of the problem. In addition, a country such as Japan (a principal target of the legislation) would likely respond by voluntarily restricting its exports rather than by eliminating import barriers.

so that regardless of the movement of exchange rates, they will experience difficulty penetrating the Japanese market. To the extent this is true, pressure to remove those barriers ought to continue. Removal is justifiable on the grounds that it would lead to a more economically efficient allocation of resources and production along lines of comparative advantage. Not only would this be good for American exporters, but it would be good for Japan, bringing greater productivity and income as production is reallocated to be more in line with comparative advantage. These arguments remain valid and important regardless of the level of trade or current-account balances.

The only sense in which the issues of trade barriers and trade surpluses can be rationally connected is one of international obligation. Japan ought to be a leader in the liberal trade regime that has characterized the postwar era because it has become a very large, advanced industrial economy with a large current-account surplus. However, Japan not only does not project such an image, but it has acted reluctantly and slowly to remove its trade barriers, and then only after considerable international pressure. In 1985, arguments made in Japan on the need to respond to foreign pressures emphasized preventing a protectionist response abroad that would hurt Japanese exporters instead of emphasizing the benefits to Japanese consumers and the economy as a whole from liberalization. There is no rule that countries with trade surpluses should dismantle trade barriers and that deficit countries can be forgiven for erecting them. However, a sense that this is fair pervades much of the bilateral dialogue. Because Japan has large surpluses, it is incumbent upon it to support liberalization more actively. Whether or not this assumption is justified, it consciously or unconsciously underlies many of the criticisms voiced in the United States.

International Financial Liberalization

Since the financial structure and the regulations within which institutions operated included very tight controls over all foreign exchange transactions, the new economic conditions of the 1970s and 1980s necessitated institutional alterations. The record of the years since 1973 shows rapid change, though somewhat constrained by the nature of the decisionmaking process. With these changes, the framework of tight controls has given way to one of considerable freedom. Not only have the large net outflows of capital been accommodated but so have much larger gross flows.

Pressures for Change

Pushing Japan in the direction of greater international openness have been the need to accommodate the altered financial flows resulting from the economic environment of slower growth and the need to respond to pressures from abroad to allow foreign financial institutions greater participation in Japanese financial markets (and to allow foreign nonfinancial companies greater access to funds from Japan). The Japanese are well aware of these separate pressures. One article, for example, referred to the two *kokusai* as driving the process of changing the way the financial institutions are regulated (both the word for "government bonds" and the word for "international" are pronounced as "kokusai").[16] As chapter 4 noted, foreigners were a relatively peripheral concern in designing changes that could be considered largely domestic, acting more as catalysts for pressures inside Japan. For some of the changes affecting international capital flows, however, the foreign element has been more central and more influential.

Early in the postwar period Japan was saddled with an exchange rate set under the Bretton Woods system that considerably overvalued the yen, leading to a tendency for current-account deficits and some chance of the international humiliation of devaluation. To deal with the situation, Japan imposed severe restrictions on all foreign exchange transactions. In addition to that economic motivation, nationalism was important—foreign capital flow into Japan was restricted as part of the desire to prevent foreign corporate interests from dominating the economy. These controls kept the corporate sector in Japanese hands, and by minimizing potentially disruptive international capital flows kept the yen pegged at 360 to the dollar. Such restriction became incompatible, however, with the need to accommodate large capital outflows in the 1970s and 1980s.

During the 1960s Japan also acquired new international obligations. Although it was already a member of the General Agreement on Tariffs and Trade and the International Monetary Fund, it maintained reservations to Article 11 of the GATT, enabling it to maintain a variety of controls on

16. "Keizai Hakusho 12 no Pointo" (Twelve Points in the Economic White Paper), *ESP*, no. 149 (September 1984), p. 38.

foreign trade, until 1963 and to Article 8 of the IMF agreement, permitting it to impose strong restrictions on international financial transactions, until 1964. In addition, it joined the Organization for Economic Cooperation and Development in 1964 and accepted the OECD position on liberalizing capital controls. Its first tentative steps toward capital liberalization came in 1968, but most changes occurred in the 1970s and 1980s.

The increased capital flows of the 1970s could take a number of forms—direct investment, bank loans, portfolio equity purchases, or purchases of foreign debt instruments—that would expand the business of different types of Japanese financial institutions. Therefore, liberalization had to be filtered through the Ministry of Finance decisionmaking process, taking into consideration questions of competitive balance among institutions. But pushing the process along was the belief on the part of Japanese government officials that the world was moving toward closer financial integration. Whether they embraced the idea of greater integration or not (and they had reasons to oppose it), many saw it as inevitable.

Pressure from abroad was directed at ensuring that foreign institutions would not be excluded from consideration as the ministry made its decisions. For foreign financial institutions, Japan in the 1980s represented the most exciting development since the OPEC dollars had to be recycled in the 1970s. Not only was there the potential for a great deal of business as the country relaxed its foreign exchange controls, but many foreign institutions regarded themselves as far more experienced at managing international portfolios than their Japanese competitors. Even in a completely deregulated environment, however, the bulk of the money would flow through Japanese financial institutions, given their well-developed domestic position; Japan was far more advanced financially than the OPEC members. Nevertheless, open competition would give foreign institutions a significant share of the business. For foreign nonfinancial companies Japan was a potential source of financing. From time to time these companies had complained that access to inexpensive financing gave their Japanese competitors an unfair advantage (although the overall cost of capital to American and Japanese firms is a subject engendering great controversy among analysts). They wanted either to have access to those same low interest rates or to ensure that liberalization integrated Japan into international markets sufficiently that the interest rate differential between it and other countries would narrow.

Foreign pressures were not always independent of domestic pressures. Groups in Japan have often found foreign pressure useful in that external criticism or threat can be used to create a sense of crisis, as discussed in chapter 4, which can increase the chance that adjustments to the financial system will be made. This approach especially characterized the May 1984 bilateral accord on international financial issues, commonly known as the Yen-Dollar Agreement.

Despite the advantages for the Japanese in manipulating foreign pressure and the belief among foreigners that heavy pressure is absolutely necessary to achieve any progress, the strategy carries some dangers. In far too many cases foreigners bear the blame for controversial decisions when substantial domestic reasons existed to support those decisions.[17] Concessions are portrayed as necessary because of world power structures or international hierarchy, and this allows domestic opposition groups to transfer their anger from the government to the foreigners. Is this good for Japan's relations with other countries? One would expect the tactic to increase antagonism both in Japan and the United States, with the Japanese seeing the United States as a bully and Americans seeing Japan as having a recalcitrant, obstructionist, closed system. This does seem to characterize the feelings of government officials in the two countries in the 1980s but oddly enough does not appear to have affected broader public opinion.[18] Whether this state of affairs will continue is unclear.

International pressure has had another impact. Japan's financial markets have moved toward greater use of market-determined interest rates and new financial instruments. Offering concessions on international financial issues became a way to further this movement, because greater ease of international capital flow meant that interest rate controls or other restrictions at home increasingly led to capital flight to international markets, thereby highlighting the need for domestic decontrol. This connection was one reason that the United States chose to push for development of the Euroyen markets, correctly perceiving that the markets would provide pressure for change in domestic Japanese markets as well.

---

17. The intrusion of the foreign element as a catalyst seems to go back very far—without much exaggeration as far even as the Meiji Restoration of 1868. Pressure from Commodore Matthew Perry and the subsequent trade negotiations between Japan and the major industrial powers spurred the coalescence of opposition to the Tokugawa government that had been building for years. Considering the government unable to hold off the foreign threat (among other failings), revolutionary forces overthrew it and established a true central government to protect the nation.

18. William Watts, *The United States and Japan: Eyes Across the Pacific* (Washington, D.C.: Potomac Associates, 1982).

The Ministry of Finance Response

To keep the value of the yen pegged under the Bretton Woods system, Japan enacted the Foreign Exchange and Foreign Trade Control Law in 1949, establishing an extensive system of restrictions on all foreign exchange transactions. The principle underlying this law was that such transactions were prohibited unless approved by the government. But the yen, overvalued in the late 1940s, gradually became undervalued by the late 1960s, the result of successful industrialization, rapidly rising productivity, and increasing price competitiveness for Japanese exports. As overvaluation disappeared, strong capital controls were no longer necessary, and liberalization began to seem desirable.

Liberalization since the early 1970s has been neither smooth nor steady. After exchange rates were allowed to float in 1973, the Ministry of Finance tried to continue using controls to influence the inflow or outflow of capital and thus affect the rates. Nevertheless, the system has generally moved toward greater openness for capital movement in both directions. The last major attempt to use capital controls for exchange rate policy (1977–79) demonstrated that liberalization had already made the remaining controls less effective.

By the end of the 1970s, progress on international liberalization had reached the point that the Foreign Exchange and Foreign Trade Control Law no longer reflected the actual state of administrative practice. It was thoroughly amended in 1979. Under the revision the guiding principle of prohibiting transactions unless specifically approved by the government was transformed into a principle of free transactions unless specifically restricted. Although this reversal was more symbolic than real, it did ratify the ongoing process of liberalization.

The Yen-Dollar Agreement of 1984 provided another point at which gradual changes could be codified and progress toward deregulation ratified. The agreement laid out an agenda of changes promised over several years. Unlike some of the merchandise trade liberalization packages, most of the promises have been kept (albeit in some cases only with additional prodding from the United States).

By the mid-1980s capital flow into and out of Japan was relatively free. However, transactions remained more restricted than in such countries as the United States and more restricted than many Japanese and foreign financial firms wanted them to be. But because the United States obtained much of what it demanded, the issue became less important for bilateral negotiations. Even without continuing heavy U.S. pressure, further progress remains likely because of the domestic dynamics of the issue.

MOTIVATIONS. Faced with the need to respond to pressures for liberalization, the Ministry of Finance was influenced by the same motivations, constraints, and goals that shaped its management of domestic deregulation—the desire to avoid winner-take-all situations, a tendency to seek consensus decisions, and a tendency to take fewer risks than Americans and to avoid uncertainty or surprises. In this context the ministry has tried to maintain a rough balance among different kinds of domestic financial institutions and to ensure the safety and stability of the financial system by carrying out deregulation cautiously.

Although liberalization was piecemeal, a consensus converged upon it, so that by the 1980s the process was virtually irreversible. Nevertheless, decisionmaking remained cautious. Limits on certain kinds of transactions were lifted gradually, and new kinds of financial instruments were often surrounded by so many qualifying conditions that their initial appeal or usefulness was negligible. These breakthroughs were, however, usually followed by incremental easing of the conditions. For example, in 1984 only a very few Japanese corporations were allowed to issue Eurobonds. The regulations were closely tied to the controls on who could issue domestic corporate bonds, and as controls on domestic bonds were slowly eased, so were those on Eurobonds. In 1985, withholding taxes levied on interest payments for Eurobonds issued by residents and held by nonresidents were abolished, and the number of eligible issuing firms was increased (and increased again in 1987). Floating interest rate bonds were also allowed in 1985, with rates pegged to the London interbank offered rate, a standard benchmark in Eurocurrency markets.[19]

19. General Accounting Office, *International Finance: Implementation of the Yen/Dollar Agreement*, NSIAD-86-107 (GAO, June 1986), p. 20; *Japan Economic Journal*, January 25, 1986; Makoto Kawazoe, "Financial Liberalization Policy: Loosening Up the Market Alters Scope of Financial Institutions," *Tokyo Financial Markets*, vol. 24 (November 1986), p. 7; and *Japan Economic Journal*, June 18, 1985. The pace of change decelerated in 1986. The further expansion of eligibility was confidently predicted at the beginning of the year, but did not materialize until February 1987. It may have been held up by the reluctance of the MOF to allow a general use of private bond-rating systems to replace its own scrutiny of each potential issuer. Rather than allowing various ratings (and higher interest rates for higher-risk bonds), the ministry has had, in effect, a single rating. Any company meeting the MOF's stiff eligibility requirements for a bond issue has the highest possible rating. The change to a private-sector system for rating bonds would diminish

Liberalization of international markets was further characterized by the desire to balance competing interests. Besides a concern for maintaining fair competition and market shares among institutions, the MOF tried to control the impact of deregulation on competition in domestic financial markets. Government officials were very much aware of these connections and did not want to disrupt the carefully crafted decisions on domestic deregulation. One example of this was the "three bureau agreement" among the Banking, Securities, and International Finance bureaus of the Ministry of Finance, under which the right to lead-manage Eurobond issues was restricted to Japanese securities companies. Thus Japanese banks could participate in the underwriting, but the securities firms could preserve a superior position.[20]

One Japanese economist has suggested that the concern for balance has shaped policy in another way. In the 1960s when exchange controls were extensive, only a limited number of banks—the 13 city banks, 3 long-term credit banks, 7 trust banks, 2 government-owned banks, and 45 regional banks—were authorized to engage in foreign exchange transactions. By 1986 the list included 167 institutions, with more regional banks and some of the sōgo and shinkin banks, but most of these smaller institutions have only limited international involvement. The desire to maintain the dominance of the traditional foreign exchange banks as this list expanded may be one of the reasons officials took so long to make any decision about establishing an offshore banking facility in Tokyo similar to those in New York and London.[21] The idea was initially proposed as early as 1982, soon after the New York offshore banking facility began operations, but did not become reality until December 1986. When it was established, the Tokyo offshore facility was restricted by regulations that made it relatively unattractive compared with those in other countries.[22] Nevertheless, the facil-

---

ministry authority and, in particular, remove its responsibility for risk management or minimization. Japan has been moving toward use of rating agencies in the mid-1980s, but the change has been reluctant and slow.

20. Japanese banks may not lead-manage public issues of Eurobonds by Japanese residents and, if they participate as underwriters, must accept an inferior ranking among the other underwriting firms. The local securities subsidiary of a Japanese bank may lead-manage bond issues by nonresidents or for private placements, however.

21. Masataka Nakajima, "Nihon no Kin'yū Kokusaika no Genjō to Mondaiten" (The Current Situation and Problems in Japan's Financial Internationalization), *Gendai Keizai: Rinji Zōkan,* no. 45 (1981), pp. 116–24, discusses these limits to liberalization.

22. Edward J. Lincoln, "Recent Financial Developments in Japan," *JEI Report,* no. 27B (July 1982), pp. 1–2; and Shingo Tamari, "Inauguration of Tokyo Offshore Market: Ballyhooed Market to Open with Albatross of Regulations," *Tokyo Financial Markets,*

ity provided a way for smaller banks to become more active in international markets, since most of them have been too small to establish extensive overseas operations or have been restrained from doing so by MOF guidance.

CONTINUED MANIPULATION IN THE 1970s. Liberalization was just getting under way in 1973 as the era of floating exchange rates began, and the initial inclination of the Ministry of Finance was to use its powers over foreign exchange transactions as an element of exchange rate policy. Its last major attempt was the effort to encourage capital outflow and discourage inflow in 1977–78 to slow the appreciation of the yen, and to encourage capital inflow and discourage outflow in 1979–80 when the yen was depreciating. Partly because the new Foreign Exchange Control Law came into effect at the end of 1980, eliminating some forms of control, and because it was becoming increasingly obvious that controls were not having the desired effect, the MOF's manipulations for this purpose have diminished.

In 1977–78 the U.S. government encouraged dollar depreciation against the yen through what has been labeled benign neglect. Fearful of the impact of yen appreciation on Japanese exporters and motivated by a genuine concern that speculation was pushing appreciation beyond the equilibrium level, the Japanese government resorted to a number of actions, including direct intervention in foreign exchange markets and manipulation of capital controls.

—Administrative guidance on medium- and long-term bank loans denominated in foreign currencies was eased. Just as in the case of window guidance on domestic lending, the Ministry of Finance issued guidelines on the acceptable increases in overseas lending by Japanese banks.

—Interest income on yen-denominated bonds (samurai bonds) issued in Japan by international organizations and institutions guaranteed by foreign governments was exempted from income tax.

—Nonresidents were precluded from buying Japanese government bonds with a maturity of less than five years and one month.

—A reserve requirement of 100 percent on yen accounts maintained by nonresidents in Japan was imposed. These were called free yen accounts,

vol. 24 (November 1986), pp. 41–43. The main complaint was about the application of securities transaction taxes and local taxes to offshore transactions. In addition, the market is subject to restrictions on the inflow of funds and on transfers from domestic accounts to the market.

since the yen could be freely exchanged into other currencies, with limitations placed on the amount and source of money that could be placed into such accounts.

—The amount of currency Japanese travelers could take out of the country was raised, as was the amount of foreign currency that residents could hold.

—The ceiling on permissible exchange transactions related to services trade was raised.

—The ceiling on remittances to relatives abroad was eliminated. This restriction had been raised in a series of steps in previous years.

—The restriction on Japanese residents' purchases of foreign securities with maturities of one year or less was abolished.

—Restrictions on the maturity or amount of foreign exchange deposits held abroad by Japanese security, insurance, and transportation companies were abolished.

—Restrictions on the acquisition of real estate abroad that was not for direct use were abolished.

—Prior approval from the Ministry of Finance for all purchases of foreign equities as part of stocksharing plans for Japanese employees of foreign-affiliated companies in Japan was abolished.[23]

These measures were intended to increase net capital outflow, thereby reducing the demand for yen relative to dollars and, it was hoped, slow or halt the appreciation of the yen.

At the end of October 1978 the yen peaked and, under the influence of changing trade flows and the newfound desire of the United States to defend the dollar through direct intervention and alteration of domestic monetary policy, began falling. Fearful that depreciation would proceed too far, a fear reinforced by the second oil crisis in the spring of 1979, the MOF reversed many of its 1977–78 decisions and instituted others to stem the growing net outflow of capital.

—A series of steps reduced and then eliminated the reserve requirement on free yen deposits by nonresidents.

—The ban on nonresident purchases of yen bonds of less than five years and one month to maturity was changed to a ban on those of less than one year and one month, and then lifted.

23. This list and the one that follows for 1979–80 are based on restrictions reported in the International Monetary Fund, *Annual Report on Exchange Arrangements and Exchange Restrictions, 1980* (title changes in 1979 from *Annual Report: Exchange Restrictions*) (Washington, D.C.: IMF, 1980) pp. 230–31; *1979*, pp. 239–40; *1978*, pp. 239–41.

—Limitations on the allowable uses of impact loans (foreign-currency loans to Japanese companies) were eased.

—Japanese banks were allowed to issue impact loans, a market previously restricted to foreign banks in Japan.

—A ban on short-term impact loans was lifted.

—Nonresidents were allowed to participate in the gensaki market for the first time.

—Administrative guidance on foreign-currency-denominated loans by Japanese banks abroad was tightened in such a stringent fashion that these loans temporarily ceased.

—Banks, trading companies, and securities companies were required to report certain foreign exchange dealings to the Ministry of Finance.

These actions indicate the extent to which the MOF was willing to tinker with details to carry out its broad policy objectives. Officials obviously liked the idea that they still had some means to influence the exchange rate. When floating rates began in 1973, the Japanese had not been at all pleased; floating exchange rates had long been regarded as detrimental to trade because of the uncertainty that would be introduced into corporate decisions. Such an attitude had led the government to oppose vigorously not only floating rates but even the revaluation of the yen in 1971. Policies to reduce the variability of exchange rates through use of such controls as remained in existence continued until the late 1970s.

One could add a more cynical, bureaucratic explanation for the continued use of exchange controls after 1973: they justified the existence of a considerable number of ministry jobs and endowed officials with a sense of importance and power. But it would be unfair to label these people as merely power-hungry. Most truly see themselves as doing important jobs for the good of the nation. Probably the most interesting characteristic of change in Japan is not that officials opposed liberalization but that the process has proceeded relatively rapidly despite their opposition.

The MOF's actions also illustrate its fear of speculation and unpredictability. Some of the controls regulated short-term capital transactions, which the ministry has always viewed with suspicion because they are assumed to be more speculative and volatile than long-term transactions. Purchase of U.S. treasury bills is thus considered a short-term investment and purchase of U.S. corporate equity or U.S. government bonds long-term, even though equity or bond investments might be held for only a short time and used for speculative purposes. It is this fear of speculative, volatile, or disruptive capital flows that led the MOF to maintain the

Table 5-5. *Capital Flows and the Exchange Rate, by Component, Quarterly, 1977–80*
Billions of dollars

Quarter	Average exchange rate (¥ per $)	Long-term capital			Short-term capital (net)	Official foreign exchange reserves	Private monetary movements[a]		
		Assets	Liabilities	Net			Assets	Liabilities	Net
1977									
First	285.6	1.2	0.8	-0.4	0.0	0.4	0.7	0.6	-0.1
Second	275.2	0.7	0.2	-0.5	-0.4	0.4	-2.4	-3.5	-1.1
Third	266.2	1.2	0.1	-1.1	-0.5	0.5	0.5	-0.8	-1.3
Fourth	247.1	2.1	0.9	-1.2	0.1	5.0	1.5	2.1	0.6
1978									
First	237.6	2.8	3.2	0.4	0.2	6.4	1.8	3.6	1.8
Second	220.8	3.6	-0.1	-3.7	-0.1	-1.9	0.4	-2.2	-2.6
Third	192.8	3.4	-0.7	-4.1	0.6	1.9	2.7	2.5	-0.2
Fourth	190.5	5.1	0.0	-5.1	0.7	3.8	1.2	4.5	3.3
1979									
First	201.5	4.7	1.1	-3.6	0.3	-4.2	2.2	1.3	-0.9
Second	217.6	4.1	0.3	-3.8	0.1	-3.8	-0.6	-0.1	0.5
Third	218.9	4.0	1.5	-2.5	1.9	0.4	6.7	10.6	3.9
Fourth	238.6	3.5	0.5	-3.0	0.4	-5.0	-0.2	0.2	0.4
1980									
First	243.5	2.2	1.3	-0.9	2.4	-1.8	4.2	8.0	3.8
Second	232.7	1.6	3.2	1.6	-1.7	4.1	-1.0	8.7	9.7
Third	220.1	3.7	5.2	1.5	1.6	1.1	8.4	7.3	-1.1
Fourth	210.7	3.3	3.5	0.2	0.8	1.5	4.1	4.9	0.8

Sources: Bank of Japan, *Balance of Payments Monthly* (November 1986), pp. 2–4, 53–55, 59–61, 65–66; and International Monetary Fund, *International Financial Statistics Yearbook* (February 1981), pp. 222–23.
a. Includes data on authorized foreign exchange banks only.

artificial distinction between the two categories in balance-of-payments statistics. (To illustrate the absurdity of this distinction, once foreigners were allowed to engage in them, gensaki transactions were initially treated in the balance-of-payments statistics as long-term capital transactions because they technically involved the sale and repurchase of long-term government bonds, even though gensaki transactions have maturities of less than one year and most have maturities of three months or less.)

Justified or not, concern over volatile capital movements lay behind the restrictions on maturities of government bonds that foreigners could purchase, short-term impact loans, foreign participation in the gensaki market, and purchases of foreign bonds with less than one year to maturity. In each of these cases the late 1970s finally brought a reappraisal of the restrictions, and the conditions were either eased or dropped.

How effective were these controls? Most appear to have been relatively pointless or trivial. They affected only some of the ways money could flow into or out of the country, and investors were becoming sophisticated enough to find ways to circumvent controls. None of the efforts, including both capital controls and direct intervention in the exchange market, prevented the yen's appreciation from 241 to the dollar at the beginning of 1978 to a record 176 to the dollar at the end of October. This unusual and rapid increase finally ended not because of the success of Japanese policies but because of a change in U.S. policy in November 1978 and the onset of the second oil shock in 1979. Similarly, the policy to encourage inflow in 1979–80 failed to prevent a considerable depreciation of the yen.

Table 5-5 shows what happened to the exchange rate and to both long- and short-term capital movements from 1977 to 1980. The wide fluctuation in the value of the yen, based on its average value each quarter, is obvious. From an average value of 285.6 to the dollar in the first quarter of 1977, the yen appreciated to 190.5 in the fourth quarter of 1978, a 33 percent rise. This was followed by a 22 percent depreciation to 243.5 by the first quarter of 1980. These fluctuations were definitely not desired by the Japanese government. Had the effort to influence the exchange rate actually worked, the fluctuations would not have been so large.

The government's most immediate effort to influence the exchange rate came from direct intervention in the market. As table 5-5 shows, Bank of Japan foreign exchange reserves increased by more than $11 billion from the fourth quarter of 1977 through the first quarter of 1978 as the bank purchased dollars to slow the yen's rise. In the first two quarters of 1979 exchange reserves dropped by $8 billion as the bank intervened to slow the yen's fall (the decrease for the year as a whole was more than $12 billion).

Long-term capital during 1978 showed some tendency for inflow (the increase in liabilities) to slow while outflow (the increase in assets) accelerated. The accumulation of foreign financial assets, for example, rose from close to $1 billion a quarter in the first three quarters of 1977 to $5.1 billion in the fourth quarter of 1978, then fell to less than $2 billion in the second quarter of 1980. Liabilities show a less distinct pattern, but they moved from being actually negative in the second and third quarters of 1978 (an outflow of capital as foreigners reduced their holdings of Japanese financial assets) to increases ranging from $1.3 billion to $5.2 billion in 1980.

The manipulation of exchange controls may bear some relationship to these developments, but other factors were also involved, including falling interest rates (the Bank of Japan discount rate fell to a postwar low of 3.5 percent in 1978), which encouraged capital outflow, and later the desire of several Middle Eastern oil-producing countries to diversify their portfolios, bringing a surge in investment in Japan during 1980. Whatever the cause of the movement in long-term capital, the MOF's influence on the exchange rate was insufficient to prevent wide fluctuations. The movements might have been even larger in the absence of the controls, but it is difficult to imagine the yen appreciating beyond its peak of 176 to the dollar in 1978.

No breakdown into assets and liabilities is available on short-term capital flows, and detail on private monetary movements is available only for the activities of foreign exchange banks, which represent just one part of total private monetary transactions. These data, though, confuse the picture of the influence of the MOF's capital controls. In many quarters the net movement in short-term capital was opposite that of long-term capital. In the final two quarters of 1978, for example, when the government was trying to encourage capital outflow, the short-term account showed a net inflow. The net movement on private monetary flows was also sharply positive ($5.1 billion in the fourth quarter of 1978), driven mainly by a large increase in the deposits in Japanese banks owed to foreigners (up to $4.5 billion). These developments were inconsistent with the direction of government policy on capital controls, such as the 100 percent marginal reserve requirement on free yen deposits.

Consider also what happened in the fourth quarter of 1979, when the yen was depreciating sharply despite the intensive intervention in the foreign exchange market represented by the $5.0 billion decline in official exchange reserves. Although controls had been adjusted to encourage capital inflow and discourage outflow, the growth in long-term assets continued at a high pace of $3.5 billion (albeit down somewhat from previous quarters) and the change in liabilities was very small. Short-term capital and private monetary movements, however, did move in the desired direction.

The evidence does not conclusively show that the Japanese government was able to influence capital movements and the exchange rate through direct controls. Nor can the failure be explained away by the considerable amount of random noise in quarterly data. The restraints put in place could not effectively block the private sector from acting on the economic information—relative interest rates, economic growth forecasts, exchange rate expectations—available to it. When, for example, Japanese banks were told to limit their medium- and long-term lending to developing countries facing debt problems, they promptly shifted to short-term loans (they were holding 50 percent of Mexico's short-term debt in 1982).[24] Some impact cannot be denied, but even with the array of tools still available to it in the late 1970s, the ministry was unable to have as much effect as it desired.

EFFECT ON CAPITAL MOVEMENTS. Another way of evaluating the changes that have taken place in capital controls is by looking at the long-term assets and liabilities reported in the balance of payments (available sources do not separate short-term capital movements into changes in assets and liabilities). When these data are normalized by GNP, they ought to show an increase over time as Japanese and foreigners reacted to the removal of constraints on their investment choices. This development is separate from the expected observation that the growth of assets would exceed that of liabilities as Japan moved to a position of net capital outflow; the net outcome should result from higher levels of activity on both the asset and liability side.

The data in table 5-6 show that until the late 1970s the impact of liberalization on these flows was limited. From the early 1960s until the mid-1970s both asset and liability transactions were generally less than 1 percent of GNP. In fact, the first rise in assets relative to GNP came in the late 1960s; these transactions increased from 0.8 percent of GNP in 1968 to a temporary peak of 2.1 percent in 1973, a level not attained again until

24. Edward J. Lincoln, "Developing-Country Debt Problems and Japanese International Financial Policy," *JEI Report,* no. 41B (October 1982), p. 3.

Table 5-6. *Long-Term Capital Movements, 1961–86*

Year	Change in assets (outflow)		Change in liabilities (inflow)	
	Billions of dollars	*Percent of GNP*	*Billions of dollars*	*Percent of GNP*
1961	0.3	0.6	0.3	0.6
1962	0.3	0.5	0.5	0.8
1963	0.3	0.4	0.8	1.2
1964	0.5	0.6	0.6	0.7
1965	0.4	0.4	0	0
1966	0.7	0.7	−0.1	0.1
1967	0.9	0.7	0.1	0.1
1968	1.1	0.8	0.9	0.6
1969	1.5	0.9	1.4	0.8
1970	2.0	1.0	0.4	0.2
1971	2.2	1.0	1.1	0.5
1972	5.0	1.6	0.5	0.2
1973	8.5	2.1	−1.3	0.3
1974	4.1	0.9	0.2	0
1975	3.4	0.7	3.1	0.6
1976	4.6	0.8	3.6	0.6
1977	5.2	0.8	2.1	0.3
1978	14.9	1.5	2.5	0.3
1979	16.3	1.6	3.3	0.3
1980	10.8	1.0	13.1	1.2
1981	22.8	2.0	13.1	1.1
1982	27.4	2.8	12.4	1.3
1983	32.5	2.8	14.8	1.3
1984	56.8	4.5	7.1	0.6
1985	81.8	6.2	17.3	1.3
1986	132.1	6.7	0.6	0

Sources: Bank of Japan, *Balance of Payments Monthly* (March 1987), pp. 53, 59; (November 1986), pp. 53–54, 59–60; and "Main Economic Indicators of Japan," MOF *Monthly Finance Review* (December 1985); (November 1978), pp. 47, 53; (November 1970), pp. 47, 53.

1982. Since 1978, however, accumulation of foreign assets has shown an extraordinarily rapid and sustained rise, reaching 6.7 percent of GNP by 1986. The growth of liabilities rarely exceeded 0.5 percent of GNP until 1980, when they reached 1.2 percent; they remained at roughly that level until an unusual drop to close to zero in 1986.

What is the implication of these data? International capital controls had been gradually relaxed since the early 1970s. Why did they fail to have much impact on gross accumulation of foreign assets and liabilities until the end of the decade? One possibility is that the earlier changes allowed capital flows to keep up with GNP growth: in the absence of change, the rigid controls would have caused the ratio of capital flows to GNP to fall. Another possibility is that the earlier changes simply did not make much difference. Not until the late 1970s was enough red tape stripped away to lead to substantial increases in activity. Finally, the reduction in restrictions may not have been matched by a demand for financial assets. It may have been easier for foreigners to invest in Japan in the mid-1970s than earlier, but the oil-shock recession would have limited their interest in Japanese financial assets. Removal of controls has an effect on actual transactions only if those controls constrain the volume to a level below the market demand.

A related question is why most of the change takes place on the asset (capital outflow) side of financial flows. These data suggest that the process of liberalization was biased toward capital outflow, but this conclusion conflicts with evidence of substantial easing of regulations applying to capital inflow. A more reasonable explanation is that from 1980 to 1985 Japan was not a particularly attractive place to invest—interest rates were lower than elsewhere and the yen was depreciating. But even the rising yen in 1986 did not stimulate foreign investment. Another interpretation is that Japanese investors, particularly life insurance companies and other large institutional investors, had a pent-up demand for foreign financial assets that could not be fulfilled until the 1980s, whereas foreigners had no similar demand for Japanese assets. While this could be true, one would expect that stiff controls of earlier years would have led to pent-up demand in both directions. Whatever the explanation, the failure of capital inflow to expand cannot be realistically attributed to continuing controls.

Revision of the 1980 Foreign Exchange Control Law

Many discussions of Japan's financial markets attach great importance to the Foreign Exchange Control Law, assuming that it was responsible for much of the international liberalization of Japan's capital markets. C. Fred Bergsten, assistant secretary for international monetary affairs in the Treasury Department during the Carter administration, argued that from the end of 1980 the law "significantly liberalized foreign access to the Japanese capital market."[25] But according to table 5-6, the rise in capital outflow as a percentage of GNP dates back to 1978. Even the increase in capital inflow predated the implementation of the new law.

The revision of the Foreign Exchange Control Law was passed by the Diet at the end of 1979 and went into effect in December 1980. As a basic principle, the law overturned the prior rule that all transactions were to be controlled unless excepted; the principle now was that all transactions would be free of control unless excepted. In practical terms the ministerial orders implementing the new law changed requirements for prior licensing of particular transactions to a requirement of prior notification. The government, however, retained extensive powers to impose controls in situations deemed to have an adverse impact on the economy. Thus large exchange rate fluctuations or financial injury to Japanese industries could be used as a legal justification for controls.

Early evaluations found the new law had made little difference. In many cases the licensing requirement under the old law had been pro forma, so that the new notification requirement did not represent much of a change. There was, however, some concern over the very vague justification for emergency controls, which could be interpreted to apply in almost any situation.[26]

Despite the modesty of the changes as they were translated into policy, the law represented an important step in the process of liberalization. The language of the original Foreign Exchange Control Law had enabled the Ministry of Finance to preside over extensive relaxation of controls, but the relaxation of the 1970s allowed the actual status of control to become increasingly out of line with the original intent of the law. Even in a society such as Japan's, where laws can be stretched to meet the circumstances, this disparity needed correction. The revision brought the law into better conformity with administrative practice. In this sense it ratified changes that had already taken place, so that the absence of immediate further changes in administrative practice is not surprising.

By confirming the validity of previous changes, the revision also legitimized continued liberalization; in effect it was a public statement that a new consensus had formed, an acknowledgment that in turn contributed to

25. C. Fred Bergsten, "What to Do about the U.S.-Japan Economic Conflict," *Foreign Affairs*, vol. 60 (Summer 1982), p. 1068.

26. An excellent early review of the revisions and the implementing orders is in the *East Asian Executive Reports*, in a series of articles in March 1980, April 1980, February 1981, and April 1981.

the momentum for further change in the same direction. Groups within the Ministry of Finance or elsewhere in the government that had opposed deregulation or the loss of ability to manipulate capital flows would have clearly recognized this point and felt less able to make their view prevail. Put another way, in the dynamics of Japanese consensus decisionmaking, those opposed to liberalization were more likely to accept their role of losers after the revisions, resigned to trying to moderate the speed of deregulation but unable to oppose it completely.

How can this interpretation be reconciled with the broad powers given to the MOF to restrict international transactions in ill-defined adverse situations? Since all Japanese laws tend to be vague, the subsequent administrative decisions made by the ministries come to have an importance much like legal decisions in the United States: they set precedents for further decisions and interpretations. When enacted, the revised Foreign Exchange Control Law was assumed by the Japanese financial community to ratify the movement toward greater liberalization, and early administrative decisions supported that interpretation. As time passed without any precedent of using the emergency powers to impose restrictions, it became increasingly unlikely that they would be used in any situation short of a true financial crisis. The first few years after enactment were crucial to establish this record, and those in the ministry and in the financial sector who favored decontrol opposed any attempt to invoke the powers. For that reason the Japanese heavily criticized a suggestion published in 1982 by C. Fred Bergsten that Japan impose controls on the outflow of capital to reverse the depreciation of the yen on foreign exchange markets, an administrative precedent that the financial community vigorously opposed. A depreciating currency and rising current-account surplus hardly represented a national emergency in their view. (Indeed, given the desire to pursue fiscal austerity, this was a national benefit.)

The possibility of asking Japan to impose restrictions on capital outflows to strengthen the value of the yen had been raised on other occasions as well and was flawed from another standpoint. Since current-account surpluses and capital outflows result from macroeconomic forces, artificially constraining capital flow attacks a symptom rather than a fundamental cause. Were outflow to be severely restricted, for example, some domestic adjustment would have to be made to allow the absorption of those savings at home. Part of that adjustment would involve reducing interest rates to encourage domestic investment and consumption, which would widen the interest rate differentials between Japan and other countries, causing Japanese investors to engage in a determined hunt for ways to circumvent the capital controls. To be effective, controls would have to be very broad and rigorously enforced, something no longer possible in Japan by the mid-1980s.

The 1984 Yen-Dollar Agreement

The other significant event in the movement toward deregulation has been the bilateral agreement between the United States and Japan in May 1984, generally called the Yen-Dollar Agreement. The outcome of many months of negotiations, it included statements about past, present, and future deregulation of various aspects of Japan's capital markets (plus a few general statements about the need to reduce U.S. federal budget deficits). As in the case of the Foreign Exchange Control Law revision, however, it would be inappropriate to view this agreement or the negotiations that led to it as entirely responsible for the liberalization of capital controls. A large part of what happened was already under way or under discussion in Japan, so that the negotiations did more to accelerate the process or act as a catalyst where domestic forces were deadlocked than to initiate change.

BACKGROUND. A paper written in 1982 by the chief economist of the Caterpillar Tractor Company accused the Japanese government of deliberately attempting to keep the yen undervalued in order to promote Japanese exports.[27] The report contended that the government engaged in three types of policies to hold the yen artificially low: restrictions on foreign investment in Japan, encouragement of Japanese investment abroad whenever the current-account balance was rising, and direct intervention in exchange markets by the Bank of Japan. Liberalization of Japan's capital markets would supposedly eliminate the government's ability to maintain such an unfair exchange rate.

While there was a modicum of truth in all these allegations—witness the MOF's actions in 1977–78—the conclusion that these policies led to an undervalued yen was unwarranted. The analysis of the effectiveness of capital controls and direct intervention tended to be exaggerated; the authors were simply not knowledgeable about Japan. When Caterpillar tried

---

27. Caterpillar Tractor Co., "The Yen—An Undervalued Currency," unpublished paper (May 5, 1982).

to convince the Reagan administration to act on these findings, the company was flatly rejected; the administration concluded that most of the arguments were specious.

Undaunted, in the fall of 1983 Caterpillar issued a new report, written under commission by a consulting firm, that retreated from accusations of deliberate and pernicious attempts to undervalue the yen but maintained that various features of international capital control in Japan had the effect of holding the yen down. Pointing to such problems as the limited variety of financial instruments, which had a dampening effect on foreign investment in Japan, the report suggested ways liberalization might rectify the situation. This list, in fact, closely resembled the final list of items included in the Yen-Dollar Agreement.[28]

This new approach characterized the testimony of Caterpillar Chairman Lee Morgan before Congress in 1983. "The much-touted reduction of Japanese capital flow barriers," he stated, "has been one-sided. Capital now flows out of Japan much more freely than it did in the past. But there has been no commensurate increase in capital inflows. This one-sided adjustment in capital flows is a major contributor to the yen-dollar exchange rate imbalance."[29] While put in an accusatory tone, this pattern (even if it were true) did not need to be part of a deliberate attempt to undervalue the yen. One could easily draw such a conclusion from the balance-of-payments data presented earlier, although those trends cannot be clearly attributed to decontrol of outflows and continued control of inflows. Stripped of the antagonistic edge of the original argument, this new approach had greater appeal to the administration.

Meanwhile a summit meeting between President Reagan and Prime Minister Nakasone had been scheduled for early November 1983 in Tokyo. Both countries were looking for ways to avoid an unfriendly discussion of trade issues. Nakasone and his Liberal Democratic party were facing general elections for the lower house of the Diet in December, and the prime minister wanted to demonstrate that he could maintain good relations with the United States. The Reagan administration wanted to avoid causing any problems that could benefit the opposition parties. If the election turned out badly for the LDP, Nakasone could be replaced by

28. David Murchison and Ezra Solomon, "The Misalignment of the United States Dollar and the Japanese Yen: The Problem and Its Solution," unpublished paper (September 1983), esp. pp. 52–88, 104–11.

29. *U.S. Economic Relations with Japan, April 17, 1983,* Hearings before the Senate Foreign Relations Committee, 98 Cong. 1 sess. (GPO, 1983), p. 16.

someone else in the party less favorably inclined toward the United States. These concerns provided a powerful reason to keep contentious trade issues out of the summit discussions, a move that displeased a number of officials in the administration who dealt with bilateral trade problems.

Measures to further deregulate international financial transactions were already under serious consideration in Japan. During the summer of 1983 Prime Minister Nakasone had charged his government with developing a package of proposals to stimulate domestic growth and improve relations in advance of the summit. After several months of internal government squabbling, this package was ready for announcement by early October and included some proposals on international finance, among them implementing a study on the possibility of creating a market in banker's acceptances.[30]

The combination of an acceptable argument by the U.S. private sector that Japanese capital controls were keeping the value of the yen too low, a desire on the part of government negotiators to avoid contentious trade issues, and the Japanese government's proposed liberalizations all pointed to a noncontroversial joint statement on financial liberalization as a reasonable outcome at the summit. The statement as it finally emerged was related at least tangentially to trade issues. It was presented, however, in a way that avoided accusations of deliberate action by Tokyo to keep the yen low but still placated those American companies threatened by Japanese competition. The existing discussion in Japan meant that items could be included on which action was already likely to occur in the near future. During the summit meetings, therefore, Treasury Secretary Donald Regan and his counterpart, Finance Minister Noboru Takeshita signed a joint press announcement on international financial matters.

Included in the announcement were the usual vague promises by the United States to follow a responsible fiscal policy, followed by rather specific Japanese promises on particular financial reforms. This list included such items as an end to the "real demand rule," under which all forward yen transactions had to be for hedging "real" trade transactions rather than for speculation; a promise to submit a bill to end the "designated company system," by which foreign investment in eleven Japanese corporations was limited; a promise to submit a bill to allow the government to issue bonds abroad in foreign currencies (dubbed Nakasone bonds); a promise to expedite the study of establishing a banker's accep-

---

30. Yoshio Nakamura, "Japan Announces Comprehensive Economic Package," *JEI Report*, no. 41B (October 1983), pp. 1–2.

tances market; lower minimum denominations for certificates of deposit; higher ceilings on CD issues; relaxation of the guidelines on Euroyen bonds; and reconsideration of the requirement that withholding tax be paid on Euroyen bonds.[31] A bilateral working group composed of officials from the Ministry of Finance and the Treasury Department was established to monitor the implementation of these promises.

The composition of the bilateral working group could also be construed as an effort to minimize tensions. The Office of the United States Trade Representative and the Commerce Department were entirely excluded from participation, and neither the Treasury Department nor the Ministry of Finance had participated to any extent in recent bilateral trade disputes (Treasury had even argued against automobile quotas at the beginning of the Reagan administration). Thus the working group appeared to be a harmonious way to engage in discussions of technical matters not appropriate to the usual framework of trade negotiations.

This image was quickly shattered. Beginning with meetings in January 1985, the mood of the discussions immediately deteriorated and followed the pattern common to many other trade negotiations. American negotiators made angry statements about the lack of progress, including especially bitter remarks by Donald Regan in March in Tokyo.[32] Also in keeping with the pattern of other trade disputes, this one acquired a self-imposed deadline: the final report of the working group was to be ready in time for a Regan-Takeshita meeting at a Group of Ten gathering in Rome in May, so that the issues would be settled before the annual summit meeting of industrial nations.[33] With this deadline and some further posturing on both sides, a final report was produced that could be described by both sides as representing significant progress. With the intense, publicized animosity that accompanied the negotiations, the final result gave the appearance of bringing about a fundamental opening of Japan's financial markets.

The report covered twenty-two specific items, with firm Japanese promises for action of twelve, expected favorable concessions on six more, and stalemate on four items. The firm changes included many of the

31. "Joint Press Announcement," *Treasury News,* November 10, 1983.

32. Jeffrey A. Frankel, *The Yen/Dollar Agreement: Liberalizing Japanese Capital Markets,* Policy Analyses in International Economics, 9 (Washington, D.C.: Institute for International Economics, 1984), pp. 71–72, provides excerpts from that press conference.

33. See Edward J. Lincoln, "Yen-Dollar Working Group: Round Three," *JEI Report,* no. 17B (April 1984), pp. 3–4; and Lincoln, "Bilateral Yen-Dollar Report Issued," *JEI Report,* no. 22B (June 1984), pp. 1–4.

issues that had been raised in the Murchison and Solomon report and covered in the November joint press statement. The stalemate list included several issues of continuing concern: application of withholding tax to earnings on deposits and securities held by nonresidents, withholding tax applied to interest payments on Euroyen bonds issued by Japanese firms and held by nonresidents, a refusal to expand the use of treasury bills, and an inability to resolve the question of foreign seats on the Tokyo Exchange. Nevertheless, some movement occurred with respect to most of the issues under discussion.

EVALUATION. Because of the belief in the United States that existing capital controls led to an undervaluation of the yen and that if liberalization could be effected, the yen would rise in value, the working group justified the changes being negotiated in precisely those terms. According to the final report, "The Working Group expected that comprehensive measures to internationalize the yen and liberalize Japan's capital markets, which are primarily aimed at achieving world economic efficiency and fulfilling Japan's reponsibilities as the second largest economy, will lead to a stronger yen."[34] However, it is on just these grounds that the agreement is most easily criticized.

The yen stood at 231 to the dollar when the agreement was signed in May 1984 and depreciated to 252 by May 1985. If the goal of the negotiations was to produce appreciation of the yen, it failed, especially considering that by May 1985 most of the changes promised in the agreement had actually gone into effect. It was not until the coordinated push to lower the value of the dollar announced at the G-5 meeting in September 1985 that the yen began to appreciate. Appreciation thereafter was rapid but could not be attributed to liberalization in Japan.

The agreement's lack of influence on exchange rate movement in the first year could be excused on the grounds of a difference between short-term effects and long-term effects. Some argued that in the short term the impact would be a larger outflow of capital as Japanese investors bought more foreign-currency-denominated assets. In the longer run the outflow would be offset by increasing capital inflows. In the original argument for bilateral negotiations, proponents (including Lee Morgan) had accused the Japanese of liberalizing only capital outflow, but the evidence presented

34. *Report by the Working Group of Joint Japan–U.S. Ad Hoc Group on Yen/Dollar Exchange Rate, Financial and Capital Market Issues to Japanese Minister of Finance Noboru Takeshita [and] U.S. Secretary of the Treasury Donald T. Regan* (May 1984), p. 12.

earlier in this chapter demonstrates that after the yen began to fall in 1979 the policy stance was shifted to encourage inflow and discourage outflow. If these policies had had their intended result (a large assumption), the removal of controls as part of further liberalization would have led to a temporary outflow of capital. However, short-run portfolio adjustment would be offset in the longer run by new investments, which were expected to bring more inflow and less outflow because the yen would become a more attractive currency relative to the past or to other currencies.

Others proposed that the agreement could stimulate outflow rather than inflow because of the difference between domestic and international regulation. If controls held Japanese interest rates artificially low, international liberalization without a corresponding domestic deregulation of those rates would promote capital outflow.[35] But was this the situation? Although the hypothesis is intriguing, domestic deregulation had already been taking place, so that it was not at all clear whether international markets were liberalized ahead of domestic ones. For corporate bonds, such a disparity in timing did occur (as was described in chapter 4); the greater ease of issuing bonds abroad led Japanese corporations to float more than half their new issues in the Eurobond market rather than at home, which spurred the process of domestic deregulation. But this example is actually one of an artificial stimulus for capital inflow rather than outflow, since bonds issued abroad by Japanese companies are a form of foreign borrowing.

If the hypothesis has any validity, it must concern the deregulation of interest rates on bank deposits, which were assumed to be held at artificially low levels. In this scenario, low interest rates would cause individual and corporate savers to prefer higher-yield foreign investments over domestic bank deposits. But were foreign financial assets such a close substitute for domestic bank deposits that interest rate differentials would cause people to move their money overseas? The household savings behavior discussed in chapter 4 does not support this hypothesis; small savers did not abandon the banking system despite the controlled rates. The savings accounts were tax free, which meant that returns of domestic bank deposits were not as unfavorable as they seemed. In addition, international investment carries an exchange risk that most small savers would have found difficult to hedge.

Large corporate investors presumably were more sensitive to the inter-

35. Frankel, *The Yen/Dollar Agreement*, pp. 51–52.

est rate differentials, and presumably they represent most of the actual capital outflow activity. But interest rate controls on savings deposits were not as important as they might have been for these investors because they had access to a widening range of other domestic financial instruments with market-determined interest rates: the gensaki market since the early 1970s, certificates of deposit in 1979, and money market certificates in 1985, as well as deregulated interest rates on large time deposits in 1985. In the first half of the 1980s these interest rates were considerably lower than those in the United States, but not because of direct controls. If the government had the ability to influence the rates, it was through general monetary policy rather than direct control, meaning that the focus should have been on manipulation of monetary policy rather than regulation of particular interest rates.

The Ministry of Finance began deregulating interest rates on large time deposits (mostly held by corporations) in 1985, an action that could have been a response to a flight of corporate deposits to overseas financial investments. On October 1 interest rates were liberalized on deposits in excess of ¥1 billion ($4.2 million at 1985 exchange rates), with the minimum lowered to ¥500 million on April 1, 1986, ¥300 million on September 1, 1986, and ¥100 million on April 1, 1987. But most of the discussion concerning deregulation of rates concerned the competitive balance between banks and securities companies, reflecting the increased holdings of government bonds and tokkin in corporate financial portfolios (both considered in chapter 4).[36]

Table 5-7 provides data on interest rates in Japan and the United States. While the financial instruments or the data collection procedures may vary between the two countries, the table does show the gap between the two. After 1976–77, nominal interest rates in the United States have been consistently higher by several percentage points. This disparity holds for both short-term and long-term market rates. Because the Japanese financial instruments listed here carry market-determined interest rates (the call market, CDs, and the secondary market for government bonds), the rates

36. Money flowed rapidly into these deposits, which increased from ¥3.0 trillion in October 1985 ($13 billion at then-current exchange rates) to ¥17.8 trillion ($75 billion) by December 1986; see "Large Time Deposits Triple in a Year," *Japan Economic Journal*, February 21, 1987. However, investments in CD issues during the same time period were stagnant. In addition, total corporate time deposits at banks expanded by only ¥10 trillion, indicating that almost one-third of the deposits in the new deregulated accounts represented transfers from regulated accounts rather than an inflow of new money; Bank of Japan, *Economic Statistics Monthly* (February 1986), p. 71; (April 1987), p. 71.

Table 5-7. *Interest Rates in Japan and the United States, by Type of Financial Instrument, 1975–85*
Percent

Year	Japan call market[a]	U.S. federal funds[a]	Japan CD[b]	U.S. CD[a]	Japan government bonds[b]	U.S. 10-year government bonds[a]	Bank of Japan discount rate[b]	Federal reserve discount rate[b]
Nominal[c]								
1975	10.7	5.8	...	6.4	9.2	8.0	6.5	6.0
1976	7.0	5.0	...	5.3	8.7	7.6	6.5	5.2
1977	5.7	5.5	...	5.6	7.3	7.4	4.2	6.0
1978	4.4	7.9	...	8.2	6.4	8.4	3.5	9.5
1979	6.3	11.2	8.2	11.2	9.1	9.4	6.2	12.0
1980	10.9	13.4	9.6	13.1	8.8	11.5	7.2	13.0
1981	7.4	16.4	6.8	15.9	8.2	13.9	5.5	12.0
1982	6.9	12.3	7.1	12.3	7.6	13.0	5.5	8.5
1983	6.4	9.1	6.6	9.1	7.4	11.1	5.0	8.5
1984	6.1	10.2	6.4	10.4	6.5	12.4	5.0	8.0
1985	6.5	8.1	7.7	8.1	5.9	10.6	5.0	7.5
Real								
1975	−1.1	−3.3	...	−2.7	−2.6	−1.1	−5.3	−3.1
1976	−2.3	−0.8	...	−0.5	−0.6	1.8	−2.8	−0.6
1977	−2.4	−1.0	...	−0.9	−0.8	0.9	−3.9	−0.5
1978	0.6	0.2	...	0.5	2.6	0.7	−0.3	1.8
1979	2.7	−0.1	4.6	−0.1	5.5	−1.9	2.6	0.7
1980	2.9	−0.1	1.6	−0.4	0.8	−2.0	−0.8	−0.5
1981	2.5	6.0	1.9	5.5	3.3	3.5	0.6	1.6
1982	4.2	6.2	4.4	6.2	4.9	6.9	2.8	2.4
1983	4.5	5.9	4.7	5.9	5.5	7.9	3.1	5.3
1984	3.9	5.9	4.2	6.1	4.3	8.1	2.8	3.7
1985	4.4	4.5	5.6	4.5	3.8	7.0	2.9	3.9

Sources: Bank of Japan, *Economic Statistics Annual, 1985* (Tokyo: BOJ, 1986), pp. 25–26, 186–90; *1980*, pp. 82, 201; *1977*, p. 186; and Bureau of the Census, *Statistical Abstract of the United States, 1987*, pp. 463, 492–93; *1985*, pp. 504–05.
a. Average for year.
b. End of year.
c. Deflated by the consumer price index: Japanese data, 1980=100; U.S. data, 1967=100.

can be affected only indirectly by monetary policy. For call rates and CDs, the U.S. advantage has fluctuated between 3 and 9 percentage points since 1978. For long-term government bonds, the gap has been 1 to 6 percentage points since 1977.

The central bank discount rate gives an indication of the influence of monetary policy on these results. Japan did not raise its discount rate as high after the 1979 oil shock as the United States did and dropped it faster because inflation was not as high and came under control more quickly. If the comparison is made with real interest rates, the same results hold. Real interest rates in Japan were higher than U.S. rates until 1981, when they swung the other way. For the call and CD markets, real rates were higher in Japan from 1978 to 1980 by 1 to 5 percentage points. Since 1981, U.S.

rates have been higher by 1 to 4 percentage points. The same pattern characterizes long-term bonds.[37] Therefore, market-determined interest rate differentials provided an incentive for capital outflow in the 1980s that is often ignored in pronouncements about the impact of the unequal timing of liberalization measures.

Regardless of whether international liberalization preceded domestic deregulation of interest rates, that argument is used in Japan as a rationale for further change. Always looking for a foreign angle to cut through domestic impasses, ministry officials in favor of deregulation have pressed their case by playing up the threat that liberalization will shift funds away from domestic financial markets. Both the Japanese and American negotiators recognized this in focusing on Euroyen markets in the Yen-Dollar Agreement. The Americans hoped that an extensively deregulated Euroyen market would attract funds from Japan, putting pressure on Tokyo to continue domestic deregulation. Japanese government officials came to the same conclusion, but they had to be cautious about encouraging the Euroyen market for fear that it would force more domestic change than they desired.[38]

That Japan's interest rates in the 1980s were lower than those in the United States does not constitute strong evidence that international liberalization preceded domestic interest rate deregulation. From a macroeconomic standpoint the existence of surplus savings put downward pressure on interest rates, especially after the government began reducing its own demand for those funds by cutting its fiscal deficit in the 1980s, thereby creating a differential between domestic and foreign rates of a sufficient size to bring about the necessary capital outflow to provide macroeco-

37. There is some question as to whether nominal or real rates are more appropriate for making comparisons. If investors place their money abroad, their concern is with nominal returns if they intend to repatriate their earnings: if they do not use the earnings to purchase goods in the foreign country, inflation there is not of concern to them. However, real interest rates could be a rough guide to how the exchange rate will move if purchasing-power parity works in a crude sense. If inflation is higher in the United States than in Japan, the dollar should depreciate over time. If interest rates are higher in the United States than in Japan after accounting for the inflation differential, investors should believe investing in the United States is more profitable, even after accounting for the likely movement in the exchange rate. The extent to which investors are motivated by real interest rates may depend on the maturity of the investment. Real interest rates may be more important for long-term than for short-term investments because fluctuations in exchange rates bear little relation to inflation differentials over shorter time periods.

38. Taguchi, "Yūroen Torihiki Kakudai: Kin'yū Seisaku no Yūkōsei Tamotsu" (Expanding Euroyen Transactions: Preserving Effective Financial Policy), *Nihon Keizai Shimbun*, December 25, 1984.

nomic balance. The size of that differential depended on the degree to which foreign financial assets could be substituted for domestic ones, which in turn depended on the amount of information available on foreign assets and the perceptions of the risk attached to investing in them. Because domestic and foreign assets were not perfect substitutes, information on international developments was not yet well developed, and exchange risk could not be completely eliminated, Japanese interest rates should have been lower than U.S. interest rates.

Viewed from the standpoint of macroeconomic balances, the Yen-Dollar Agreement was unlikely to have much impact on net capital flows. If the measures in the agreement had no impact on savings, investment, or the government deficit, they would not affect the net outflow of capital. If one assumes that deregulation would lead to higher interest rates in Japan, then there was some possibility that savings would even fall, thereby reducing the need for net capital outflow.[39] If the Japanese are "target" savers, then an increase in interest rates reduces the annual amount they must add to those savings to reach their goals. However, even if higher interest rates would reduce savings to some extent, they might also reduce investment, which is often assumed to be more sensitive to interest rates than savings are. The reduction in investment could offset a drop in savings, maintaining the gap between the two.

Suppose further that deregulation made investment in Japan easier and more attractive to foreigners. According to the reasoning behind the Yen-Dollar Agreement, the value of the yen would increase on exchange markets as investors sold dollars to acquire yen. But the story would not end at this point. The increased investment from abroad would cause Japanese interest rates to fall, which should cause investors to rethink their choices. Furthermore, if foreigners bought more yen-denominated financial assets, Japanese savers would also readjust their portfolios. Lower interest rates might lead to greater domestic industrial investment in Japan, absorbing some of the increase in total funds caused by the inflow, but Japanese savers might also send more of their own savings overseas.

All these are only possibilities, but they imply that the simple conclusion that the Yen-Dollar Agreement would lead to decreased net capital outflow and a rise in the value of the yen against the dollar was neither obvious nor necessarily justified. The complex interactions involved in interest rate determination and international capital flows were just as likely to lead to a decrease in the value of the yen as an increase.

39. Frankel, *The Yen/Dollar Agreement*, p. 63.

If the Yen-Dollar Agreement had an ambiguous impact on the exchange rate, has the United States gained anything from it? Aside from the assumption that reduced constraints on capital flows lead to a more efficient allocation of resources around the world, the main benefit appears to have been greater access for American financial institutions. This was, in fact, one of the expressed goals of the negotiations, and the final agreement included a number of specific proposals to ease foreign entry and participation.[40] Even many of the proposals, such as allowing foreign firms to co-manage Euroyen bond issues, that were technically part of the attempt to "internationalize" the yen and raise its value were more closely related to the issue of foreign participation.

The success of the agreement is indicated by the fact that there was action on virtually all the items covered—even those to which Japan said it could not respond favorably. A follow-up study in 1986 by the General Accounting Office declared the implementation of the agreement to be mostly complete.[41] The changes made included smaller denominations and larger maximum issues of CDs, creation of MMCs, creation of banker's acceptances, lifting of quotas imposed on banks for converting foreign currencies to yen, liberalization of interest rates on large time deposits, removal of the withholding tax on Euroyen bonds, relaxation of limitations on Euroyen bond issues, establishment of short-term Euroyen CDs, relaxation of limitations on Euroyen loans, permission for some foreign banks to manage pension funds in Japan, and seats on the Tokyo Stock Exchange for several foreign securities firms. Perhaps the only agreement of substantial interest to the United States that had not been addressed conclusively by the Japanese government was to establish an open market for treasury bills.

The real value of the yen-dollar negotiations and the agreement lie in these changes. Had those negotiations not taken place, deregulation and the liberalization of international markets would have continued in Japan, but the interests of foreign financial institutions would have been slighted because they would not have been included as participants, in any meaningful sense, in the decisionmaking process.

Obtaining real evidence of a systematic government bias toward domestic Japanese institutions is difficult. Nevertheless, American financial firms, especially banks, often complain that they are prevented from pur-

40. *Report . . . on Yen/Dollar Exchange Rate*, pp. 43–44.
41. GAO, *International Finance: Implementation of the Yen/Dollar Agreement* (GPO, 1986).

suing those forms of business in which they feel they have the greatest advantage over their Japanese competition. Such behavior would fit the pattern of other cases in which Japanese agencies have attempted to limit competition from foreign firms in the areas of their greatest strength in order to favor domestic firms. How much of the situation can be attributed to a desire to hold the foreigners at bay and how much to the general conservatism and risk aversion of the Ministry of Finance is impossible to determine, but the complaint certainly has some validity.

Not only is the Ministry of Finance apt to ignore foreign concerns in the absence of pressure, but it has also traditionally feared the prowess of foreign institutions. At the same time that American banks were complaining about the difficulty of earning any profit on their business in Japan, a book warned of the competitive threat these same banks represented. Akitoshi Takatsuki concentrated on Citibank, the Bank of America, Chase Manhattan, and Morgan Guaranty Trust, describing their strength in servicing not only American clients in Japan but Japanese companies as well. Citibank's operations in Japan, he noted, ranked with those of the mid-size regional banks, a fact intended to impress upon the reader the extensiveness rather than the limited nature of the operations. While he acknowledged that the "impact" loan market, which had been the exclusive province of the foreign banks until 1979, was becoming less profitable, Takatsuki emphasized the expertise, innovativeness, and profitability of the American banks in providing diverse financial services, including credit card franchise arrangements. Befitting the emphases of the 1980s, though, Takatsuki's purpose was not to argue that foreigners should be shut out but to urge Japanese banks to become more innovative and competitive in order to face the challenge of continuing liberalization.[42]

Given at least some evidence that domestic forces in Japan were interested in liberalization for Japanese financial institutions only, such issues as access to the Euroyen market (the Ministry of Finance would have far less control over the activity of foreigners once the market developed), foreign access to trust banking, and membership on the Tokyo Stock Exchange would not have arisen in the absence of foreign pressure. One

42. Akitoshi Takatsuki, *Ginkō: Jiyūka e no Senryaku* (Banks: Strategy toward Liberalization) (Tokyo: Nihon Keizai Shimbun, 1984), pp. 118–36. According to Takatsuki's data (for 1982), Citibank ranked just behind the fifty-fourth largest bank in Japan (Oita Bank, a mid-sized regional bank) in loans outstanding. Dai-Ichi Kangyō Bank, the largest in Japan (and now the world) in terms of total assets, had outstanding loans twenty times the value of those of Citibank in Japan. For financial data on individual Japanese banks, see Ministry of Finance, *Ginkōkyoku Kin'yū Nempō*.

can also see this bias in discussions with Japanese officials; they are very sincere about the commitment to further deregulation and liberalization but have to be reminded to comment on the role of foreign institutions. They tend to see these institutions as peripheral to their main concerns for balancing interests among Japanese institutions.[43]

The market access stemming from the agreement also extended to foreign nonfinancial firms. American companies have complained that their Japanese competitors had an unfair advantage in their access to lower-cost financing than was available in the United States. (Considerable controversy surrounds the issue of the relative cost of capital to American and Japanese firms because the comparison involves far more than relative interest rates.) Some American firms wanted to raise money in Japan but found that restrictions prevented them from issuing bonds. Until the end of the 1970s the only eligible issuers were multilateral aid organizations such as the World Bank, national governments, and organizations such as railroads and electric utilities owned by foreign governments. The changes in these bond regulations and liberalization of Euroyen bond markets set in motion by the agreement led to greater opportunities for foreign firms to gain access to yen financing, although the importance of these changes was diminished somewhat by international bond interest swaps that provided a way to partly circumvent the restrictions. A problem remains, however, because while most firms envy Japanese interest rates, they do not want yen. If they borrow in yen at Japanese interest rates, they bear an exchange risk, and if they hedge the risk through the forward market, they lose the advantage of the low interest rates.

The Yen-Dollar Agreement has thus been overrated as a means to increase the value of the yen but has served a useful function in furthering the market-access concerns of the U.S. government and financial community. Because the agreement represents only one more in the long series of steps toward liberalization and deregulation that began a decade earlier, it does not stand as a point of demarcation between periods of closed, controlled markets and one of open markets, just as the revision of the Foreign Exchange Control Law in 1979 was not a point of clear demarcation. And

43. Foreign banks are so peripheral to MOF concerns that *Ginkōkyoku Kin'yū Nempō*, the Banking Bureau's principal annual publication, virtually ignores them. While it provides detailed financial information for all individual city, regional, trust, long-term credit, and sōgo banks, and somewhat less detail for individual shinkin banks and credit cooperatives, it publishes no information on individual foreign banks other than their names and national identification.

anyone seeing the agreement as a triumph of U.S. pressure would be mistaken, since most of the changes were already under consideration in Japan and took place because domestic constituencies favored them. The United States did act as catalyst to the process, however, and ensured that the concerns of foreign financial institutions would not be ignored.

Basing the rationale for the negotiations on a false assumption that "internationalization" of the yen would increase its value against the dollar was unfortunate. There was no way to predict with any certainty which way the yen would move, and the agreement held disappointment for Americans who believed this assumption. The premise also allowed the Japanese to waste time arguing the point. Finally, this focus allowed the Japanese to use the negotiations to promote changes in regulations that had little to do with access for foreign firms.

Summary

Since the early 1970s Japan's economic relationship with the rest of the world has undergone important and long-lasting changes that affected international economic transactions in trade and capital as well as the institutions shaping them. Macroeconomic forces pushed the country into a large current-account surplus. As a result, Japan became the largest creditor in the world. This outcome depended on the willingness of the rest of the world, and the United States in particular, to accept the surpluses. During the first half of the 1980s the United States accommodated and aggravated the macroeconomic developments in Japan by generating rising U.S. fiscal and current-account deficits.

This state of affairs proved very fragile. International concern over the size of the U.S. deficit and of Japan's current-account surplus was a major factor in the G-5 agreement in September 1985 that contributed to the subsequent appreciation of the yen, which promised to shrink the surplus in the second half of the 1980s.

The macroeconomic changes of the 1970s and 1980s also necessitated loosening the rigid controls on foreign exchange transactions established in the early postwar period. Pressures for change led to the closer integration of Japan into international financial markets. But these changes did not come easily, because regulation of international financial transactions had been a key component of the overall framework of heavy control and regulation characterizing government relations with financial institutions

after the war. Japanese government officials deserve great credit for pre-
siding over very substantial deregulation that decreased their ability to
affect market outcomes and eliminated part of their self-justification and
self-esteem.

This extensive record of change has, however, often failed to impress
foreign government officials and businessmen. The changes have been
carried out in the usual Japanese fashion—slow and piecemeal—reflecting
conflicting pressures on the Ministry of Finance. Foreign pressure was
required to help the ministry get around impasses and to assert the market-
access interests of foreign financial firms that would otherwise have been
systematically ignored.

Overall, bilateral relations on financial regulation have been productive, which seems surprising given the heated atmosphere in the spring of
1984 when negotiations on the Yen-Dollar Agreement were proceeding.
The answer to the puzzle lies in the domestic constituency for change in
Japan. The Japanese government did not agree to deregulation because the
United States demanded action; it responded largely because domestic
interests favored change and because officials recognized the need for
accommodating the new financial flows associated with slower economic
growth. The process has not yet run its course, and the pace of further
liberalization could be rapid.

These macroeconomic and institutional changes spurred the emergence
of Tokyo as a world financial center, which brought international interaction directly into Japan, including a heavy influx of foreign financial firms
and their personnel. Japanese financial institutions also quickly expanded
their own offices abroad, and when the yen appreciated, Japanese industrial firms began a wave of direct investment in overseas factories. These
developments thrust upon Japan a new, important international role, one
for which it was not fully equipped socially or intellectually. Adjusting to
its new status could present Tokyo with many difficulties and present the
bilateral relationship with new challenges into the 1990s.

CHAPTER SIX

Whither Japan?

NO ONE can doubt that Japan has undergone a tremendous transformation since the early 1970s. It has experienced what would seem to be a permanent shift to slower economic growth that has ended an extraordinary era of rapid growth and industrialization. This fundamental change has altered the basic macroeconomic balances in the economy, creating surplus savings in the private sector, offset first by large government deficits and then by sizable current-account surpluses. These developments in turn have contributed to the need for, and to a considerable extent the accomplishment of, significant deregulation of Japan's financial markets.

In the mid-1980s Japan has become a successful, mature industrial economy. Its personal income levels are equal to or higher than those in the United States, it no longer lags behind the advanced industrial nations technologically, and it has lost the sense of inferiority that pervaded it in the early postwar era. The Japanese can say with justifiable pride that their nation has coped rather well with the problems that faced all industrial nations in the wake of the 1970s oil crises. Although its initial response to the unexpected international developments in 1973 was characterized by panic and poor policy decisions, once the government and private sector overcame their initial confusion, economic performance was better than in other industrial nations.

But Japan is by no means in a comfortable, stable position in the mid-1980s. Indeed, the nation is just beginning a new phase of adjustment necessitated by the rapid appreciation of the yen since 1985 that could prove very difficult. Eventually, the appreciation will reduce Japan's external trade surplus by discouraging exports and increasing imports. Expanding external surpluses provided the outlet for excess savings and fueled economic growth earlier in the 1980s, but in the final years of the decade either some other outlet must be found or the savings surplus will

267

have to diminish. The Japanese government did little to address this problem until 1987, and even then its efforts were weak.

How serious is the need to adjust? One common Japanese attitude has been that industry will adapt quickly to the stronger exchange rate, with profitability maintained through increasing productivity in export industries. The belief in this ability to adapt is an indication of how confident the Japanese have become of their economic success.[1] Companies are vigorously attempting to deal with the stronger yen through a combination of technological change, pay cuts for both management and blue-collar workers, and pressure on subcontractors to cut prices. The ability of some firms to do this successfully is not surprising, since the reduction in the trade surplus does not mean that all firms must find exports unprofitable. However, this strategy has limits for any firm and is not equally feasible for all.

While Japan's trade surplus will contract, the contraction may take place fairly slowly for two reasons. First, Japanese firms with established positions in foreign markets are loath to lose their market shares. Their strategy may be to establish production capabilities overseas if exporting is no longer profitable enough. But building production facilities takes time, and in the interim the firms may have to accept losses on exports in order to maintain market shares. Second, the dollar-denominated price of oil has fallen at the same time that the value of the yen has risen, bringing a tremendous decrease in the cost of imported oil. In 1986 the yen-denominated value of exports fell 16 percent, but the value of imports fell 31 percent, so that the trade surplus was actually 26 percent larger than in 1985.[2] The contraction of Japan's trade surplus cannot be delayed perma-

1. In one poll of manufacturing firms, 70 percent of respondents said they could cope with an exchange rate of 150 yen to the dollar within two years, and another 20 percent thought they could cope within three years. "Yen-Buffeted Firms Set Cost Cutting as Top Goal," *Japan Economic Journal*, February 28, 1987.

2. Susan MacKnight, "Japan's 1986 Trade Figures: Has the Surplus Peaked?" *JEI Report*, no. 5B (February 1987), p. 10. Japan's trade and balance-of-payments data can be measured in either dollars or yen, and the dollar figures are the ones most commonly published. However, to understand the impact of exchange rate movements for Japanese firms, it is the yen-denominated figures that matter. Much of the decrease in yen-denominated exports was attributable to price-cutting (evidenced by a decline in the wholesale price index for exports), supporting the hypothesis that Japanese firms would accept reduced profits or even losses to protect foreign market shares in the short run. In dollar terms Japan's exports in 1986 rose by 19 percent and imports declined by 2 percent, causing the trade balance to jump 79 percent to a surplus $83 billion. The disparity in the two sets of figures comes from what is known as the J-curve effect. Even though Japan's exports

nently, however. Japanese firms will increasingly move toward overseas production, and 1987 saw the end of falling oil prices.

Changes in the services account of the balance of payments will partially offset the effects of the contraction in the merchandise trade surplus on the current account. Net foreign assets will continue to expand rapidly, causing the enormous increase in net income from abroad discussed in chapter 5. In addition, the stronger yen means that every yen invested abroad will translate into larger dollar investments and larger dollar earnings. Firms that relocate some manufacturing production abroad will also rapidly increase their income from fees and royalties, and those already licensing their technology abroad will earn more. Thus the decline in the trade balance will not decrease the current-account surplus by a similar amount; the substitution of fees and investment income for exports is not one for one. A company that relocates production abroad through direct investment or licensing to local firms does not generate a flow of receipts in the balance of payments equal to the former value of exports.

None of these developments would take place if the yen were once again to depreciate against the dollar, which many Japanese would undoubtedly like to have happen so that there would be no need for dramatic economic adjustment. Is this likely?

The initial appreciation of the yen in 1985 and 1986 was not accompanied by major alterations of economic policy or macroeconomic balances in either the United States or Japan. An exchange rate is a price, and if the price is inconsistent with underlying economic conditions, it cannot be sustained. The key in this case is the United States. If the United States continues to decrease its federal budget deficits, the pattern of stronger yen–weaker dollar will easily continue. Lower fiscal deficits mean less pressure on interest rates in U.S. capital markets and less excess demand for real goods and services in the economy, which would reduce the U.S. current-account deficit and capital inflow. These developments would be fully consistent with a weaker dollar (reduced capital inflow decreases the demand for dollars in international exchange markets). The passage of the Gramm-Rudman-Hollings Act at the end of 1985 provided a crude indication that the United States would move in this direction. Even though the guidelines prescribed in the law have not been met, the movement toward

---

declined (from the yen-dominated perspective of Japanese firms), the exchange rate shift was even larger, boosting the dollar-denominated figures. Over a longer time period, however, the dollar figure should also show a decline in exports.

smaller federal deficits did begin in 1986. If this trend continues, any depreciation of the yen against the dollar becomes increasingly unlikely.

Since the strong yen appears permanent, the external adjustments will continue. Even if the changes in merchandise trade take time to develop and the current-account adjustment is more moderate than it would be if it depended only on changes in trade, Japan's current-account surplus will shrink. As measured in the national income accounts, the surplus was falling throughout most of 1986 and 1987. And as the opening of foreign manufacturing operations by Japanese firms accelerates, the contraction in the surplus should also quicken. A shrinking trade and current-account surplus is a drag on the economy, and Japan now faces the hard necessity of finding some other way of dealing with excess domestic savings.

Policy Options

Japan has two options to ease domestic adjustment: it can reduce the private-sector imbalance between savings and investment or increase the government deficit by following a more expansionary fiscal policy. Neither will be easy to realize. Nevertheless, implementing one or both will be necessary if the external constraint remains binding.

Reducing Private-Sector Savings

The proposition that a country saves too much sounds odd. How can an act that is universally held to be a virtue be a vice? Besides, many in Japan see a pragmatic need to keep savings rates high to support the steadily increasing percentage of nonworking elderly. But in the interest of bringing about a better balance of savings and investment, and thus a better international balance and economic growth based on domestic demand, government policies should discourage saving.

CHANGING TAX POLICY. Despite the failure of previous tax reform attempts, the tax reform bills of 1987 once again addressed the imbalance of savings and investment by proposing to eliminate the tax advantages of personal saving. This time the proposal met with success. The changes have eliminated the tax-free status of savings accounts and imposed a flat 20 percent tax rate on all interest income.[3] The effect of these changes

3. "Tax System Reform Is Established," *Asahi Shimbun* (September 20, 1987), p. 3.

was, however, not certain. Rather than lowering the overall savings rate, the tax could cause people to invest in other assets that remain tax free or in those with higher rates of return.

But regardless of uncertain outcomes, continuing to encourage savings through tax policy was inconsistent with any policy to reduce current-account surpluses or stimulate domestic demand. If savings were taxed and if people chose to save just as much as they did before, then the tax benefits of the old system were not needed in the first place. It is encouraging therefore that Japan has now taken this step.

One other proposal—the value-added tax—that was part of the original version of the 1987 tax reforms, however, was inconsistent with a policy of reducing savings. Any such measure is a tax on consumption and encourages saving relative to consumption. The value-added tax represented an odd direction for Japan to take. Even though it would have been combined with cuts in marginal tax rates and the elimination of tax benefits for savings, it would certainly have maintained or restored the bias in the tax system toward encouraging saving. In addition, to lower marginal tax rates and thereby increase disposable income is to alter an entirely different class of tax—changing an income tax does not affect choices between consumption and saving. Given these inconsistencies, the failure of this part of the proposal was welcome.

EASING CONSUMER CREDIT. Another way to discourage saving might be to encourage consumer spending by improving the availability of credit information on borrowers or by further popularizing credit cards. Japan has moved rapidly in this direction. Outstanding household liabilities for example, rose from 33 percent of disposable income to 56 percent between 1975 and 1984. However, in 1985 the corresponding ratio in the United States was almost 84 percent, suggesting that Japanese households still had considerable room to expand their liabilities and that government could do more to encourage the process.[4] Were further change to take place, Japanese consumers would presumably more often borrow to purchase durables than save up for purchases.

4. Management and Coordination Agency, *Japan Statistical Yearbook, 1986* (Tokyo: MOF, 1986), pp. 531, 543. Data are based on average household income and liabilities as measured in the family income and expenditure survey. U.S. data are from John F. Wilson and others, "Major Borrowing and Lending Trends in the U.S. Economy, 1981–85," *Federal Reserve Bulletin* (August 1986), p. 522, and represent total debt divided by total disposable income for all households. Both the Japanese and U.S. data cover all forms of consumer debt, including mortgages. Japanese data do not permit the breakdown of debt into mortgage and installment credit components.

This approach to reducing savings has flaws, however. First, the effect would be temporary because greater use of consumer credit implies postponing saving, not eliminating it—a point few people recognize. The repayment of consumer loans is a form of saving because it reduces consumer debt; that is, greater use of credit implies a shift of saving from before a purchase to after it. In the short run, saving might decrease as people borrowed to consume more, but the longer-term effect could be very small as the acquisition of new loans came into greater balance with the repayment of old ones.

Second, easier credit might not lead to a large increase in consumption because the factors limiting purchases in Japan are not primarily related to the availability of credit. The lack of space in Japanese houses and apartments, for instance, may be more important in determining purchases of consumer durables than credit availability. And purchases of automobiles may be constrained by the lack of parking space, the ready availability of good public transportation, and heavy traffic congestion in urban areas. Government policies to expand highway construction and encourage housing investment could thus be more effective means to stimulate demand for durable goods.

Encouraging consumer use of credit may also not have much impact on total household savings for another reason: Japan can no longer be called a nation with a poorly developed consumer credit market. In just the five years from 1979 to 1984, the number of credit cards in use more than tripled, from 23.6 million to 73.8 million.[5] The use of automatic equipment for checking credit cards in retail outlets also spread rapidly. Nevertheless, further encouraging consumer credit availability would be consistent with other strategies to reduce savings. Policy measures could include promoting credit information bureaus, which remain poorly developed because of a general unwillingness to divulge any credit information.

REDUCING HOUSING DOWN PAYMENTS. The largest consumer durable, of course, is housing, and one hypothesis is that Japanese savings behavior is motivated by the large down payments required. Even if mortgages were as available in Japan as they are in the United States, the size of down payments relative to income would be larger because of the higher average cost of housing in Japan and, until recently, the lower incomes—a

5. Economic Planning Agency, *Kokumin Seikatsu Hakusho, 1985: Sengo 40 Nen: Seijuku no Jidai ni Mukete* (White Paper on the People's Life, 1985: 40 Years after the War: Facing an Age of Maturity) (Tokyo: MOF, 1985), p. 384.

prudent bank extends credit only up to a certain multiple of a borrower's annual income.[6] As a result, Japanese households must save more than American households before purchasing a house.

One way to reduce such savings would be to devise policies that subsidize or lower down payment requirements. However, no such policy could be pursued without a major commitment of funds by the central government. These could be provided through tax expenditures—mortgage interest payments could be made deductible on individual income tax returns. Such a change would increase the maximum size of the mortgage a bank would be willing to provide to a household with any given level of income, thereby reducing the proportion of the total price that would have to be met through a down payment.

INCREASING LEISURE TIME. Japanese school children still attend school for half a day on Saturday, and few businesses grant employes every Saturday off.[7] Japanese workers are also widely believed to underuse annual vacation time out of fear that to use it would jeopardize their career advancement. Virtually every government report since the early 1970s has deplored this pattern of behavior and has called for increased leisure time to improve the quality of life. A popular theory in Japan, one reflected in the Maekawa report, is that increased leisure would also stimulate domestic demand and thus reduce savings. In effect, it is argued, households save so much because they have too little time to spend what they earn.

While use of vacation time and choices about Saturday work are a matter for companies and their employees, government policy could pro-

6. According to Economic Planning Agency, *Kokumin Seikatsu Hakusho, 1983: Yutori Aru Kakei to Atarashii Kazokuzō o Motomete* (White Paper on the People's Life, 1983: Seeking a New Family Image under Affluence) (Tokyo: MOF, 1983), p. 54, the average price of a new dwelling unit in metropolitan Saitama, Tokyo, Chiba, and Kanagawa prefectures was ¥44.8 million ($180,000) in 1982. Directly comparable data for the United States are not available, but the median (not average) price of a single-family dwelling unit in the United States in 1982 was $69,300. While this figure would be considerably higher in such metropolitan regions as New York, Boston, and Los Angeles, prices in Japan are likely to be much higher still. Bureau of the Census, *Statistical Abstract of the United States, 1987* (GPO, 1986), p. 707.

7. In 1984, 77.1 percent of Japanese workers in firms of thirty or more workers had some version of a two-day weekend. However, only 27 percent had every Saturday off; the other 50 percent were under a variety of plans that gave them one or two Saturdays a month; Economic Planning Agency, *Kokumin Seikatsu Hakusho, 1985*, p. 100. It might be added that 57 percent of Japanese employees in 1981 worked in businesses employing one to twenty-nine workers and that the two-day weekend is probably much less widespread in this category. *Japan Statistical Yearbook, 1986*, pp. 124–25.

vide a powerful stimulus to increase leisure time. In 1987 it was doing just that by considering legislation to establish a forty-hour workweek instead of the present forty-eight hours. This would promote Saturday holidays by necessitating overtime pay on Saturday for anyone already working Monday through Friday. In addition, the government could counter the vacation problem by mandating more national holidays, and especially by expanding the "golden week," the period at the end of April and the beginning of May that now contains three holidays.[8] Filling in the gaps would create a full week of enforced vacation time.

How much increased leisure would encourage consumption and reduce savings is unclear, but the effect ought to be positive. It should also lead to increased investment in leisure industries and could have regional benefits as longer blocks of free time allowed households to travel farther into the countryside. The overall effects might not be large, but they would be consistent with the need to stimulate domestic demand. The principal obstacle to implementing these changes comes from an attitude, mostly among older Japanese, that improving the quality of life is simply synonymous with encouraging laziness.

Increasing Investment

The net surplus of savings could also be reduced by policies that stimulate investment. This was the emphasis of the concept of minkatsu (private-sector vitality) explored in chapter 3. However, although a number of policies could help increase investment, many would lead to reduced tax revenues or increased government spending.

DEREGULATION. The concept of minkatsu is based on the assumption that individual investment in housing and corporate investment in plant and equipment is being constrained by regulations that could be eliminated. As is often the case, the concept sounds good but the details of practical application remain fuzzy. A policy statement by Keidanren in October 1984 epitomized the situation:

> The ratio to GNP of public investment by the central and local governments is high in Japan compared with other countries, and pump-priming measures are losing their effectiveness. . . . Finding

8. These are the emperor's birthday (April 29), Constitution Day (May 3), and Children's Day (May 5).

ways to put private-sector managerial resources to effective use in consolidating Japan's infrastructure will thus be a major task in the future. To do this requires the introduction of private-sector vitality, centered on urban redevelopment projects, by easing government regulations.[9]

The statement goes on to make the dubious point that deregulation could give such a strong boost to minkatsu that investment would rise even if government expenditures on social infrastructure were cut back to reduce deficits. As thin and undefined as the concept remains, however, it has a convincing ring to it and seems widely accepted.

What could Japan deregulate that would lead to greater investment? The most promising targets would be rules that restrict housing investment, including those limiting the size or height of residential buildings (established mainly to protect the "sunshine" rights of surrounding dwellings), restraints on land reclamation, regulations keeping some government-owned land in unproductive uses (*chōsei chiiki*), and tax rules that promote holding land in inefficient uses while waiting for it to appreciate. Were these regulations to be eased or eliminated, more land would become available for residential use. This would help stabilize housing prices because land costs constitute a large part of the cost of building a new house.[10] If the government also raised the low property taxes on agricultural land, made property sales easier, and deregulated land use, even more housing investment might result.

How much deregulation could be achieved, however, is debatable. Elimination of sunshine rights might encourage strong investment in multistory condominiums in areas now dominated by one- and two-story dwellings, but would the public stand for such a change? Sunshine is important to Japanese households because of the limited distribution of clothes dryers and the practice of airing bedding on a regular basis. The same sorts of barriers protect other targets for deregulation, such as the Large-Scale Retail Store Law passed in 1974 and strengthened in 1978. By requiring permission from the Ministry of International Trade and Indus-

9. "An Anatomy of the Japanese Economy: Prescription for Administrative and Fiscal Reform," *KKC Brief*, no. 23 (October 1984), p. 7.

10. Economic Planning Agency, *Kokumin Seikatsu Hakusho, 1983*, p. 48. Because land prices are so high, households hold a very large share of their nonfinancial assets in the form of land. In 1981, land was 72 percent of household nonfinancial assets, while dwellings were only 23 percent and durable goods 5 percent. In the United States the share for dwellings is much higher and that for land much smaller.

try, which in turn requires the concurrence of local councils that include small shopkeepers, the law has considerably slowed (but not completely blocked) the construction of large discount stores.[11] Were the law to be rescinded, investment in these stores would expand but would be at least partially offset by disinvestment in small shops. More importantly, small store owners support the Liberal Democratic party and will be increasingly important as the LDP seeks to shift its base of support from rural areas to more urban ones. Probably neither the store owners nor the LDP would accept liberalization of this law.

These examples imply that deregulation is unlikely to proceed as far as its proponents desire and that it will not have as much impact on investment as is supposed. Because deregulation also strikes at important vested interests, it cannot be accomplished quickly. Even the opening of limited competition in telecommunications, which was tied to the privatization of Nippon Telegraph and Telephone, took five years from the start of the administrative reform movement. Most of the deregulation goals discussed in Japan are admirable and would lead to a more efficient and rational use of economic resources, but the time involved and the small impact of many of the changes imply that deregulation cannot be relied on as a means of significantly reducing the imbalance between savings and investment.

INVESTMENT TAX CREDITS. The Japanese tax code provides no general investment tax credit, despite frequent pressure from corporations and groups such as Keidanren to institute such a policy. An investment tax credit would be consistent with encouraging private-sector investment, but studies in the United States cast some doubt on its ability to induce investment that would not have taken place otherwise, and the recent U.S. tax reform eliminated it. More important, however, since it embarked on fiscal austerity in 1979, the Ministry of Finance has been so opposed to any policy that would reduce government revenue that a proposal such as this has little chance of success. Furthermore, changes in corporate tax policy since the early 1970s have tended to eliminate the special corporate tax breaks that had been instituted in the 1950s and 1960s to encourage

11. The share in total retail sales held by stores employing fifty or more people slipped slightly from 1974 (21.2 percent) to 1982 (20.0 percent) after having expanded rapidly in the 1950s and 1960s (from 9.1 percent in 1954). Management and Coordination Agency, *Japan Statistical Yearbook, 1986*, p. 322; and Edward J. Lincoln, "The Japanese Distribution System," *Council Report*, no. 18 (June 1979), esp. table 4.

investment in particular industries. Ministry opposition to the credits shows no signs of weakening.

Initiating investment tax credits would also invite international criticism. Japan's problems with its trading partners have been caused by perceptions that it is competing unfairly in manufactured products. It would not be wise to adopt policies that encourage plant and equipment investment, and presumably increase competitiveness, in the midst of these problems.

In lieu of an investment tax credit the initial tax reform proposal of 1987 provided for a modest decrease in marginal corporate income taxes by dropping the rate on retained earnings from 43.3 percent to 37.5 percent over several years, while raising the tax on dividends from 33.3 percent to the same 37.5 percent.[12] But in the final version of the tax reform that became law, this was scaled back. Indeed, the only drop in corporate taxes came from a failure to renew an expiring 1.3 percent surcharge on corporate income taxes. This will do little to stimulate corporate investment.

MORTGAGE INTEREST DEDUCTIBILITY. Japan does not allow individuals to deduct mortgage interest payments from their income taxes. Allowing such deductions might stimulate housing investment by making larger mortgages more affordable. As noted earlier, this would also lower the household savings necessary to meet down payments for housing purchases, thus conveniently affecting both savings and investment. People could either purchase more expensive houses or purchase their houses sooner. However, this policy too would face strong opposition from the Ministry of Finance because tax revenues would decrease. The tax reform of 1987 did not include a provision for mortgage interest deductibility, nor was one seriously discussed.

GOVERNMENT HOUSING INVESTMENT. In a broader sense the government has long subsidized housing through the Jūtaku Kin'yū Kōko (Housing Loan Corporation) and the Jūtaku Toshi Setsubi Kōdan (Japan Housing and Urban Development Corporation). These organizations borrow from the government through the Fiscal Investment and Loan Program, which funnels funds from postal savings deposits and several other pro-

---

12. Masaaki Homma, "An Overview of the Tax Reform in the U.S. and Japan," paper prepared for the Japan–U.S. Symposium, Tokyo, January 1987, pp. 30–31.

grams through the Ministry of Finance to government-related financial institutions and other public policy organizations. The Housing Loan Corporation then provides mortgage loans and the Japan Housing and Urban Development Corporation builds subsidized housing. The best indication of the government's real attitude toward housing investment is provided by the funding of these two organizations. After reaching ¥3.7 trillion ($15.6 billion) in fiscal 1983, authorized borrowing by the Housing Loan Corporation stagnated; it was ¥3.8 trillion in fiscal 1986. For the Japan Housing and Urban Development Corporation the change came earlier and was stronger, peaking at ¥962 billion ($4.2 billion) in fiscal 1980 and dropping sharply to ¥849 billion ($5.0 billion, a rise caused by exchange rate movements) by fiscal 1986.[13] These facts speak louder than the rhetoric about deregulating land use to stimulate investment.

No consideration of housing policy can ignore these government-owned organizations. As table 6-1 shows, in fiscal 1983 they provided 43 percent of all new mortgage lending, which represented 31 percent of all new housing investment for the year (once down payments are included). This involvement is largely a result of changed social demands in the 1970s. Government institutions provided less than 4 percent of housing investment funds in the mid-1960s, although they accounted for more than 50 percent of total financial institution lending for housing. What this means is that far more housing investment took the form of cash payments in the 1960s and less was in the form of mortgage loans. The government, then, can do a great deal to affect the level of investment in housing. The Ministry of Finance and others who favor continued reduction of government deficits could justify increasing funds to the Housing Loan Corporation because the funds do not come from the general account budget. In 1987 the MOF finally allowed an 8.1 percent increase in borrowing by both the Housing Loan Corporation and the Housing and Urban Development Corporation to stimulate housing investment, an encouraging sign but still quite modest.

One final aspect of housing loans should be considered. A major argument raised in Japan in the first half of the 1980s was that increased funds for housing would raise land prices without bringing a rise in real investment. While exaggerated, this problem deserves consideration. Increased funds for housing would be more effective if accompanied by a strong effort to change the tax and regulatory environment to enable an expansion of investment that would not be eaten away by land price

13. Ministry of Finance, *Zaisei Tōkei, 1986* (Fiscal Statistics, 1986), pp. 292–304.

Table 6-1. *Supply of New Housing Loans, by Type of Lender,*
Fiscal Years 1966–83
Billions of yen unless otherwise specified

Fiscal year	Private-sector financial institutions	Government-owned financial institutions	Government loans as percent of total housing loans	Government loans as percent of total housing investment
1966	77	79	50.6	3.6
1967	140	95	40.4	5.0
1968	294	128	30.3	3.8
1969	583	153	20.8	3.7
1970	788	260	24.8	5.4
1971	1,147	292	20.3	5.6
1972	2,632	385	12.8	5.5
1973	3,253	561	14.7	5.7
1974	3,093	953	23.6	9.9
1975	4,203	1,268	23.2	11.4
1976	5,257	1,381	20.8	11.2
1977	5,967	1,655	21.7	12.6
1978	7,075	2,504	26.1	18.1
1979	7,412	3,301	30.8	21.2
1980	5,904	3,430	36.7	22.7
1981	6,273	3,674	36.9	24.8
1982	6,068	4,380	41.9	28.8
1983	5,851	4,413	43.0	31.4

Source: Ministry of Finance, *Ginkōkyoku Kin'yū Nempō, 1984* (Banking Bureau Finance Annual, 1984) (Tokyo: Fiscal and Monetary Research Group, 1984), p. 89.

inflation. Such changes could include those mentioned earlier in the section on deregulation.[14]

INTEREST RATES. Investment could also be stimulated by easing monetary policy, which would bring a reduction in interest rates (and might

14. Japanese claims about the inefficacy of stimulating housing investment are also exaggerated. It is true that land prices are high and that roughly three-quarters of housing investment costs go to land purchase rather than dwelling construction. But the Japanese wrongly point to the recent high inflation of Tokyo land prices (close to 100 percent in 1986) to buttress their fears that additional housing investment will simply drive up the price of land, having little or no impact on stimulating domestic demand. The inflation in Tokyo is not characteristic of the rest of the country; land prices have been stable nationwide. In addition, the presumption that the portion of housing investment that goes to purchase land is wasted assumes that those who sell their land for new housing projects simply save all the money they receive. While they may indeed choose to save a large portion, it is highly unlikely that they would save all of it. If they spend part of their proceeds, then they provide a positive impact on domestic demand.

discourage saving as well). This policy has been pursued, but its effectiveness has been limited, and by early 1987 interest rates were so low that further reductions would be difficult. In addition, use of monetary policy was constrained by international conditions.

As Japan recovered from the oil shock of 1979 and inflation clearly remained under control, the Bank of Japan eased monetary policy. The resulting lower interest rates widened the differential between domestic and foreign rates, leading to greater capital outflow. Fearful that increased capital outflow and a weaker yen would bring strong protests from the United States, the Bank of Japan avoided domestic pressure to further reduce interest rates. From December 1981 to October 1983 the discount rate remained at 5.5 percent; it then fell to 5.0 percent, where it remained until the beginning of 1986. Only after the September 1985 Group of Five agreement, when the yen appreciated rapidly and U.S. interest rates fell, did authorities feel that they could ease monetary policy. The discount rate was gradually decreased to a postwar low of 2.5 percent by early 1987.

Lower interest rates increase the profit from plant and equipment investments and should stimulate mortgage demand. However, in Japan such investment does not appear as sensitive to interest rate changes as it is to other influences. Although interest rates fell in 1977–78 investment did not benefit; industry was still adjusting to the deceleration of economic growth and the excess capacity created by that transition. When rates fell in 1986 the economy was being buffeted by the strengthening of the yen, which discouraged investment in export-oriented or import-competing industries.

LIBERALIZING IMPORT RESTRICTIONS. A final possibility for stimulating investment would be to liberalize import restrictions. Compared with people in other industrialized nations, Japanese consumers spend a relatively large portion of their incomes on food because strong barriers against imported agricultural products protect a very inefficient domestic agricultural industry.[15] Were those barriers to fall, demand for services and manufactured products might rise as people spent less on food. This increased consumption would then stimulate investment. The net impact of such a policy would depend on what happens to domestic agriculture. If it were reorganized into more efficient units, the positive effect on total domestic

15. In 1984 food represented 27.4 percent of total consumer expenditures; in the United States the level was only 19.8 percent. Management and Coordination Agency, *Japan Statistical Yearbook, 1986*, p. 532; and Bureau of the Census, *Statistical Abstract of the United States, 1987*, p. 422.

spending for manufactures would be stronger than if there were simply disinvestment in agriculture, which would lower consumption—at least temporarily—by agricultural households. Lower food costs could also be achieved by deregulating the retail industry, allowing greater expansion of discount stores. However, as mentioned before, there are strong political forces working against the rapid implementation of such a policy.

Some have suggested that liberalizing import regulations on products other than food could also stimulate investment. Removing tariffs and quotas on plywood and other lumber products would reduce building costs, which might increase investment in housing. This effect is likely to be small, though, in comparison with what could be achieved through increased financial support for homebuyers and deregulation of land use. Investment did seem to be stimulated in 1984 when corporations were allowed to buy foreign communications satellites. Combined with regulatory changes allowing competition in the domestic telecommunications market, investment in data communications increased, resulting in additional purchases of foreign equipment. As in the case of agriculture, however, these benefits must be weighed against the potential flight of investment from import-competing industries.

Foreign observers of Japan often assume that lower import barriers will cause the Japanese to save less as they increase consumption of imports. This is unlikely. Falling barriers will lead to a reallocation of consumption—away from food and toward manufactured products, for instance—but will have little effect on the overall level of consumption or investment. Lower import barriers are an admirable goal for many reasons, but solving the macroeconomic dilemma is not one of them.

Increasing Government Deficits

Although new policies to reduce savings and increase investment would be desirable, most would appear either of limited value or politically difficult to implement. Those with the greatest potential seem closely related to government tax and spending policies, so that action on savings and investment cannot be truly divorced from government fiscal policies. However, in broad terms the alternative to reducing the private-sector imbalance would be to increase fiscal stimulus, which could be supplied through a decrease in taxes, an increase in government spending, or a combination of the two. As discussed in chapter 3, both possibilities ran into decisive opposition after 1979 from the Ministry of Finance and from other groups that supported austerity. That opposition has shown some signs of weakening since 1985 but remains strong.

The first indication that Japan might change its fiscal policy did not come until the summer of 1987, when a mildly expansionary supplementary budget was passed. Touted as a major effort to stimulate domestic demand, it did little more than reverse the direction of policy from increasingly austere to neutral. The original fiscal 1987 budget had anticipated a further drop in deficit spending, and the supplement reversed that to produce a very small increase.[16] While this development is encouraging, the size of the movement implies that the MOF's basic opposition has not abated. Much more can be done either to reduce taxes or increase spending, although spending increases represent the more promising and appropriate route to pursue.

TAX REDUCTION. One can question whether a tax reduction would be the proper move for Japan. Taxes remained low compared with those of other industrial countries in the 1980s. OECD data for 1982 show the ratio of Japanese government revenue to GNP at 30.2 percent; it was 32.0 percent in the United States, and levels ranged up to 50 percent or more in some European countries. No other OECD member country had a ratio as low as Japan's.[17] To reduce taxes when they are already low by international standards would be an odd policy. This statement, though, applies more to individual than corporate income taxes. By the mid-1980s, increases had made the corporate tax burden greater than that in the United States.[18]

---

16. The original budget for fiscal 1987 called for issuing ¥10.5 trillion in government bonds, a drop of 8.6 percent from fiscal 1986, thereby continuing the trend of increasing austerity. This was accomplished by stringent limits on expenditures (up only 0.5 percent overall) and included a 12.4 percent cut in public works spending. The supplementary budget increased expenditures, with public works up enough to more than restore the initial cuts and yield a 7.1 percent rise. Spending was to be financed by both higher anticipated revenue and an expanded bond issue. With the changes, bond issues would rise to ¥11.9 trillion, up ¥1.4 trillion from the original budget. However, because the original budget had decreased deficit spending, the comparison with fiscal 1986 indicates only a ¥366 billion ($2.5 billion at 145 yen to the dollar) increase in the deficit. The real shift in fiscal policy from 1986 to 1987, therefore, was very small. Data are from Ministry of Finance, *Monthly Finance Review*, no. 166 (April 1987), p. 28.

17. Organization for Economic Cooperation and Development, *The Role of the Public Sector: Causes and Consequences of the Growth of Government*, OECD Economic Studies, 4 (Paris: OECD, 1985), p. 29.

18. See, for example, Jane Gravelle, *Comparative Corporate Tax Burdens in the United States and Japan and Implications for Relative Economic Growth*, report no. 83-177 E (Congressional Research Service, September 1983), pp. 3-11.

Although lower taxes are certainly an option, the original tax reform proposals of 1987 were based on strict revenue neutrality, and opponents feared that the MOF would even compromise this neutrality by pressing for increases in the tax rate after initial implementation of the reforms. The ministry introduced a minor benefit by calling for implementation of the value-added tax six months after the other provisions of the reform were to go into effect, allowing a very temporary decrease in taxes. Only after the original tax reform package failed did serious talk of a tax cut emerge.

The revised tax bill that finally became law in 1987 did represent a real tax cut, while it also made some alterations in tax structure through reducing the number of tax brackets and eliminating the tax-free savings system. Overall, however, the changes were minor, with most of the reductions offset by the new revenues that will result from eliminating tax-free savings. The revised bill thus cannot be construed as a significant shift in policy, even though it represents a more positive step than the original reform proposal.

INCREASED GOVERNMENT SPENDING. Even though opposition to increases in discretionary government spending was intense from 1979 to 1985, Japan has room to expand many forms of spending that would be very useful for society. Chapter 3 pointed out that as a percentage of GNP Japan's expenditures on social programs remained lower than those of most other industrial countries. Social spending rose rapidly during the 1970s, but by the mid-1980s housing standards, the diffusion of sewer systems, the number and quality of public libraries, the availability of park land, and the proportion of paved roads all lagged behind other advanced industrial countries. Most power and telephone lines in urban areas remained above ground (utility poles in the middle of narrow sidewalks constituted a pedestrian hazard as well as an eyesore). Subway and train stations had few escalators or elevators for the elderly or handicapped, not to mention weary riders of all ages. The situation ought to have been a source of national embarrassment.

One of the many surprising aspects of Japan during the late 1970s and early 1980s was the public's passive acquiescence in the campaign for fiscal austerity and the consequent stagnation in spending for social goals, but that acquiescence has to have limits beyond which the Liberal Democratic party cannot push without losing support. Therefore, not only would an increase in government spending greatly benefit the general welfare, but it ought to help the political fortunes of the LDP as well. The party could declare victory in the administrative reform movement, claiming (with some justification) that government had become more efficient, and then move on to support spending increases.

Increased spending on social infrastructure could especially address the coming needs of an aging society. More nursing homes, hospitals, recreation centers, libraries, local parks, and other facilities will all be necessary to accommodate the larger proportion of elderly in the population. So will easier physical access to public transportation and safer sidewalks. The need for these investments is building, and investment should be stepped up now.

Public spending would also spur private-sector investment. Greater investment in housing would likely lead to increased purchases of other consumer durables, stimulating sales and investment in those industries. Similarly, better roads or more expressways could improve domestic car sales.

One of the chief arguments raised by opponents of fiscal expansion is that once begun it is difficult to curtail. Embarking now on new social programs, they fear, would be dangerous because the aging population will require rapid increases in government spending for social security, health, and other programs in the future. However, some forms of spending avoid this problem. The stock of social capital could be significantly improved to meet the needs of society, after which such expenditures could be cut as others rise with demographic change. An expanded stock of social capital would entail new maintenance costs, but the costs would be far lower than the initial construction costs, and in some cases, such as housing and sewer systems, maintenance costs would be borne privately.

A policy of increased government spending would thus seem to be the most effective approach to take. Taxes are already low, and the government has an ample array of programs and responsibilities on which it could spend more. Such a policy would directly benefit the Japanese people's welfare, absorb more of the private sector's surplus savings, and encourage private-sector investment. Considering such obvious benefits, the continuing opposition of the MOF is a mystery.

Controlling External Surpluses

The yen appreciated against the dollar rapidly and strongly after the Group of Five announced in September 1985 that the dollar was overvalued. Many hailed the autonomous appreciation as the solution to the problem of U.S. deficits and Japanese surpluses on merchandise trade and the current account. However, the anticipated adjustments were slow to materialize. Fearful that continued Japanese surpluses strengthened the possibility of retaliatory protectionism in the United States, some Japanese observers proposed more direct actions to control international imbalances.

One proposal was for a broad set of voluntary export controls. Behind it lay the following reasoning: the problem in bilateral relations stemmed from the imbalance in trade; neither the United States nor Japan was willing or able to alter fiscal policy significantly; therefore, direct control over Japan's exports was the only way to lower the imbalance and hold American protectionism at bay. However, would such a policy work? The main effect of voluntary restraints imposed on automobile exports in 1981 was that, although fewer cars were shipped, they produced the same export value, creating higher profits for Japanese auto producers. And as with yen appreciation, such controls would work only if the initial reduction in exports were matched by adjustments in the private-sector savings-investment balance or increased government deficits. If not, the policy would not change the overall outcome. A voluntary reduction in exports would be matched by a reduction in imports.

Besides doubts about their economic efficacy, export controls present serious political problems. The rationale for controls assumes that the trade imbalance per se has been the core of difficulties in bilateral relations in the 1970s and 1980s, an assumption that may not be correct. A more convincing interpretation is that deteriorating relations have resulted from Japan's surpluses in combination with the perception that Japan is a reluctant importer or recalcitrant participant in the liberal trade system. Under this assumption, imposing voluntary export controls would only reinforce the image of Tokyo as endeavoring to avoid liberalizing import restrictions and deflecting foreign criticism by containing its export growth (in a way that would not really harm its export industries because of the increased profits created by scarcity). Reaction against Japan could be swift and harshly protectionist.

It would be unfortunate if Japan were to impose broad export restraints rather than to tackle the necessary changes in fiscal policy or savings and investment incentives. Yen appreciation has constituted an important incentive for facing these policy needs even though it has worked slowly. Artificial constraints would only deflect attention from these needs, especially if they maintained profits in export industries.

U.S. Policy

Given Japan's options, what bilateral approach should the United States have pursued in the first half of the 1980s and what policies should it consider in the final years of the decade? If one accepts the assertion that the large Japanese current-account surpluses, U.S. deficits, and the trade imbalance heighten economic tensions, then macroeconomic policy should be a key consideration of bilateral meetings. U.S.–Japanese discussions of macroeconomic issues were, however, conspicuously missing from the Reagan administration's agenda during its first term—a time when Japan's surpluses were rising very rapidly. Even in 1985 little was done, and the few relevant remarks of Secretary of State George Shultz indicated no serious focus on the problem. No important bilateral government meetings pursued macroeconomic discussions. However, it must be recognized that discussion with Japan on macroeconomic policies could not have proceeded without a commitment to alter U.S. policy. Not only did the trade imbalance need to be attacked at both ends, but since the Japanese blamed most of it on the United States, they would be very unwilling to undertake policy adjustments without prior U.S. action. In that respect the passage of the Gramm-Rudman-Hollings Act in 1985 placed the United States in a stronger bargaining position. Even without strict enforcement of the law, U.S. officials could legitimately claim that the federal deficit was falling and that Japan could and should alter its own policies so as to decrease its current-account surplus.

A common objection to including macroeconomic topics in bilateral negotiations is that to do so constitutes an unfair intrusion into sovereign domestic policy. That objection has little merit. When domestic policies have an important impact on international relations, they become a proper item for discussion and negotiation. Under the Bretton Woods system of pegged exchange rates, domestic macroeconomic policy was always a legitimate international topic. When the world moved to floating exchange rates in 1973, the necessity for considering the international implications of domestic policies was supposedly removed, but they proved to be stronger and more unpalatable than anticipated. The damage to U.S. export and import-competing industries in the first half of the 1980s and the increased friction between the two countries that resulted from their domestic macroeconomic policies became much more severe problems than anyone would have expected in the early 1970s. Thus the underlying domestic policies ought to be discussed.

The proposition that macroeconomic issues should be subject to bilateral discussion should not be taken to mean that the locus of consideration should shift from microeconomics to macroeconomics, however. Both approaches are needed to achieve a balanced policy that will contain tensions. To deal with Japan's external surpluses and U.S. deficits without accompanying action on Japan's import barriers would be to ignore important contentious problems. Conversely, dealing with import barriers without addressing macroeconomic issues would leave American companies at a competitive disadvantage.

Discussing macroeconomic policy in the bilateral context is hardly a new idea. From 1977 to 1979 the United States put extensive pressure on Japan to follow policies to stimulate domestic growth under the rubric of the "locomotive theory," which held that the best method for extricating the world from the prolonged stagnation following the first oil shock was for the United States, Japan, and West Germany to stimulate their domestic economies simultaneously. This concerted effort would act as a locomotive to drag the rest of the world to renewed growth. The United States pressed Japan to accept its responsibilities during negotiations in the fall of 1977, which led to the Strauss-Ushiba agreement in January 1978 in which Japan "promised" to make real GNP grow by 7 percent during fiscal 1978. The particular agreement was foolish: no government can make sustainable promises about what will happen to its economy, and Japanese government forecasters are no better at predicting the future than Americans. But establishing a target did imply Japan would adopt stimulative policies in hopes of reaching it.

The pressure came at a time when the Japanese government was seriously divided over fiscal policy. The Ministry of Finance favored austerity; the Ministry of International Trade and Industry (among others) favored increased spending. Thus American pressure became a tool for domestic Japanese forces to use in their own effort to stimulate the economy, and Japan did grow more quickly in fiscal 1978. The economy would, in fact, have grown at a 7 percent rate except for the depressing effect of a decline in the current account, a delayed result of the strong appreciation of the yen in 1977–78 and the onset of the second oil crisis.

The negative effect of this episode was that the United States once again became the scapegoat for the policies adopted. Considerable unfavorable publicity, including charges of unfair interference in domestic Japanese policy, was heaped on it and its negotiators. A common result of bilateral relations, this problem may be unavoidable.

Since 1985, Reagan administration policies toward Japan have returned to a somewhat more balanced approach. Reinforced by the Gramm-Rudman-Hollings Act and by the administration's new willingness to focus on exchange rates, macroeconomic policies and developments became important to bilateral (and multilateral) talks, while pressure on microeconomic trade barriers continued unabated. During 1986 the administration repeatedly called for Japan (and West Germany) to stimulate their domestic economies. Even if the calls were not initially successful in changing policies, the issues were thrashed out in public. As the United States renewed its interest, though, officials exhibited a puzzling willingness to accept Japanese statements and promises at face value. When the Maekawa report—short and vague, with calls for "internationalization" and stimulation of domestic demand that mainly reiterated the miscellaneous positions of previous reports—was issued in the spring of 1986, the United States interpreted it as a very promising change of direction.

Reactions to Japan became even more puzzling later in 1986. Bilateral meetings between Treasury Secretary James Baker and Finance Minister Kiichi Miyazawa in the fall of 1986 and in early 1987 resulted in U.S. acceptance of Japan's assurance that it was working to stimulate domestic demand. But Japan was doing nothing of the kind. After the first meeting, it passed a supplementary budget that cut government spending. It then compiled a budget for fiscal 1987 that was even more austere. In early 1987 Tokyo again promised rapid consideration of a package of policies to stimulate domestic demand, when, in fact, no such package would materialize until after the austere budget was passed. The nation also remained absorbed in the tax reform bills, so that consideration of other economic policies was postponed. Perhaps most puzzling of all was the U.S. silence on tax reform in Japan. The insistence of the Ministry of Finance on revenue neutrality and the inclusion of the value-added tax could have been heavily criticized but was not. When, in the summer of 1987, the Japanese government finally did propose a package to stimulate demand, it was warmly received by the United States, even though the claim of a ¥6 trillion ($40 billion at 150 yen to the dollar) impact on the economy was grossly overstated.[19]

19. The ¥6 trillion included a variety of items not directly connected to the central government budget. Increased government spending included in the supplementary budget

U.S. statements following the Baker-Miyazawa meetings also expressed a satisfaction with current exchange rates that was intended to stabilize the rates. They appear to have had that effect. Yet if Japan was doing little to stimulate its economy at that time, why should the United States have agreed to a statement intended to stabilize the exchange market? Japan's extreme reluctance to alter its domestic policies suggests that the United States should have called for a further strengthening of the yen to induce those changes.

How can one evaluate these recent events? That macroeconomic issues have returned to the agenda is encouraging. That the United States has not dealt with Japan more forcefully is not. Policy initiatives such as tax reform that could and should have been criticized were not. Japan's vague promises to stimulate demand were accepted when they should have been recognized as empty. The result has been further delay in Japan's policy response to the stronger yen, a delay that is in the interest of neither country. The U.S. government should rely more heavily its own analyses of Japan's policy options so that the presentations by Japanese government officials are not accepted as fact. It should be willing to push its own view of what Japan can and should do. The Department of the Treasury, which bears primary responsibility for dealing with Japan on these issues, has been rather gullible.

Conclusions

Japan is certainly different from the United States, as is amply demonstrated by the sharp disparity in the macroeconomic balances of the two economies. The Japanese often take these differences as evidence that their country is unique and impossible for foreigners to understand. That argument provides a convenient excuse for denying foreign demands and ultimately hurts Japan internationally by enhancing the impression in other countries that it is a reluctant participant in the world community, that it wants to keep itself in a unique and insulated position for its own benefit. If the United States is to deal adequately with this close ally, the Japanese

---

came to only ¥2 trillion, and the increase in the government deficit, as noted earlier, only ¥1.4 trillion when compared with the initial budget for the year, or an even smaller ¥366 billion when compared with the previous year.

should not be given the opportunity to say that no one understands them. This book has tried to add to that understanding.

Better understanding does not mean accepting all Japanese justifications for not doing what the United States asks in bilateral negotiations. It does mean approaching bilateral relations with a realistic knowledge of what is happening in Japan and a clear-eyed appraisal of how to press problems of concern to a successful solution. Pressure from the United States, for example, will never bring the Ministry of Finance to adopt bold, sweeping measures of financial deregulation, but pressure will keep piecemeal change moving along.

Success is more likely when domestic groups in Japan support the changes desired by the United States. That condition certainly prevailed on macroeconomic policy issues in the mid-1980s. There was lively debate on the direction policy should take, but in the absence of strong support from abroad the proponents of change were having a difficult time. The conditions were right to apply pressure. Returning discussion of macroeconomic issues to the bilateral dialogue was entirely correct, but was not pursued vigorously.

The alterations in the macroeconomic fabric of Japan stemming from the deceleration in economic growth that was the consequence of catching up with the industrial world have been profound. Japan has managed to adjust successfully to those alterations for a decade but faces a serious test in the second half of the 1980s. The government's unwillingness to bend fiscal policy very far calls into question the country's future success. It might muddle through without a recession, but growth could be disappointing and well below its potential. And the public could fail to realize the full personal benefits of living in an advanced industrial society. Success brought on by the transition to economic maturity in the 1970s by no means guarantees that Japan will do as well in the 1980s and beyond. The initial indications are not encouraging.

Index

291